MOUNTAIN OF FAME

• • • • • JOHN E. WILLS, JR. • • • • • • • • • • • • •

Mountain of Fame

• • • • • •

PORTRAITS IN
CHINESE
HISTORY

• • • • • •

PRINCETON UNIVERSITY PRESS, PRINCETON, NEW JERSEY

Copyright © 1994 by Princeton University Press
Published by Princeton University Press, 41 William Street,
Princeton, New Jersey 08540
In the United Kingdom: Princeton University Press,
Chichester, West Sussex

Library of Congress Cataloging-in-Publication Data
Wills, John E. (John Elliot), 1936–
Mountain of fame : portraits in Chinese history /
John E. Wills, Jr.
p. cm.
Includes bibliographical references and index
ISBN 0-691-05542-4
1. China—Biography. I. Title.
DS734.W63 1994
920.051—dc20   93-46773

This book has been composed in Janson
Designed by Jan Lilly

Princeton University Press books are printed on
acid-free paper and meet the guidelines for permanence
and durability of the Committee on Production
Guidelines for Book Longevity of the
Council on Library Resources

Printed in the United States of America

2   4   6   8   10   9   7   5   3   1

To my students at the
University of Southern California

CONTENTS

• • • • • •

ILLUSTRATIONS

• • • • • •

MAPS

FIGURES

When I have completed this book,
I shall deposit it in the Mountain of Fame,
so that it can be handed down to men
who will understand it, and penetrate to the
villages and great cities. Then although
I should suffer death from ten thousand cuts,
what regrets should I have?

Sima Qian, c. 91 B.C.E.

PREFACE

• • • • • •

THIS IS a book that introduces the history of a great people through the prism of that people's own historical memories. The epigraph is drawn from a letter by Sima Qian, China's greatest historian, in which he describes how he suffered mutilating punishment and stayed alive and working in order to complete the great history his father had begun and to transmit knowledge of China's past and its great men to later generations.

Cang zhi ming shan, literally "store it name mountain," is a cryptic enough phrase even by the standards of literary Chinese. "Name mountain," *ming shan*, probably was not the name of a mountain; it may have been an expression used to refer to the imperial archives. The phrase also represents the intersection of two images that have great resonance in Chinese culture. Real and metaphorical mountains have had great power over the minds of the Chinese at many times and in many ways. Buddhist monasteries often were built in mountainous areas. Some sacred mountains were ancient centers of pilgrimage and veneration. Emperors were buried in real mountains, like the tomb of Empress Wu and her husband, or in great tomb mounds that were *called* mountains, like the famous tomb of the First Emperor of Qin. Landscape paintings were and are called "mountain and water paintings." Water always flows on and away, like time or one's life, but mountains have weight, endure. Men might change the course of a river, but they could scarcely scratch the surface of a mountain. The solitary viewer in a landscape painting was delighted by implacable heights and cliffs beyond the power of human meddling. Even men, at least the greatest man, Confucius, might seem to their disciples as elusive and awesome and solid as a mountain.

The word *ming*, "name," comes even closer to the heart of the culture. Confucius taught that the world could be restored to order and virtue if only people conformed to the traditional roles designated by the names of their positions in society. "Name" in the sense of an individual's "good name" or fame was terribly important, not just for oneself but because it cast glory back over parents and ancestors and might survive one's own death and conquer the ceaseless flow of time.

Stories of *mingren*, "name people," "famous people," were even more important to the Chinese than to other traditional cultures as expressions of their sense of the past and their deepest values. The stories that were told were largely of high-status individuals, but they definitely were shared and beloved by many of China's common people. Confucianism was thought of as the teaching of a very real and vulnerable human being who tried to revive a way of life created by other men, the sage kings and early Zhou kings. Traditional lore about the medieval loss of the north to foreign invaders centered not on a "lost cause" but on stories of the tragic hero Yue Fei. Even Maoism was a variation of "impersonal," "objective" Marxism inseparable from the life, leadership, and words of one man. The optimism about human potentialities that runs through the Chinese tradition from Confucius to Mao has been inseparable from stories of the realization of the highest values in actual lives. Moreover, all these famous people, even legendary ancestors and heroes who after their deaths became gods, were conceived of as real, mortal, limited human beings, living in society and dependent on others, not gods on earth. Often their stories can be read at many levels, so that their moral and intellectual brilliance is not lost sight of, but the complexities, the hidden chains of cause, the flaws of heroes, and the unwanted consequences of virtuous action also are revealed. It is, I suspect, in large part because of its obsession with the stories of its famous people that Chinese culture is so rich and varied in its moral imagination, so at home, indeed delighted, with the complexities and ambiguities of human character and action. About half the length of the great historical work that Sima Qian planned to store in the Mountain of Fame is taken up by biographies of individuals.

This book, then, reflects and makes use of the Chinese fascination with famous people. It is intended for people who never have paid much attention to China and now want a quick and graspable introduction to some main themes in its stirring history. In writing it I have had in mind a tourist who is about to go there; a practical person whose main interest is in understanding and dealing with China today; a scholar wondering what a Chinese perspective might do for his own thinking about religion, philosophy, history; a young person of Chinese ancestry trying to find some clues to a heritage only dimly perceived; or just a reader who likes good stories. For all these readers and more, an approach through biography has a number of advantages. Since every individual has a family (ancestors, even if not descendants), lives under some kind of government, makes a living, has a place in society, suffers pain and disappointment, and dies, a look at a well-chosen life can give us some sense of the family and class structures, economics, politics, religions, and philosophies of an age, and how they interacted in individual experiences and historic trends. Biography satisfies a very deeply rooted taste for stories with beginnings and endings, and it appeals to our need to make sense of our own lives.

There is no shortage of overviews of China's past, of all lengths and qualities. But a balanced overview of such a vast subject either is too long and complex for rapid assimilation or is such a breathless rush of strange names, dates, and ideas that the reader gets little sense of the real drama and importance of the subject. This book does not aim to be balanced, but rather to give the reader a deep enough encounter with some key people, ideas, and times to really engage his or her attention and moral imagination. The biographical approach inevitably underemphasizes abstract reasoning and beliefs in gods and other worlds, none of which were in short supply in China, and discussion of large impersonal trends in history, which most modern historians would want to emphasize much more than this book does. The latter limitation can be overcome to a degree by focusing not just on individual lives but on the backgrounds and contexts that shaped these individuals and constrained their thoughts and actions. I have hoped that by making this a book about lives *and times* I could overcome some of the limitations of a general biographical approach and make this book somewhat better rounded as a brief introduction to main themes and trends in Chinese history. But it makes no pretense at being fully rounded, and occasionally I will point out to the reader major themes that are getting short shrift in it.

This book provides some introduction to the great religious traditions, to philosophy, and to the arts, but it gives fullest attention to some long continuities in politics and political culture. Here the study of lives and times turns out to be singularly powerful, and the results help us to explicate some trends in nonpolitical philosophy and some very general traditional values. A few sentences of anticipatory summary may help the reader keep track of these political continuities and transformations as they surface repeatedly in the chapters that follow. We will see the emergence in the age of Confucius of a set of definitions of political life that focused on "the Way of the Ruler and the Minister" (*jun chen zhi dao*), the one-to-one relation between a hereditary sovereign and the individual, usually of good family but with no hereditary right to office, who sought to prove his selflessness, learning, and practical adeptness and thus to gain employment as a minister. The ruler's most important task was to find good ministers and then give them sufficient responsibility to carry out their duties, and to listen to their advice even when it was unpalatable. The minister, especially the scholar-minister bearing the lore of tradition and all its good and bad examples, had great moral authority but no autonomous power; he could be dismissed at any time. Chinese moral thought has devoted a great deal of attention to the complexities and ambiguities of the minister's position.

Chinese political history down to our own century can be read as a succession of developments in the nature of the ruler-minister relation, including shifts in the balance of power between the two, in bureaucratic organization, and in modes of recruitment to the bureaucracy. The chapters that follow contain stories of lives expressing and reshaping Chinese concepts of these roles, and thus the ways in which political action could be conceived, of people gaining power or losing it by acting out or violating these traditional roles. In modern times the ruler–minister relation could not provide the mobilization of the common people or the solidarity of ruler and ruled that modern nation-building require, but large elements of the moral styles and modes of personal relations associated with it survive even today.

That is only one way of finding a connecting thread in the rich fabric I have sought to present here. Readers are invited to find their own, to see continuities and confrontations among the people and stories presented here, to remember stories I should have included but did not. In developing the approaches that have gone into this book, I have learned a great deal from the reactions of the more than one thousand students who have studied these lives with me, from the various kind Chinese hosts who took me to see places connected with these lives and discussed them with me, and from the specialists in various fields who have shaped my understanding of the large range of subjects touched on here. My greatest and least repayable obligation is to the dead, to the men and women who lived these lives and told these stories over the centuries. This book is one more small indication that their names live on and their stories still are told.

ACKNOWLEDGMENTS

• • • • • •

IN ADDITION to my central debts to my students, my Chinese friends, and the shapers of the Chinese historical tradition, I owe special thanks to Jonathan Spence, Ch'un-shu and Shelley Chang, and Charlotte Furth, who gave me searching readings of most of the chapters; Edwin Perkins, who went over a partial draft with the eye of a shrewd outsider and experienced editor; Arline Golkin, who taught several times the course in which this book was developed, and who passed on to me comments from many students and the results of her own careful reading and empathetic teaching; and Wu Jiaxun, who was my teaching assistant, research assistant, and key source of the insights of a modern intellectual deeply involved with the literary heritage of his people. I also am grateful for the insightful and supportive comments of Yü Ying-shih, Kwang-ching Liu, and an anonymous reader for Princeton University Press. Expert guidance on individual chapters was supplied by Peter K. Bol, Perry Link, and Stephen F. Teiser. Margaret Case encouraged me to submit this project to the Press, gave astute advice, and stood by patiently while I took much too long to get it done. Lauren Osborne has given exemplary professional guidance in the final stages. Anita O'Brien, Jane Low, and Jan Lilly of the Press also made important contributions. Illustrations two through eight are the work of Bel Lin. Illustration nine is reproduced courtesy of the Gest Oriental Library and East Asian Collections, Princeton University. Illustration ten was supplied by and is reproduced with the permission of the Department of Party History, National Party of China (Kuomintang), Taipei. Illustration twelve is reproduced courtesy of Fallander/Sipa Press. The maps were designed by Chase Langford.

I gratefully acknowledge permission to reprint the following materials:

Excerpts from Confucius, *The Analects*, D. C. Lau, tr., 1979. Used by permission of Penguin Books. Ltd.

Excerpts from *Tao Te Ching* by Lao-tzu, translated by Victor H. Mair, translation copyright © 1990 by Victor H. Mair. Used by permission of Bantam Books, a division of Bantam Doubleday Dell Publishing Group Inc.

Excerpts from Li Yu-ning, ed., *The Politics of Historiography: The First Emperor of China*, International Arts and Sciences Press, 1975. Used by permission of M.E. Sharpe, Inc.

Excerpts from Nancy Lee Swann, *Pan Chao: Foremost Woman Scholar of China*, published by Century, 1932. Used by permission of Gest Oriental Library and East Asian Collections, Princeton University.

Excerpts from Luo Guangzhong, *Three Kingdoms: China's Epic Drama*, trans. and ed. by Moss Roberts. Used by permission of the Regents of the University of California and the University of California Press.

Excerpts adapted from Michael A. Fuller, *The Road to East Slope: The Development of Su Shi's Poetic Voice*, 1990. Used by permission of Stanford University Press.

Excerpts from Mary Backus Rankin, *Early Chinese Revolutionaries: Radical Intellectuals in Shanghai and Chekiang*, 1902–1911. Cambridge, Mass.: Harvard University Press. Copyright © 1971 by the President and Fellows of Harvard College. Reprinted by permission of the publishers.

Excerpts from *The Poems of Mao Tse-tung*, translated by Willis Barnstone, published by Harper and Row, 1972. Used by permission of Willis Barnstone.

Excerpts from Burton Watson, *Ssu-ma Ch'ien: Grand Historian of China*, 1958; Burton Watson, tr., *Records of the Grand Historian of China*, 1961; Philip B. Yampolsky, tr., *The Platform Sutra of the Sixth Patriarch*, 1967; Burton Watson, tr., *Su Tung-p'o*, 1965; and W. T. de Bary et al., ed., *Sources of Chinese Tradition*, 1960. All used by permission of Columbia University Press.

NOTE ON ROMANIZATION

• • • • •

ALMOST ALL English-language books about China written between about 1900 and the mid-1970s use the Wade-Giles system, devised in the mid-1800s. It distinguishes between voiced and unvoiced pairs of consonants by putting an apostrophe after the voiced one. Thus *ta* sounds like *dah*, *t'a* like *ta*. The pinyin system, adopted in the People's Republic of China and used in most press reports about China today, is used in this book. It does these pairs, for example, as *da* and *ta*, uses odd letters to fill out the Chinese consonant system, and uses the letter *i* to represent two completely different sounds, "uh" and "ee"; you can tell which only by the preceding consonant.

Here are some examples from this book:

Pinyin	*Rough English pronunciation*	*Wade-Giles*
Kong Zi	Koong Dzuh	K'ung-tzu
Qin	chin	Ch'in
Zhou	joe	Chou
xiao	shiau	hsiao
Sima Qian	Suhmah Chien	Ssu-ma Ch'ien
Su Dongpo	Soo Doong Poh	Su Tung-p'o
Zheng Chenggong	Juhng Chuhng Goong	Cheng Ch'eng-kung
Hong Xiuquan	Hoong Shio Chwahn	Hung Hsiu-ch'üan
Cixi	Tsuh Shee	Tz'u-hsi
Mao Zedong	Mow (as in brow) Dzuh Doong	Mao Tse-tung

Pinyin is not used in the twentieth-century chapters for four personal names, one organizational name, and one place name for which different forms are very well known and still in current use in English. Sun Yat-sen and Chiang Kai-shek are more or less Cantonese versions of Sun Yixian and Jiang Jieshi; Chiang Ching-kuo equals Jiang Jingguo; Lee Teng-hui stands for Li Denghui; Kuomintang (frequently abbreviated KMT) is used for Guomindang; and Taipei is used instead of Taibei.

A SUMMARY TIME LINE

• • • • • •

	Major Periods	Individuals Discussed
2000 B.C.E.	Xia, 2205–1766 (trad.)	Yu, 2280?–2197
	Shang, 1766–1122 (trad.)	
1000 B.C.E.	Zhou, 1122–249	
	Chun Qiu, 771–401	
		Confucius, 551–479 (trad.)
	Warring States, 401–221	
	Qin, 221–206	First Emperor, 259–210
	Early Han, 206–9 C.E.	Sima Qian, 145–87?
0	Xin, 9–25 C.E.	Wang Mang, 33 B.C.E.–23 C.E.
	Later Han, 25–220	Ban Zhao, c. 48–120
	Three Kingdoms, 221–280	Zhuge Liang, 181–234
	Jin, 280–304	
	Northern and Southern Dynasties, 304–589	
	Sui, 589–618	
	Tang, 618–907	Empress Wu, 630?–705
		Hui Neng, 638–713 (trad.)
1000 C.E.	Five Dynasties, 907–960	
	Northern Song, 960–1125	Su Dongpo, 1037–1101
	Southern Song, 1127–1279	Yue Fei, 1103–1141
	Yuan, 1279–1368	Qiu Chuji, 1148–1227
	Ming, 1368–1644	Wang Yangming, 1472–1529
	Qing, 1644–1911	Zheng Chenggong, 1624–1662
		Qianlong Emperor, 1711–1799
		Hong Xiuquan, 1813–1864
	Republic, 1911–1949	Sun Yat-sen, 1866–1925
		Liang Qichao, 1873–1929
	People's Republic, 1949–	Mao Zedong, 1893–1976
		Deng Xiaoping, 1904–
2000 C.E.		

MOUNTAIN OF FAME

YU

ALL PEOPLES, it seems, have ideas of how the world and humankind began. For some large-scale literate cultures these ideas are of great importance. The vision of immensely long cycles of cosmic creation and destruction is somewhere near the heart of Hinduism. Medieval European scholars endlessly refined their understanding of the creation story and compiled their knowledge of the physical world in "Hexamerons" divided according to the days of the creation. Today there still are Christians who believe that the survival of their teachings depends on "Creationist" refutation of scientific cosmogonies and theories of evolution, while "big bang" theories attract much interest among scientists and amateurs of science.

The Chinese had their own ideas about the origins of the cosmos. In one of them, heaven and earth once were completely mixed up together. Then the light and bright in this mass began to separate from the heavy and dark, and a primeval and perhaps proto-human monster called Pan-gu began to grow between them. After his death the various parts of his body formed the world we know: his breath became the wind and clouds, his skin and body hair the plants and trees, and the parasites on his body human beings. In another the origins of the cosmos are less clear, but it is a female deity called Nü-gua that first brought order out of primeval chaos. One may find the Pan-gu myth's picture of humankind as fleas on the cosmos a bit disconcerting, but one also can see in it evidence for the ready acceptance of a human's small place in the universe that was an enduring and frequently very impressive feature of Chinese culture. This myth also is a clear expression of a tendency to think in terms of light and dark, heavy and light, and to conceive of them as *complementary* principles in an organic harmony rather than opposites at war with each other.

But the most interesting point about these myths is that they do not seem to have been very important in the earliest stages of Chinese culture for which there exist extensive records. There is no trace of them in the sayings of Confucius. Most of our scant knowledge of them comes from texts of the second or first centuries B.C.E.[1] or later, and at no time were they, or any other ideas about the origins of the cosmos, as important to traditional Chinese as Hindu and Judeo-Christian ideas were to participants in those traditions. What really mattered to the Chinese were not the origins of the cosmos or of humankind, but the origins of human society. This may seem to be a strange bias, but today we probably are closer to understanding the big bang than we are to a coherent account of the nature of mind and morality.

The Chinese had many myths of the origins of society and of various human inventions, and later thinkers used them in numerous ways. Perhaps the best place to begin is a passage from one of the texts linked to the *Yi jing*. A mysterious and enormously influential work, part divination manual, part guide to the subtle harmonies and interplays of action and passivity, success and failure, light and darkness, an understanding of which is supposed to make possible a life of wholeness and integrity, this classic is one of the many keys to Chinese culture that I cannot fit into this book. It offers guidance to the decisions and hazards of life based on "hexagrams," combinations of divided and undivided lines arrived at through various kinds of random choice. According to an appendix or commentary to this work, in ancient times humankind was ruled by a succession of sage emperors, who invented and bestowed on their people the inventions and social forms that made them genuinely human, different from the animals. These sages got the inspiration for their inventions from the patterns of positive and negative forces to which the *Yi jing* offers the key. The first of them was Fu-xi, whose name means "subduer of animals" or, in one alternative name, "cook and sacrificer." He invented nets and baskets for fishing and hunting, first domesticated animals, and taught his people to enter into proper marriages instead of coupling like animals. His invention of nets was inspired by the *Yi jing* hexagram *Li*, which looks something like a net. In some versions of these legends Nü-gua appears as his wife or sister; she invented many of the feminine arts and patched a rip in the fabric of heaven.

The next important figure was Shen-nong, the Divine Farmer, who invented agriculture and herbal medicine and taught his people how to hold periodic markets to trade their goods.

With the next important figure in the series of sage emperors, the twin cores of Chinese social values—family and bureaucracy—come clearly into focus. He is called Huang-di, the Yellow Lord. The character *di*, "lord," was used in some ancient texts in the compound Shang-di, "Lord on

---

[1] "B.C.E." and "C.E.," "Before Common Era" and "Common Era," are used in this book instead of the more familiar "B.C." and "A.D." as more appropriate to a study in which Christianity makes only a late appearance and where the use of a dating scale of Christian origin is solely a matter of convenience.

1. The hexagram *Li* of the *Yi jing*

High," which may have referred to departed ancestors or to a shadowy high god; later it would be part of the phrase translated as "emperor." Yellow was the color of the earth in ancient Chinese thinking and in the dry yellow-brown of the north Chinese plains, and also the color symbolic of the imperial position, from the yellow cloak thrown around a usurper's shoulders to the yellow tiles of the palace roofs of Beijing.

The Yellow Lord had to summon his vassals to suppress a great rebel and put him to death. He opened up roads so that people in various areas could communicate with each other, and he appointed superintendents over the many small principalities and over the common people. He distributed grain at the proper times, made clear tables of knowledge of the heavens and of nature, and appointed officials to help him in all these tasks. His exertions were great, and he was very sparing in his expenditures. In one important account all the later rulers down through the Zhou were his descendants in one branch or another. After him came some rather dim figures, and then three important rulers named Yao, Shun, and Yu.

From the last centuries B.C.E. down to our own times, educated Chinese believed that humanity had reached a peak of order and well-being about 2350–2200 B.C.E., in the reigns of the emperors Yao, Shun, and Yu. The belief in this real and very human felicity in the past was one of the most important elements in a Chinese optimism about what man could be that survived all experience of what man really was. It also was very closely tied to the idea that the best government was a government of the best men. Yao was supposed to have come to the throne after his brother, who was "not good" and may have been deposed. Like the Yellow Lord, Yao appointed officials to superintend agriculture, to make astronomical observations, and so on. Then he began to search for a successor, asking his officials about the qualifications of various people. Rejecting all his suggestions, they finally told him of a man named Shun, who dwelled in obscurity in a remote part of the country but was becoming known for the great virtue he showed in living in harmony with a nasty and quarrelsome family. Yao then decided on a supreme test of Shun's family virtue, giving him Yao's two daughters to be his wives; Shun also passed this test, maintaining perfect harmony in his family. A sage to be sure! Yao gave him higher honors, and Shun's blind father and his step-brother grew more and more jealous. They set fire to the granary when Shun was repairing its roof, but he held on to two big straw sun hats and leaped down safely, becoming the world's first parachutist as well as a sage. He made tours of inspection around the country, appointing men to various duties; he performed the royal functions on behalf of Yao and eventually succeeded him on the throne.

Shun is the great example of a man who rose by virtue from humble origins. The great Confucian thinker Mencius wrote: "When Shun lived in the depth of the mountains, he lived among trees and stones, and had as friends deer and pigs. The difference between him and the uncultivated man of the mountains was slight. But when he heard a single good word, witnessed a single good deed, it was like water causing a breach in the dikes of the Yangzi or the Yellow River. Nothing could withstand it."

Among the officials Yao appointed was one Gun, who was supposed to control a great flood then ravaging the world. Gun labored mightily at his task but made little progress, and when Shun saw this on one of his tours of inspection he had Gun thrown in prison, where he died. Shun then appointed Gun's son Yu to continue his father's work. Aggrieved by his father's failure and punishment, Yu assembled the necessary labor forces and for thirteen years hurried from place to place supervising the work, living very frugally, even passing the door of his own house without stopping. Instead of trying to dam and dike the waters away from fields and houses, he had his workers dig channels that would allow the waters to run off to the ocean more quickly. Many of China's major rivers, including the Yellow River, were rechanneled by his efforts. When the work was done, the plains were repopulated, agriculture flourished, and Yu set out on a great tour of the empire, writing down for each area the nature of its soil, the rate of its land revenues, and the special local products that it ought to contribute to the imperial court; the results of his survey have survived in a long document called the *Yu Gong* (Tribute of Yu). In another document Yu is shown planning an expedition against a rebellious people called the Miao, and eventually winning them over by sheer virtue and charisma, without a fight.

After Yao died, Shun succeeded him on the royal throne. He sought the advice of Yu and other great ministers about the basic principles of government. In the texts that record these dialogues, Yu is not represented as the most articulate of the ministers, but in several passages he is shown sounding a base note of caution and conscientiousness. If the ruler and the minister will both realize how difficult their tasks are, then all will be well. It is important to work at those tasks every day. It is important to pay attention to problems and deviations in their first beginnings. Around this core of the psychology of the conscientious ruler and minister, other participants in these dialogues are portrayed as developing a picture of equilibrium in public life of great power and beauty. Shun tells Yu, "The mind of man is

2. From a Han dynasty image of Yu

perilous; the mind of the True Way is hard to discern. Concentrate! Be single-minded! Hold fast to its center." The virtuous man, says a minister, is gentle but firm, outspoken but respectful, straightforward but warm and mild, hard but just, strong but principled. The harmony of perfect government includes both a beneficent Heaven and a respectful people; "Heaven sees and hears as our people see and hear." The music master Kui describes how, in the court of a virtuous ruler, the ceremonial music evokes a cosmic harmony in which the imperial ancestors descend, the lords all take their proper places, and the male and female phoenix perform their stately dance in the court.

Shun now was convinced that Yu was the best man, and he named him his successor, despite Yu's protests that he was not worthy. Seventeen years later Shun died, and after three years of mourning Yu retired from the court, seeking to leave the throne to Shun's son. But the people of the empire deserted the son and turned to Yu, so that he assumed the throne and ruled for another ten years. He hoped to leave the throne to a virtuous minister, but that minister died before him. Then he named as his successor another minister, who had not served him for very long. Yu died while touring the lower Yangzi region and was buried there. His designated successor left the court as Yu had done, seeking to relinquish the throne to Yu's son Qi. This time the people accepted the son, saying "Our prince is the son of Emperor Yu." The change was permanent; the descendants of Yu ruled China by hereditary right for four hundred years, and Yu was honored as something he had never intended to be, the founder of China's first dynasty, the Xia.

The importance of this story for Chinese political values can scarcely be exaggerated. The ideal of the minister who works very hard for the honor of his family and the benefit of the common people, the organizing of labor for water-control works, the self-conscious balance and concentration in moral effort and self-cultivation, the importance of the ruler's search for the best ministers—all appear here full-blown. In this golden age the supremely good and able minister might even be selected to succeed his lord on the throne. The end of that pattern and the transition to dynastic inheritance at the death of Yu was the Chinese tradition's closest analogue to the expulsion from the Garden of Eden. Later thinkers worried about it, found it inadequately explained in the traditional accounts, but could do no better than to explain that Yu's succession to Shun had been the will of Heaven, and so had been Qi's succession to Yu.

The story of China's most ancient times told here was believed by all literate Chinese, as far as I know, down to this century. The idealization of the "age of Yao, Shun, and Yu" remained a constant in Confucian thought. Studies of historical geography took the *Tribute of Yu* as their first document. One important historical geographer adopted a personal name, Zuyu, which literally means "one who takes Yu as an ancestor." Textual scholars of the seventeenth century and later called into question the authenticity of some of the texts quoted above, but not the fundamentals of the story they told.

The fate of all this ancient lore in the twentieth century is a strange and fascinating story. In the 1920s and 1930s, modern historians and folklorists, adding new methods and iconoclastic zeal to the monumental textual researches of Qing classical scholars, began to show that Confucius had concentrated on the early Zhou rulers and had only occasionally referred to Yu. It was thinkers after him who had built up the idealization of Yu and then tried to go even farther back and buttress their positions with references to the Yellow Lord and the Divine Farmer.

They also showed how fragmentary texts reflected more mythological, less "humane" versions of many of the culture heroes. They told, for example, how Gun was executed by the Lord on High at a dark place far off to the north, his body remained intact for three years, and then someone cut his belly and Yu emerged. Yu then changed into an animal, possibly a yellow bear, and set out to tame the floods, helped by a yellow dragon that dragged its tail on the ground to mark where the channels should go. His travels took him to the place where the sun comes up, to a land where the people had wings, and to another where they wore no clothes. He once convened a great assembly of spirits on a mountaintop. Different myths of Yu had different regional associations, including some with Sichuan and some with the wetlands of the lower Yangzi. Out of all this, modern scholars were quite ready to conclude that the traditional picture of China's most ancient past was a fabrication compiled from many sources by later scholars, and that nothing could be reliably known about anything prior to the early Zhou, around 1100 B.C.E.

But in the same decades, other modern scholars and scientists were beginning to uncover archeological remains suggesting a reliable basis for some of the ancient stories. In the 1920s and 1930s, scientific excavations revealed tombs, building foundations, splendid bronze vessels, and "oracle bones"—animal bones used in divination and inscribed with records related to it—from the Shang dynasty, about 1700–1100 B.C.E., which followed the Xia in the traditional account. In those same decades some important Chinese Neolithic sites were excavated. In the People's Republic a nice conjunction of inherited scholarly interests, Marxist focus on material factors in history, and very thorough administrative control of the countryside has produced an on-going flowering of archeology that is far and away contemporary China's greatest achievement in the study of humanity. There are major new discoveries every year. We now can see the emergence of several centers of village agriculture between 6000 and 4000 B.C.E., and then a linked set of changes in all of them characterized by the emergence of forms of pottery ancestral to the art forms of Shang, by villages with walls, which suggest the prevalence of warfare, and by sharp differentiations in the wealth of goods with which people were buried, indicating the emergence of an elite of rulers and/or priests. Carbon 14 dates for this shift, K. C. Chang's "Lungshanoid horizon," place it about 2500 B.C.E., strikingly close to the traditional 2600 for the Yellow Lord and 2350 to 2200 for the reigns of Yao, Shun, and Yu. Chang and many Chinese scholars think some very early bronze-age sites in the province of Henan may match some of the traditional historical geography of the Xia dynasty.

Should we, then, expect the Chinese archeologists to announce some day the discovery of the tomb of Yu or a duty roster from one of his drainage canal projects? No; it would be truly amazing if any evidence were uncovered of the reality of Yu as a historic individual. But the rough fit between the traditional and archeological dates of the emergence of a recognizably Chinese form of society and politics is one of many signs of the excellent and realistic historic sense of the early Chinese. Other early texts, for example, show a sound understanding of the basic sequence from hunter-gatherer cultures to agriculture with stone implements to the use of metals. Above all, there endures a historic sense that sees human civilization not as a gift of the gods but as an achievement of the moral insight, inventiveness, and hard work of people, and sometimes, as after the death of Yu, as the product of chance.

But the humanization of spirit-figures in these stories will seem most surprising to anyone familiar with the reverse process of the divinization of human heroes in many other cultures, and sometimes in later Chinese culture. It will be a little more understandable if we notice that ancestral lineages were very important to the Chinese. Then we might think of these spirit-figures as ancestral totems, gradually being shorn of their supernatural traits as their descendants cite that lineage to claim their place alongside other noble families as descendants of rulers and ministers in one great, unified political order. The development of that political ideal will become clearer in relation to the next lives I shall discuss, but much of the mystery of this early humanization will remain.

The ideal of a selfless ruler working without cease, changing the earth, bestowing benefits on the people is one that echoes on down to the vast labor mobilizations for public works in the People's Republic, to Chairman Mao and his homilies on "serving the people" and his stories of the foolish old man and his descendants who moved a mountain shovelful by shovelful, basket by basket. In Beijing, facing Mao's mausoleum, there is a large and excellent Museum of Chinese History. In each hall of the museum stands a large statue of a hero of that age. In the first hall, devoted to China's prehistory, the statue is of Yu.

2

CONFUCIUS
(Kongzi)

. . . . . .

CONFUCIUS was a scholar who idealized the government and culture of an age five hundred years before his own, and who sought to convince the rulers of his time that all would be well in their states if they would concentrate on winning the trust of their people and setting a good example for them, would keep warfare and corporal punishment to a bare minimum, and would place scholars like him in charge of the governing of their states. In a time of rapid social, economic, and political change and of increasing warfare among the states of the Chinese world, it is not surprising that he failed. In his old age his only hope to influence the future lay in his scholarship, his students, and the presentation in his own life and in his teachings of an image of human goodness and steadfastness in adversity that can move even those who do not share his dreams. Out of his bitter failure he had made a moral triumph, and his life and his teachings are at the heart of Chinese optimism about what man can be and can accomplish in this world. In his recorded sayings we seem to get a picture of a real person, afraid, frustrated, moved by music, growing old, convinced that each of us can be truly humane at any moment if only we will really try. I think it is the oldest piece of literature in the world in which such a human portrait emerges.

Confucius's idealization of the past was rooted in reality and in ideas about ruling and goodness that had begun to develop long before his time. Yu's death marked, in Chinese tradition, the shift to transmission of rule by inheritance, in dynasties. Nothing reliable is known about the first dynastic transition, from Xia to Shang. The reality of that from Shang to Zhou, around 1100 B.C.E., is unquestionable, and it is very important for Chinese political ideas. The rulers of the new Zhou dynasty came out of the Wei River valley in Shaanxi, the location of modern Xi'an, on the fringes of the old core of Chinese culture but destined to be its political center for much of the next two thousand years. Some of the texts in the Chinese classical books that appear to be of earliest authentic date are those in the *Shu jing* (Classic of Documents) in which the Zhou conquerors justify their rule to the former subjects of the Shang:

> Your last Shang king abandoned himself to indolence, disdained to apply himself to government, and did not bring pure sacrifices. Heaven thereupon sent down this ruin. . . . Heaven waited for five years, so that his sons and grandsons might yet become lords of the people, but he could not become wise. Heaven then sought among your numerous regions, shaking you with its terrors to stimulate those who might have regard for Heaven, but in all your many regions there was none that was able to do so. But our king of Zhou treated well the multitudes of the people, was able to practice virtue, and fulfilled his duties to the spirits and to Heaven. Heaven instructed us, favored us, selected us, and gave us the Mandate of Yin [Shang], to rule over your numerous regions.[1]

The consolidation of this regime is supposed to have required about fifty years and the suppression of a major uprising in the old Shang heartland. The credit is given less to the kings than to the duke of Zhou, who guided the Zhou state as regent for a child-king who was his nephew. The focus on the duke of Zhou is to some degree a product of the same later idealization of the ministerial role that made Yu so much more interesting as a minister than as a ruler, but recent archaeological finds and historical studies confirm much of the traditional story of the Zhou founding, and it is likely that the duke of Zhou was a historical figure.

Later texts made of the early Zhou state a feudal utopia, with many hereditary lines of local rulers owing ceremonial allegiance to the Zhou kings, elaborate hierarchies of officials, schools, roads and irrigation ditches, and equitable systems of land distribution and revenue collection. Much of this is a reflection of idealizations of systematic bureaucracy that only became influential after Confucius's time. But study of reliable sources, especially the inscriptions on great bronze vessels cast in the early Zhou, make it clear that it was in fact a society with a considerable amount of bureaucratic centralization, in which control was maintained in part by royal visits and the dispatch of royal inspectors to various areas, and by ties of kinship; many local rulers were offshoots of the Zhou ruling house or were intermarried with it. Another important source of unity was the way in which the ceremonial deference of local rulers to the Zhou kings was balanced by the kings' favors to them and confirmation of their positions. Each local ruler had his own ancestral temple and probably also an "altar of earth and grain" symbolizing his territorial sovereignty. Even the royal

---

[1] H. G. Creel, *The Origin of Statecraft in China* (Chicago, 1970), pp. 83–84.

house of Shang was allowed to maintain its ancestral temples, and was granted sovereignty over the small state of Song. Some other ruling houses of small states claimed descent from more ancient rulers of all of China (which probably contributed to the transformation of totem-monsters into sage rulers). Grants of territory and other royal honors frequently were commemorated by the casting of magnificent bronzes; one such bronze, which must have required hundreds of hours of highly skilled labor, records the king's gift to a local lord of part of the game from a royal hunt in which the lord had joined. An ancestral temple full of such bronzes must have been a most impressive reminder of the ties that bound a local ruler to the Zhou order.

The historical record and archaeological record suggest a complex picture of flux and disorder after about 900 B.C.E. The decadence of traditional styles of bronze vessels is striking. From about 700 B.C.E. on, the picture is strikingly different: the Zhou kings have moved from the Wei Valley to Luoyang on the Yellow River out on the north China plain, and they are no longer able to control their vassals, some of whom are beginning to expand their territories and encroach on their neighbors. The Zhou kings are supposed to have moved east after barbarian invasions of the Wei Valley, and it is likely that increasingly tense and complex relations between peoples who participated in the early Zhou culture and those who did not did much to stimulate the emergence of the more warlike competitive states of the following centuries. Bronzes from after about 600 B.C.E. show a striking variety of developments and influences, again suggesting the increasing importance of relations among peoples of a variety of cultural heritages.

The period after 723 B.C.E. is called the Chunqiu age, after a chronicle of the State of Lu, the *Chunqiu* (Spring and Autumn) that begins in that year. An even more important source for these centuries is the *Zuo zhuan* (Chronicle of Zuo), a much longer and more complex work traditionally treated as a commentary on the *Chunqiu*. These sources are full of difficulties and later accretions, but they tell a great deal about political changes from about 700 down to about 450 B.C.E. Out of the many-layered dispersal of power and sovereignty in the early Zhou order, a few centers began to grow in power, to encroach on their neighbors, and to develop the institutions of centralized state power—military command structures, taxes on land, state exploitation of mineral resources, the administration of newly conquered territories by officials serving at the ruler's pleasure rather than by hereditary feudatories. The best-known centers of these developments were the north-central state of Jin; Chu in the south, with a complex cultural heritage quite distinct from that of the north; and Qi in the east, where records of state-building measures were linked to stories of a capable and ruthless prime minister named Guan Zhong. Even Confucius, who deplored all departures from the early Zhou order, believed that Guan Zhong had saved China from being overrun by barbarians.

By Confucius's time, power in many of the states had shifted from the rulers' families to great ministerial families. The latter maintained themselves for several generations and frequently encroached on the prerogatives and powers of the ruling families, but themselves had no standing in the old Zhou feudal order. In some cases it is clear that these families rose to power in the state-building process and maintained themselves through control of new state organs, especially military commands. The dominance of people who rose as ministers and remained ministers in form—like Guan Zhong—is an important source of the idealization of the ministerial role that emerged in these centuries and was associated with the memory of the duke of Zhou. In some states several families struggled for dominance while neighboring states sought to fish in the troubled waters. Diplomacy was intricate and formal, with much attention to the formalities of meetings and oaths and to the persuasive use of classical texts, but also cynical and brutal. Some *shi*, men of aristocratic but modest background, were beginning to make names for themselves as administrators, diplomats, military adventurers. The rise of the *shi* is one of the most important trends of Confucius's times and the two centuries after.

This, then, was the world into which Confucius was born in 551 B.C.E., a world that he deplored and sought to reform but that gave him and his disciples opportunities they would not have had in the early Zhou order they idealized. Confucius was a native of the state of Lu, which was by no means powerless but was somewhat in the shadow of Qi to the north, Chu to the southwest, and Jin to the northwest. Lu had a strong sense of special connection to the early Zhou order; its ruling family were descendants of the duke of Zhou. "Confucius" is a Latinization of "Kong Fuzi," "Master Kong," which has been used by Western students of China since the seventeenth-century Jesuit missionaries. His personal name was Kong Qiu; "Kong Zi," a shorter form of "Master Kong," is the form of reference most readily recognized by Chinese today.

No coherent biography of Confucius has survived from his own times, and those written in later centuries obviously incorporate many legendary elements. His collected sayings, the famous *Lun-yu* (Analects), are by far the best source of knowledge of him, but they are fragments of his teachings and his conversations with his disciples, sometimes loosely organized around a theme, sometimes completely random in sequence, never dated or in chronological order. A few important passages can be found in the *Zuo zhuan* and in the book of the philosopher Mencius. Thus a modern reader can get a convincing sense of some of Confucius's deepest convic-

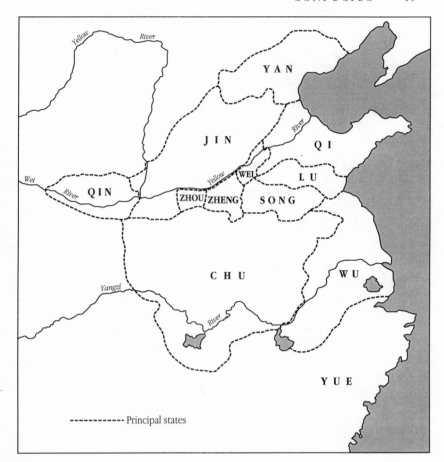

Map 1. China in Confucius's time

tions and emotions, but can know only fragments of a chronology of his movements and political involvements.

In one of his most famous passages of self-revelation, Confucius said: "At fifteen I set my heart on learning; at thirty I had a place to stand; at forty I came to be free from doubts; at fifty I understood the decree of Heaven; at sixty I could hear [that decree] and submit; at seventy I followed my heart's desire without overstepping the bounds" (II, 4).[2]

---

[2] All quotations from the *Analects* are followed by a reference to chapter and section in this form, following the numbering and in general following the interpretations in D. C. Lau's translation. There are occasional slight differences in the numbering used in other translations and in Chinese texts.

If one works from the traditional birthdate of 551 B.C.E., and especially if we suggest that sometimes the reference to age is not exact and may be better read as, for example, "in my fifties," not "at fifty," this sequence of ages can be seen to fit surprisingly well with a few things we do know about Confucius's life. Probably he was of modest aristocratic heritage, but, having no wealth or good personal connections, he had to make a career for himself. We have his own testimony that because he was of humble station when he was young he had acquired many menial skills, and that he had been a storekeeper and a supervisor of herds. He was not proud of these experiences, but his background must have contributed to his lifelong conviction that poverty was no disgrace and should pose no obstacle to obtaining an education or being considered for a position at court.

Confucius sought to rise in the world by becoming an expert on ceremony, genealogy, and ancient lore; the first plausible story about him in the *Zuo zhuan* has him, at the age of about twenty-seven, seeking out a visiting official who could teach him some arcane lore about the naming of officials in the time of the Yellow Lord and his successor. The great historian Sima Qian wrote that Confucius had visited the capital of the powerless Zhou kings, and it is quite plausible that a scholar of ancient lore should have been eager to go there, to see the altars and the ritual vessels. Perhaps it was as a low-ranking officer with ceremonial duties that he "had a place to stand" some time around 520. Later he spent some years in Qi, perhaps seeking employment, perhaps avoiding the impossible situation in Lu, where the three great ministerial families held all the power and the legitimate duke had fled into exile. In Qi he heard the court music of the sage emperor Shun and was so moved that "for three months I did not notice the taste of the meat I ate" (VII, 14). For him knowledge of the ancients had become much more than a useful specialization for an aspiring official; it was the central revelation of man's deepest emotions and highest possibilities. He dreamed of the duke of Zhou.

He also saw in knowledge of the ancients the key to a solution to the political ills of his time. The Zhou founders had devised a harmonious social and political hierarchy, its ranks constantly displayed in distinctions of ceremonial display, forms of greeting, even tombs and coffins. Now both these ceremonial orders and the realities they represented were being constantly flouted. In Lu the legitimate dukes had been ciphers under the power of three great ministerial families for all of Confucius's life, and the most powerful of them, the Ji, used eight rows of dancers at a ceremonial dance in their courtyard, which was a prerogative of the Zhou kings granted to the dukes of Lu because of their descent from the duke of Zhou. "If this can be tolerated," said Confucius, "what cannot be tolerated?" (III,

1). When Duke Jing of Qi asked Confucius about government, he replied, "Let the ruler be a ruler, the subject a subject, the father a father, the son a son." That is, let everyone play his proper role in the traditional order inherited from early Zhou and in the natural order of the family, and all will be well (XII, 11). After he reached the age of forty, he "had no doubts" about the relevance of the early Zhou order to the political ills of his time, and the urgency of reviving it in Lu by placing men like himself in charge of the state. "If anyone were to employ me, in a year's time I would have brought things to a satisfactory state, and after three years I should have results to show for it" (XIII, 10). Asked about one of the most solemn sacrificial ceremonies, he denied understanding of it and said that "whoever understands it will be able to control the world as easily as if he had it here," and pointed to the palm of his hand (III, 11). "Lu, at one stroke, can be made to attain the [true ancient] way" (VI, 24).

Already Confucius had begun to gather around him a group of men, some of them not much younger than he, who took him as their teacher. It was apparently through one of these students, Zi Lu, that he got a chance for a more substantial position in Lu. In 502 a revolt by several military adventurers against the domination of the Ji family in Lu failed. It probably was after this that Zi Lu became chief steward of the Ji, and by his influence obtained a series of modest posts for his master, including one as a junior official in charge of the punishment of criminals. We know what he thought of the ceremonial usurpations of the Ji, and if he also was beginning to develop his later antipathy to the use of punishments, it is hard to imagine a less congenial political situation. But it was a way to serve Lu and to try to gain some influence over its affairs.

In 500 Confucius is said to have assisted the duke of Lu at a diplomatic meeting with the duke of Qi. A Qi adviser, thinking Confucius an expert on ceremony but not brave, had some savage local people appear at the meeting, hoping to take the duke of Lu captive and force him to agree to Qi's wishes. When the savages appeared Confucius advised his lord to withdraw, saying to the duke of Qi that the intrusion of armed savages on a friendly meeting between rulers was no way to persuade the rulers of other states to do the bidding of Qi. He then guided the Lu negotiators in insisting that Qi return some border lands to Lu if it wanted Lu's agreement to send troops to assist in any Qi expedition outside its borders, and he gave good advice on several points of ceremony and protocol. Most Chinese scholars have rejected this story, finding its picture of Confucius as a clever diplomatic tactician at odds with his uncompromising idealism. But it seems to me that this is a good example of the combination of eloquence, loyal service, and specialized knowledge of ceremonies that made

Confucius a valuable minister at this time and made many of his disciples employable then and later. Also, his cleverness was not in the service of just any state but of Lu, which to him had a special heritage and special destiny. Opportunism and clever tactics may well have seemed justified to support the interests of this very special state and to enhance the influence in it of Confucius and his followers. Confucius's search for political influence in Lu even led him to be tempted to join a survivor of the earlier rebellions who seemed to have a chance of gaining power. "If his purpose is to employ me, can I not, perhaps, create another Zhou in the east?" (XVII, 5).

In records of the year 498, Confucius appears on the fringes of an attempt instigated by Zi Lu to demolish the fortified strongholds of the three great ministerial families. These strongholds, evidence of the families' long domination of the affairs of the state, actually had become liabilities to them, held in defiance of them by rebellious vassals. Their demolition ostensibly would be a step toward the restoration of the rightful power of the duke of Lu, but also would serve the interests of Zi Lu's patrons the Ji and the other two great families. The attempt failed. Zi Lu and Confucius lost their positions and had to flee from Lu, not to return for thirteen years.

It is hard to get any sense of change or development in the ideas of Confucius. The passages in the *Analects* are not dated. To later Chinese, Confucius was a sage, who despite his very human emotions, or perhaps in part because of them, had perfect insight and absolute moral pitch, and knew everything he needed to know from the beginning. I suspect, however, that there was development in his ideas, largely as a result of the change from efforts to gain influence in his native state, with its special heritage, to seeking a ruler, any ruler, who would listen to him and adopt his ideas. In Lu the special heritage of the state had justified opportunism in its service and in search for power within it. Failure there may have taught Confucius that there were no quick fixes, no possibilities of the restoration of ancient institutions within a few years. And there was even less prospect for such a change in other states, where the early Zhou heritage was not so well preserved or highly esteemed.

It seems possible to put together a coherent reading of his moral and political teachings that shows them becoming more general, less tied to details of the early Zhou, more absolute in their moral demands. Confucius himself is seen in such a reading becoming less a man of Lu struggling to shape the special destiny of his native land, more a would-be minister of any ruler who would employ him, with no power base, no selfish goals, nothing to offer except the fearsome integrity of himself and his teachings, who threatened not political intrigue or a coup but embarrassing and uncompromising criticism. Eventually he made a principle of this free-floating search for employment with integrity: "While the gentleman cherishes virtuous rule, the small man cherishes his native land" (IV, 11). "It is a shameful matter to be poor and humble when the Way prevails in the state. Equally, it is a shameful matter to be rich and noble when the Way falls into disuse in the state" (VIII, 13).

His progress toward these views, in this reading, was gradual. At the beginning of his exile Confucius may have taken some kind of minor post under Duke Ling of Wei, who was not a moral ruler but had good ministers (XIV, 19). He even submitted to an interview with the notoriously evil Nan Zi, wife of the duke, exclaiming afterward, "If I have done anything improper, may Heaven's curse be upon me! May Heaven's curse be upon me!" (VI, 28). His views of what Wei needed were sensible and moderate; as he traveled through the state, he remarked to the disciple who was driving his chariot, "What a flourishing population!" The disciple asked, "When the population is flourishing, what further benefit can one add?" "Make the people rich." "When the people have become rich, what further benefit can one add?" "Train them" (XIII, 9). But when a distant relative of Zi Lu offered to obtain for him a higher position, he refused, saying "There is the Decree." Perhaps he no longer wished to make the compromises with corrupt power he had been willing to make in Lu and when he first arrived in Wei. Perhaps this situation and his exile from Lu were convincing him that it was Heaven's decree that he preserve the ancient Zhou moral teachings at all costs, including the risk of never achieving political power.

It was in his fifties, between 501 and 492, that Confucius said he had come to understand the decree of Heaven. In addition to his experiences in Lu and Wei politics, his sense of his destiny and mission were profoundly shaped by a number of incidents during his exile when he and his disciples were in physical danger and very much afraid. The first may have happened on his first trip from Lu to Wei, when the local people in a place called Kuang, mistaking him for one of the military adventurers who had sought power in Lu and also raided in this area, surrounded his little band. To be in danger was bad enough; to be in danger because one is mistaken for someone else must be unbearable. "When under siege in Kuang, the Master said, 'With King Wen dead, is not this Literary Heritage invested here in me? If Heaven intends this Literary Heritage to be destroyed, those who come after me will not be able to have any part of it. If Heaven does not intend this Literary Heritage to be destroyed, then what can the men of Kuang do to me?'" (IX, 5). "Literary Heritage" is my translation for the word *wen*, the same as in the name of King Wen, basically meaning "writing." Often used in contrast with *wu*, "martial virtue," *wen* implies the arts and virtues of scholarship and nonmilitary governing. The Zhou heritage that Confucius had dreamed of reviving in Lu was of course known through written records, but it is interesting that Confucius in this famous and important passage referred to the Literary Heritage itself, not to the ceremonies and institutions for which it provided evidence. I suspect that for him the beauty and moral power of the texts themselves were becoming more important, the early Zhou institutions and ceremonies less.

In their wanderings in exile Confucius and his disciples also were attacked by one Huan Tui, and the Master said, "Heaven is the author of the virtue that is within me. What can Huan Tui do to me?" (VII, 23). Confucius may have held office briefly in the small state of Chen, but it also was in that state that he and his group ran completely out of food and were so weak that they could not walk. Zi Lu asked, "Are there times when even gentlemen are brought to such extreme straits?" The Master replied, "It comes as no surprise to the gentleman to find himself in extreme straits. The small man finding himself in extreme straits would throw over all restraint" (XV, 2).

Perhaps Confucius's most interesting encounter during his years of exile was with the governor of She, a highly intelligent and successful official of the southern state of Chu, a rising power in the Chinese world with a distinctive culture that many other Chinese considered barbaric. The governor was trying to set up a sort of satellite state of former subjects of the small state of Cai who had not fled as Chu conquered their homeland. A "barbarian" and no respecter of the traditional sovereignties of small states, the governor nevertheless was interested in discussing government with Confucius. The essential, Confucius said, was to "Ensure that those who are near are pleased and those who are far away are attracted" (XIII, 16). Here Confucius anticipated a common theme of a number of schools of political thought in the next two centuries—the importance, in a world of competing territorial states, of keeping the common people prosperous and contented and attracting immigration from other states to strengthen the economy and provide more recruits for the armies. Another discussion developed a more specifically "Confucian" theme. The governor of She told Confucius about a man in his native place who was so upright that when his father stole a sheep he gave evidence against him. Confucius answered, "In our village those who are straight are quite different. Fathers cover up for their sons, and sons cover up for their fathers. Straightness is to be found in such behavior" (XIII, 18).

Confucius's years of exile ended with another visit to Wei, where he was treated with respect by Kong Yu, the minister who was the actual ruler of the state on behalf of a child duke. Confucius was revolted by a violent struggle within the ruling family and by the cynical way in which Kong Yu manipulated his own marriage connections. When Kong Yu asked Confucius's advice on how to attack a noble who was dishonoring his marriage to Kong's daughter, Confucius replied that he knew all about ceremonies but nothing about military matters, and left Wei. This was in part an excuse for getting out of an impossible situation and in part a statement of fact and principle; Confucius is not known to have ever offered advice about military matters, and he consistently downplayed the importance of military affairs in the politics of his time.

Confucius and his disciples now were able to return to Lu, about 484, and he spent the last five years of his life there. Another of his disciples, Ran Qiu, now was steward of the Ji family, so Confucius returned to an uncomfortable situation much like the one he had occupied fifteen years before. Ran Qiu consulted him about a proposal to tax lands in the state, and Confucius replied by urging light taxation; if the rulers were not greedy the traditional taxes would be enough, but if they constantly wanted more revenues not even the proposed land tax would satisfy them. Ran Qiu ignored his advice, taxes were increased, and the angry old man said to his disciples, "He is no disciple of mine. You, my young friends, may attack him openly to the beating of drums" (XI, 17).

Confucius was given an honorary position as a counselor of the lowest rank. When the duke of Qi was killed by one of his ministers, Confucius took his position seriously enough to request formally a Lu expedition to chastise the assassin. He seems to have expected that no one would want to listen to him, saying, "I have reported this to you simply because I have a duty to do so" (XIV, 21). He was more listened to on questions of ceremonial proprieties for noble funerals. He spent much time teaching his disciples, working on the editing of early Zhou classical texts, and completing (according to tradition) the *Chunqiu* chronicle. Confucius's conversations with Duke Ai of Lu and with Ji Kang Zi, the current head of the Ji family and apparently Confucius's most important patron, give the fullest picture of the uncompromising demands he made on rulers and of his immense faith in the power of moral example in politics. It also should be noted that there is no reference to early Zhou ceremonies and institutions in these passages.

Duke Ai asked, "What must I do before the common people will look up to me?"

Confucius answered, "Raise the straight and set them over the crooked and the common people will look up to you. Raise the crooked and set them over the straight and the common people will not look up to you."

Ji Kang Zi asked, "How can one inculcate in the common people the virtue of reverence, of doing their best, and of enthusiasm?"

The Master said, "Rule over them with dignity and they will be reverent; treat them with kindness and they will do their best; raise the good and instruct those who are backward and they will be imbued with enthusiasm." (II, 19, 20)

Ji Kang Zi asked Confucius about government. Confucius answered, "To govern is to correct. If you set an example by being correct, who would dare to remain incorrect?"

The prevalence of thieves was a source of trouble to Ji Kang Zi, who asked the advice of Confucius. Confucius answered, "If you yourself were not a man of desires, no one would steal even if stealing carried a reward."

Ji Kang Zi asked Confucius about government, saying, "What would you think if, in order to move closer to those who possess the Way, I were to kill those who do not follow the Way?" Confucius answered, "In administering your government, what need is there for you to kill? Just desire the good yourself and the common people will be good. The virtue of the gentleman is like wind; the virtue of the small man is like grass. Let the wind blow over the grass and it is sure to bend." (XII, 17, 18, 19)

These last years were marred by the death at an early age of Confucius's favorite disciple, Yan Hui, who did not allow his poverty to affect his delight in the Way, always was eager to learn, and never faltered in putting his Master's teachings into practice. When he died, the Master cried. "Alas! Heaven has bereft me! Heaven has bereft me!" His disciples protested that he was showing undue sorrow. "Am I? Yet if not for him, for whom should I show undue sorrow?" (IX, 9, 10).

At sixty, while wandering in exile, he finally had been able, he said, not only to understand the decree of Heaven but to submit to it; at seventy, back in Lu, he could follow his heart's desires without overstepping the bounds. But old age took its toll: "Great indeed is my decline! For a long time now I have not dreamed of the duke of Zhou" (VII, 5). He died in his seventy-fifth year, in 479. The duke of Lu, in a proclamation of ceremonial mourning for him, violated the ceremonial proprieties so dear to Confucius by calling himself "I the One Man," an expression supposed to be used solely by the Zhou Son of Heaven.

This sketch of Confucius's life and of some of the ways in which it may have shaped his teachings has not yet led to some of his deepest and most important ideas. In the passages of the *Analects* in which they are developed, explicit references to the great men and institutions of earlier ages are not common, but none of his teachings is fully comprehensible apart from Confucius's fascination with antiquity. Confucius once insisted that he was "a transmitter but not a creator" (VII, 1); I would prefer to take seriously his vocation as a transmitter of an ancient culture but also to insist that he was a highly creative transmitter. He created the role of the scholar-minister, studying and passing on an ancient heritage and holding it up as a mirror to his ruler's conduct. He changed, universalized, moralized the meanings of some words found in the early Zhou texts. Above all, he created a world view of profound optimism about the goodness of human nature and the possibility of benign government, which he and later Confucians could not have sustained if they had not been so thoroughly convinced that human moral and political perfection actually had existed in the early Zhou and in the days of Yao, Shun, and Yu.

Confucius's search for a ruler who would listen to him and employ him was very near to the core of his values. He would have been shocked by present-day dismissals of "just politics" and "just like a politician." For him there was no higher calling than government, and the man who was not involved in government was radically incomplete. In the words of Zi Lu, "Not to enter public life is to ignore one's duty. Even the proper regulation of old and young cannot be put aside. How, then, can the duty between ruler and subject be set aside? This is to cause confusion in the most important of human relationships simply because one desires to keep one's unsullied character. The gentleman takes office in order to do his duty" (XVIII, 7). The Confucian aspired to be recognized by a ruler and chosen as a minister. The ruler should "Set an example for your officials to follow; show leniency to minor offenders; and promote men of talent" (XIII, 2). The common people, as we have seen, had to be looked after and allowed to prosper, but they played a fundamentally passive role, grass before the wind of the teaching of their superiors. The basic grammar of politics here defined was generally accepted from Confucius's time down to our own century: a common people politically passive except in times of gravest crisis, officials watching over them who were morally independent but politically completely dependent on appointment by a ruler. It also was generally accepted that government produced nothing, that its revenues represented a dead loss to the people, and thus that taxes should be kept as light as possible. This, the selection of good officials, and the setting of good moral examples should suffice to keep order. "The Master said, 'Guide them by edicts, keep them in line with punishments, and the common people will stay out of trouble but will have no sense of shame. Guide them by virtue, keep them in line with ceremonies, and they will, besides having a sense of shame, reform themselves'" (II, 3).

The disciple Zi Gong asked about government. Confucius said, "Give them enough food, give them enough arms, and the common people will have trust in you." Zi Gong then asked, "If one had to give up one of these three, which should one give up first?" "Give up arms." Which next? "Give up food. Death has always been with us since the beginning of time, but when there is no trust, the common people will have nothing to stand on" (XII, 7).

Rulers listening to such advice may have recognized that it embodied basic wisdom from which they could learn much, but at the same time they knew that it was no substitute for advice on what to do *right now* about bandits descending on peasant villages or the army of a neighboring state poised to invade. A bias toward fundamental analysis of problems and the proposal of long-run solutions was characteristic of many Confucian statesmen down to our own time. It could be a source of great strength of systematic administration in times of stable government, but it could produce absurd impracticalities in times of flux and crisis. We might agree that good men, rulers and ministers, were the most basic and long-term solution to political problems and still sympathize with the ruler who needed advice of more immediate applicability.

If I am right that Confucius became disillusioned about the possibility of a quick return to the early Zhou system, the long-run solution he came to focus on had at its center the idea that every ruler, every minister or would-be minister, should aspire to be a gentleman, a *junzi*. There are many sayings about the gentleman in the *Analects*. Quite a few of them are brief and contrast the attitudes and behavior of the gentleman with those of the "small man." Some of this is apt guidance for anyone's moral striving:

> The gentleman is troubled by his own lack of ability, not by the failure of others to appreciate him. (XV, 21)

> What the gentleman seeks, he seeks within himself; what the small man seeks, he seeks in others. (XV, 21)

> The gentleman is easy of mind, while the small man is always full of anxiety. (VII, 37)

Others are more specific to the situation of the minister or would-be minister, and these help to fill out an understanding of ministerial ethics. The minister should not associate with others to amass power or limit the ruler's freedom of decision: "The gentleman enters into associations but not cliques; the small man enters into cliques but not associations" (II, 14). "The gentleman is not a vessel" (II, 11). In the latter passage, of just four characters, "vessel" (*qi*) means especially a sacrificial vessel, something with a specialized and ornamental use. The gentleman is not a specialist but a moral generalist, and he must be given real responsibility, not just made an ornament of a court. *Qi* also means "tool" or "instrument," and the gentleman must be treated as a morally autonomous individual, not just a tool of the ruler who employs him.

That is quite a lot to pack into just four characters! The expression *junzi* itself packs a complex history and set of associations. The characters literally mean "son of the prince," and that and the frequent contrast with the "little man" make it clear that this term has a background of class feeling, of contrast between the values and actions appropriate to rulers and those for the ruled, much like the history of "gentleman" in English and many other important moral terms. In early Zhou texts *junzi* usually simply means "the ruler." It was Confucius's great achievement to insist that not only those who had a hereditary right to office could aspire to be gentlemen, but anyone who sought education, moral growth, and involvement in governing; his gentleman is a highly appropriate ideal for the rising class of the *shi*, the lowest aristocracy with no hereditary right to office. Certainly there was a great deal of class feeling left in the term, and he probably intended it to apply more to impoverished *shi* like himself and Yan Hui than to farmers and artisans, but it was basically an ideal of moral striving open to anyone.

Men from modest backgrounds could aspire to the life of the gentleman only if they could obtain the necessary education. One of Confucius's greatest achievements was his emphasis on education. The *Analects* paints a picture of a teacher who would accept any student, no matter how meager the gift or payment that student was able to make (VII, 7). This teacher was thoroughly aware of the varying abilities and temperaments of his disciples and of the different ways in which they needed to be taught: some needed to be held back, others to be urged on (XI, 22). The future of his great cause depended entirely on its transmission to the next generation; this made him reverent, loving, demanding:

> I never enlighten anyone who has not been driven to distraction by trying to understand a difficulty or who has not got into a frenzy trying to put his ideas into words. When I have pointed out one corner of a square to anyone and he does not come back with the other three, I will not point it out to him a second time. (VII, 8)

> It is fitting that we should hold the young in awe. How do we know that the generations to come will not be the equal of the present? Only when a man reaches the age of forty or fifty without distinguishing himself in any way can one say, I suppose, that he does not deserve to be held in awe. (IX, 23)

Another famous passage literally says "In teaching no classifications" (XV, 39); traditionally it has been taken to mean that in education there should be no class distinctions, but it also has been read as making the very different but important point that in teaching there should be no separation into hard and fast categories or specializations.

In China Confucius has always been known as the First Teacher. His example is at the root of the extraordinary respect for education and teachers still to be found in all Chinese communities today. The First Teacher set an example for his students by being himself constantly engaged in learning, in the study of ancient texts and the application in his own life of the moral lessons to be found in them, and in learning through discussion. The human mind might have the roots of goodness in it, but they were better developed by these forms of learning than by absorption in the solitary mind. The process was demanding, but it also brought the joys of growing understanding and of encounters with the great men and great writings of the past.

> I once spent all day thinking without taking food and all night thinking without going to bed, but I found that I gained nothing from it. It would have been better to spend the time in learning. (XV, 31)

> Is it not a pleasure, having learned something, to try it out at due intervals? Is it not a joy to have friends come from afar? Is it not the way of a gentleman not to take offence when others fail to appreciate your abilities? (I, 1)

> Even when walking in the company of two other men, I am bound to be able to learn from them. The good points of the one I copy; the bad points of the other I correct in myself. (VII, 22)

The term that best sums up the focus of Confucius and his disciples is "the Way" (*dao*). "The Master said, 'He has not lived in vain who dies the day he is told about the Way" (IV, 8). For Confucius and his followers this meant, among other things, the Way of the Former Kings, the institutions and moral examples inherited from Yao, Shun, Yu, and the Zhou founders. But, as seen in the stories about the sage kings, this Way was neither an accidental human invention nor an arbitrary command of god or gods, but the result of the discovery by the sages of the basic patterns of nature and human nature and the elaboration of a way of life based on them that made it possible for people to be fully human, to live in harmony with nature and their fellow human beings. Chinese thinkers also came to call these basic patterns the Way—the way of nature, the way the world works. There was no radical distinction between the two; the Way of the Former Kings was firmly rooted in the Way of Nature.

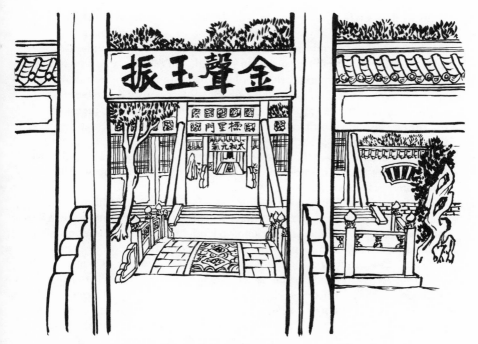

3. Memorial arches at the Confucius Shrine, Qufu

This is especially clear in Confucius's treatment of the very important complex of values and customs referred to by the awkward phrase "filial piety," which involved the obedience of young people to their parents, kind and generous care of aged parents, prolonged and heartfelt mourning after their deaths, and reverence for earlier ancestors in the male line. Filial piety sometimes is thought of as a repressive and unnatural system, and it certainly produced some bizarre phenomena in later centuries, but in the view of it that Confucius helped to shape, it was a life-enhancing expression of natural emotions. When one of Confucius's disciples suggested that the traditional three years of mourning for a parent (actually twenty-seven months) was too long, Confucius said that if he really would feel at ease going back to ordinary life after just one year he should do so. But after the disciple left Confucius said, "How unfeeling Yu is! A child ceases to be nursed by his parents only when he is three years old. Three years' mourning is observed throughout the Empire. Was Yu not given three years' love by his parents?" (XVII, 21). In several other passages he emphasized that it was the genuineness of reverence for aged parents and of grief over their deaths that counted most, not the food given them while they lived or the details of the funeral ceremonies (II, 7; II, 8; II, 4).

This attitude toward funeral ceremonies is an excellent example of Confucius's attitude toward ceremony in general. He may have lost his early faith in the political changes that could be brought about by restoring the early Zhou ceremonial order, but he always took seriously the usefulness of traditional ceremonial patterns for regulating relations among members of the ruling class and diplomacy among states. Expertise in these matters was the most important asset that made Confucius and his disciples employable. "If it is really possible to govern countries by ceremony and yielding, there is no more to be said. But if it is not really possible, of what use is ceremony?" (IV, 13).

Confucius contributed to the emergence in his time of a unified understanding of ceremony (*li*) that has been accepted by most Chinese down to our own time. It included two friends bowing and exchanging courtesies when they met; a son making sure his father's coffin was appropriate to his rank and then mourning for him for twenty-seven months; two rulers and their ministers subtly adjusting indications of relative status before a diplomatic encounter; ministers taking their places before their ruler according to their ranks; rulers performing sacrifices to Heaven, Earth, spirits of local places and natural forces, and their own royal ancestors. In this unified understanding, all these forms of ceremony were manifestations of the interactions of the Way of Nature and the Way of the Former Kings, and kept them meshed in one patterned harmony of feelings, acts, and the natural cycles of the seasons and the transitions of human life and death. Confucius advanced this unified view by taking family ceremonies and proprieties and ceremonies of political hierarchy very seriously as foundations of political order, and by turning resolutely away from the preoccupation of many of his contemporaries with the use of ceremonies to manipulate the forces of the spirit world and ward off supernatural disasters. Moreover, ceremony played a large part in the development of the human capacities of the gentleman; their orderly beauty gave him great joy, and at the same time the necessity of performing ceremonies correctly was a form of conquest of oneself (XII, 1). The same combination of form, discipline, and emotion is to be found in music, which Confucius also loved.

The reader will have noticed that Confucius's Way does not include much of what we would most easily identify as religion. It was not that he scorned traditional beliefs or tried to argue that there were no supernatural realities, but that he put his emphasis elsewhere:

> Fan Chi asked about wisdom. The Master said, "To work for the things the common people have a right to and to keep one's distance

from the ghosts and spirits while showing them reverence can be called wisdom." (VI, 22)

Ji Lu asked how the spirits of the dead and the gods should be served. The Master said, "You are not yet able to serve man. How can you serve the spirits?" "May I ask about death?" "You do not yet understand life. How can you understand death?" (XI, 12)

The Master was seriously ill. Zi Lu asked permission to offer a prayer. The Master said, "Was such a thing ever done?" Zi Lu said it was. The prayer offered was as follows: "Pray thus to the gods above and below." The Master said, "In that case, I have long been offering my prayers." (VII, 35)

Heaven had a purpose for him and a care for the fate of mankind, but "What does Heaven ever say? Yet there are the four seasons going round and there are the hundred things coming into being. What does Heaven ever say?" (XVII, 19).

The highest realization of the Confucian Way, and the closest approach of his teaching to the sense of something always available to us but too deep for us to grasp steadily, which many in Western traditions express in terms of the relation between God and mankind, is found in Confucius's sayings about benevolence (*ren*). The very simple character is composed of the characters for "man" and "two." In early Zhou texts it sometimes means something like "manly" or "handsome." "Benevolence" is perhaps the least unsatisfactory of many inadequate translations, which at least has the merit of suggesting the roots of this highest realization of man in desire to do good and to treat others with kindness.

The concept of benevolence always carried a strong sense of a quality that was rooted in human nature and readily accessible to people if they would only look for it, and of the importance of twoness, of self and other. It was closely associated with a more commonsense idea of reciprocity or selflessness: "Do not impose on others what you yourself do not desire" (XV, 24). "Zhong Gong asked about benevolence. The Master said, 'When abroad behave as though you were receiving an important guest. When employing the services of the common people behave as though you were officiating at an important sacrifice. Do not impose on others what you yourself do not desire'" (XII, 2). Benevolence was simply the sum and summit of all the particular virtues, and in that way could be closely tied to ceremony.

To return to the ceremonies through overcoming the self constitutes benevolence. If for a single day a man could return to the observance of the ceremonies through overcoming himself, then the whole empire would consider benevolence to be his. However, the practice of benevolence depends on oneself alone, and not on others. (XII, 1)

Is benevolence really far away? No sooner do I desire it than it is here. (VII, 30)

Is there a man who, for the space of a single day, is able to devote all his strength to benevolence? I have not come across such a man whose strength is insufficient for the task. There must be such cases of insufficient strength, only I have not come across them. (IV, 6)

In his heart for three months at a time [Yan] Hui does not lapse from benevolence. The others attain benevolence only by fits and starts. (VI, 7)

The view of Confucius developed above relies almost entirely on the *Analects*. Followers of Confucius's teachings in later centuries also drew on many other sources. In some biographies he was represented as a child prodigy, a man of great height and strange appearance, an expert on all kinds of abstruse ancient lore, a semidivine figure of great historical destiny, a high official in Lu who brought good order to that state in a very short time; all quite a distance from the magnificent portrait of moral fervor and human frustration in the *Analects*.

Less at variance with the attitudes found in the *Analects* were the teachings ascribed to him and his favorite disciples in a number of short texts that were more connected in exposition and more abstractly philosophical than the *Analects*; traditional Chinese scholars accepted these texts as records of Confucius, but modern researchers believe them to be of later date and not reliable records of the Master's words. In the *Xiao jing* (Classic of Filial Piety), Confucius is shown explaining this key virtue: "To establish yourself and follow the Way, exalting your name to later generations, and thus casting glory upon your father and mother, is the beginning of filial piety." The *Da xue* (Great Learning) made dogmatically clear the Confucian emphasis on the priority of study and moral effort:

Only when affairs are investigated is knowledge extended; only when knowledge is extended are thoughts sincere; only when thoughts are sincere are minds rectified; only when minds are rectified are our persons cultivated; only when our persons are cultivated are our families regulated; only when families are regulated are states well governed; and only when states are well governed is there peace in the world.

The *Zhong yong* (Doctrine of the Mean) showed benevolence as the sum of all the virtues, the fullest realization of what it is to be a human being, but also went beyond this to an ideal of sincerity (*cheng*), or perfect harmony of word and actuality, in which this moral sincerity opened the way to a harmony with the cosmos:

> Only those who are absolutely sincere can fully develop their nature. If they can fully develop their nature they can fully develop the nature of others. If they can fully develop the nature of others, then they can fully develop the nature of things. If they can fully develop the nature of things, they can assist in the transforming and nourishing process of Heaven and Earth. If they can assist in the transforming and nourishing process of Heaven and Earth, they can thus form a trinity with Heaven and Earth.

Despite the great power and beauty of these texts and their teachings, nothing in them quite matches the depth of insight into the human condition that comes from reading and rereading the *Analects* in all their disorder and diversity. In the *Analects*, even an exploration of the most abstract and mysterious of Confucius's teachings, that on benevolence, leads right back to the beloved disciple Yan Hui whose early death he mourned so bitterly. Confucius seems to have found it altogether appropriate that his disciples should know of his joys and sorrows, his angers at abuses of power and his own terrible frustration about his failure to obtain office. He let his disciples see him as a man, not as some kind of near-divine being standing above human desires and frustrations. And the disciples who put together the *Analects* thought it fitting that they should preserve these very human expressions of emotion by their Master.

If Confucius had succeeded in his search for political office he might be remembered as one of a number of wise statesmen of the Chunqiu period, or as the author of an interesting experiment in restoring the early Zhou order in Lu. It was because of his failures and frustrations that he concentrated more on teaching and scholarship, developed the ideals of the gentleman and benevolence. He valued worldly success, but also knew how to make something even greater than success out of frustration and grief, and he gave us a teaching and a human example that can sustain us in success and in failure. In the words of the great disciple Zeng Zi, "A gentleman must be strong and resolute, for his burden is heavy and the road is long. He takes benevolence as his burden. Is that not heavy? Only with death does the road come to an end. Is that not long?" (VIII, 7).

For Confucius time flowed ceaselessly, like a river: "While standing by a river, the Master said, 'What passes away is, perhaps, like this. Day and night it never lets up'" (IX, 17). People missed chances, mourned, died. But that made the joys of being human nobler, keener. At a particularly bitter and discouraging moment in his travels, the governor of She asked the disciple Zi Lu about Confucius, and Zi Lu told his master he had not known how to answer. The Master said, "Why didn't you simply say something like this: He is the sort of man who forgets to eat when he tries to solve a problem that has been driving him to distraction, who is so full of joy that he forgets his worries and who does not notice that old age is coming on?" (VII, 19). As we read him and come to our own understanding of his teaching—and we must, for no summary does it justice, and it is above all the sense of a man we must confront—we may come to feel about his Way as did the gifted Yan Hui, whose early death almost broke Confucius's heart: "The more I look up at it the higher it appears. The more I bore into it the harder it becomes. I see it before me. Suddenly it is behind me. The Master is good at leading one on step by step. He broadens us with culture and brings us back to essentials by means of the ceremonies. I cannot give up even if I wanted to, but, having done all I can, it [his Way] seems to rise sheer above me and I have no way of going after it, however much I may want to" (IX, 11).

THE FIRST
EMPEROR OF QIN
(Qin Shihuang)

• • • • • •

THE CHINESE always have seen their history as full of lessons, of good and bad examples. For all but a few premodern Chinese, the First Qin Emperor was the greatest of bad examples, demonstrating that totalitarian enforcement of law, repression of dissent, and heavy burdens of taxes and forced labor will lead swiftly to the collapse of the government that seeks to impose them.

Bad examples often make good stories. Lao Ai and the dowager queen, Jing Ke, sent off with a song, the emperor's decaying corpse being hurried toward the capital, village conscripts claiming the Mandate of Heaven—the story of Qin bursts with coarse will and individuality. This is not just the story-teller's art; today one can sense some of the same energy in the army of life-size terra-cotta soldiers and horses made to guard the emperor in his tomb. Every one is individual, the faces returning our gaze boldly.

The Qin state was a product of and a reaction against the anarchic vigor of politics, commerce, and thought that characterized the Warring States period. One of the most important foundations of the basic changes in all these spheres was the rapidly expanding use of iron, already visible in Confucius's lifetime and continuing all through this period. Once the higher temperatures needed to smelt iron ore were attained, iron was much more abundant than the copper and tin that made bronze. Probably because they already were expert in firing fine pottery, the Chinese skipped the forged-iron stage and went straight to cast iron, using kiln-heated molds, two thousand years ahead of Europeans. One result was an immense increase in numbers of metal weapons. But weapons are useless unless soldiers can be fed and clothed, and the appalling war-making capacity of the great states of this period depended on their vigorous economic growth and on efficient methods of taxation. Iron made iron plowshares and axes for clearing forests, tools for craftspeople, kettles for preparing dyes, drugs, salt, and

4. The Qin Terra-cotta Army

food, as well as weapons. Large cities developed with specialized quarters for various crafts.

States contributed to economic growth by building roads and by digging canals both for transport and for irrigation. Interregional trade made it possible for various regions to produce their own characteristic products in larger quantities for wider markets—a situation probably reflected in the "Tribute of Yu" text—and produced for the first time some very wealthy and powerful merchants. Private individuals bought and sold land; states still bestowed on great men grants of land and the families who farmed it, but this no longer was the only way in which rich people held land. As a result, systems had to be devised for taxing land regardless of who owned it, so that part of the product of privately owned fields still would go to support the government, and a bureaucracy had to be developed for this complicated task. Confucius himself in his last years had opposed the introduction of a land-tax scheme in Lu. Rulers and political thinkers also worried about ways of taxing the growing wealth of artisans and merchants. In a world of competing states and mobile people, rulers had to balance their need for tax revenue against their desire to attract, not repel, wealthy merchants and productive artisans and farmers. Confucius had advised the governor of She to "ensure that those from far away are attracted."

Rulers also were eager to attract wandering *shi* to their states. *Shi* sometimes is translated "knight," and many of the wandering *shi* were exceptional archers, swordsmen, strongmen, tacticians, or simply those crazy suicidal "war-lovers" who have their uses in every military establishment. Others sought employment as bureaucrats, by their numbers and skills making possible the organization of huge public works projects (canals, roads, walls), the administration of big cities and complicated tax systems, and the gradual spread from one state to another of the practice of administering outlying areas as *xian*, direct dependencies of the central government under appointed salaried magistrates, not hereditary feudal lords living off the revenues of the areas they ruled. In the records of this period, it is amazing how securely centralized these states seem, how rarely local divisions appear to affect their politics, and how interchangeable their officials were; men moved from state to state at all levels, sometimes even as prime ministers, and no one seems to have reproached them for disloyalty to their native lands. Here as in so many other ways, Confucius can be seen to have anticipated a theme of Warring States politics, acting out in his years of exile a singularly high-principled version of the wandering *shi* searching for a prince who would employ him: "While the gentleman cherishes benign rule, the small man cherishes his native land" (*Analects*, IV, 11).

There were seven great states: Yan in the northeast, Qi, Chu, Qin, Wei, Han, and Zhao—the latter three states formed by the breakup of Jin. Wu, in the lower Yangzi area, was a rising power on the edge of the world of Chinese culture. Shifting alliances and cynical betrayals were the order of the day, as political intriguers moved from state to state seeking office and offering new strategies, new tricks. There were major invasions and battles almost every year. Each of the seven states could put in the field an army of 100,000 or more. Slaughter of defeated armies was the rule. No one paid any attention to the Zhou high king; all the rulers of the great states now called themselves kings (*wang*). Everyone involved in politics seems to have expected that out of the chaos one of the states would emerge supreme and impose some kind of new order, but no one expected it to be a re-creation of the Bronze Age order of the early Zhou. A wide variety of formulas for political success seemed plausible.

It was this sense of a total breakdown of the old order and of the many possibilities of a new one that made the years of the Warring States the years of the "Hundred Schools," the most vigorous, creative, and varied period in all of Chinese intellectual history. Some wandering *shi* were less swords for hire or would-be bureaucrats than wandering scholars—again like Confucius—offering to the rulers of their time a remarkable variety of ideas about man, nature, government, and the good life. Rulers of the states listened with interest to any scheme that might improve their prospects for survival and ultimate victory. They also gained prestige as patrons of culture by supporting scholars at their courts, listening to their debates, and encouraging their efforts to compile ancient texts, histories, and the writings of various schools. By the end of the period there was even one great merchant playing the culture-patron game.

Some of the thinkers of the Hundred Schools produced writings longer and more connected in argument than the *Analects* of Confucius and matching them in depth and uncanny beauty. There is quite a lot of intelligent discussion of them in Western languages, excellent translations are available, and several of them are worth repeated readings or even a lifetime of study. Here I shall discuss them only as the background to the rise of Qin and to anticipate a few ideas developed in later chapters.

In some of these thinkers the focus on politics and ethics is obvious. This is true of the two great followers and developers of the teachings of Confucius, Mencius (Meng Zi) and Xun Zi. Mencius emphasized the potential goodness of human nature, and the way it could come to realization under selfless rulers and institutions like those of the early Zhou. Xun Zi, much less optimistic about human nature, still thought it could be disciplined and socialized by moral effort and ceremony. The political focus also is easy to see in the teachings of Mo Zi, who shared the Confucians' moral approach to politics and opposition to the extinction of small states and other abuses of the power of rulers, but deplored the expense and waste of time of elaborate funerals and other ceremonies. Mo Zi condemned the drift of the Confucian school away from concern with the spirits and belief in a Heaven that intervened in human affairs, believing that people needed to be motivated by the hope of supernatural benefits and rewards.

The political element is also there, but harder to find, in the wonderful texts of the Daoist masters, so called from their frequently cryptic, metaphorical, elusive exaltation of the harmony of the individual with the Way (*dao*) of Nature. In the book called the *Dao de jing* (Classic of the Way and Its Power), also known as the *Lao zi* after its mythical author, the Way is described as "nebulous yet complete, born before Heaven and Earth, silent, empty, self-sufficient and unchanging, revolving without cease and without fail," while the followers of the Way have their own kind of political and moral insight:

> Not exalting men of worth
>> prevents the people from competing;
> Not putting high value on rare goods
>> prevents the people from being bandits;
> Not displaying objects of desire
>> prevents the people from being disorderly.

For these reasons,
> The sage, in ruling,
>> hollows their hearts,
>> stuffs their stomachs,
>> weakens their wills,
>> builds up their bones,
> Always causing the people
>> to be without knowledge and desire.
> He ensures that
>> the knowledgeable dare not be hostile,
>> and that is all.

Thus,
> His rule is universal.

Similarly, the magnificent text called the *Zhuang zi*, full of the richest imagery of the changes and wonders of nature, showing with dazzling wit the relativity of all knowledge, also makes its anti-Confucian message clear:

> Once Zhuang Zi was fishing in the Pu River when the king of Chu sent two of his ministers to announce that he wished to entrust to Zhuang Zi the care of his entire domain.
> Zhuang Zi held his fishing pole and, without turning his head said: "I have heard that Chu possesses a sacred tortoise which has been dead for three thousand years and which the king keeps wrapped up in a box and stored in his ancestral empire. Is this tortoise better off dead and with its bones venerated, or would it be better off alive with its tail dragging in the mud?"
> "It would be better off alive and dragging its tail in the mud," the two ministers replied.
> "Then go away!" said Zhuang Zi "and I will drag my tail in the mud!"

In an age of much construction and many new tools and processes, it is not surprising that there were some very influential thinkers who shared the Daoists' preoccupations with the Way of Nature but were much more optimistic about the possibilities of naming and explaining natural phenomena and exploiting knowledge of nature for human economic or political ends. The classifying and explaining of natural phenomena also appealed to wandering *shi* trying to relate what they saw in new places to the mountains, rivers, weather, and plants of their native places. Some thinkers elaborated a dualism of *yin* and *yang*—female and male, passive and active, dark and bright—that has been influential throughout the Far East down to the present.

Others developed a scheme of five powers or movers—earth, wood, metal, fire, water—that looks a little like the Greek four elements but conceives the fundamentals less as substances than as dynamic configurations that succeed one another in a predictable order. Various classes of natural phenomena were classified according to the five powers. Correlating and contrasting are basic functions of the human mind, and much good observation of nature came to be organized in terms of the five powers theory. Rulers wondering how to succeed or survive and which among them would manage to shape a new unified order to replace the Zhou were especially attracted by one branch of this kind of correlative thinking:

> When some new dynasty is going to arise, Heaven exhibits auspicious signs to the people. During the rise of the Yellow Lord, large earthworms and large ants appeared. He said, "This indicates that the Power of Earth is in the ascendant, and our affairs must be placed under the sign of Earth. . . . During the rise of King Wen of the Zhou, Heaven exhibited Fire, and many red birds holding documents written in red flocked to the altar of the dynasty. . . . Following Fire there will come Water. Heaven will show when the time comes for the Power of Water to dominate. Then the color will have to be black, and affairs will have to be placed under the sign of Water.

In addition to whatever guidance or reassurance these theories gave to rulers, they seem to have had a poetic fitness; it is not hard to see Qin as an implacable black flood.

The five powers theory developed especially in the eastern states of Yan and Qi. In the same area, sometimes loosely allied with it, traditions developed of esoteric arts that would put the human body through some kind of metamorphosis so that it stopped aging and decaying and became immortal. Some believed that a drug of immortality could be obtained from the mysterious eastern islands of Penglai, which were said to be inhabited by immortals, but no one had ever gone to those islands and come back. Some passages in the Daoist texts referred to such immortals, and eventually the quest for physical immortality became a basic feature of an elaborate Daoist religion.

The final victories of Qin and its transformation of the whole Chinese world into a new type of political order took place entirely within the years of rule of the man who became the First Emperor; its collapse occurred just four years after his death. These decades mark one of the most important turning points in Chinese history. Their shifts and contradictions are baffling until we view them in light of the long trends and many-sided cultural developments of the Warring States period; then almost everything falls into place. It still can seem surprising that it was Qin, not Qi or

Chu, that emerged supreme, but even that can be made comprehensible with the help of a map and a bit of chronology.

The future rulers of Qin seem to have had their origins as herders of cattle far out on the northwest frontier of the Chinese cultural area. In the wake of the "barbarian" attacks that forced the Zhou kings to move from the Wei River valley out onto the central plain, the Qin suppressed the "barbarians," established their capital near the old capital of the early Zhou, and were recognized by the Zhou high kings as feudal rulers of that area. It may be that they were in fact among the "barbarian" attackers, and that after driving out the Zhou they emerged supreme and began to adopt Chinese ways of ruling. Their neighbor and rival to the east, across the Yellow River, was Jin, the most powerful and politically creative state of the 600s. The Qin rulers already were sending troops to intervene in the struggles of the central plain and were dreaming of achieving recognition as the supreme feudal lords and protectors of the Zhou kings. But Jin, closer to the central plain and more highly developed politically and economically, was far more successful in such interventions. Nevertheless, Qin, inferior to Jin in population, wealth, and political sophistication, won as many battles between the two as it lost in the 600s and 500s. Jin was the only dangerous neighbor Qin had, while Jin faced danger in all directions. Jin's greater wealth, better-developed and more complex government, and older and more entrenched nobility made its internal politics less stable than Qin's. Qin manipulated the quarrels of the Jin court, and losers sometimes fled to take service in Qin. Then in the 400s the internal conflicts led to the breakup of Jin into three states, Han, Wei, and Zhao. The basic strength of Jin had been so great that each of these fragments still was a powerful contender among the Warring States. Qin now frequently was able to play them off against each other or to shift its military pressure from one to the other, and it continued to attract talented defectors from their courts into its service.

One such defector from Wei, named Shang Yang, is associated with a series of great reforms in the mid-300s that set Qin on its road to supreme power and anticipated many of the features of the regime it would impose on the entire empire. A closer look at the records of Qin in the early 300s reveals many anticipations of Shang Yang's reforms, but the whole pattern of the new order is best seen as it was brought to completion under him. Feudal inheritance of rank and office, never highly developed in Qin and weakening everywhere, was abolished; henceforth rank and honors were to be given only for merit in battle. Vestiges of feudal restrictions on the buying and selling of land were wiped out. The common people were to be rewarded for productive activity in farming, weaving, and other crafts, and punished for nonproductive activity, such as trading. The whole state was divided up into centrally administered *xian*. Whereas the old order had little use for written law and exempted nobles from its jurisdiction, Qin now established a single, strict, detailed code of laws that applied to everyone in the state. To make sure that the common people obeyed the laws, they were organized into groups of five families, all of which would be punished if any one among them broke the law. The whole purpose of this new order, reflected in a work that may be of later date called the *Shang jun shu* (Book of Lord Shang), was to "enrich the state and strengthen the military" so that Qin could defeat its rivals and emerge supreme; whatever civilian activity contributed directly to equipping and feeding the army was good, military merit was the only kind of merit that counted, and the whole state was under something approximating military discipline. The idea of a rigid and unambiguous code of law applied to everyone in the state was so central to this form of statecraft that later Chinese called it the School of Law (*fa jia*), and Western scholars call it Legalism.

Shang Yang's reforms had many parallels in the other Warring States, but they seem to have been unique in their thoroughness, coherence, and ruthlessness. Qin, already a rising power, was from the 340s on the great power of the Chinese world. Would-be experts in diplomacy went from state to state presenting elaborate schemes for accommodating with Qin and taming it—"détente" or "appeasement" in twentieth-century terms— or for uniting all the other states in containment of its menace. Many of them were tried at least briefly; none had much success or was followed for very long. Cavalry warfare developed rapidly among the "barbarians" of the northwest frontier and their Chinese neighbors, especially Zhao and Qin; Qin does not seem to have had much trouble controlling its border regions, and it probably was able to draw some excellent cavalry from them into its armies. In 316 it took advantage of its geography in another way, marching south across difficult mountain country to conquer the small, half-Chinese states of Shu and Ba in the great Sichuan basin—rich in iron ore and agricultural potential, and easily defensible—giving Qin an excellent strategic position upstream on the Yangzi from its great rival Chu. In 288 Qin and Qi put forward a claim to divide sovereignty over the Chinese world between themselves, taking for their kings the new title of "Lord," *di*. Qin's enemies forced Qi to back down, and Qin was not yet strong enough to claim sovereignty for itself alone, so it too backed down. In 260 a huge Zhao army surrendered to Qin and was massacred; the standard account gives the scarcely credible figure of 400,000 men buried alive. Two branches of the Zhou ruling house were wiped out in 256 and 249, and no one was left to claim succession as the Zhou Son of Heaven.

In 246 B.C.E., soon after the last Zhou Son of Heaven was pushed from his throne, the future First Emperor became king of Qin, but he was only thirteen years old, and the real power in the state was in the hands of the prime minister, Lü Buwei. Lü was an immensely wealthy merchant and an important patron of scholars; an important book of philosophy and speculation about nature and government, entitled the *Lü shi chunqiu* (Spring and Autumn of Mr. Lü), was compiled under his patronage and has been preserved. The story of his rise and fall told by the great historian Sima Qian portrays him as a clever and totally unscrupulous persuader, and the regime he served as morally decadent and illegitimate. These stories must have been widely known and very welcome at the court of the Han, who succeeded the Qin and of whom Sima Qian was a loyal minister. Lü Buwei, it is said, found in the capital of Zhao a Qin prince, Zi Chu, kept there as a hostage for the good behavior of Qin toward Zhao. Since the two states were often at war, Zi Chu was badly treated. One of more than twenty sons of the crown prince of Qin, he had little prospect of succeeding to the throne there. Lü, who saw in him a "precious commodity" of which he could make good use, treated the miserable young prince with great generosity. Lü had a magnificent troupe of dancing girls; when Zi Chu saw them and was particularly attracted to one of them, he asked Lü to give her to him. She was Lü's personal favorite, but he would do anything to keep his "precious commodity" happy and dependent on him, so he agreed. He and the girl managed to conceal from Zi Chu the fact that she already was pregnant by Lü, and when a boy baby was born Zi Chu accepted him as his own son. Thus, Sima Qian relates, Lü Buwei was the real father of the future First Emperor.

The favorite concubine of the crown prince of Qin was childless. When Lü Buwei went to her with rich presents and praise of Zi Chu, she adopted Zi Chu as her heir, and when the crown prince succeeded to the throne Zi Chu in turn became crown prince. Three days later the new king died, Zi Chu became king, and Lü Buwei became prime minister. Lü's power grew even greater three years later when Zi Chu died and his son—or rather Lü's son, if the story is true—succeeded to the throne of Qin. Lü was granted an estate of 100,000 households as well as supreme power. The only difficulty was that he had resumed his sexual liaison with his former concubine, now the dowager queen of Qin, and feared discovery and disgrace. Seeking to get out of this situation by diverting the lady's avid attentions to someone else, he organized a lewd entertainment at which one Lao Ai appeared with his outsize penis thrust through the center of a wooden wheel. Sure enough, the dowager queen heard about it and summoned Lao Ai. A fake condemnation to the punishment of castration was arranged, so that Lao could have free access as a eunuch to the women's quarters of the palace. He became the constant companion of the dowager queen, and eventually she secretly bore two children by him. He became more powerful than Lü Buwei, deciding all affairs of state and maintaining huge troupes of retainers. When the king eventually learned of all this, Lao Ai was pushed into revolt, and he and all his relatives were exterminated. Two years later, in 237, Lü too fell from power as a result of his role in the Lao Ai affair, and in 235 he took poison.

All this scandal and disorder at court does not seem to have seriously slowed the Qin war machine or threatened the unity of the state. Qin, with little entrenched nobility or educated elite, always had been the most hospitable of the states to men from other states seeking high office. Another newcomer now rose to power, a man from Chu named Li Si who became the real mastermind of the final unification and the transformation into centralized imperial institutions. Li Si was not an abstract thinker, but the extant examples of his arguments on policy are clearly and powerfully written. He had studied under the great Confucian advocate of discipline and hierarchy, Xun Zi.

One of Li Si's fellow students under Xun Zi, Han Fei Zi, did not serve Qin but became the greatest and most articulate theorist of the new centralizing Legalist statecraft. In long, coherent essays, he argued against the Confucian delight in the examples of ancient times; little could be certainly known of those times, and in any case times had changed, especially as the population had become more dense and the struggle for survival harsher, so that ancient examples were irrelevant. The intelligence of the common people was not to be relied on; the government had to force them to do what was in their own best interests. Neither should scholars be listened to who had no practical contribution to make to the wealth and power of the state but used their stories of ancient times to gain fame and office for themselves and to oppose the rulers. The state of Han sent Han Fei Zi as an envoy to Qin in 234; Li Si had him thrown in prison, where he soon died.

In addition to the focus of its rulers on wealth and strength, Qin, giving land as rewards for military merit and having no feudal limits on landholding, seems to have been unusually successful in attracting immigrant farmers who increased its food supply and were available for its armies. It also made as good use as any state of the new technology of the time. An immigrant engineer designed a superb irrigation system for the Qin homeland in the Wei River valley that made it much more productive. Across the mountains in Shu, the Qin official Li Bing built a magnificent irrigation system, parts of which are still in use 2,200 years later.

Nothing, it seemed, could stop Qin. In 227, with Qin's territory already reaching to the frontier of Yan, a plot was hatched in Yan to send a great swordsman named Jing Ke to assassinate the king of Qin. The king was very well guarded, but Jing Ke could gain entry if he brought along maps of strategic regions of Yan and the head of a general who had defected from Qin. So great was the general's hatred of Qin that he slit his own throat so that his head could be used in the plot. The crown prince of Yan and all his associates saw Jing Ke off at the river that marked the frontier, all dressed in white, which is the color of mourning in China. Jing Ke sang:

> Winds cry *xiao xiao*,
> Yi waters are cold.
> Brave men, once gone,
> Never come back again.

Then he shifted to a military tune, and his companions stopped weeping and their hair bristled inside their caps as he drove off. He did manage to gain access to the king of Qin, bearing a casket containing the general's head and a roll of maps with a sword concealed inside it. But his first lunges at the king failed, and although he pursued the panic-stricken king around the pillars of his throne hall and eventually threw the sword at him, he missed and eventually was cut down by Qin soldiers.

Qin conquered Yan in 226, Wei in 225, Chu in 223, Qi in 221. Now, in 221, it ruled the entire Chinese world and was ready to make that world over in the image of the state of Qin. Already in 288 it had demonstrated that the old title of king would not be enough for its rulers; now it added *huang*, "sovereign," to the word "lord" it had previously proposed, and it proclaimed that henceforth its rulers would be *huang-di*, "sovereign lord," which is usually translated as "emperor." The old custom of a successor king granting a posthumous title to his father was condemned as an unfilial practice of the younger generation passing judgment on the older; henceforth each ruler would simply be known by his number in a succession that was to have no end. The king of Qin thus became the First Emperor or First Sovereign Lord, *Shihuangdi*; his successor would be the Second Generation Emperor, and so on. In the five powers theory water extinguished fire, which was the ruling agent of the house of Zhou. Qin now emphasized that it ruled under the power of water, changing some terms and names and changing its flags and court robes to black, the color of water.

Some officials proposed that the emperor make his sons princes over some of the newly conquered outlying areas, but on Li Si's advice he rejected this proposal and divided the entire country into *xian* administered by magistrates appointed by the central government. Several *xian* were combined into a commandery (*jun*). There was no single official in charge of a commandery; control over it was divided among a civil governor, a military commander, and an inspector. A similar three-way division of power among civil, military, and supervisory or inspecting arms was developed in the central government. The fundamentals of this pattern of bureaucratic government persisted, with many permutations, down to the end of imperial rule in 1911 and have echoes even in the party–army–ministry structure of power in the People's Republic. In its combining of firm central control with a system of checks and balances that made it very hard for any one official to accumulate enough power to challenge the ruler, the Qin order was a work of political genius. We can see clear anticipations of parts of it in the governing of the state of Qin. Some aspects of it had been developed in the course of the military occupations of the various states; others may be the inventions of Li Si. Chinese historians see this change from a long-dying feudal (*feng jian*) order to one of bureaucratically administered commanderies and prefectures (*jun xian*) as the central feature of the great transformation of 221.

Qin statecraft since before the time of Shang Yang had been oriented to the greatest possible mobilization of the resources of the state against its enemies: high burdens of taxation, labor service, and military service; uniformity of laws; implacable punishment of lawbreakers. When the rival states had been swallowed up, the mold was not easily broken. Taxes remained high, laws detailed, punishments severe, and about one man in ten was drafted for military or labor service. For several years a large part of this power and wealth was devoted to consolidating the actual and symbolic dominance of Qin over its former rival states. Their elite families were forced to move to the Qin capital. All metal weapons were confiscated, melted down, and cast into great statues set up in the palace and great bells. A replica of the palace of each conquered state was built near the Qin capital. From 220 on, the emperor made great journeys to many parts of his empire, which allowed the court to live off the resources of areas richer than the old state of Qin, inspect the other areas at first hand, and receive the homage of local leaders. On these journeys the court constantly asserted its sovereignty and legitimacy, paying homage to sacred mountains and setting up stone tablets bearing inscriptions that justified his rule in quite traditional ways:

> In the twenty-ninth year in midspring, the start of the sunny season, the emperor made a tour of inspection in the east, ascended Mount Chifu and reached the ocean. His subjects, following in his train, think of his illustrious virtue and recall the beginning; under the Great Sage's rule, laws were set down, principles made manifest. He taught other states, shed the light of his kindness abroad to illumine the right. The six states, insatiable and perverse, would not make an end of slaughter, until, pitying the people, the emperor sent troops to punish the wicked and display his might. His penalties were just, his actions true, his power spread far, all submitted to his rule. He wiped out tyrants, rescued the common people, brought peace to the four

corners of the earth. His enlightened laws spread far and wide as examples to All Under Heaven until the end of time. Great is he indeed! The whole universe obeys his sagacious will; his subjects praise his achievements and have asked to inscribe them on stone for posterity.[1]

It was on one of these expeditions that the emperor had a thousand divers search the bed of the Yellow River for the great bronze vessel symbolic of Zhou sovereignty that supposedly had been thrown in the river when the Zhou royal house was overthrown; his failure to find it was taken by later generations as a sign that Qin was not really the legitimate successor to Zhou. Stories also were told of the emperor's terrible rages against anything human or natural that caused him trouble; when a windstorm on the Yangzi was blamed on the goddess of a certain mountain, he had all the trees on that mountain cut down.

These "irrational" actions should not surprise us. The First Emperor and his court were not guided solely by Li Si's drive for systematic central control or by Han Fei Zi's relentless logic and contempt for the past. They were heirs to almost every strand of Warring States culture. We already have seen some quasi-Confucian moral elements used in the inscriptions to justify Qin's subjugation of the other states, and Qin's use of the five powers theory in symbolizing and legitimizing its succession to Zhou. Ideas that political power could be assured and personal health and longevity sought through correspondence with the forces of nature also lay behind the continual building of great complexes of palaces, ceremonial halls, and the emperor's future tomb.

But what if the emperor could cheat death entirely? The magicians of Yan and Qi had long insisted that a man could make himself physically immortal by the right food, the right bodily regimens, the right herbs and fungi. On one of his journeys to the east the emperor heard of the Penglai Islands out in the ocean where immortals lived off divine herbs. Men and boys were sent off to find them, and every report of herbs and fungi of special power was followed up. But no one returned from Penglai, and no herbs or fungi of immortality were found.

About 216 B.C.E., as the quest for herbs of immortality intensified, the Qin state also turned its immense resources of revenue and manpower outward, beyond China's northern and southern frontiers. All through the Warring States period the northern states had been worried by conflicts with nomadic peoples of the steppes to their north, moving about following their herds, perfecting their skills in mounted archery and cavalry warfare. A people the Chinese called the Xiongnu developed large-scale polit-

---

[1] Translations from the Basic Annals of the First Emperor are taken, with slight modifications, from Li Yu-ning, ed., *The Politics of Historiography: The First Emperor of China* (White Plains, N.Y., 1975), pp. 261–96.

ical organizations under great warrior kings; they were the great power on those steppes for about four hundred years and may have been the "Huns" who descended on Europe thereafter. After the establishment of the Qin Empire, Meng Tian, son and grandson of Qin generals, led a force of as many as 300,000 warriors and transport workers into the grasslands. The Xiongnu were driven out of the borderlands and withdrew far to the north, beyond the Gobi Desert. Meng Tian then directed the building of a great road leading north and west from the capital into the steppes. That road was used to move laborers and food supplies north for more great construction works, in which defense walls that had been built by the various states were linked together. Traditionally this has been seen as the first time a single structure was built to divide the realm of the nomads from the agricultural-bureaucratic Chinese Empire; that is, the first Great Wall of China. We now understand that the modern Chinese and Western concepts of a millennial and unchanging Great Wall are complex myths, and that for most of Chinese history there was no such unified structure of walls. But the Qin wall was real; traces of the road and of the wall still can be seen. It was much farther north than the present Great Wall, much of which dates from the Ming dynasty, and was built of pounded earth, a much more modest structure than the Ming wall. It seems clear that the Qin rulers were altogether the equals of their Roman contemporaries as builders of roads and other public works.

The Qin rulers also sent troops and colonists south from the Yangzi valley, establishing their domination over local peoples all the way to the area of modern Guangdong and Guangxi provinces. More roads were built to the south and southwest. A canal was cut joining the headwaters of a tributary of the Yangzi to one of the West River in Guangxi; it still is in use today.

The removal of the Xiongnu menace for several decades and the building of roads and canals in the long run should have been beneficial to the general population and especially to the merchants whom Legalist theory despised. Qin centralization also led to thoroughgoing standardization of weights, measures, and the writing system, potentially of great benefit to interregional trade within the empire. But in the short run it seems that the burdens of harsh administration and heavy taxation and labor service were more apparent, and there was much resentment. It must have intensified as the emperor used conscripted labor to build more and more palaces and the massive tomb. In a few years these resentments would explode in the rebellions that would bring down the Qin. Trouble for Li Si and his emperor came first, however, from a quite different kind of problem.

The great Qin bureaucracy would have been unthinkable without an abundant supply of would-be officials. Loyalty to native land or moral conviction was no barrier to many from conquered states and many whose principles of political morality were completely at variance with Qin's taking service under it. Qin was ready to accept all kinds of would-be office-holders, confident that its rigorous legal and administrative system could control them; in this way Legalism did not reject the Way of the Ruler and Minister but accepted its basic structure while denying the moral autonomy of the minister. No doubt many officials simply hoped to survive until the Qin collapsed and to give themselves advantageous positions in the struggle that would follow. Others, however, had that Confucian penchant for criticizing tyrants to their faces as a matter of principle, regardless of the consequences, seeking to change their minds solely through reason and moral fervor. This was especially obvious and the consequences especially dire in a famous debate in 213 in which a scholar named Chunyu Yue cited the precedents of Shang and Zhou feudal decentralization to argue that feudal lords with a vested interest in the survival of the dynasty would support it if it faced a military challenge; the emperor, he said, should abandon Qin's basic principle of total bureaucratic centralization and institute hereditary feudal rulers in some outlying areas. Li Si replied:

> The Five Emperors did not emulate each other nor did the Three Dynasties adopt each other's ways, yet all had good government. This is no paradox, because times had changed. Now Your Majesty has built up this great empire to endure for generations without end. Naturally this passes the comprehension of a foolish pedant. Chunyu Yue spoke about the Three Dynasties, but they are hardly worth taking as examples. In times gone by different barons fought among themselves and gathered wandering scholars. Today, however, the empire is at peace, all laws and order come from one single source, the common people support themselves by farming and handicrafts, while students study the laws and prohibitions.
>
> Now these scholars learn only from the old, not from the new, and use their learning to oppose our rule and confuse the common people. As prime minister I must speak out on pain of death. In former times when the world, torn by chaos and disorder, could not be united, different states arose and argued from the past to condemn the present, using empty rhetoric to cover up and confuse the real issues, and employing their learning to oppose what was established by authority. Now Your Majesty has conquered the whole world, distinguished between black and white, set unified standards. Yet these opinionated scholars get together to slander the laws and judge each new decree according to their own school of thought, opposing it secretly in their hearts while discussing it openly in the streets. They brag to the sovereign to win fame, put forward strange arguments to gain distinction, and incite the mob to spread rumors. If this is not prohibited, the

sovereign's prestige will suffer and factions will be formed among his subjects. Far better put a stop to it!

I humbly propose that all historical records but those of Qin be burned. If anyone who is not a court scholar dares to keep the ancient songs, historical records, or writings of the hundred schools, these should be confiscated and burned by the provincial governor and army commander. Those who in conversation dare to quote the old songs and records should be publicly executed; those who use old precedents to oppose the new order should have their families wiped out; and officers who know of such cases but fail to report them should be punished in the same way.

If thirty days after the issuing of this order the owners of these books have still not had them destroyed, they should have their faces tattooed and be condemned to hard labor at the Great Wall. The only books which need not be destroyed are those dealing with medicine, divination, and agriculture. Those who want to study the law can learn it from the officers.

The emperor approved this proposal.

In the later Chinese tradition this incident has become the most famous of the bad examples of Qin. The "burning of the books" has come to stand both for repression of principled dissent and for impiety toward the past, and the rapid collapse of Qin has been taken to prove that no government that behaves in this way can expect to endure.

In the years that followed, the emperor's interest in immortality and in avoiding assassins seems to have intensified. New palaces were built, modeled on the symmetries of the heavens, linked by walled roads. Remembering Jing Ke and several other would-be assassins, and informed by a scholar that he would be more likely to avoid evil spirits and to encounter immortals if he moved his residence regularly, the emperor built more and more palaces and moved restlessly among them. The penalty for revealing his whereabouts was death. His great tomb also seems to have been planned to provide for extraordinary power and wealth beyond the grave. Its chamber contained a relief map of the empire in gold and silver, its rivers and seas flowing with mercury, a chart of the heavens sparkling above. Nearby were vast armies of terra cotta soldiers and horses to guard the emperor in death. But resentment of the vast levies of supplies and labor continued, and no immortals or divine herbs were found, so that new openings emerged for elite protest. Sima Qian tells the story as follows:

> The scholars Hou and Lu took counsel together, saying "The emperor is stubborn and self-willed. Starting as the prince of one state, he conquered the whole empire, and now that all his ambitions are

realized he thinks no one since time immemorial can compare with him. He relies solely on the law officers, whom he trusts. Although there are seventy court scholars, their posts are just sinecures for he never listens to them. The prime minister and other high officials only deal with routine matters on which the decisions have already been made, leaving all to the emperor. He loves to intimidate men with punishments and death, so that to avoid being charged with crimes those who draw stipends dare not speak out loyally. The emperor, never hearing his faults condemned, is growing prouder and prouder while those below cringe in fear and try to please him with flattery and lies. According to the law of the realm, no man may practice two arts and anyone who fails in his task may be executed. No fewer than three hundred astrologers are watching the stars, but these good men, for fear of giving offence, merely flatter the emperor and dare not speak of his faults. It is he who decides all affairs of state, great or small. He even has the documents weighed every morning and night, and will not rest until a certain weight has passed through his hands. How can we find herbs of immortality for such a tyrant?" And so they ran away.

When the emperor learned of their flight he flew into a passion. "I collected all the writings of the empire and got rid of those which were no use. I assembled a host of scholars and alchemists to start a reign of peace, hoping the alchemists would find marvelous herbs. But I am told no more has been heard of Han Zhong and those who went with him, while Xu Fu's crowd has wasted millions without obtaining any elixir—all I hear of them is charges of corruption! Handsomely as I treated Lu and the other scholars, they are libelling me, making out that I lack virtue. I have had inquiries made about the scholars in the capital and I find that some of them are spreading vicious rumors to confuse the black-headed people."

He ordered the chief counsellor to try the scholars, who incriminated each other to save their own necks. Over four hundred and sixty, found guilty of breaking the law, were buried alive in Xianyang as a warning to the whole empire. Even more were banished to the frontier regions.

Even the emperor's eldest son and heir protested, but he was ignored and sent off to the northern frontier to "supervise" Meng Tian's armies.

In 210 B.C.E. the emperor went on another great tour, this time to the southeast. He paid homage at the mountain where the Great Yu was supposed to have been buried. Still obsessed by reports of isles of immortals, he traveled along the coast. He dreamed that he fought with a sea god, and later he killed a great fish. But then he fell ill and soon died. His chief eunuch, Zhao Gao, conspired with Li Si to put their favorite son of the emperor on the throne, but in order to do so they would have to get back to the capital without anyone, especially the heir apparent off in Meng Tian's camp, knowing that the emperor was dead. The body was kept in the emperor's great enclosed traveling carriage, and trusted servants continued to go in with meals at the proper times. But after a few days it was obvious to anyone downwind from the carriage that all was not well. The plotters then had a cart of salt fish drawn along behind the imperial carriage, so that anyone smelling a bad smell would think it was bad fish, not a very dead emperor. They succeeded in their plot, set their candidate on the throne as Second Emperor, and killed many princes and high officials. In the next year revolts broke out, and in the year after that Zhao Gao had the great Li Si executed.

The revolts against the Qin spread rapidly, and by 206 it had been completely overthrown. Many of the rebels were commoners and aristocrats who hoped to restore the old separate states; this kind of sentiment was especially strong in Chu. But the first revolt is supposed to have begun in perfect retribution for the excessive rigor of the Qin code of laws: a group of conscripted laborers had orders to report for duty on the construction of the Great Wall on a certain date, and the penalty for reporting late was death. When they became bogged down by heavy rains and flooded rivers and could go neither backward nor forward, some bold spirits among them decided that if their lives were forfeit in any case, they might as well risk them in the "Great Enterprise" of revolt.

Turning its back on the lessons of antiquity, exalting the rule of law, silencing high-principled scholars, imposing heavy burdens on the common people, the Qin was seen by most later Chinese political thinkers as the antithesis of good government. For them and for many Western students of China, the "Legalism" of Shang Yang, Han Fei Zi, and Li Si was the polar opposite of "Confucianism." Some Chinese scholars always have realized that this contrast was much too stark, and have acknowledged the permanent contribution of the Qin to Chinese history. As we follow the development of "Confucian" roles and ideas in the political order founded by the "Legalist" Qin, we will find many ways in which these two strands of statecraft needed each other, completed each other, and many ways in which the melodramas of Qin continued to echo in the Chinese imagination.

SIMA QIAN

THE HAN dynasty ruled over all of China for more than four hundred years, from 202 B.C.E. to 220 C.E., with only one interruption, a sixteen-year period of usurpation and civil war ending in a Han restoration. From its first days to its last, the history of the Han is full of great events and great people, of stories that continue to echo in the Chinese mind. The Chinese identification with the Han is so persistent that "Han nationality" is used in China today to refer to the people who use the Chinese language and who share the culture and ethnic heritage we call Chinese, in contrast to the other "nationalities" or ethnic groups, such as Mongols and Tibetans, who also are citizens of the Chinese state. For the Chinese the Han is full not only of good stories but of good and bad lessons: the shrewd, uncouth founder, a great judge and employer of men; protesting scholars and their repressors; usurpers and loyal martyrs; poets and magicians.

One of the creators of the mystique of Han, the great recorder and shaper of the stories of its first hundred years, was the Grand Historian Sima Qian, already encountered in the epigraph and introduction of this book. Sima Qian approached history not as an isolated scholar seeking after pure knowledge, but as the heir of a great family tradition of record-keeping, knowledge of the lore of Heaven and Earth, and service at court. He was himself a participant in and victim of the politics of an age of crucial transformation, in which the open-ended possibilities and unprecedented innovations of the Warring States and the rise and fall of Qin yielded to a new, coherent, amazingly long-lasting pattern of the mutual dependency but recurring hostility of rulers and ministers in a single-centered imperial system. I know of no better way to view this vital era than through the prism of the writings and experiences of this great man. In drawing on his great *Shi ji* (Records of the Grand Historian) we also fulfill as so many Chinese readers and writers have, his desire to make a difference to the future, to save something from humiliation and oblivion by means of the writings he left behind.

The *Records of the Grand Historian* begins with a long chronology of rulers and dynasties, from which I already have drawn some of the story of Yu and the rise and fall of Qin. The Qin story is followed immediately by Sima Qian's greatest achievement as a storyteller, the account of the rise of Han. The first emperor of Han, posthumously known as Emperor Gao, had been a village constable and never entirely lost his rough rural manners; he once replied to a tiresome lecture by a Confucian scholar by seizing the man's silk hat and urinating in it. But he was quick-witted and courageous, tried to limit the effects of war on the common people, and knew how to judge and make good use of human talent. Starting out as one of many leaders of local rebellions, he was the first to occupy the Qin capital in the Wei valley. He preserved it from pillage and immediately proclaimed the abolition of the harsh and detailed law code of Qin. But then Xiang Yu, his nominal superior and great rival, entered the area and turned his troops loose to burn and kill. From that point on the story as Sima Qian tells it is one of war to the end between Xiang Yu and the future Emperor Gao, full of dramatic personal confrontations and hairbreadth escapes. Neither one called for the restoration of the states of the Warring States; Xiang favored a league of a larger number of states, with himself as first among equals, while Emperor Gao after his victory maintained the Qin centralized order for about half the empire, granting the rest as semi-autonomous kingdoms to his great ministers and generals. A more important reason for Emperor Gao's success and Xiang Yu's defeat, in Sima Qian's view, was their different ways of dealing with their subordinates. Xiang Yu was jealous of men of ability, never gave them adequate rewards, and never admitted that he had made a mistake. Emperor Gao admitted that he was not a match for his great ministers and generals in leading troops, devising strategies, or organizing the logistics of a great campaign, "but it is because I am able to make use of them that I gained All Under Heaven."

Emperor Gao reigned for only seven years after his final victory over Xiang Yu. Several of the allies whom he had set up in kingdoms revolted, and he personally led campaigns to put them down. The most important of the kings was seized, pardoned, moved to a different area, then accused of plotting revolt and executed. When Emperor Gao died only one kingdom remained not in the hands of relatives of the imperial family. His successor, Emperor Hui, died young, and after his death Emperor Gao's widow, the Dowager Empress Lü, was the real power behind a succession of child emperors. There were signs that the Lü family might seize the throne for itself, but after the empress's death in 180 B.C.E. the princes of the Han imperial family wiped out the Lü and consolidated the Han succession. The next two Han rulers are portrayed as presiding over a government that, inspired in part by the bad example of Qin and in part by Daoist principles of noninterference in the natural courses of man and nature, kept taxes very low and avoided military action inside and outside the empire. Sima Qian comments that even among the intrigues of the rise and fall of the Lü family, "the common people succeeded in putting behind them the sufferings of the age of the Warring States, and ruler and subject alike sought rest in surcease of action. . . . Punishments were seldom meted out and evildoers grew rare, while the people applied themselves to the tasks of farming, and food and clothing became abundant."

There were several reasons why this admirable situation could not last. First, the Han Empire still confronted on its northern frontier the well-organized and highly mobile threat of the nomadic Xiongnu. Emperor Gao once had been surrounded and almost captured by Xiongnu invaders. He and his successors chose to placate them, sending Han princesses to marry their rulers and giving them large presents of the cloth and other fine consumer goods they did not make for themselves. The cost was not unbearable, but the potential for further extortion was considerable. From 177 on there were many Xiongnu border raids, always ending in some kind of patching up of apparently peaceful relations. Eventually many Han statesmen came to see these policies as craven and humiliating, as well as unsuccessful. A more aggressive foreign policy would require higher taxes, more conscription of manpower. Second, as the kingdoms came into the hands of Han princes of the second and third generations, the family ties were loosened and the number of intrafamily grievances increased, so that peace among the kingdoms and between them and the imperial court no longer was assured. Third, the consequences of prolonged prosperity for the single-centered empire were paradoxical. More men had the wealth and leisure to prepare for and aspire to active roles in politics. Some forms of wealth, especially commerce and such vital regional products as iron and salt, could be easily tapped by anyone hoping to influence the politics of the empire.

These changes came together in dangerous combinations as disaffected rulers of outlying kingdoms began to exploit the resources of their territories and to assemble large numbers of ambitious young men at their courts. The most important of these new centers of power was the kingdom of Wu, in the lower Yangzi. There, Sima Qian relates, the king "set about inviting fugitives from all over the empire to come to his kingdom, minted cash from the copper ore in ever-increasing quantities, and boiled the sea water to extract salt, so that he was able to dispense with the head tax, and his kingdom enjoyed great prosperity." Another dangerous development was the disaffection of the king of Zhao, on the northern frontier where he could easily make alliances with the Xiongnu. Less menacing was the king who assembled large numbers of Confucian scholars at his court. Sima

Qian, never one to leave a good tale untold, tells of other kings who used their wealth to indulge their private whims, including one who loved to play policeman in his capital city and others entirely given over to homosexual or heterosexual lust.

The kingdoms and lesser marquisates were held at the pleasure of the emperor, who could deprive a ruler of all or part of his territory at any time but usually would not do so without some apparent justification. The emperor also decided if one son of a dead king would inherit the whole kingdom or if it would be divided among several heirs. If a king left no male heir his kingdom was abolished and turned into centrally administered territory. Kings could be summoned to the capital to participate in ceremonies or to explain their conduct, or central government officials could be sent to conduct investigations in their capitals. The prime minister of each kingdom was appointed by and responsible to the emperor.

Still, it was not at all clear that these controls would be sufficient to check the rising power of the kingdoms. From about 170 B.C.E. on, an official named Chao Cuo, a student of the books of Shang Yang and other Legalists, urged the Han emperors to take more forceful measures to limit the power of the kingdoms. He also was very much concerned about the growing power of the Xiongnu. Although the connection is not made in his surviving writings, internal centralization and an activist foreign policy often went together in imperial China; centralization would limit the ability of regional rulers to ally with dangerous foreigners and would supply the manpower and resources needed for strong defenses or conquest beyond the frontier. When the king of Wu rebelled in 154 and six other kings joined him, they demanded the execution of Chao Cuo. The emperor sought to buy peace by having Chao killed, but the rebels continued their advance, only to be stopped and defeated in a few months by brave marches and stubborn defenses by imperial generals and by other kings who remained loyal. The rebel kingdoms were abolished or divided up among other imperial relatives.

The succession to the throne in 141 B.C.E. of a fifteen-year-old boy, very much under the influence of the relatives of his grandmother, the Grand Dowager Empress Dou, was the unpromising beginning of one of the most critical periods of change in all of Chinese political history. The new emperor, posthumously entitled Emperor Wu, reigned until 87. His posthumous title means "martial"; his reign was one of China's greatest ages of expansion and conquest. It also was a time of great change in the ceremonies and ideologies of the state and of the conclusive victory of the centralizing imperial power over the regional kings. The first act recorded for the reign was an order for all regional officials to send to the capital men of learning and good character to be tested for their suitability for appointment as officials. There had been several orders of this kind earlier in the Han, but none so comprehensive and ambitious. There was a great need to absorb into the service of the imperial court ambitious men who had found ample chances to study in the peace and prosperity of early Han, and especially those who had been and still could be tempted into service at the courts of the kings. This first effort was abortive; when the candidates sent to the capital were ordered to write essays on problems of public policy, most wrote in a Legalist vein. The Dou family were devoted to Daoist teachings of minimal government and personal quest for transformation; the Legalist would-be officials were sent home. The call for officials was renewed in 135 after the death of the Grand Dowager Empress Dou, with more positive results. This time many of the men summoned and tested went on to careers in the high bureaucracy. At the same time some more senior scholars were named learned academicians (*bo shi*), charged with the teaching of a particular classical text to young men at the capital; this was the nucleus out of which an Imperial Academy would grow. Soon a pattern emerged of recommendation by local officials, further study under the learned academicians, examination for selection for service as a "court gentleman," and eventually appointment as a local official or for other special duty.

We have seen a combination of esteem for scholarship and ambition for office as early as Confucius and his disciples, and I have noted that the First Emperor of Qin does not seem to have lacked would-be officials, even though some of them disagreed fundamentally with his policies. Thus it is not surprising that Confucian teachings, not very influential in the Legalist-Daoist confrontations in the first decades of Han, became very influential in this changing bureaucracy. Modern scholars call these teachings "Han Confucianism"; in many ways they were quite different from the teachings of the Master. They are first seen in the writings of Gongsun Hong, a wonderful example of the way in which men from modest backgrounds sometimes could rise to the heights of the Chinese bureaucracy.

Gongsun Hong had been a prison official in eastern China, but had been dismissed for some offense and had made his living raising pigs. When he was over forty he studied the *Chunqiu* and the teachings of the various schools. He was sent to court in 141 in response to the emperor's call for men of character and learning, soon was dismissed, but was sent again in 130. In setting the question for the candidates to write on, the emperor showed a great interest in stories of an ancient past in which the *yin* and *yang* were in harmony, grain and domestic animals flourished, and so on. Gongsun Hong's reply, which the emperor judged the best of all the candidates, argued that if minds were in harmony then the forces of nature would be in harmony, and all the effects the emperor wished would follow.

He also argued that in the days of Yao and Shun rewards and noble ranks were few and punishments were light but the people did not rebel; this was because the rulers dealt with them in good faith. Gongsun Hong had a distinguished career, rising to the highest offices. Even more famous, though less influential as an official, was Dong Zhongshu, who also won notice as a scholar in the early years of Emperor Wu's reign and wrote a commentary on the *Chunqiu* that is one of the most important documents of Han Confucianism.

Confucius himself had not been much interested in nature or the supernatural, but part of what he included in ceremony was viewed by many as intended to maintain the harmony of the cosmos or to propitiate ghosts and dangerous spirits. Various schemes for explaining and controlling natural phenomena and for correlating their changes with each other and with those of the human world had been worked out in the Warring States period. There exist only fragments of information on the ways in which interests in nature lore, in ceremony as transaction with cosmos and spirits, and Daoist quests for physical immortality and fascination with the magical powers of recluses interacted with each other in the third and second centuries B.C.E. What is clear is that a wild variety of products of such interaction was carried to the imperial court in the 130s and 120s by seekers for office and other forms of influence. There were various efforts to reconcile these ideas into a single structure appropriate for the ideology of a unified empire. Dong Zhongshu and others used Confucian principles to systematize some of these ideas because they legitimized imperial rule and gave moral glamour to office-seeking.

Also, the records of ancient times that had been studied by Confucians since the Master himself, with the *Yi jing* added to the list, now were recognized as "Classics" (*jing*) and the fundamentals of the curriculum of the Imperial Academy. The resulting Han Confucianism by no means lost the Confucian earnestness about self-improvement or penchant for criticism of abuses of power, but took very seriously the idea that the policies and personal conduct of the emperor and his proper performance of an annual round of ceremonies were essential to maintain the proper harmony of the realms of Heaven, Earth, and humanity. Unusual weather, freak births, changes in the heavens, and so on were considered to be serious signs that something was out of joint between the realms of Heaven and humanity. An eclipse of the sun (*yang*, masculine), for example, might be taken to indicate an excess of feminine power in the imperial palace.

Confucian scholars were useful in devising legitimating ceremonies, drafting state papers, and educating the next generation of officials, but they did not determine the main directions of state policy, and frequently opposed them. Emperor Wu's regime was inclined to take aggressive action in all directions as soon as it was free of the restraining influence of the Grand Dowager Empress Dou. A Han ambush of a large party of Xiongnu in 134 was followed by annual Xiongnu raids along the border. These expansionist policies were opposed by many officials, including one Zhufu Yan, who had risen from poverty-stricken origins in Qi and who used Confucian arguments but also cited some wise counsel given by Li Si to the First Emperor of Qin. But in 127 Zhufu Yan changed his tune, urging that the Han reoccupy the territory within the northward bend of the Yellow River, restoring the Qin line of defenses in that area. His recommendation was followed, and the Han armies were successful. Zhufu Yan also urged a general policy of dividing up the territories of marquises among their heirs, on the Confucian grounds that this would encourage warm family feelings and filial piety, and accused the kings of Yan and Qi of personal moral offenses. Both kings committed suicide, neither had an heir, and their kingdoms came under central control. The linking of efforts to strengthen central power and calls for an aggressive foreign policy, the use of Confucian moral concerns to justify "Legalist" centralization, are striking. Zhufu Yan may have changed his views on foreign policy because he sensed what Emperor Wu and the powerful generals wanted to hear. His days of success as a policy adviser were short, however; the king of Zhao accused him of corruption and he was executed.

An even more decisive step toward centralization was the suppression of the rebellion of the king of Huainan in 122, which Sima Qian describes in a long, complex, and gripping narrative winding through four generations of violence and revenge in the imperial family. The first king was a son of Emperor Gao who killed a high minister responsible for an unjust accusation of his mother; the lady had killed herself because of the shame. The king was exiled and died; his son inherited the kingdom but harbored a deep desire for revenge. His large and rich territories enabled him to manufacture large quantities of arms, accumulate reserves of money, and send "bribes and gifts to wandering knights and men of unusual ability in the provinces and other feudal kingdoms. The rhetoricians and strategists came forward with the most reckless and absurd pronouncements in order to flatter the king who, delighted with their words, awarded them large sums of money and plunged even deeper into plans for revolt." (These were not the only kinds of wandering experts who gathered at the Huainan court; there also were Daoist thinkers of the highest quality, contributors to the collection of Daoist teachings that bears the name *Huainanzi*.) The son and heir of the king was active in the plans for revolt; the imperial court was informed of these plans by a grandson of the king whose father had been excluded from the favors bestowed on the crown prince. A grandson of the minister killed by the first king was close to Chancellor Gongsun

Hong and urged action. All the plotters were arrested before they could call out their troops. The king killed himself, the others were executed, and the kingdom was abolished. Another revolt in a neighboring kingdom also was nipped in the bud.

The abolition of these kingdoms in 122 B.C.E. seems to have been decisive in breaking the power of the kingdoms. In 112 almost all the marquisates that had been inherited since the reign of Emperor Gao were abolished. By that time the share of the empire ruled by kings was much smaller than it had been in 141. In 106 a new system of regional inspectors sent out by the imperial court was created to maintain closer supervision over the larger numbers and wider distribution of commanderies and prefectures. Equally important were the measures the court now took to tap for its own purposes the wealth of the empire. From the 120s on, growing military expenses had strained state finances. Rich people were rewarded by state honors when they made contributions of money and grain, but still the officials noted the prevalence of rich merchants and idle landlords while the local officials' treasuries were empty. Moreover, revenues from mines, salt works, and trade had supported the rebellious intentions of Wu and Huainan. New taxes were instituted in 119. In 113 the court prohibited any minting of coins, mining of metals, or manufacture of salt by any private party, and it created new offices to manage the resulting state monopoly of these industries. This was followed in 98 by a state monopoly of the manufacture and sale of alcoholic beverages. A new type of official soon was noticed, frequently from a merchant background, expert in manipulating currency and trade, making excellent careers for themselves and great sums of revenue for the imperial treasury.

These new revenues now made possible the rapid expansion of Han armies in all directions. A spectacular burst of military activity began in 121. The Xiongnu, defeated in 121 and in 119, retreated north, beyond the Gobi Desert. The Xiongnu retreat from the upper reaches of the Yellow River allowed the Han to move into that region and on out along the "Silk Road," the oasis trade route that linked China with Persia and the Roman Orient. New commanderies were set up on that frontier from 108 to 104. Explorations to the northwest under Zhang Qian culminated in the Han conquest of Ferghana, beyond the present northwest frontier of the People's Republic, in 104. A series of conflicts in the northeast led to the establishment of full Han rule over much of the Korean peninsula in 108.

From Qin–Han times down to the eighteenth century, relations with the nomadic warriors of what is now Mongolia were an unavoidable problem for the agrarian governments of north China. It is not clear that the early Han conciliatory policy really had been found unworkable, but there were good arguments for the shift to the offensive against the Xiongnu, and the extensions of power to the northeast and northwest could be rationalized as efforts to cut the Xiongnu off from access to possible allies and trading partners. The almost equally spectacular expansion to the south can hardly be seen as anything but a manifestation of a restless will to power and a government with vast resources at its disposal. A Qin general had conquered the area of the modern province of Guangdong, then had turned it into the autonomous kingdom of Southern Yue; Han armies conquered it in 111, with the help of a pro-Han local faction, and brought it under full-scale imperial administration. The difficult mountain country of what is now Guangxi and Yunnan provinces already was coming under Han pressure from the north; the new invasion routes upstream from Southern Yue now led to the incorporation of this area in the Han Empire as well. Thus by 100 B.C.E. the Han were in control of pretty much everything within the boundaries of modern China except Tibet and, oddly, the area of modern Fujian Province. They faced episodic local resistance in many of these areas, held on to them at great cost, and were much criticized by Confucian officials for the expenditure of tax revenues and the loss of life involved.

Given the insistence that all changes in the realms in Heaven, Earth, and humanity were closely intertwined, the rise of a state of such immense wealth and power was bound to lead to a sense that a monarchy so powerful must be particularly favored by the supernatural realm, and that this favor must be acknowledged in new ceremonies and other symbol-laden practices. Sima Qian, in a long and rich account of these matters, suggests that Emperor Wu himself was deeply interested in them. At the very beginning of his reign scholars sought to advise him on changes of the calendar and the performance of two great ceremonies at Mount Tai called *feng* and *shan* but the Daoist allegiances of the Dowager Empress Dou stopped these discussions. People won fame and fortune by claiming that they had the secrets of physical immortality and by advising the emperor to establish ceremonies honoring the Grand Unity (Tai Yi) as well as the Lords of the Five Directions (Wu Di). About 121 a man convinced the emperor that he could summon the spirits of the dead, including that of a beloved concubine, but was executed after the emperor realized that all his magical arts were fraudulent. Then a spirit medium, called the Spirit Mistress, attracted the emperor's attention.

Perhaps it was in part to draw the emperor's attention away from this sort of thing, to draw within the emerging Han Confucian synthesis the emperor's fascination and that of much of his court with symbols and the supernatural, that the officials began proposing new ceremonies and symbolic initiatives. Zhou kings and Qin and Han emperors had simply counted the years from the beginning of their reign: "the fifth year of

Emperor Gao" and so on. The two emperors before Wu had started over in the middle of their reigns, giving themselves "middle" and "later" years. The officials now proposed that special two-character expressions be adopted to count the years, beginning with Establishment Origin (*jian yuan*) for the first part of Emperor Wu's reign, with two others to commemorate later auspicious occurrences—the appearance of a mysterious bright light and the capture of a one-horned animal. Then in 113 a great ancient bronze cauldron was unearthed. The officials, recalling stories of nine great vessels cast by Yu and much more lore about ancient bronzes, declared this a sure sign that the emperor enjoyed the favor of Heaven. Soon 113 was declared to be the first year of another new reign period, Origin Cauldron (*yuan ding*). The use of such "year designations" (*nian hao*) or reign periods, to count time and to reinforce the symbolic legitimation of a particular government, continued down to 1911 in China, and continues in Japan to this day.

The discussions of ceremonies at Mount Tai that had been so quickly suppressed in the first year of the reign of Emperor Wu now resumed. These were believed to have come down from the age of Yao, Shun, and Yu, or at least from the great days of early Zhou. They had their roots in ancient worship of mountains, but there is no reliable evidence for these specific ceremonies from even as early as the time of Confucius. The *feng* and *shan* ceremonies were to take place at Mount Tai, the great sacred mountain near Confucius's home in Lu. But the versions of the *feng* and *shan* that interested the emperor were like that of one Master Shen, who said that "of all the seventy-two rulers who attempted the *feng* and *shan*, only the Yellow Emperor was able to ascend Mount Tai and perform the *feng*. . . . The ruler of Han also will ascend the mountain and perform the *feng*, and when he has done this, then he will become an immortal and will climb up to Heaven." The emperor ordered his Confucian scholars to search ancient records for the correct ways of performing these ceremonies, but it seemed to them that since the last performance had been so long ago, it was very hard to be sure, and they could not produce any detailed information. If they thought this would keep the emperor from performing some completely unclassical ceremony in search of personal immortality, they were wrong. In 110 the emperor called a halt to their discussions and set out toward Mount Tai in a huge procession. He ascended Mount Tai with only one attendant, performed the *feng*, then descended and performed the *shan* at its foot. These ceremonies eventually would be incorporated in a fully Confucianized imperial regimen, but it is hard to see this episode as anything other than a defeat for the Confucian scholars.

The emperor performed the *feng* again in 106. In 104 he adopted a new year designation, Great Beginning (*tai chu*). There had been many proposals that the Han change the calendar, as ancient dynasties supposedly had done when they came to power, but down to this time the former Qin calendar had remained in use. Now the emperor also ordered changes in the calendar and a change of the color of flags, robes, and so on to yellow, much as the Qin had made them all black, and again based on a theory of succession among the natural powers.

It is in connection with these changes that the family of Sima Qian appears in the historical record. According to family tradition, the Sima had been astronomical officials under Yu and court historians in the early Zhou, but there is no independent evidence for this. Surnames like this, consisting of two characters, two syllables, were much more common in Han times than they are today. Meaning roughly "master of horse," "Sima" probably indicated that the surname originally was taken by an ancestor who was a military officer. Sima Qian's father, Sima Tan, held the office of *tai shi*, usually translated as "grand historian," at the court of Emperor Wu. Since early Zhou times officials bearing this and related titles also had kept records of heavenly phenomena and advised on their interpretation; in view of the importance of these matters in Han elite culture, a more appropriate translation of the title might be "grand astrologer." Sima Tan was the author of a remarkably clear and sensible summary of Warring States thought, called "The Discussion of the Essentials of the Six Schools," which found that the Confucians dealt with essentials of proper relations between ruler and minister and so on, but "their discipline is difficult to carry out to the fullest"; he preferred the Daoists, whose teaching "embraces all things," including the best of the other schools: "Its principles are simple and easy to practice; it undertakes few things but achieves much success."

Sima Qian apparently was born about 145 B.C.E. He says he spent some of his youth on a farm, and that by the age of ten he could read the ancient writings. Around the age of twenty he went to Wu and looked for the cave that was supposed to contain the tomb of the great Yu. He also traveled to Confucius's home area in Lu and saw the carriage and other relics of the Master's life. He traveled widely in the Yangzi valley, and he says he was sometimes in some danger. Then he became a court gentleman, probably aided by his father's substantial position at court, and in that capacity took part in a military expedition to the south of Ba and Shu, in modern Sichuan.

Sima Qian's account of the ceremonial and symbolic changes of Emperor Wu's court contains a number of references to his father's active participation. But when the emperor went to Mount Tai in 110 to perform the *feng* and *shan*, "the grand historian was forced to stay behind at

Zhounan and could not take part in the ceremony. He was filled with resentment over this and lay on the point of death." It seems likely that although he found the Confucians rather limited he had sided with them in this case, finding as an official historian that there were no adequate precedents to guide the performance of the ceremony, and had been excluded from planning or even attending to the great event as a result.

Sima Tan had been working on a great compilation of documents relating to the duties of his office, but had not finished it. As he lay dying, he said to his son, "Now the Son of Heaven, following the tradition of a thousand years, will perform the *feng* ceremony on Mount Tai, but I shall not be able to be present. Such is my fate! Such indeed is my fate! After I die you will become grand historian. When you become grand historian, you must not forget what I have desired to expound and write." He went on to quote part of the text known as the *Classic of Filial Piety*: "To establish yourself and follow the Way, exalting your name to later generations, and thus casting glory on your father and mother, is the beginning of filial piety." Recalling the great men of ancient times, and how some of the records of them had been lost in the disorder of the Warring States, he told Sima Qian, "I have been grand historian, and yet I have failed to set forth a record of all the enlightened rulers and wise lords, the faithful ministers and gentlemen who were ready to die for duty. I am fearful that the historical materials will be neglected and lost. You must remember and think of this!" Qian bowed and wept, and replied, "I, your son, am ignorant and unworthy, but I shall endeavor to set forth in full the reports of antiquity which have come down from our ancestors. I shall not dare to be remiss!"

Sima Qian became grand historian in 107. He was deeply involved in the discussions leading up to the calendrical and ceremonial changes of 104, but he also had his mind on the completion of his father's great historical project. He recalled that his father had wanted to establish the correct transmission and texts of the *Yi jing*, the *Chunqiu*, and other ancient texts. "Was this not his ambition? How can I, his son, dare to neglect his will?" He was particularly interested in the *Chunqiu*, a chronicle of the state of Lu that many Han scholars believed had been written by Confucius and embodied in its cryptic entries his judgments of the good and evil rulers of his time. He denied that he was creating a work or passing judgment on his age, insisting that his goal was simply to preserve and transmit records of the past. But this denial probably was an attempt to shield himself from the anger of the emperor and some officials, since there is in fact a great deal of implicit criticism of his age and its rulers in his great book.

Earlier Chinese books sometimes bore the name of the person whose teachings were collected in them, like the *Mencius*, or the person under whose patronage they were compiled, like the *Spring and Autumn of Mr.*

Lü. But Sima Qian's great *Shi ji* (Records of the Grand Historian) is the earliest surviving Chinese book in which the author acknowledges authorship and speaks directly to the reader in the text. Nevertheless, his intent to preserve and transmit also led to the incorporation of large pieces of earlier texts, such as the *Tribute of Yu* section of the *Classic of Documents*. It was a massive compilation; a complete translation into a Western language would fill two to three thousand pages. Where earlier books had been more or less random in organization, the *Records of the Grand Historian* has a distinctive organization into five major parts:

1. Basic annals (*ben ji*), a court-centered, year-by-year chronicle of the succession of rulers and other main political events, beginning with the earliest sage emperors, including a separate chronology of Xiang Yu as well as one of the victorious founder of the Han.
2. Chronological tables (*nian biao*), an intricate and very helpful set of chronological tables showing the genealogies of the sage emperors, synchronizing the chronologies of the various states of middle and late Zhou, and listing in tabular form the dates of the establishment, alteration, and abolition of the kingdoms and marquisates of the Han.
3. Studies or treatises (*shu*), topical essays on matters of special importance to the Han court, such as ceremony, the calendar, the *feng* and *shan* ceremonies, astronomy, water control, and state controls over the economy. The last is the most important source on the new economic measures of emperor Wu's reign.
4. Hereditary houses (*shi jia*), chronological accounts of the rulers of the most important late Zhou states, Han kings, and, oddly, Chen She (the first rebel against the Qin) and Confucius. (The latter is so full of legendary elements that it is of little use in attempting to understand Confucius's own life and teachings.)
5. Memoirs (*lie zhuan*), literally the "classified transmissions," *zhuan* being the word Sima Qian used in his evasive insistence that his intention was to transmit records but not to create or to pass independent judgment. These chapters make up over half of the total length of the *Records of the Grand Historian*. Most of them are biographies of individuals; there also are a few chapters of topically organized collective biography, and several devoted to Han relations with various foreign peoples.

This is a complex way of organizing a historical work, and it requires a good deal of time and effort to get the maximum benefit from it. No one part of the book gives all the most important points about a major development. For example, for the story of the collapse of Qin and the victory of Han, the reader must read the overlapping basic annals of Qin, Xiang Yu, and Emperor Gao, the hereditary house chapters on the first rebel and several of the allies of Emperor Gao who later were made kings; and several memoirs on other important ministers of the Han founder. Thus this immensely important transition is seen not just from the perspective of the winner but also from those of the loser and of the great men whose advice and assistance were essential to Emperor Gao's victory. This is not history for someone who wants to read a book once and get a single story, a neat answer as to what it was all about, but is for living with, coming back to over and over, continuing to think about and learn from, as every educated Chinese was supposed to do down to our own century. This way of writing history is an important source of the awareness of multiple perspectives and the fondness for complexity that have characterized the Chinese understanding of politics and human action ever since. The form of the *Records of the Grand Historian* was adopted, with a few small modifications, by the writers of the accepted standard or official history that was written after the fall of every major dynasty, from the Han down to the *Draft History of the Qing* written in the 1920s.

How do we explain such a breakthrough, the sudden emergence of a form of such power and sophistication? The most important clue is that it was the work of court historians, father and son, who frequently were called upon to provide information and precedents for court deliberations. The organization of this work is very close to a plausible way of organizing documents for ready retrieval when so called upon, a filing system if you will. Does the emperor want to discuss a report of a shooting star and divine what heaven might be telling him? Here is the file on astronomy. Does he want to decide what to do about disturbing reports from the kingdom of Huainan? Here is the file on that kingdom, the successive generations of its kings and their relations with the imperial court. And it is important to note that for many crucial topics more than one file will be available, and the emperor and his ministers will be encouraged to see events from more than one perspective, as all good policymakers should.

Such an origin of the organization and contents of the work, and Sima Qian's own insistence that one of his goals was to transmit and preserve ancient materials, help to account for the apparent copying into the book of many documents of earlier origin. It also is likely that much of the biographical material in this and later histories was compiled by descendants of the biographee as an act of filial piety, and at most somewhat edited by the compiling historian. But in many of its parts the *Records of the Grand Historian* is far from being an impersonal document. In many passages we find masterful strokes of the storyteller's art: Lü Buwei holding on to his "precious commodity," seeds of vengeful retribution coming down through the generations of the kings of Huainan. It is clear that the telling of tales to rulers, frequently linked to some teaching about clever strategies, was well-developed in Warring States times. By this time such storytellers may also have found audiences in the houses of the rich and in the markets of the great cities. Did the grand historians listen and record as such storytellers appeared before Emperor Wu? Or were they themselves expected to be masters of this art? We have no way of knowing; Sima Qian was at least a connoisseur of the art, and more likely a master of it himself.

Sima Qian also placed brief introductions at the heads of his chapters, which sometimes explained his understanding of a topic or his reason for including it. More important, at the end of many of his important chapters there appears a short section beginning "The grand historian remarks" in which he writes for himself and gives his own views on the events he has just recounted. One of the meanings of the character *zan*, here translated as "remarks," is "praise" or "eulogy"; perhaps the grand historian, upon completing the presentation of a text to the emperor, was expected to provide a brief summary, often taking the form of a eulogy of the person whose biography had been presented, or praise of the particular accomplishment of the imperial ancestors that had just been recounted. But Sima Qian's remarks are very far from conventional or obsequious; they are in fact some of the most personal and moving parts of his work. I already have drawn on his assessment of Xiang Yu and his startling remark that the sordid palace intrigues in the days of Empress Lü did not keep it from being a period of relaxation and prosperity for the common people. He also mixed comments on his own investigations with his evaluations. Writing on Han Xin, who served emperor Gao but eventually rebelled against him, he writes:

> When I visited Huaiyin one of the men of the place told me that even when Han Xin was still a commoner his ambitions were different from those of ordinary men. At the time of his mother's death he was so poor that he could not give her a proper burial, and yet he had her buried on a high, broad plain with room enough for ten thousand households [grave tenders for the tomb of a person of highest rank]. I went to see Han Xin's mother's grave, and it was quite true.
>
> If Han Xin had given thought to the Way and been more humble instead of boasting of his achievements . . . how fine a man he might have been! For his services to the house of Han he might have ranked with the duke of Zhou. . . . Yet he did not strive for such things but, when the world was already gathered under one rule, plotted treason instead. Was it not right that he and his family should be wiped out?[1]

[1] All translations from the *Shi ji* are from Burton Watson, tr., *Records of the Grand Historian* (New York and London, 1961).

Commenting on the biography of Shusun Tong, an unusually change-able and supple Confucian scholar who once served at the Qin court and later became influential at the court of Emperor Gao, he writes,

> Shusun Tong placed his hopes in the world and calculated what was needed; in planning ceremonies and in all his other actions, he changed with the times, until in the end he became the father of Con-fucian scholars for the house of Han. The greatest directness seems roundabout, people say. Even the Way itself twists and turns. Is this perhaps what they mean?

The most piercingly personal of Sima Qian's remarks are about death and fame. Commenting on Bo Yi and Shu Qi, who were praised by Confu-cius for having fled to the mountains and starved to death out of loyalty to the fallen Shang dynasty rather than "eat the grain of Zhou," he writes that there are many examples of men who violate all the proprieties and live in great luxury, while others live the most carefully moral lives but meet with disaster.

> I find myself in much perplexity. Is this so-called Way of Heaven right or wrong? . . . Bo Yi and Shu Qi, although they were men of great virtue, became, through Confucius, even more illustrious in fame. . . . The hermit-scholars hiding away in their caves may be ever so correct in their givings and takings, and yet the names of them and their kind are lost and forgotten without receiving a word of praise. Is this not pitiful? Men of humble origin living in the narrow lanes strive to make perfect their actions and to establish a name for themselves, but if they do not somehow attach themselves to a great man, . . . how can they hope that their fame will be handed down to posterity?"

Finally, commenting on a gifted general who served first Xiang Yu and then Emperor Gao, he writes,

> He suffered punishment and disgrace and became a slave and did not commit suicide. Thus in the end he became a renowned general of Han. Truly the wise man regards death as a grave thing. When slaves and scullion maids and such mean people in their despair commit suicide it is not because they are brave; it is because they know that their plans and hopes will never again have a chance of coming true.

Another innovation, less direct than the remarks but equally powerful, is the inclusion in the memoirs of several chapters of what might be called collective biographies. In each of these chapters Sima Qian tells about sev-eral men who played roughly the same role in history and society. Here he moves beyond the traces of his official function as grand historian to a highly personal variation on the biographical format. His views on the good and bad effects of the prevalence of each of these roles sometimes are made explicit in his remarks at the ends of these chapters, but are even more effectively presented in the grouping and in the details of the stories. A historian of our own times might get something of the same effect, for example, by composing pointed collective biographies entitled "Movement Organizers," "Media Stars," "Billionaires," and "Indicted Politicians."

Out of sympathy with the way in which the imperial court seemed to be drawing all wealth and ambition into its own orbit in his time, Sima Qian especially enjoyed himself in his collective biographies of two kinds of men who were more independent, the wandering knights and the money-makers. The wandering knights stories are all from the Warring States period, when this type thrived and always could find employment. Sima Qian notes that Han Fei Zi condemned them and the Confucians as two subverters of the centralized state.

> As for the wandering knights, though their actions may not conform to perfect righteousness, yet they are always true to their word. What they undertake they invariably fulfill; what they have promised they invariably carry out. Without thinking of themselves they hasten to the side of those who are in trouble, whether it means survival or destruction, life or death. Yet they never boast of their accomplishments but rather consider it a disgrace to brag of what they have done for others. So there is much about them which is worthy of admiration, particularly when trouble is something that comes to almost everyone some time.

The money-makers were merchants or craftspeople who provided the people with things they wanted, without the interference of government. Various products were produced in different areas, but "once these exist, what need is there for government directives, mobilizations of labor, or periodic assemblies? Each man has only to be left to utilize his own abilities and exert his strength to obtain what he wishes." One man sold silks to the border tribes, who paid him in livestock at ten times the price ratio prevalent in China; he did this over and over again until he had so many herds that "he could only estimate their numbers roughly by the valleyful." A widow inherited a mercury-ore cave and "used her wealth to buy protection for herself so that others could not mistreat or impose upon her." The First Emperor of Qin honored her. Another sent his slaves out peddling fish and salt, so that even the slaves managed to become prosperous. The desire for wealth, Sima Qian says, is a part of human nature. None of these people used any titles or gifts from the government to get ahead, "nor did they play tricks with the law or commit any crimes to acquire their fortunes. They simply guessed what courses conditions were going to take and acted accordingly. . . . There was a special aptness in the way they adapted to the times."

The collective biography of the Confucian scholars is most valuable for the information it gives on how the texts of the classics were restored and transmitted after the chaos and book burning of the rise and fall of Qin. The view of their accomplishments as Han officials is negative: Gongsun Hong was a flatterer who always told the emperor what he wanted to hear, and none of the others discussed was much better. So bleak was Sima Qian's view of the government of his own times that his collective biography of the reasonable officials, those who governed wisely and treated the common people kindly, draws examples only from the centuries before the Qin. The corresponding collective biography of the harsh officials is entirely devoted to men who served the Han. One who served Emperor Wen was harsh but loyal and incorruptible, very useful in curbing the power of local wealthy families. The stories of harsh officials who served Emperor Wu get more and more bitter as the chronological list continues. As the officials grew harsher in enforcing the law, the people grew more clever in evading it. One Zhang Tang had shown his harsh and punitive nature as a boy, putting on trial and executing a rat he had caught stealing meat in his father's house. He helped organize the new salt and iron monopolies and prosecuted the king of Huainan for the emperor. Despite Zhang Tang's harshness, Sima Qian still was able to acknowledge his effectiveness, and noted that after his death it was found that he had accumulated only the small amount of money he had received as salary. Others ruled the common people harshly but did not bother the powerful local families. The last official discussed in this chapter, Du Zhou, was responsible for sixty to seventy thousand arrests after some popular unrest, and also prosecuted some of the most powerful men at court. He became very rich, and his sons and grandsons all held high offices.

Sima Qian himself was among the victims of the vicious politics of the later years of Emperor Wu's reign; it is possible that Du Zhou was among his accusers. The circumstances are described in a biography of the famous general Li Ling that appears in the later *History of Han* (Han shu), not in the *Records of the Grand Historian*, but is such a vivid tale of heroism and betrayal that it may actually have been written by Sima Qian. Li Ling was the grandson of one of the greatest of Emperor Wu's generals and already had many successful battles behind him when in 99 B.C.E. he was sent out against the Xiongnu with a force of only five thousand infantry, perhaps the first time foot soldiers had been sent out into the steppes. The force was intended to lure the Xiongnu closer to the Han frontier, where reinforcements would come up to attack and annihilate them. Li won some victories against great odds, then retreated toward the frontier, fighting as he went. The Xiongnu were wary of a full-scale assault, until a traitor informed them that it seemed that no reinforcements were coming. Then they surrounded Li Ling's forces in a mountain valley. Most of the Han soldiers died fighting, and only about four hundred of the original five thousand got away and reached the border. Li Ling surrendered to the Xiongnu. The emperor took no action, now regretting his failure to send the necessary reinforcements. But in 98 someone informed him that Li Ling was training the Xiongnu in the Chinese arts of war. The emperor condemned Li to death and exterminated his family. Li Ling later insisted that the person who had been training the Xiongnu was not he but one Li Xu. He could have returned after a general pardon but refused to do so, dying among the Xiongnu.

There was no particularly close tie of friendship or loyalty between Sima Qian and Li Ling, but still in 98 the grand historian took the extraordinary step of defending Li against the accusations of treason, insisting that he must have surrendered in order to "try to seek some future opportunity to repay his debt to the Han." The enraged emperor turned Sima Qian over to the legal authorities for trial for the capital crime of defamation of the imperial court. A conviction was a foregone conclusion. In his case, the death sentence was reduced to the most severe of the mutilating punishments, castration. One does not have to be an orthodox Freudian to suspect that fear of and revulsion at castration is deeply built into the male psyche. In Chinese tradition this revulsion was reinforced by the dictates of filial piety, in which one of the child's first duties is to preserve intact the body received from the parents. Anyone, and especially anyone of honorable standing in society, would be expected to commit suicide, keeping the body whole to death, rather than submit to castration. Sima Qian shared these beliefs and feelings, but also was deeply committed to another side of filial piety. He had promised his father that he would complete his great work, preserving the names and deeds of the great men of antiquity and assuring the fame of the Sima family. And filial piety required not the effacement of self but its fulfillment: "Establish yourself and follow the Way, exalting your name to later generations, in order to shed glory on your father and mother." In the great work he was struggling to complete for the sake of family and self, the most distinctive personal notes were condemnation of the harsh and cynical government of his own time and nostalgia for a time when good, brave, and clever men were not hemmed in on every side by an all-encompassing state. His hatred of that state now had been horribly confirmed by his own experience. We already have noticed his opinion in one of his remarks that suicide is most appropriate for "slaves and scullion maids and such mean people" who believe that "their plans and hopes will never again have a chance of coming true." So he rejected the possibility of suicide and submitted to the excruciating and humiliating punishment.

Sima Qian's talents were not lost to the emperor; he became a highly valued eunuch official of the Palace Secretariat, frequently accompanying the emperor on his travels.

In 93 B.C.E. an old friend, Ren An, was accused of some crime, as most officials were sooner or later in those years. He wrote to Sima Qian, "instructing me in my duty to recommend men of ability and work for the advancement of worthy gentlemen," which seems to be a veiled plea for intercession on Ren An's behalf at court. Sima Qian's letter of reply is the most personal and one of the greatest pieces of writing we have from him. Since he was "a mutilated being who dwells in degradation," anything he would try to do would be rejected and laughed at, and would only injure the person he had sought to help. But still, he could not put off writing in reply, for if Ren An died, "it would mean that I would have no opportunity to unburden to you my bitterness and anguish." Once he had served honorably at court, but "Alas, alas! A man like myself—what can he say now? What can he say now?"

In the Li Ling affair, he wrote, "I took the chance to speak of Li Ling's merits in this way, hoping to broaden His Majesty's view and put a stop to the angry words of the other officials. But I could not make myself fully understood. Our Enlightened Ruler did not wholly perceive my meaning. . . . So I was put into prison, and I was never able to make clear my fervent loyalty." Perhaps he still could not fully recognize the emperor's savagery, and in any case it was not safe to mention it even in a private letter.

He continued:

My father had no great deeds. . . . He dealt with affairs of astronomy and the calendar, which are close to divination and worship of the spirits. He was kept for the sport and amusement of the emperor, treated the same as the musicians and jesters, and made light of by the vulgar men of his day. If I fell before the law and were executed, it would make no more difference to most people than one hair off nine oxen, for I was nothing more than a mere ant to them. The world would not rank me among those men who were able to die for their ideals, but would believe simply that my wisdom was exhausted and my crime great, that I had been unable to escape penalty and in the end had gone to my death. Why? Because all my past actions had brought this on me, they would say.

A man has only one death. That death may be as weighty as Mount Tai, or it may be as light as a goose feather. It all depends upon the way he uses it. Above all, a man must bring no shame to his forbears. Next he must not shame his person, nor be shameful in his countenance, nor in his words. . . . Lowest of all is the extreme penalty, the "punishment of rottenness" [castration].

I grieve that I have things in my heart which I have not been able to express fully, and I am shamed to think that after I am gone my writings will not be known to posterity.

Many men had made use of terrible adversity to leave a great work behind; Confucius had been in distress and danger many times, and had completed the *Chunqiu*.

I too have ventured not to be modest but have entrusted myself to my useless writings. I have gathered up and brought together the old traditions of the world which were scattered and lost. I have examined the deeds and events of the past and investigated the principles behind their success and failure, their rise and decay, in 130 chapters. I wished to examine into all that concerns heaven and man, to penetrate the changes of the past and present, bringing to completion the great task of one family. But before I had finished my rough manuscript, I met with this calamity. It is because I regretted that it had not been completed that I submitted to the extreme penalty without rancor. When I have completed this work, I shall deposit it in the Mountain of Fame, so that it can be handed down to men who will understand it, and penetrate to the villages and great cities. Then although I should suffer death from ten thousand cuts, what regret should I have? . . . I have brought upon myself the scorn and mockery even of my native village and I have soiled and shamed my father's grave. With what face can I again ascend and stand before the grave mound of my father and mother? . . . Only after the day of death shall right and wrong at last be determined.[2]

Sima Qian died sometime after 86 B.C.E. Little is known of the last years of his life. His book did survive, and it has shaped the ways history is written and thought about in China, Japan, and Korea down to the present. He succeeded in passing on the great stories of the heroes and villains of the past, and in ensuring that his own delight in human bravery and cleverness, his own bitterness and anguish, would not die with him.

[2] Burton Watson, *Ssu-ma Ch'ien, Grand Historian of China* (New York, 1958), pp. 57–67.

5

WANG MANG

••••••

About two hundred years after the founding of the Han, a high official named Wang Mang began to elaborate a vision of the restoration of the utopia of order and justice that many scholars of his time believed had existed in the early Zhou. Land would be distributed in equal plots to all farmers. No one would suffer in slavery or any other form of bondage. Confucian learning would be supported, and the correct texts and interpretations of the Classics would be determined once and for all. Farmers in their fields and children in the alleys would sing in praise of the Great Peace. Even the place names and the coinage of the early Zhou would be restored.

These dreams were not just one man's; in one form or another much of the elite of the first century B.C.E. shared them. But these idealistic scholars had confronted the same dilemma of Confucian politics that had frustrated the Master himself: They conceived of and presented themselves as selfless ministers, entirely dependent on recognition and appointment by the ruler, scarcely able to think of combining to seize power on their own. Unless they could completely convert a ruler to their principles, they would have to choose between betrayal of their dreams and the risks and frustrations of idealistic opposition. But rulers came to power by heredity, intrigue, or war, not by proving their selfless commitment to the general interest; the age of Yao, Shun, and Yu was long gone.

Only once in all of Chinese history did a man become Son of Heaven who seemed to be perfectly committed to the ideals of the Confucian scholar-officials. That man was Wang Mang. Rising in power as a minister, not a possible successor to the throne, he emerged in the role of the duke of Zhou, guarding dynastic interests when there was no adult successor to the throne, then became emperor in his own name, and went on to try to realize his dream of an institutionalized Zhou revival. Even apart from his usurpation, the politics and policies of his regime were widely deplored. Floods and droughts were the last straw. Widespread rebellion against his regime led to terrible civil wars and finally to the restoration of the Han dynasty. If many had seen the rapid fall of the Qin as proof that no such amoral and antitraditional totalitarian regime could survive, Wang Mang's fall did much to demonstrate, as Confucius himself may already have learned, that the institutional forms of an idealized past could not be revived.

After the death of Emperor Wu in 87 B.C.E., the state-building policies and politicians deplored by Sima Qian remained in control of the court, but Confucian opposition to them was increasingly articulate. The pressure on the economy of court expenses and the incessant military campaigns was said to be very great. In addition to a rather modest land tax, adult males had to pay an annual "counting tax" in copper cash, which rarely or never was canceled even in areas stricken by flood or drought. Many small farmers sought protection from it by becoming tenant farmers or personal retainers of some great man who had sufficient influence to shield them from the tax collectors. Some destitute farmers even sold themselves or their children into slavery. Thus a few great families acquired vast estates and swarms of slaves and retainers, on which they paid few or no taxes. About 100, the great Confucian scholar Dong Zhongshu had unsuccessfully urged Emperor Wu to set limits to the concentration of land in private hands that was resulting from private money-making and from the distribution of land as the kingdoms and marquisates were reduced.

In 81 there was a great debate at court on the monopolies, of which there is an excellent record called the *Yan tie lun* (Discourses on Salt and Iron). The Confucian scholars condemned the burdens imposed on the people by the monopolies, the domination of the court by money-grubbing officials, and above all the greed of the court itself, which should keep its expenses as low as possible and should not "contend with the people for profit." Chancellor Sang Hongyang answered them by pointing to the necessity of expensive border defenses against the Xiongnu and others, and by scorning the advice of bookish idealists who never had to worry about the consequences of their actions and were not competent to manage anything. Sometimes his speeches sound a bit like a certain kind of American businessman laughing at the ideas of a professor who has never had to meet a payroll. The *Discourses* are one of the finest documents we have of the complex tension in Chinese political culture between altruistic moral passion, frequently somewhat impractical, on one side, and realistic statecraft, often cynical and egoistical, on the other.

In the short run, the debate did little to shake the power of Sang Hongyang and his colleagues. An unworkable monopoly on the brewing of liquor was abolished after the debates. Except for a brief interruption in 44–41 B.C.E., the rest of the monopolies remained in force. Nor is there much evidence for continuation of Dong Zhongshu's opposition to the concentration of landholding. Instead, the Confucian tradition of protest found expression in condemnations of perversions of the ruler–minister relation and improprieties within the palace, and in speculations about possible changes in the mandate of heaven.

The instabilities and conflicts of Han dynastic politics were often the results of one of the basic difficulties of a hereditary monarchy. Sometimes it would produce a child sovereign or an adult one who was not a very capable or energetic ruler. Who would control the imperial institution in those circumstances? Frequently it would be the dead emperor's widow, the dowager empress, and her male relatives. This domination of the court by "outside relatives" (*wai qi*) was one of the most persistent difficulties of Han politics, and it plagued many later dynasties as well. The Han already had experienced an almost fatal case of outside relative power with Empress Lü, widow of Emperor Gao, and a far less threatening one in the Dowager Empress Dou who dominated the first years of the reign of Emperor Wu. In the last years of the reign of Emperor Wu the families of two of his consorts, Wei and Li, intrigued and occasionally fought in the streets. The old emperor responded by leaving neither of them in a position to exercise outside-relative power after his death, naming an infant related to neither as his heir, and leaving the highly capable senior official Huo Guang in charge as regent. "I want my youngest son set up, with you to act the part of the duke of Zhou." Huo controlled the court in cooperation with Sang Hongyang and other generals and officials until 80, then accused them of plotting to depose the emperor and install one of the regional kings, and exterminated them and their families. In 74 a successor was installed who seemed to be in the hands of the Li family, outside relations from the reign of Emperor Wu. Amid repeated references to Yi Yin (the minister who deposed the first ruler of the Shang dynasty) and the duke of Zhou, Huo Guang secured the consent of the dowager empress (his own fifteen-year-old granddaughter) and the capital officials in deposing this emperor and putting a child on the throne. Highly competent and ruthless, little interested in the supernatural or in Confucian moral platitudes, Huo dominated the court unchallenged until his death in 68. His relatives were driven from power and exterminated in 66.

Huo Guang had shown that the duke of Zhou mystique provided an alternative to outside-relative domination of the court of a young or weak emperor. Outside-relative dominance remained, however, the more "natural" and persistent pattern. It was especially unchallengeable when the emperor was a child and his mother dominated the selection of officials who would rule as his regents until he came of age. But even an adult emperor owed filial deference to his mother. Outside relatives won choice assignments as generals and provincial officials, were given noble titles and large estates in the provinces, and used their influence to secure appointments, tax exemptions, and so on for lesser men who followed their lead and served their interests. For the idealistic Confucian, the power of the outside relatives was a deplorable violation of the ideals of selection and promotion of officials on the basis of merit and of decision making based on principled discussion of the issues. A more distant and more cynical observer might conclude that it was at least a kind of solution to the inherent problems of hereditary monarchy and was to a degree inherently self-limiting. As an emperor came to adulthood, his empress and her relatives would form a faction of their own. Sooner or later the dowager empress would die, her relatives would lose their ultimate source of support within the palace, and the relatives of the present empress would have a chance to expel and replace them. Thus a kind of circulation of outside relative cliques followed the passing of the generations.

In opposing the influence of empresses, other palace women, and their relatives, Confucian scholars relied on the wide acceptance at this time of the idea of correspondences and mutual influences among the realms of Heaven, Earth, and humanity. Especially useful were the ideas of the balance and harmony of *yin* and *yang*. Since Warring States times, Chinese thinkers had frequently made of the idea of complementary cosmic forces of *yin* and *yang*, of which the oldest meanings may be "shady side" and "sunny side," but which also imply "moist" and "dry," "cool" and "hot," "soft" and "hard," "inside" and "outside," "passive" and "active," and "female" and "male." Some of the connections of these contrasts to feminine and masculine sexuality are fairly obvious, but others are more obscure. Why, for example, should *yin* be square and *yang* round? In any case, for Han thinkers any event could be interpreted as a mixture of these two forces, and any natural phenomenon in which they seemed out of their normal harmony was seen as heaven's warning of a similar imbalance in the human realm. Too much rain at the wrong time of year indicated an excess of *yin*. So did an eclipse of the sun, which is *yang*. Han emperors had no intellectual or cultural defenses against this kind of criticism. They repeatedly proclaimed their own anxiety over unusual signs in the heavens or in the weather, and they requested their ministers' opinions as to what kind of reform was necessary. A few visionaries interpreted omens as announcing the need for radical institutional changes, a move of the capital, or even the transfer of the mandate to a new dynasty; the life expectancy for prophets of this kind was very low.

All this anxious peering at the heavens and interpreting of omens can best be seen as one manifestation of an intense and varied religious life in this period that modern scholars are just beginning to understand. We already have encountered in the age of Emperor Wu the quest for physical immortality and the desire to summon spirits. Divine powers, propitiated by rulers and ordinary people alike, were associated with various directions, seasons, and human needs. At the end of the first century B.C.E., we get occasional hints of mass religious fervor and expectation associated with one or another of these deities. In 3 B.C.E. there were prophecies of the arrival of a deity called the Queen Mother of the West (*Xi wang mu*), who was supposed to dwell in the high mountains far to the west and could assist people in the search for immortality. Huge masses of people came from the east to the capital. In the capital people were singing and dancing, or were climbing on the roofs, lighting fires, and beating drums, hoping to greet the goddess. Eventually the excitement died down, but this was not an isolated development; there are quite a few representations of the Queen Mother of the West, with a leopard's tail, a tiger's teeth, and tangled hair, on stone monuments that have come down to us from the Han.

Many members of the elite no doubt shared in these religious hopes and excitements. Some of them, and some who adhered more closely to Confucius's focus on life and morality in this world, also were involved in important developments within the Confucian tradition. Study at the Imperial Academy was more widely recognized as an important way to get ahead in the bureaucracy. The number of students increased, as did the number of specialists in various classics who taught them. It became more important to settle disputes of wording and interpretation among various lines of transmission of the classics. New texts of various classics, supposedly hidden away to save them from the Qin destruction, came to light. They were written in the Old Text (*gu wen*) of the Warring States period and frequently differed from the New Text (*jin wen*) texts written down after the Qin–Han wars in the script of that time and accepted in the first century of Han. Officials were sent out on tours of investigation to find as many classical texts as possible. All this contributed to the importance of classical scholarship, but also to a skeptical sense that it was hard to know exactly what the teachings and examples of the sages were, and that to a degree people had to think for themselves in evaluating competing heritages. There was increasing interest in a few passages, some of them in modern-script texts that had been known for a long time, that presented a picture of historical cycles. In one, for example, it was said that Confucius, in editing historical records, had made distinctions appropriate to the progress of humanity from an age of disorder to one of "small tranquility" to the all-encompassing "great peace" (*tai ping*) inaugurated by his own teachings. The implication was that a similar progress toward a great peace could be made in later ages by following Confucian teachings in the proper way.

One Old Text text first noticed in these years, the *Zhou li* (Ceremonies of Zhou), presented an idealized picture of a perfectly planned and peacefully prosperous empire in early Zhou that had only a shaky relation with the realities of those long-gone times but would have immense influence over Chinese political thought from the time of Wang Mang down to the present century. Reforming Confucian officials brought about major changes in the imperial ceremonies to the great cosmic powers, discarding the worship of the Lords of the Five Directions and of the Great Unity that had come down from Emperor Wu's time, and adopting rites of homage to Heaven and Earth that they believed to be closer to early Zhou models.

All these strands of change, enthusiasm, and prophecy seemed to flow together in a strange crisis in the capital in 5 B.C.E., when an obscure individual from the provinces presented a text that he claimed was a revelation from the Lord of the Red Essence, red being the color of the Han dynasty. According to it, the dynasty had come to a period of decay and was in danger of losing the mandate of heaven. It must renew the mandate, and all people in the empire must renew themselves morally. The year period should be changed to "Initiation of the Great Beginning," echoing Emperor Wu's "Great Beginning" in 104. The emperor should take the new title of "Emperor of the Great Peace [*tai ping*] Who Shows Forth the Sage Virtue of the Liu Family" (the Han imperial house). Soon thereafter the presenters of this prophecy were urging that all the current officials should be dismissed and the prophets appointed in their places; soon after that they all were dead. Despite their failure, they had brought together a widespread belief in omens, expectations of a breakthrough to some kind of a better world, and a sense that the Han dynasty's mandate was by no means secure. Wang Mang, in political eclipse in 5 B.C.E. but well placed to resume his rise to power shortly thereafter, would bring together these factors and others noted above in a more potent and successful mixture.

Wang Mang rose to power as an outside relative of an empress, the mother of Emperor Cheng, who reigned from 33 to 7 B.C.E. The Dowager Empress Wang was the center of power in her son's reign, since Emperor Cheng was not much interested in the hard work of ruling the empire. One after another of her brothers and cousins was appointed marshal of state and general in chief and effectively controlled the central administration. The dowager empress was not involved in the details of government, but her position was the ultimate source of her relatives' power. Her contribution was simply to be there, to stay alive; she died in 13 C.E. at the age of eighty-four, her long life having made possible the rise of Wang Mang through many twistings and turnings to his ultimate seizure of the imperial throne.

Wang Mang was born in 45 B.C.E., son of a brother of the future Dowager Empress Wang. His father died before he could receive the noble title, gifts, and estates that his brothers received when their sister was a reigning empress. Making a virtue of his relatively modest circumstances, he became a humble and conscientious person, serving his mother and his uncles devotedly, raising an orphaned nephew, and avoiding the lavish consumption displayed by his uncles and cousins. He cared personally for his uncle Wang Feng, the first of the Wang regents in the reign of Emperor Cheng, in his last illness, and the uncle recommended him to his sister the dowager empress. As a result, Wang Mang was given a position in the palace guards in 22 B.C.E. and was made a marquis with revenue from a large estate in 16.

From beginning to end, Wang Mang's public life was full of demonstrations of his humility and selflessness, and also of ambition, political skill, and ruthlessness. We have to come to terms with this mix of personal traits if we are to understand his actions, his appeal to the people of his times, and his ultimate failure. Our efforts are considerably complicated by the biases of the most important source on his career, a long chapter in the *History of Han* by Ban Gu, written in the first century C.E. Ban Gu was a member of an extremely devoted and eminent family of ministers of the Later Han, which rose out of the collapse of Wang Mang's regime. A Confucian moralist explanation of the fall of Wang Mang and the success of Later Han had to show that Wang was brought down by his own moral failings, not by bad luck or events beyond his control. Ban Gu's account presents, very skillfully and insidiously, a picture of Wang as a power-hungry hypocrite. It records Wang's many selfless deeds very matter-of-factly, and it is only gradually that Ban Gu argues that none of Wang's acts of selflessness were sincere, that all were calculated to make the best possible impression and to advance his career. Also, Ban Gu has a good deal to say about Wang's fascination with omens. Writing in an age when a skeptical temper was more widespread in the elite, he makes these interests seem bizarre and eccentric when in fact they were almost universal in the elite of Wang's time.

Four brothers and cousins of the Dowager Empress Wang served in succession as chief minister at the court of Emperor Cheng. When the last of them resigned in 8 B.C.E., the only possible successor of that generation did not have a good reputation, so it was natural for the dowager empress to turn to the next generation of the family. Wang Mang was by far the best known and most promising of that generation, so he became chief minister and virtual regent of the empire at the age of thirty-seven. He did not have time to accomplish anything distinctive before Emperor Cheng died in April of the year 7 and was succeeded by a nephew known posthumously as Emperor Ai. The new reign was full of confusing possibilities and initiatives. The powerful families of the emperor's mother and grandmother sought to play the now familiar outside-relative role. The emperor's homosexual lover was very powerful at court. A high minister proposed limits on concentrations of landholding. The abortive prophecy of the great peace in 5 was followed by the expectation of the Queen Mother of the West in 3. In this uncertain and overexcited time, Wang Mang and his grandmother, now the grand dowager empress, had the good sense to keep a low profile, she ordering him to resign his post and retire to his estate and he obeying despite the protests of his many admirers at the capital. Wang Mang eventually was allowed to return to live quietly in the capital, and he and the grand dowager empress were ready to act when Emperor Ai died without an heir in 1 B.C.E., leaving the imperial seals in the hands of his lover. The Grand Dowager Empress Wang rushed to the imperial palace, secured the imperial seals, summoned Wang Mang, and threw Emperor Ai's lover in prison, where he soon killed himself. The one appropriate heir among the descendants of Emperor Cheng's father was summoned from the provinces and enthroned; he is known as Emperor Ping. He was only nine years old. His mother and her family, the Wei, were not allowed to come to the capital with him. The Wangs, aunt and nephew, now were in unchallenged power.

From 1 B.C.E. to 9 C.E., Wang Mang advanced through a series of stages from a conventional regency for a child emperor to the proclamation of a new dynasty with himself as first emperor. Ban Gu shows him pursuing his goal of usurpation single-mindedly from the beginning, manipulating the politics and arranging portents and expressions of public support that carried him to the throne, amid endless sham refusals and insincere protests that he was unworthy and incapable. There certainly was a strong element of convention in his protests and refusals, and some of the portents must have been manipulated. At some point, however, Wang Mang must have come to believe that Heaven had a very special destiny for him. But he also was led on by the logic of the situation, in which alternatives to his taking power in his own name disappeared one by one. He made an excellent impression by his masterful handling of the dangerous succession crisis in 1 B.C.E. His governing thereafter gained wide admiration for its competence and public spirit. Given the culture of those times, it was inevitable that this admiration frequently was expressed in the form of reports of portents of Heaven's favor. His own sense of destiny and his dedication to a moral transformation of government soon took the form of one stage after another of efforts to recreate the early Zhou utopia depicted in the *Ceremonies of Zhou*.

In 1 B.C.E. envoys from a foreign people came to the capital and presented a white pheasant. It was an auspicious sign; foreigners had presented a white pheasant to the duke of Zhou. In 1 C.E. various courtiers proposed that the grand dowager empress should grant him new honors, including the title "Duke Who Brings Peace to the Han" (*An Han gong*). Wang declined repeatedly, insisting that others were more worthy than he. After his closest associates all had been granted lesser honors, he finally accepted and was given full power to control the government and make decisions on behalf of the boy emperor. In 2 C.E. the elaborate process was begun that would lead to the selection of a wife for the boy emperor. Wang Mang firmly and repeatedly refused to have his daughter included among the young women considered, but hundreds of officials urged that she be selected, and finally he gave in. Now if the boy lived to adulthood there would be a new Empress Wang, and the family's power as the ultimately successful outside relatives would be unchallengeable.

The normal Han practice was to grant the father of a new imperial wife a large amount of land and gold; emperors, after all, were supposed to set an example of filial piety and generosity to their relatives. Wang Mang accepted these gifts, but lived much more frugally than most of the great men of his time. He abstained from meat and rich dishes at any time when there was a food shortage in the empire, advised the grand dowager empress to dress more simply, and made large contributions of money and land to relief of the poor and hungry. Many other great men, it was said, followed his example in making such contributions. Wang also used his own funds to support large numbers of scholars at the capital, which enhanced his reputation for generosity and put some of the best talent in the empire at his disposal.

In 4 C.E. Wang Mang discovered that his son Wang Yu was in secret communication with the Wei family, relatives of the emperor's mother. Wang Mang did not allow the Wei family to reside at the capital; Wang Yu seems to have felt it was better to try to work out a reconciliation than to let enmity continue to grow between the Wei and Wang families. Wang Yu was thrown in prison on his father's orders, and drank a fatal dose of poison. Wang Mang went on to exterminate the Wei family and some of the most prominent of his other opponents.

Until this crisis Wang Mang had relied primarily on his own good reputation and the power of his good example. Now he seems to have decided that more active measures must be taken to enhance his fame and to present him as a great moral teacher. He wrote his own book of admonitions to sons and grandsons and had it distributed to all officials in the empire, to be taught in all the schools. Officials soon sent in requests that those students who could recite Wang Mang's admonitions should be placed on a register for preferential official appointment, just as those were who could recite the *Classic of Filial Piety*. All this was very much in accord with

Family	Family	Family
Family	Public	Family
Family	Family	Family

5. The well-field system

the Confucian conception of the primacy of moral teaching among the functions of government. So was the dispatch soon thereafter of eight officials to tour the empire and observe the customs of the common people. The general idea of "observing the customs" was that if the teaching influence and example of the rulers was working as it should, nothing improper would be found, but if brawls, unfilial sons, lewd songs, and so on were observed, some extra measures of correction might be necessary. The inspectors brought back with them eight thousand letters from common people, all of which urged that Wang Mang and his family should receive the highest ranks and the greatest estates. "The duke of Zhou's seven sons all were granted fiefs."

In the same great flurry of activity in 4 c.e., Wang Mang took his first steps toward transforming the empire according to the model of the book called the *Ceremonies of Zhou*. This book is the perfect expression of a strand in Chinese political culture of what might be called bureaucratic idealism, which envisions a realm in which all major facets of human life are organized according to neatly nesting hierarchies of bureaucratic terms, boundaries, and practices. The result is not totalitarian repression but social equity, spontaneous good order and generosity, and ceremonies maintaining proper order among men and between the cosmic and human orders. A bureaucratic and institutional expression of the optimism about human nature best expressed in the teachings of Mencius, it has fascinated many down to our own times; echoes of it will be found among eleventh-century reformers, nineteenth-century revolutionaries, and perhaps even in the disastrous Great Leap Forward of 1958.

The *Ceremonies of Zhou* envisioned a symmetrical layout of territories, beginning from the capital of the Son of Heaven and continuing through territories governed in less and less direct ways to the land of the outer barbarians. Main roads and canals had their branches which had their branches, each level being designated by a special term, leading to a descending hierarchy of types of towns and villages, each with its officials and schools also fitting into a neat hierarchy spreading out from the capital. The foundation of this tidy world, and the core of Chinese fascination with this vision, was a system of local landholding called the well-field (*jing tian*) system. It already had been mentioned by Mencius and used by Dong Zhongshu to support his argument for land reform. The character for "well" (*jing*) is shaped like a tic-tac-toe game; with the addition of outer lines, it gives a tidy nine-squared pattern for the land distribution system.

According to this scheme, each family had a square to farm for itself, keeping the entire crop. The public field (*gong tian*, which also might mean "lord's field") was cultivated by the eight families working together, or each family cultivated a ninth of it and their houses were on the ninth share; here details differ. The produce from the public field went to the rulers, so assuming equal effort and productivity there was a tax on agricultural production of one-ninth or one-tenth. Young men were granted fields as they came to adulthood, and returned them for redistribution when they reached old age; ultimate ownership of land rested not with the cultivator but with the sovereign. Chinese scholars have recognized for at least a thousand years that such a system could work equitably and efficiently only on flat land of fairly uniform fertility. It is possible that accounts of the well-field system reflect some kind of primitive system of distribution of land, perhaps associated with shifting cultivation, that was practiced in the early Zhou or earlier, but the schematic uniformity of the system clearly is the product of later bureaucratic idealizations.

Wang Mang eventually would make use of the tradition of the well-field system to legitimize his effort to stop the concentration of landownership in the hands of a few great families, but only after he had seized full power in his own name. In 4 C.E. he concentrated on symbolic and ceremonial aspects of the *Ceremonies of Zhou* heritage, ordering the construction of a Spirit Tower, a Round Moat School, and a Bright Hall. All of these were buildings that were supposed to have had key roles in the early Zhou order of ceremonies and teaching. The Spirit Tower was a platform for observing the weather and the heavens, the Round Moat School the highest academy in a neatly organized hierarchy. The Bright Hall (*Ming tang*) was by far the most important and the most problematic. Emperor Wu had had one built at the foot of Mount Tai in connection with his great ceremonies in 110; there it had been associated with his quest for immortality and for connection with transcendent powers. The version of the Bright Hall that interested Wang Mang seems to have been a more Confucian one, in which great ceremonies of homage to all the Han imperial ancestors were performed. It also is likely that it expressed a Han Confucian preoccupation with proper relations between the human and cosmic realms, having several halls with the appropriate colors and symbols that were used for audiences and ceremonies at the appropriate seasons.

The building of these buildings was accomplished in about twenty days, by a special labor levy of 100,000 people. At the same time, other ambitious measures were pushed forward. Scholars who could assist in the reconstruction and editing of various classical texts were summoned from all over the empire. Place names were changed to fit the names used in the *Ceremonies of Zhou*. Housing was built for 10,000 students of the Imperial Academy. A "constantly full granary," presumably storing supplies for a year of bad harvests, was built near the capital.

When Wang Mang refused further imperial gifts of land, ordinary people presented memorials to the throne urging that he accept them. A total of 487,572 such memorials were received. The inspectors of customs brought back reports of songs of praise for Wang Mang being sung by the common people. Wang himself reported that there were no thieves or hungry people in the empire, and that things dropped by the road were not picked up. A member of the Han imperial family proposed that Wang should formally become regent, performing most of the ceremonies of the imperial position. According to tradition, Shun had filled this position when Yao first ceded the throne to him, Yu had done the same for Shun, and the duke of Zhou had even performed some of the ceremonies of the Son of Heaven.

At the end of 5 C.E. Emperor Ping fell gravely ill. Wang Mang, again imitating the duke of Zhou, placed a prayer in a metal box imploring Heaven to take him, not the emperor. But the emperor died in February of 6 C.E. Wang Mang later was accused of poisoning Emperor Ping, but this seems unlikely. As long as the emperor was alive and Wang's daughter was empress, Wang's position was absolutely secure, and he could proceed cautiously, with many ostentatious refusals, toward taking the regent's position for himself. Now he had to find a new Han heir and prevent the emergence of new sets of outside relatives who might challenge his position. He placed a child on the throne, arguing that the new successor could not perform the ceremonies to his predecessor unless he were from a generation junior to his. The Dowager Empress Wang quickly approved of Wang becoming regent.

A white stone was found with red writing on it proclaiming that Wang Mang should become emperor. At this time, however, Wang simply accepted the position of regent. His regime easily crushed a rebellion led by a member of the Han imperial family. In 7 a rebellion led by a provincial official, who accused Wang of murdering Emperor Ping, aroused somewhat wider response, but was suppressed by the end of the year. Wang now took the new and unprecedented title of temporary emperor, but still insisted that he planned to relinquish power to the Han prince when he grew up. He gave noble titles and fiefs to many who had helped him against the rebellion. The Confucian scholars at his court praised him for his support of scholarship. In his "taking Heaven as his model, searching out ancient ways and modifying them," he was like Confucius after he heard the music of Shun. "If he had not had the utmost of sage wisdom, how could he have accomplished all this?"

It is not easy to explain Wang Mang's decision to abandon his declared intention to return power to the Han prince some day and to take the throne himself. The grand dowager empress was still alive as the ultimate guarantor of his power. In 9 C.E. he had the Han prince married to one of his granddaughters, setting the stage for a still longer continuation of outside-relative power. Perhaps Ban Gu is right, and usurpation had been his goal all along. Perhaps there were weaknesses in his position that we cannot see from our limited sources that impelled him to this step. We do know that at the end of 8 there was a great rush of reports of portents that Wang should become emperor. Messengers from Heaven appeared to various people in their dreams. As a message on a stone was being examined, a wind arose, and when the cloud of dust subsided there was a pattern of silk on the ground that was interpreted as another message from Heaven. An official proposed a reinterpretation of the abortive prophecies of 5 B.C.E. to mean that a regent would change the reign period. Finally, a metal box was presented to the ancestral temple of Emperor Gao, founder of the Han, in which there were two documents, one reporting that the Lord of Heaven was sending a seal to Wang Mang, the other reporting that the Red Emperor, Emperor Gao, was transmitting the mandate to the Yellow Emperor. When this was reported to the court, Wang Mang rushed to the temple of Emperor Gao and declared that he finally was convinced that he no longer could evade Heaven's command that he should take the throne and found a new dynasty. The name of his dynasty, in fact, was to be New (Xin).

Ban Gu asserts that the documents in the metal box were faked, and he gives the name of the man who did it. But the symbolic power of these portents cannot be so easily dismissed. One document recalled the feverish expectations of transformation and "great peace" of 5 B.C.E. The second document fit Han reasoning about the five powers and the way they would succeed one another: red was the color of fire, which would be succeeded by earth, the color of which was yellow. Beyond that, Wang Mang claimed that his family was descended from the mythical Yellow Lord (Huang Di, not the same huang as that in the expression for "emperor"). And in Han religion the Yellow Lord had become a central divinity, especially important in the quest for immortality, so that the Daoism of the time often was referred to as "the Way of Huang and Lao." Thus in his response to these portents, whatever the mix of opportunism and conviction may have been, Wang Mang was tapping currents of religious enthusiasm far more powerful than those reflected in his imitations of the duke of Zhou and his following of the *Ceremonies of Zhou*.

It was to the *Ceremonies of Zhou* and other real and imagined Zhou precedents that Wang now turned to guide a series of far-reaching policy initiatives. First steps toward several of these policies seem to have been taken before Wang's final usurpation in 9, but they all came together in full force at this time. Several different kinds of coins, some of them replicating the knife and spade shapes of some of the late Zhou states, were instituted and made compulsory for certain transactions; it seems clear that the proportion of valuable metal in some of the new coins was lower than in the previous Han coinage, and that this was in fact a debasement of the coinage. Most people refused to accept the new coins, and the policy was widely resented. The government monopoly on coinage was revived and strictly enforced. In 10 it was followed by a series of new monopolies on the production of salt, iron, liquor, and so on. Han Confucians usually had been bitterly opposed to such monopolies; Wang justified them by a very strained reading of a passage in the Classics.

Wang also granted a great many noble titles and fiefs. Although early Zhou society had been feudal, at this time he does not seem to have made systematic use of a model from the *Ceremonies of Zhou* or any other text in his enfeoffments. Some fiefs were simply granted to those who had supported him against the rebellion in 7. Others went to heads of great families that claimed descent from various sage emperors of high antiquity, so that they could maintain the proper veneration to their august ancestors. Others were part of an elaborate scheme of ceremonial guardians for Mount Tai and other sacred mountains.

Most important of all was his proclamation that henceforth there would be no private landholding; all land would be known as the king's fields and would be subject to confiscation and redistribution. Immediately, rich families having more than one hundred *mou* (about thirty-three acres) of land were to distribute the excess over that amount to their distant relatives or neighbors. Slaves were not freed, but it was forbidden to buy or sell them. Wang justified these measures as first steps toward the restoration of the well-field system, which he said had been inhumanely destroyed by the Qin. Little is known about what measures were taken to enforce this remarkably sweeping change. We are told that the buying and selling of slaves was pretty effectively disrupted. It also is clear that these measures aroused the opposition of the entire landed elite. Wang was forced to rescind them in 12 C.E.

Later Chinese usually have seen the failure of this effort to restore the well-field system as a warning against idealistic efforts to restore ancient institutions, no matter how wonderful they may have been in the days of the sages. From the viewpoint of a cynical analysis of outside-relative politics, Wang might be seen as seizing any means and any justification to break the power of a landed elite that would tend to be loyal to the Han, to entrench his own supporters and stop the circulation of outside-relative elites, and to increase the revenues of his government. How could Wang have thought he could succeed in such radical changes? Perhaps he had in fact come to believe his own portents and propaganda.

With the important exception of the opposition to the regulations on land and slaves, Wang's rule seems to have been reasonably well accepted in its first years. A few plots by real and pretended members of the old Han imperial house were quickly suppressed. According to Ban Gu, Wang's foreign relations were much less successful. He himself relinquished the title "emperor" invented by the Qin and called himself "king." Since the Son of Heaven had no equal, this led to the fashioning and dispatch to foreign rulers who paid homage to the Han of new seals that demoted them from "king" of this or that people to "duke" or "count." The Xiongnu, Ban says, were outraged and began to raid the borders of China. Wang rejected many opportunities for compromise settlements and behaved arrogantly toward all foreign peoples. The great military expeditions he sent out against them were a basic cause of the heavy burden of his regime on the common people and their eventual revolt. Modern scholars have questioned this story in various ways, in particular pointing out that the conflicts with the Xiongnu do not seem to have extended into the years of decline and civil war at the end of Wang Mang's life.

The Grand Dowager Empress Wang died in 13 C.E. That should not have had much impact on Wang's power, since as first emperor of the Xin dynasty he now claimed many other sources of legitimacy in addition to his membership in a great outside-relative family. Still, it was from about this year that his regime seems to have been in ever-increasing trouble, and that his inability to come to grips with the realities of his situation seems to have become incurable. Perhaps the grand dowager empress herself had provided a measure of prudence and political realism that could not be replaced. No doubt his decline was in part the result of long-term difficulties: resentment of his usurpation, disaffection over the abortive land reform, abuses of monopolies and currency innovations. To this list one of the most important modern scholars on this period, Hans Bielenstein, would add the impact of floods of the Yellow River.

The Yellow River carries a huge load of silt out of the mountains of China's northwestern provinces. Before the building of the great Sanmen dam in the 1950s, it dropped much of this load of silt as it came out on the north China plain and slowed down, raising and shifting its own bed. In recent centuries, imperial governments devoted much money and conscripted manpower to the construction of great dikes confining the river to its channel. Since all the silt was deposited in that channel, the river bed gradually rose, forcing the construction of ever-higher dikes. Although the Han government struggled to prevent floods and shifts of course along the Yellow River, not even the wealthy and powerful state of Emperor Wu was able to keep it permanently contained. The regimes of his successors, more hesitant about public expenditures and with less adequate revenue bases, did even less well. There was a great flood and shift of the river's lower course about 3 C.E., in which part of its flow began to enter the ocean south of the Shandong peninsula. This was followed in 11 by a catastrophic shift in the river's course from a mouth near the modern city of Tianjin to one just north of the Shandong peninsula. Residents who were not killed in the floods fled to other parts of Shandong or farther. Relief systems like Wang's "constantly full granary" were completely inadequate for the needs of so many destitute people. "Wandering people" caused trouble and joined in banditry and rebellion all over the empire. There was a major rebellion along the lower Yangzi. In the area of modern Shandong province, a rebellion broke out in 17 under the leadership of a woman who was called "Mother Lü." The area seems to have been the center of the Queen Mother of the West excitement a few years before, and it has remained a center of religious prophecy and subversion down to recent times. A far larger outbreak called the "Red Eyebrows" followed in the same area in 18. The red paint on the rebels' foreheads certainly served to identify them, probably also to declare their loyalty to the Han, and perhaps also to tap the power of fire and of the Red Lord. We know very little about them; they seem to have been poorly organized but very numerous and very destructive.

As all these dangers piled up around him, Wang Mang in 14 continued his pursuit of the *Ceremonies of Zhou* utopia and of a fixed and frozen political order. All provincial offices were changed from rotating bureaucratic appointments to permanent, inheritable noble titles with fiefs. In addition to changes in all titles of offices, many place names were changed and changed again in an effort to conform to the geography of the *Ceremonies of Zhou*. Ban Gu remarks that Wang "thought in detail about geographical arrangements, the institution of ceremonies, and the composition of music. . . . He discussed [these matters] for successive years without coming to decisions, so that he did not have time to examine law-cases, decide complaints of injustice, or to settle the urgent business of the common people."

Another round of enfeoffments and granting of noble ranks followed in 17. By now it was said that Wang had granted so many titles and fiefs that the income from them was insufficient to maintain the grantees. Those who held semibureaucratic office were confronted by such complex rules on the income they were supposed to receive that they could not decide what was legal and what was not, and simply took what they needed or wanted without restraint. The disruptions by the floods and the swarms of refugees on the roads no doubt made many landholdings less valuable than they would have been in peaceful times. Extra taxation to support the huge armies Wang sent against the rebels and the Xiongnu, and the depredations of passing forces, added to the general misery. Several years of insufficient rainfall compounded it. Starvation was widespread, and there were reports of cannibalism.

All this detail, of course, is from Ban Gu's partisan account. And Ban, the great skeptic about portents in favor of Wang Mang, did not hesitate to record any number of omens of his collapse and portents of Han restoration in these years. Still, the chronology speaks for itself: in 23 C.E., just ten years after the death of the grand dowager empress, Han loyalist troops took the capital, and Wang Mang was killed in the fall of the city.

Ban's account of Wang's last years shows an increasingly tyrannical government, arresting thousands of people for violating the monopoly on minting coins, conducting executions the year round (in gross violation of the harmony of Heaven and humanity, which restricted them to autumn, the season when the natural world dies). Wang is shown as more and more out of touch, not wanting to hear about rebel advances, but refusing to allow his commanders to mobilize or move their troops on their own initiative. Pursuing the lore of omens and correspondences that had justified his seizure of power, in 21 he ordered a wide search in the empire for women to enter his household: "Because the Yellow Lord had 120 women, he became an immortal." He also sent men to violate the temple of Emperor Gao of the Han, chopping up its doors and windows, whipping its walls with the whips used to whip criminals. He spent vast sums on splendid ceremonies at the temples of his ancestors; he had come a long way from the times when he did not eat meat if there was hunger anywhere in the empire. Even in these late years, however, Ban records one case in which Wang paid attention to a comprehensive denunciation of his policies and followed one part of its recommendations. The monopolies were abolished, but at the end of 22, much too late.

By the end of 23 Wang was dead and Han loyalist troops were occupying the capital. They were driven out by the Red Eyebrows early in 25. Appalling massacre, looting, and burning followed. Later in 25 more Han restoration forces entered the capital, and the first emperor of the Later Han was enthroned.

Ban Gu ends his account of Wang Mang by comparing him to the First Emperor of Qin. The Qin burnt the books in order to establish their policies, while Wang "chanted the six arts in order to ornament his evil words." "They came to the same result but by different paths." Like dragons flying too high, they exceeded Heaven's will for them and were destroyed.

BAN ZHAO

· · · · · ·

WANG MANG had presented himself as an idealistic Confucian scholar and a patron of other Confucian scholars seeking education and opportunity at the Imperial Academy, but he actually had risen to power as a relative of a dowager empress, and in power he had sought to limit political mobility by making the highest offices hereditary. The restoration of the Han, inaugurating what is called the Later Han (25–220 C.E.), was based on an establishment reaction against Wang's usurpation and his radical policies, motivated by loyalty to the Han, by the family feeling of the very large and powerful Han imperial family, and by defense of property in land and slaves. Yearnings for an egalitarian "great peace," more clearly expressed in the religious enthusiasms and elite dreams and symbols of the years of Wang's rise than in anything we know about the Red Eyebrows and other popular rebels against him, were completely discredited in the political elite, but survived in the broad popular culture.

Several descendants of the Han emperors, and others who falsely claimed such descent, headed rival restoration factions. The man who finally emerged supreme and became the first emperor of the Later Han, posthumously Emperor Guangwu, was a member of a branch of the imperial family that had fallen to modest provincial elite status, and had himself served at the court of Wang Mang. His regime, firmly founded on the bureaucratic ambition and conservative moral earnestness of the best of the provincial elite, was one of the most seriously Confucian regimes in all of Chinese history. There were solemn annual ceremonies in memory of Confucius. The emperor himself went to pay homage at Confucius's home at Qufu and began the custom of giving noble rank to his senior male descendant, a custom that continued down to the Revolution of 1911. Serious efforts were made, against much resistance from large landowners, to conduct an accurate survey of landholding and to keep land taxes low and fairly distributed. Partly in reaction to the use Wang Mang had made of Old Text versions of the Classics, the court supported some of the most conscientious and detailed scholarship on classical texts that has ever been written. Young men again sought to make their careers through study of the Classics at the Imperial Academy.

The result was a regime of impressive unity and stability, which could and did mount major military campaigns into areas that now are on the far northwestern frontier of China and beyond the Chinese-Vietnamese border in the south. Textual and archaeological evidence suggests that in these decades of good government and prosperity the fine crafts and lavish spending that characterized the Earlier Han capital spread to provincial cities and the estates of great landlords.

Provincial magnates presented themselves to the Later Han court as selfless ministers, scholarly, skilled in literary expression, inspired by the teachings of Confucius and the examples of sage rulers. Their households were important centers of the study and teaching of the classical texts, literary composition, and Confucian moral values. Discipline, order, and propriety within the family were thought of as vital training for disciplined and moral participation in political life. And of course teaching of this kind also would do much to insure that the sons of these families would advance in the imperial bureaucracy, renewing the prestige of the family and protecting its property from excessive taxation or confiscation. We will note many changing forms of this interweaving of ministerial idealism, family propriety, and careerism, right down to the end of the empire. In the particular mix of these values in these centuries, with its great emphasis on family propriety and discipline, it is not surprising to find that an unusual amount of attention was devoted to the importance of women as teachers and examples of virtue. The oldest surviving collection of lives of virtuous women, for example, was compiled by Liu Xiang, a great scholar who served Wang Mang.

Perhaps the finest example of the qualities and achievements of this Later Han elite was the Ban family. Ban Gu, the historian who wrote the very negative account of the rise and fall of Wang Mang, has already been discussed. His twin brother Ban Chao was one of the greatest frontier generals and administrators in Chinese history. Their younger sister Ban Zhao was a poet, a scholar and teacher at the imperial court, an advocate of education for women, and an articulator of a Confucian vision of woman's role in family and society as subtle and intricate as the fine needlework she used as a key metaphor in one of her poems.

The Ban family traced its origins to the state of Chu. In the turmoil of the fall of Qin and the rise of Han a member of the family migrated to the northern frontier, where he became very rich in cattle and sheep. The real foundation of the family fortunes did not come until after about 30 B.C.E., when a daughter was taken into the palace of Emperor Cheng. It was said that she refused to ride in the same carriage with the emperor, so that she would not distract him from his duties. She also was a scholar and writer, one of whose poems has been preserved and is still admired today. This was a time when many previously unknown ancient books or new texts of known books were being found (or faked) and presented to the imperial court. Ban You, a brother of Palace Lady Ban, participated in some of this collecting and editing work, and as a reward the emperor presented to him duplicate copies from the imperial collections of some old books that previously had been inaccessible outside the palace. Palace Lady Ban was a highly respected figure but does not seem to have been among those whose families sought to control the court in this period; it was those documents, and the scholarly and literary accomplishments of Palace Lady Ban and her brothers, that set the family on a slower and less risky path toward eminence through scholarship and ministerial service.

The Ban family seems to have managed to avoid too conspicuous association with the regime of Wang Mang. Ban Biao, a nephew of Ban You and of Palace Lady Ban, spent much time with the family treasure-trove of documents, and also collected materials for a continuation down to his own time of Sima Qian's great history. He wrote an essay asserting that the effects of the Wang Mang regime had not reached down to the common people, all of whom continued to long for a Han restoration. He served for a time on the staff of Dou Rong, head of a family descended from relatives of the Dowager Empress Dou who had held power at the beginning of the reign of Emperor Wu. The Dou, natives of the same district as the Ban, were immensely powerful on the northwestern frontier and had provided crucial support to Emperor Guangwu. From this time down to the death of Ban Gu the fortunes of the Ban were linked to those of the Dou. Emperor Guangwu asked Dou Rong who was helping him write his state papers, and Dou mentioned Ban Biao's name; Ban was recommended for office but never held a position of power and continued his collecting and editing of historical materials down to his death in 54 C.E. His twin sons Gu and Chao were born in 32, his daughter Zhao in about 48.

A classical education was supposed to be a preparation for a moral life, but especially for service as a minister of the emperor. Since women did not serve in the bureaucracy, the incentives to give girls such an education were not so strong. But it seems likely that Ban Zhao received almost as good an education as her brothers. In an age when the importance of good order and good example within a great family was widely acknowledged, such an education of an upper-class girl may have been more common than it was later. But the Ban family had an exceptional heritage—the erudite Palace Lady, the documents from the palace, Biao's historical researches— and there cannot have been very many women who got such a thorough classical and literary education. It began under her father's direction, and after his death her much older brothers probably helped to teach her and find teachers for her.

Then at the age of fourteen she was married to a man of the Cao family. Nothing more is known of him or of his family. Surely she had been well instructed about the delicate situation in which she now would find herself. A new daughter-in-law above all had to please and serve her mother-in-law. She also had to win the friendship or at least toleration of her husband's brothers and sisters. The birth of a son, an heir to her husband's family, would do much to strengthen her position. Toward her husband she was expected to be gentle and obedient, but too strong and emotional a relation between bride and bridegroom might actually impair her ability to weave the complex net of new roles and ties she needed if she were to play a proper, harmonious role in her husband's family.

The very young Mrs. Cao, formerly Ban Zhao, did not have many years to practice this role. Her husband died at an early age. She never remarried. Strict Confucian principles required her to remain in her late husband's family. For some time she probably did so, serving her mother-in-law and raising at least one son. Her widowed mother and her brilliant brothers had moved to the capital about the time she was married. It probably was some time after 75, when Ban Gu became a highly respected adviser at the court of a new emperor, that she joined his household there. Perhaps she did so so that her children could study with their uncle. Very probably she was more at ease in their household and in the refined literary and intellectual society of the capital than in the provincial home of her husband's family.

Ban Gu had begun his search for fame and fortune about 58 by writing a remarkably sycophantic letter to a prince of the imperial family, whom he compared to the duke of Zhou. He may have served on that prince's staff before taking a modest and ill-paid position at the capital. His twin brother Chao had to take very low-ranking scribal positions to help meet the family's expenses. He hated this humble, boring life and dreamed of following the example of Zhang Qian, the great conqueror of Inner Asia in the reign of Emperor Wu. In 73, perhaps owing to the patronage of Dou Xian, who was organizing a massive offensive against the Xiongnu, he obtained a low-ranking position accompanying a Han envoy to the distant oasis states of what is now Xinjiang.

Ban Chao would not return to the capital for almost thirty years. Leading a party of only thirty-six men, he probed for ways to revive Chinese influence along the trade routes from oasis to oasis. In his biography we sense little or nothing of the ethnic and cultural complexity of the region, with its Turkic and Indo-European peoples, its memories both of the Chinese armies and, not too much farther west, of those of Alexander the

Great. Buddhism had put down roots in some of the Inner Asian states, and it was being brought to the Han capital by their merchants and envoys. The biography describes, in terms no doubt made more vivid by many retellings, how Ban Chao made use of antagonisms within and between the various oasis states to mobilize the armies of some of them against others, reestablishing Chinese influence and excluding that of the Xiongnu. One exploratory expedition he sent out reached the shores of the Caspian Sea, or perhaps the Persian Gulf. The biography of Ban Chao is one of the greatest of those stories of heroism, astuteness, and guile that contributed so much to the faith of later generations of Chinese in their ability to overawe and outsmart any foreigner, "using barbarians against barbarians." Ban Chao rarely received reinforcements from the capital, and his announcements of his victories arrived there as if from another planet. He contributed nothing to his family's power base but a great deal to its prestige.

When a new emperor came to the throne in 75, he frequently summoned Ban Gu to the palace to assist him in his studies. Crucial support for Ban's position came from the steadily growing power of the Dou family: Dou Xian already was very influential in war and foreign policy, and in 78 a Dou lady became empress. Ban now accompanied all imperial hunts and other journeys, writing elaborate poems to commemorate them, including many exclamations about the "flourishing age." In 79 the emperor ordered a great conference of the best scholars of the empire on the correct texts and interpretations of the Confucian Classics, and placed Ban Gu in charge of editing the official conference report, the *Bo Hu Tong* (Comprehensive Discussions in the White Tiger Hall), which remains one of the most important landmarks in the history of scholarship on the Confucian Classics. But much of the time Ban was free to carry on his father's work on a history of the Earlier Han, and now he had all the power of the imperial court behind his efforts to collect materials.

Ban Zhao now was about thirty. Little is known about her life in this period. Her later achievements as a teacher and her ability to finish some of the most intricate portions of the history after Ban Gu's death prove that she was sufficiently erudite to assist him in his historical work and make it likely that she already was an active contributor to the project in the 70s and 80s. A later poem of hers marveling at a great bird sent from Inner Asia shows that she also had the literary talent needed to help her brother provide ornamental poetry for court occasions. She may also have found time to teach her own children, Ban Gu's, and any that Chao had left behind. She was eminently qualified to teach history, literature, the Classics, and astronomy to all of them. The daughters and nieces would have gotten more, including stories of eminent women from earlier collections and the family history project, fruits of her meditations on her own experiences as a daughter-in-law, and detailed instruction in household management—servants, food supply, weaving, sewing, embroidery. Young men were being educated to contribute to their families by pursuing their wonderful careers as scholars, politicians, or soldiers. Young women were being trained to provide order, good management, and moral example within the family. For a big elite household that wove its own cloth and made its own clothes, skill with a needle was a central practical requirement, not an ornament for idle hands. Ban Zhao wrote a famous poem:

NEEDLE AND THREAD
Chill autumn gleam of steel,
Fine, straight, and sharp,
You thrust your way in and gradually advance,
So that things far apart are all strung into one.
Needle and thread, your orderly traces
Seem to have no beginning, but join far and wide.
Going back, twisting, flaws are mended,
As smooth as the fine coat of a lamb.
How can we measure your work?
All of it makes your memorial stone.
You're found in the village home,
And in the great noble hall.[1]

Ban Gu made excellent progress on his history of the Earlier Han. It would follow the basic pattern of Sima Qian's great work, but would not need to have a separate section for hereditary lords, since they were of little importance in the unified empire. He explicitly criticized his great predecessor's respect for Daoism and fondness for adventurers and money-makers; his own work would be much more strict in its adherence to Confucian standards. His political position seemed more secure than ever after 88, when the emperor died and the Dowager Empress Dou and her brother Dou Xian became the real rulers on behalf of a child emperor. Ban Gu was not much involved in politics and policy making, but several times used his historical and literary skills in support of Dou Xian. Dou Xian favored diplomatic and military intervention in Inner Asia. He led a successful campaign against the Xiongnu in 89. Ban Gu supported these policies against those who argued for a more cautious defensive stance. He even participated in a minor and rather confused way in the next expedition. But then the young emperor came of age and laid plans to free himself from the

[1] These translations are based on translations and Chinese texts in Nancy L. Swann, *Pan Chao: Foremost Woman Scholar of China* (New York and London, 1932).

heavy hands of the dowager empress Dou and her brother. In 92 Dou Xian and his followers were accused of plotting to kill the emperor and imprisoned; they committed suicide. The dowager empress was not killed but lost all power. Ban Gu was arrested, ostensibly because of a minor infraction by one of his servants but actually because of his Dou connection, and executed.

News had just been received of Ban Chao's greatest victories, and he had been granted new honors. In any case, he was beyond the reach of the new regime at court. Ban Zhao was just a woman, not worth killing, but now without influence or protection in the capital. In 95 her son was assigned to a minor official post in the provinces. She accompanied him to his new post. This certainly was exile, and possibly a prelude to some further action to dispose of these inconvenient remnants of the previous regime. Ban Zhao had every reason to believe that the lives and good names of herself and her son were in jeopardy. She wrote a long poem, of which only parts can be given here.

JOURNEY TO THE EAST
. . . .
Dawn comes and still no sleep.
My heart slows and skips.
I pour a cup of wine to ease my thoughts.
Stifling my feelings, I sigh and blame myself.
. . . .
Longing for the capital I sigh in secret,
But it's a "small man" who cherishes a favorite place,
As the old books tell us.
. . . .
We come to Kuang, and my thoughts are far away,
Recalling how Confucius was in danger.
In that chaotic time the Way was lost,
And not even a sage was safe.
. . . .
Honor, dishonor, wealth, or poverty cannot be sought.
Body straight, I follow the Way, and wait for better times.

The better times came surprisingly soon. In 96 or 97 Ban Zhao was back in the capital, beginning the golden years of her influence and prestige at court. The turnabout was the result of more shifts in the politics of the emperor and his palace women. One Lady Deng, member of a family that had given early support to the founder of Later Han, entered the palace in 96. She was a well-educated young woman with an excellent reputation for virtuous conduct, diligence, and filial piety. Her entry into the palace, or her later rise in the hierarchy of palace women, may have resulted from the emperor's efforts to work out a respectable and controllable set of relations to his ladies and their relatives. Ban Zhao could be of great assistance in such an effort. Her biography states that the emperor often summoned her to the palace, where "he ordered the [future] empress [Lady Deng] and the ladies of honorable rank to treat her as a teacher." She taught the Classics, astronomy, and mathematics. She also was commanded to compose poems on unusual gifts and other special occasions, like this one on a great bird sent by Ban Chao.

> THE BIRD FROM THE FAR WEST
> We honor the land where the great birds dwell,
> Born on the mystic peaks of Kunlun.
> Another has the same name but is much smaller;
> This one can be compared to the phoenix.
> Cherishing virtue, he returns to righteousness.
> He comes ten thousand *li* on his great wings.
> He comes to rest at the Imperial Court.
> He roams at ease, rejoicing in its air of harmony.
> High and low work together and are fond of each other.
> They listen to the deep chords of the classical songs.
> From east and west, from north and south,
> All come eager to submit.

The emperor also ordered Ban Zhao to come to the imperial library and use its documents to complete her brother's history. The sections left unfinished at his untimely death included the table of high officials and the essay on astronomy. Ban Zhao completed these very difficult sections. She explained them and the rest of the history to court scholars who found parts of it hard to understand; one of them assisted her in the final editing work. She seems to have been a full participant in the literary and intellectual activity of the court, discussing texts and issues with men and women and teaching their sons and daughters. It is recorded that one of her Cao sisters-in-law wrote essays disputing some of her views, and that the wife of one of her sons edited her literary works after her death. In 101 Ban Zhao interceded with the emperor to obtain permission for Ban Chao, over seventy and in bad health, to return to the capital.

In 102 the emperor dismissed his empress and her relatives and named Lady Deng his new empress. In 106 he died; the Dowager Empress Deng arranged the succession of a small child and, after he died, of an older boy. Even after that boy came of age she remained a leading power in the court until her death in 121. She survived so long in part because she and her male relatives sought only modest measures of power and wealth, avoiding the resentment of outside-relative excess that was so common earlier and later. In these political maneuvers and in her maintenance of an orderly and cultured court, Ban Zhao was her key adviser. This is most strikingly seen in an incident in 110. A senior Deng relative wanted to retire from office to mourn his mother. The dowager empress was reluctant, and some of the other Deng males may also have objected; he was a key figure in their power outside the palace. But Ban Zhao submitted a memorial to the dowager empress, arguing that "there is no greater virtue than that of yielding to others" (*rang*). Confucius had taught that it ought to be possible to govern a state through ceremony and yielding. If the Deng relative was not allowed to retire, the Deng family might never again be able to gain a good name for yielding to others. The dowager empress was convinced, and several of the Deng relatives retired to their estates. As the biography of Dowager Empress Deng puts it, "At one word from Mother Ban, all the great men withdrew."

Ban Zhao's son was given noble rank and an important official position. In 112 the dowager empress established a formal school in the palace for sons and daughters of the imperial family, which she supervised personally. It would be nice to think of the aging Mother Ban still giving an occasional special lesson. When Ban Zhao died about 119 or 120 the Dowager Empress Deng wore mourning for her, and the court went into mourning.

Ban Zhao had made of her life a fine embroidery of scholarship, personal integrity, and a political astuteness that owed much to her reading of history and all that she heard from her brother and other participants in capital politics. But she also was the product of a long tradition of ideals of feminine behavior and of her own experiences as a daughter-in-law. Women should be modest, retiring, diligent in their household duties. It is up to them to keep peace in the household, winning the acceptance of the mother-in-law by modesty and diligence in waiting on her, earning the respect and friendship of brothers- and sisters-in-law. A good name is more important than anything else. Frivolity, gossip, loud chatter with women friends are to be avoided.

Ban Zhao embodied and taught, especially to Dowager Empress Deng, a pattern of integrity, of modesty and yielding in inter-personal relations, of not overreaching or wanting too much power, that was rooted in these feminine virtues and that served her and her imperial pupil very well. She also wrote, for the younger generation and for generations yet to come, a famous statement of these principles called the *Nü Jie* (Admonitions to Women). Its eloquent and elegant summary of this feminine ideal, full of quotations of Confucius and the Classics, was much admired and had great influence in later centuries. Somewhat simpler and more direct than some of her erudite poems, it is meant to be understood by readers who did not have all her educational advantages. In it she brought up one issue on which she found herself out of step with her own time and on which later generations heeded her much too seldom. Here the language is so direct that we almost flinch at the sharp tongue of Mother Ban, especially as she makes sarcastic use of the Confucian ideal of the gentleman (*jun zi*):

> Now look at the gentlemen of the present age. They only know that wives must be controlled and that [the husband's] rules and precedence must be established. They therefore teach their boys to read texts and commentaries. But they do not understand that husbands and masters must also be served, and that proper relationships and ceremonies should be maintained. But if one only teaches men and does not teach women, is that not ignoring the essential relation between them? According to the *Ceremonies*, children are taught to read beginning at the age of eight, and by the age of fifteen they should be ready for thoughtful study of the Classics. Why should [the education of girls as well as boys] not be according to this rule?

In traditional China there always were upper-class women who got solid educations along with their brothers. But at no other time did the social and cultural situation produce as much attention to the problem of the education of women or as many socially prominent and politically and culturally active women as in the Later Han. Ban Zhao's writings are among the very small number of works of women authors that have been preserved from premodern China. Her arguments for the education of women were generally ignored in recent centuries, when literacy rates were much lower among women than among men. Only in our own century has political and social support for the education of women really expanded.

Nor did the excellent examples of Mother Ban and Dowager Empress Deng have any permanent effect on Later Han court politics. By the mid-120s, just a few years after their deaths, another empress dowager was trying to manipulate the succession, and the life and succession of the only son of the previous emperor was saved only by an armed coup staged by the palace eunuchs. This brought the eunuchs to unprecedented power and opened the way to decades of intrigue and violence.

7

ZHUGE LIANG

• • • • • •

In the Chinese tradition Zhuge Liang represents one of the supreme embodiments of the heroic minister. Content in his withdrawal from bad times and his quest for the secrets of nature, independent and not at all eager for office, he responded to the urgent plea of his true lord and showed immense gifts as a persuader and tactician. He fought in few battles, but even after death his name struck terror in his enemies. His lord was the legitimate successor of the Han emperors, served by two great warriors bound to him not by his having selected them as ministers but by the three heroes having found each other at a country inn and sworn to stay together until death. The legitimate Han rule they served prevailed only in one part of the empire and was constantly at war with two other great states; hence, the period is known as the Three Kingdoms. The outcome was tragic; the Han cause was defeated, and the heroes were not even able to die together. Their efforts were doomed by their flaws of character, closely tied to their heroic virtues, that led them into fatal errors of tactics and judgment at crucial points in the story. They knew each other's flaws but were committed to each other by oath and cause; unlike the isolated heroes of Greek tragedy, these men are represented as heroes of a tragedy of *interdependence*.

Many stories about the heroes of the Three Kingdoms were circulated in their own time and were drawn together in the *San Guo zhi* (Studies of the Three Kingdoms), completed about 290, which came to be accepted as the standard dynastic history of the period. But the heroes' impact on the Chinese consciousness, and the inclusion of one of them in this book, is much more a result of their portrayal in a wonderful historical novel, the *San Guo yanyi* (Romance of the Three Kingdoms), written by Luo Guanzhong in the late 1300s. Characters and scenes from this novel have been among the most popular sources for the traditional dramas and storytelling performances that still can be seen in China. Many thoroughly modern young Chinese will smile at a mention of the story of borrowing the arrows, or will recall a children's book or comic book about Zhuge

Liang. To understand the warlords who dominated China in the first decades of this century, we should put away our political science texts and read the *Romance of the Three Kingdoms*. Mao Zedong may have been more deeply shaped by it than by Marx and Lenin. I would make it the second book, right after the *Analects* of Confucius, on any short list of books to read in order to understand the Chinese people.

The relation of the story told in the *Romance* to the actualities of the world of the end of the Han is imperfect at best. Little comes through of the diverse and intense cultural world of visionary revolt, magical practice, Daoist speculation, Buddhist beginnings, and efforts to preserve some Confucian fundamentals in an inhospitable world. The politics and economics of a state dominated by great landed families are nowhere to be found. However, the novel does reflect the actualities of the uncertainty and fluidity of politics and the constant resort to arms that made this period so different from the bureaucratic debates and maneuverings of a stable, unified empire. It was in fact the decline of such an empire, the Later Han, that led to the turmoil of the Three Kingdoms.

As we have seen, the discretion of Empress Deng and Ban Zhao had provided only a brief respite from the quarrels of factions of the relatives of empresses. The deadly intrigue within the inner palace was accompanied by massive corruption and favoritism, so that these families and their allies got all the best offices and accumulated vast estates on which they paid few or no taxes. When finally an emperor managed to throw off the power of one great family in 159, he did so only with the aid of the palace eunuchs, who had emerged as another group contending for power in the capital. Conscientious officials and students at the Imperial Academy, many of them from families of modest provincial landholders, protested more and more vehemently the manipulation of the imperial family by relatives of empresses and by eunuchs. In 166–169, efforts of a leader of the Dou family, with support of the officials and academicians, to extirpate the eunuchs were defeated. Some leaders of the effort were killed or exiled. Many more found themselves and their relatives and descendants permanently barred from office or even from residence in the capital.

The inequity of the rural social and economic order and the sordid intrigues at the court no doubt both contributed to episodes of attempted rebellion from the 140s on. One leader proclaimed himself Emperor of the Great Beginning, another Black Emperor, two Yellow Emperors. There were reports of appearances of yellow dragons. The official sources indicate that all these rebellions were suppressed, but they were parts of a growing movement of religious practice and organization worshipping a deified Laozi and drawing on Daoist practices of healing and search for physical immortality. Communities were formed under leaders who knew the sacred formulas that would cure the sick. The old prophecy of the coming of the "great peace" now took the form of the coming of the Yellow Heaven, which would emerge at the beginning of a new sixty-year cycle, in 184 C.E. The rebels who rose in that year to overthrow the Han and welcome the Yellow Heaven wrapped yellow scarves around their heads. The rebellion of the Yellow Scarves was fairly quickly suppressed, or at least dispersed to the point where it no longer threatened court and capital, but Yellow Scarves groups and others calling themselves Black Mountain, White Wave, Yellow Dragon, Thunder Lord, and so on continued to pop up here and there in the following decades. Better organized and more persistent was the Five Pecks of Rice Daoist organization, which controlled the Han River valley and much of Shu (modern Sichuan) for decades. Evidence can be found for the survival of some of these communities in the countryside, and for elite efforts to limit their power, as late as the 400s.

The Han court of 184, eunuch-dominated and massively corrupt, was in no condition to face the challenge of the Yellow Scarves. It had no choice but to give wide authority to the provincial leaders, many of whom had been excluded from the court for over a decade, to raise troops on their own. These leaders were eager to suppress a movement that had no place for Confucian officials or, at least in some of its branches, for landlords. Thus the effects of the Yellow Scarves rebellion confirmed a trend made possible by the prosperity of Later Han and accelerated by the exile of the officials and academicians, away from a court-centered politics and culture and toward one that focused on the power and patronage of great provincial landholders with their own retinues of students, private soldiers, and unfree tenants and craftsmen. This structure underlay the turmoil of the Three Kingdoms period and was basic to Chinese politics and society from this time until after the Sui–Tang reunification around 600.

Some scholars had reacted to the sordidness of the Han court and to their own forced withdrawals to the countryside by reviving Daoist idealizations of the life of the gentleman hermit who scorns the illusions of politics and seeks the secrets of the Dao. Others, often citing the teachings of the Legalists and other realistic statesmen of the Warring States period, reacted by insisting that order must be imposed on society by thorough enforcement of the laws, without any of the considerations of family and personal connection that had so corrupted Later Han court and society. It was the latter type who had the most immediate role to play in the turmoil of the end of the Han. The emerging provincial leaders joined forces in 189 to eliminate eunuch power in the court. Then they fought among themselves until 200, when the great Cao Cao vanquished his last rivals in north China.

The portrayal of Cao Cao in the *Romance of the Three Kingdoms* is one of that work's more unfortunate oversimplifications. He is portrayed as intelligent, devious, and power-hungry, which he was, but hardly anything is shown of his thoughtful efforts to revive the power of the central government, and his achievements as a poet are rarely alluded to. His most important policy innovation was the settling of people on land that formerly had been occupied by the Yellow Scarves or otherwise had been left uncultivated after the civil wars. His main aim was an adequate supply of grain for his court and troops, but of course this measure also contributed to a general economic revival.

Cao Cao never took the imperial position for himself, preferring to maintain a puppet Han emperor. He faced continued opposition from the Five Pecks of Rice movement and from various regional leaders in the Yangzi valley. The most important of these were Liu Biao, a member of the Han imperial family based in Jingzhou in the central Yangzi valley, and Sun Quan, based in the rich lowlands of the lower Yangzi. In 208 he sent his forces into the Yangzi valley but was defeated in a great river battle at a place called Red Cliff by an alliance of Sun Quan's forces with the much smaller forces of another Han kinsman, Liu Bei. Liu Bei's forces then moved up-river into Shu, modern Sichuan, at the invitation of another imperial kinsman, and soon took full control of that rich area. Cao Cao died in 220, and his son soon proclaimed the passing of the mandate of Heaven from the Han and the founding of a new dynasty, the Wei. Liu Bei responded by claiming that the legitimate Han succession continued in Shu, with himself as the next emperor. Administrative power in Shu was in the hands of Zhuge Liang, who proved to be an effective, tough state-builder whose policies were not very different from Cao Cao's. Sun Quan made himself first emperor of Wu. Thus the three kingdoms of Wei, Shu Han, and Wu were explicitly established. Both Wu and Shu Han were based in rich areas hard to attack from the north. They could have threatened the power of the Wei in the north if their alliance had remained firm, but the two states were intermittently at war with each other over claims to the Jingzhou area. The Shu Han regime made some advances against the Wei and against the Five Pecks of Rice bases in the Han River valley. Zhuge Liang died on a campaign into the Wei River valley in 234. The Shu Han regime carried on under Liu Bei's son, but never again was a threat to its rivals. It finally was extinguished in 265, and Wu in 280. In the north a new dynasty, the Jin, replaced the Wei in 265 and ruled over a unified empire from 280 until the early 300s, when it was driven from the north by invasions of non-Chinese peoples.

That is a very simple outline of developments about which much more can be written from reasonably good sources. But if we want to understand the place of the Three Kingdoms in the Chinese sense of the past, we must focus not on the historical record but on the *Romance of the Three Kingdoms*, which follows a historically verifiable outline but leaves out much that can be known and adds elaborate and wonderful stories that have little or no foundation in sources available to us. As so often happens in historical fiction or drama, institutions, trends, and complexities are slighted, the focus on individual character and action becomes stronger, and there is a tendency to clearer distinctions between heroes and villains than can usually be found in political reality. But there still is plenty of room for portrayal of conflict between private and public commitments, for heroes laid low by the faults of their virtues or by the faults of those to whom they are bound by ties of sworn brotherhood. Most of all, in the *Romance* the sense of reenactment of human emotion and action is so vivid that I cannot resist telling the whole story in the present tense.

The *Romance* opens with a poem:

> On and on the Great River rolls, racing east.
> Of proud and gallant heroes its white-tops leave no trace,
> As right and wrong, pride and fall turn all unreal.
> Yet ever the green hills stay
> To blaze in the west-waning day.
>
> Fishers and woodsmen comb the river isles,
> White-crowned, they've seen enough of spring autumn tide
> To make good company over the wine jar,
> Where many a famed event
> Provides their merriment.[1]

This is followed by another reminder that all things are transitory: "The empire, long divided, must unite; long united, must divide." It was so for the Zhou and for the Qin, and now the story to be told is of the time when the Han was reaching its end. A review of the Han decline quickly gives way to the story of the chance meeting at a country inn of three heroes: Liu Bei, an impoverished distant relation of the Han imperial family; Guan Yu, who had to flee his home after he killed a local notable who was tyrannizing the ordinary people; and Zhang Fei, a hot-tempered warrior. The three take a famous oath in a peach orchard, vowing to repay their obligation to the reigning dynasty and to work for the welfare of the common people. "We three, although of separate ancestry, join in brotherhood here, combining strength and purpose, to relieve the present crisis. We will perform our duty to the Emperor and protect the common folk of the land. We

---

[1] These translations follow Moss Roberts, tr., *Three Kingdoms* (Berkeley, Los Angeles, and Beijing, 1992).

dare not hope to be together always but hereby vow to die the selfsame day. Let shining Heaven above and the fruitful land below witness to our resolve. May Heaven and man scourge whoever fails this vow." This "Peach Orchard Oath" echoed in the Chinese tradition as the prototype of a form of relations among individuals that was egalitarian, not hierarchical; voluntary, not determined by birth into a particular family; and governed by the allegiance of each to all the others and to a cause larger than all of them. The brothers' chance meeting is the first of hundreds of important chance meetings in Chinese fiction, echoes of that interest in the role of chance in human affairs we saw first in the story of the succession of Yu's son.

In the long, complex development of the novel, the characters of the heroes are gradually revealed. Liu Bei, by his membership in the imperial family the "elder brother" and eventual claimant of the Han succession, is shown to be a paragon of conscientiousness, scruple, and generosity, who would have been truly sagely as the third emperor of a great dynasty but lacks the guile and ruthlessness required to rebuild the fortunes of the Han. Zhang Fei is the first of a long line in Chinese fiction of short-tempered, loud-mouthed, good-hearted warriors who will cause a great deal of trouble for their associates if not carefully watched; for the reader or hearer, he is good for a laugh, a release of fantasies of uncontrolled anger, yelling and fighting, instant and guileless redress of wrongs. Guan Yu, by far the most interesting of the three, is another warrior, fearless in battle, more controlled and a better counselor than Zhang, above all a man who will defend his own honor and will honor at all costs his obligations to others. His red-faced, beautifully bearded statue stands today in many temples and house shrines; he has become Lord Guan (Guan Di, Guan Gong), the God of War in Chinese popular religion.

In the opening chapters of the novel the three brothers share in victories over the Yellow Scarves and campaigns against the warlords, finding that among the warlords ostensibly supporting the Han life is no less dangerous, and that it is a good deal harder to distinguish the forces of good and evil than it had been when fighting the Yellow Scarves. A particularly difficult alliance with one Lü Bu is upheld by Liu Bei's noble and trusting spirit but then scuttled by Lü's trickery and Zhang Fei's impetuous reaction to it, so that finally Liu Bei and his sworn brothers are forced to seek the protection of Cao Cao and to live at the court of Cao's captive Han emperor. Cao puts Liu Bei in charge of troops and sends him on an expedition, but then sends a man to arrange his assassination. When Zhang Fei and Guan Yu uncover the plot and kill the plotter, Zhang goes on to massacre the man's family, and Liu Bei flees to join the forces of Cao's leading enemy. Guan Yu is persuaded to return to the capital instead of fighting to the death against Cao's superior forces, so that he can keep watch over Liu

Bei's wives and avoid a separate death that would break the Peach Orchard Oath. Cao tries to drive a wedge between Guan and Liu by assigning only one room to Guan and Liu Bei's wives, so that scandalous rumors will reach Liu, but Guan sits outside the door of the room all night, candle in hand, sword drawn, eyes wide open.

After the defeat of the armies opposing Cao Cao, Liu Bei flees to the Jingzhou area in the middle Yangzi. The forces under his command are small, and his position is very insecure. When Guan Yu learns where he is, he sneaks away from the capital to join him. Cao Cao catches up with him, tries to persuade him to turn back, but allows him to leave; Guan goes to join his true lord, but also has a sense of obligation to Cao for treating him honorably and letting him go.

Liu Bei and his sworn brothers now set out to find men who can advise them how to strengthen their position in the middle Yangzi. They are told repeatedly of a mysterious person named Zhuge Liang, whose main concern is the Daoist pursuit of immortality and the secrets of nature, but who also is wonderfully well versed in the great strategists of the Warring States period. Twice they go to the small thatched house where the great man lives, only to find that he is off in the mountains somewhere. When they come a third time, he is at home but is taking a nap. Liu Bei stands respectfully waiting for him to awaken, while Zhang Fei becomes livid with rage and suggests awakening him by setting fire to his thatched roof. When Zhuge Liang finally awakens he is all politeness and apology. He appears to be "singularly tall, with a face like gleaming jade, a plaited silken band around his head. Cloaked in crane down, he had the buoyant air of a [Daoist] spiritual transcendent." Soon he and Liu Bei settle down to serious discussion of strategy. Zhuge Liang has a map, which shows the importance of taking Jingzhou as a strategic base and the possibility of moving from there up the river into Shu. Liu Bei is delighted, and Zhuge Liang abandons his spiritual pursuits to become Liu's strategic adviser. Guan Yu and Zhang Fei remain suspicious, especially as it becomes clear that Zhuge Liang will devise his strategies from a tent at headquarters and will not lead troops into battle. Liu explains that "For brains I have Kongming [the courtesy name frequently used for Zhuge Liang in the *Romance*], for courage you two. They cannot be interchanged. . . . Plans evolved within the tent decide victory a thousand leagues away."

Zhuge Liang soon proves his worth to Liu Bei not only as a tactician but as an adviser and persuader of others. The key human problem in the area is the power of Liu Biao, holding the key city of Jingzhou, aging and unwell, torn between an oldest son who should be his heir and the relatives and son of a second wife. Cao Cao's armies are advancing on the area. Liu Biao seems ready to resolve the situation by making Liu Bei his heir, but

Bei refuses. Zhuge Liang asks why he turned him down. "[Biao] has treated me with consummate grace and etiquette. To exploit his moment of peril to seize his estate would be too cruel." Zhuge Liang sighs, "What a kind-hearted lord!" Then, in a very funny scene, Zhuge Liang tries to salvage something from the situation by giving good advice to Liu Biao's oldest son, repeating that he cannot presume to give advice on a family quarrel but allowing himself to be trapped in an inner room where he can't escape the young man's pleas. Little is accomplished, however; Liu Biao dies, leaving his office and territory to his younger son, and the second wife's relatives soon open the gates to Cao Cao.

Zhuge Liang now gets his first chance to prove how much can be accomplished by "plans evolved within the tent." Units of Liu Bei's forces go out to confront a larger Cao army, appear to retreat, and lure the Cao army into a valley where they are suddenly surrounded by flaming dry reeds. Parts of the fleeing army stumble into ambushes expertly laid by Zhang Fei and Guan Yu.

Still the Cao forces' superiority in numbers is clear; Liu Bei's cause is doomed unless he can find a strong ally. An emissary arrives from the court of Sun Quan, lord of the lower Yangzi, which is divided between those who want to acknowledge the supremacy of Cao Cao and those who want to find other allies and resist such subjection. Zhuge Liang volunteers to go to Sun Quan's court and persuade him to take the latter course: "Trust to my three inches of limber tongue." The *Romance*'s account of his visit to Sun Quan's court is a complex little masterpiece, showing him making good use of all kinds of information, always seeing farther ahead than his opponents, like a superb verbal chess-player. To Sun Quan's ministers he uses moral arguments, emphasizing the offense of Cao Cao reducing the Han emperor to a puppet and the high moral qualities of Liu Bei. In his interview with Sun Quan he emphasizes the numerical superiority of Cao Cao's forces, urging him to decide quickly whether he should submit or whether he can find the forces and allies to resist. Liu Bei, he makes it clear, will remain loyal to the Han as a matter of principle. Sun Quan is insulted by the implication that he is less brave and principled than Liu Bei, but this has the desired effect, making him more ready to listen to any plausible anti-Cao strategy, and soon he has agreed to an alliance with Liu Bei. There still is resistance among Sun's ministers. On her deathbed, Sun Quan's mother had urged her son always to listen to the advice of one minister, Zhou Yu. Zhuge Liang tells Zhou:

> When I was in residence at Longzhong, I heard that Cao was building a new tower on the banks of the Zhang. It was called the Bronze Bird Tower—an absolutely magnificent edifice, and elegant! He has

searched far and wide for beautiful women to fill the chambers. Cao, who is basically of the type inclined to wantonness, has known for some time that the Southland [Wu] patriarch Qiao has two daughters, beauties whose faces would make fish forget to swim or birds to fly, abash the very blossoms and outshine the moon. He has vowed, "First I'll sweep the realm and calm it and build an empire; then I'll possess the Southland's two daughters Qiao of Wu and install them in the Bronze Bird Tower so that I may have pleasure in my later years and die without regret."

He goes on to recite a fine poem by Cao Cao's son Cao Zhi on the Bronze Bird Tower. Zhou Yu is outraged; one of the daughters of the Patriarch Qiao is his own wife. "Cao, old traitor, you and I cannot share footing on this earth. So I swear."

So the Sun Quan–Liu Bei alliance is settled, and the stage is set for the climactic confrontations on the Yangzi, leading up to the Battle of Red Cliff. There was such a battle, in 208, and broad outlines of it are clear from reliable sources. Cao Cao's forces were badly handicapped by their inexperience in warfare on the wide and treacherous river. Their defeat was decisive; Cao had lost his last real chance to reunify the empire. The author of the *Romance* has embroidered these events with foggy night, fiery disasters, the pride and rage of Cao, and supreme portrayals of Zhuge Liang as master of the forces of nature and uncanny trickster.

Zhou Yu now is committed to resistance against Cao Cao but is repeatedly astonished by Zhuge Liang's ability to see through complicated situations, anticipate what would happen next, and stay three steps ahead of his rivals in his plans. Finding him too dangerous a rival for power in the new alliance, he seeks a way to do away with him without incurring the wrath of Sun Quan and Liu Bei. He asks him if he can provide 100,000 arrows for the coming battles. Zhuge Liang replies, astonishingly, that he can do so within three days, and would accept the death penalty if he did not fulfill his promise. Then he asks another commander to provide "twenty vessels with a crew of thirty each. Lined up on either side of each vessel I want a thousand bales of straw wrapped in black cloth. But if you tell Zhou Yu this time my plan will fail." On the third night there is a thick fog on the river, which Zhuge Liang, master of natural lore, has anticipated. He has the ships pass Cao's camp in single file, the crews shouting and beating the drums as loudly as they can. Cao's archers shoot as rapidly as they can at the sources of the menacing sounds in the fog. As the fog lifts in the morning, the vessels pass again at a greater distance, their crews shouting their thanks to Cao Cao for donating such a fine supply of arrows to his enemies.

Cao Cao still has every reason to believe that his forces will win any

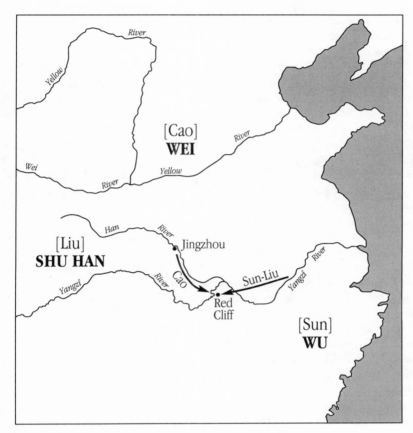

Map 2. Centers of Three Kingdoms, campaign of 208 c.e.

battle. He assembles his officers for a banquet on his flagship. Boasting of his past victories, he looks forward to installing the two daughters of Patriarch Qiao in the Bronze Sparrow Tower. He chants one of his own poems, concluding:

> The moon is bright, the stars are few,
> The magpie black as raven.
> It southbound circles thrice a tree.
> That offers him no haven.
>
> The mountaintop no height eschews,
> The sea eschews no deep,
> And the duke of Zhou spat out his meal
> An empire's trust to keep.

A loyal officer protests ill-omened words in Cao's song, and Cao in a drunken rage spears him to death on the spot, but the next day he is overcome with remorse.

The Sun–Liu alliance, its forces inferior in numbers and arms, now prepares large numbers of ships full of wood, straw, and explosives to be sent drifting down into Cao's anchored ships. To make sure that the Cao fleet cannot get away, they send a double agent to Cao, who advises that he can deal with the seasickness his northern soldiers are suffering on their ships by chaining the ships together so that they will not move so much in the water. The double agent, something of an artist with his three inches of limber tongue, convinces Cao. Cao knows of the fireships being prepared by his enemies but thinks them no threat, since they are downriver to the southeast of his base, and at that time of year the prevailing winds are from the north and west.

Now it is time for Zhuge Liang to demonstrate his mastery of the secrets of summoning the powers of nature. He has a three-tiered altar built. On the bottom tier are twenty-eight flags for the twenty-eight solar mansions, on the next sixty-four flags for the hexagrams of the *Yi jing*, on the top four men dressed in the colors appropriate to the four directions. In the robes of a Daoist priest, barefoot, long hair loose down his back, Zhuge Liang ascends and descends his altar, in silent prayer. Soon a wind begins to rise out of the southeast. The fire ships are lit and set adrift. They bear down on Cao's base like flaming arrows. It is too late to try to loosen the chains that fasten all the ships. The fire spreads rapidly from one to another, and all are lost.

Cao Cao's forces now do the best they can to organize for the retreat to their north China bases. Zhuge Liang sends Guan Yu to guard a key pass that is Cao's most likely route of retreat. Guan has assured him that despite his sense of obligation to Cao he will not let him pass. But when Cao does appear at the pass, all he has to do is say "You have been well, I trust, General, since we parted?" He goes on to remind him of the great importance of fidelity to private obligations. Guan turns his forces aside, and Cao passes to regroup and consolidate his power in the north.

The story then winds on through the consolidation of the Shu Han regime and its expansion into some key areas in the Han River valley. The breakdown of the alliance between Shu Han and Wu is explained by a story of Guan Yu's rejection of Sun Quan's proposal to marry his son to Guan's daughter: "My tiger lass married off to a mongrel? . . . Speak of it no more." The insulted Sun Quan sends his armies west and takes Jingzhou. Guan dies in battle, and soon his spirit appears to warn Liu Bei of impending trouble and then to thoroughly frighten Cao Cao. After the death of Cao Cao, his son's proclamation of the new Wei dynasty, and Liu Bei's proclamation of his claim to the Han succession, Zhang Fei insists that the Liu Han armies must first attack Wu to avenge the death of Guan Yu; the bond of brotherhood takes precedence over the possibility of a united struggle against the usurper regime in the north. But on the campaign to the east two soldiers whom Zhang had flogged sneak into his tent and stab him to death. Liu Bei's ministers now argue for a revival of the alliance with Wu, but Liu's personal desire for vengeance takes precedence over the imperatives of dynastic power: "Sun Quan I hate. To ally with him now would betray my fraternal covenant. We will destroy Wu first, and then Wei."

This is one of a number of ways in which the *Romance* shows that Liu Bei no longer is the potentially ideal sovereign he once was. He no longer seeks Zhuge Liang's advice, even on matters of military strategy. In the campaign against Wu he gets his forces in a very badly exposed position, his camps are attacked by fire spread by a southeast wind, and he barely manages to escape. But Zhuge Liang has prepared an uncanny maze of rock walls on the route followed by the pursuing Wu commander. The commander enters the maze, and when he tries to leave winds rise, he can see nothing but jagged peaks against the sky, and the great river rolls like war drums in the background. A strange old man finally appears and shows him the way out, and he retreats as fast as he can.

Liu Bei dies, and Zhuge Liang manages the peaceful succession of his son. He tries to do the best he can pursuing the Han cause in face of the isolation of the Shu Han regime and the mediocrity of the successor. He makes some progress in the Han River valley, but has to retreat to the city of Hanzhong after a serious defeat. Seeing vastly superior Wei forces approaching, he has the main gates of the city opened and twenty men placed at each to sweep the road. Zhuge Liang himself puts his white scarf around his head, his crane feather cloak around his shoulders, and sits on the city wall with two boys, playing a *qin*, a stringed instrument. The Wei general, convinced that Zhuge Liang never takes chances and knowing his skill in setting traps, looks at this astonishing spectacle and orders a general retreat. Zhuge Liang drives on into the Wei River valley, but an attack on the enemy using burning wheels sent rolling down hillsides to block a pass fails when a sudden rainstorm puts the fires out. Heaven is turning against him.

Zhuge Liang is exhausted from trying to make all the plans and decisions. His vitality is at low ebb. He has soldiers with black flags stand around his tent while he prays to the Northern Dipper, asking that his life be prolonged for the sake of the Han cause. If the lamp in his tent stays lit for seven days, he may have gained a year of life. But on the sixth night a soldier dashes in, accidentally kicks over the lamp, and it is extinguished. Zhuge Liang now dictates his deathbed memorial to his emperor: "I humbly beg that Your Majesty keep an honest mind and limit your desires, disciplining yourself and caring tenderly for the people. Serve the late Emperor in a spirit of filial piety; show humane generosity throughout your kingdom. Promote those not in the pubic eye to advance the cause of true excellence; deny access to the vicious and depraved to strengthen the moral tone of the realm"

He also orders that after his death there is to be no outcry of mourning, for the enemy will be watching. He has had a life-size figure of himself carved of wood; it is to be put in a chariot and sent out the next day at the head of the Shu Han army. After his death, his orders are followed. The Wei forces see his figure in the chariot, think he is still alive, and flee.

The novel continues to the Jin reunification of 280, ending with a repe-

6. A dough figure of Zhuge Liang

tition of its first sentence about the alternation of unity and disunity, but it seems to me that Zhuge Liang's last trick, his cheating of death itself, is the real conclusion of the story, and one of the finest evocations in Chinese literature of the power of fame, of a great name, to outlive death and even to turn the tide of war.

In April 1985 my wife and I were playing tourist in Xi'an, where the Qin terra-cotta army and the Zhou, Han, and Tang tombs make the air thick with the Chinese past. Xi'an is in the Wei River valley, scene of Zhuge Liang's last campaign. At a craft shop for tourists there was a counter where a man was making tiny figures out of dough with the traditional features of Lord Guan and many other heroes. "What," I said, "No Zhuge Liang?" "You want Zhuge Liang? I'll make you one." In minutes, with no reference to any pattern, he rolled tiny strips of dough onto a stick about three inches long to make his head, his purple cloak, an odd purple scarf around his head, a long scarf of yellow and white feathers around his shoulders, a feather fan in his hand. His eyes are alert and shifty. He seems to be about to speak, once again to set a trap or change the fate of states with his three inches of limber tongue.

HUI NENG, THE SIXTH
PATRIARCH

• • • • • •

UP TO NOW we have been following stories of lives and teachings that despite our best efforts may seem a little remote. Confucius can and does
speak to us across the immense gulfs of time, language, and mentality.
There are many in East Asia today who insist that his teachings and values
still are very relevant to their lives, but their "Confucianism" has little of
the Master's magnificently impractical idealism and none of his desperate
nostalgia for a golden past. In this chapter we turn to a kind of experience
and teaching that is as hard to grasp as any, but to many people in both East
Asia and the United States is alive today, full of wisdom and psychological
healing power. We are most likely to know of it under the Japanese pronunciation, *zen*. (One of the great uniting features of East Asian civilization
is that the peoples of China, Japan, Korea, and formerly Vietnam can read
a character and get the same meaning from it even though they pronounce
it differently. The standard Chinese pronunciation of the character that
the Japanese pronounce *zen* is *chan*.) In the United States it has been influential among artists and poets, and the network of monasteries and teaching centers across the country has developed to such an extent that their
head monks have to have regular meetings to coordinate policies and agree
on translations of terms and texts.

Chan Buddhism is an extremely serious, tough-minded, and irreverent
form of religious life. Scriptures, disciplines, teachers have their places, but
only as ladders to be kicked away once you have reached your goal. It
assures one that one has within oneself that which one seeks, and quite
mercilessly leaves one without any other resource when one thinks one
needs help most. There is nothing like it in the other religions of the
world. Even if you cannot agree with the basic principles of Buddhism, as
I cannot, Chan will challenge you to think of what might be built out of
your basic principles that would equal its toughness and directness.

Buddhism had its origin in India, in a way of dealing with questions of
life and death that became very widespread in Indian religion in the age of

Confucius, Socrates, and the Hebrew prophets. The idea that our souls are reborn in new bodies after the death of the present body and that the happiness or misery of that rebirth are determined by our conduct in this life helped to explain and justify a social order in which most people had their status fixed by birth. Some people find this idea fascinating. But from the beginning, many have found it appalling. Sooner or later, each of us confronts our own limitations, not just physical and mental, but of morals and character, and we suspect strongly that we will not be able to overcome them. In the Judeo-Christian-Muslim tradition one may pray for strength or forgiveness or salvation; but whatever one can or cannot do, the books are closed and all is settled with death. To many it is quite simply a release. But in the Hindu-Buddhist view deeds in this life determine an immediate rebirth, and strivings and frustrations and griefs *continue*. If some by their good deeds are reborn in favorable conditions, others pass lives and lives in misery and degradation. This reaction to the idea of transmigration led many to seek somehow to escape the cycle, by mystic practices that would lead to the extinction of the separate soul or bundle of causes that persists from incarnation to incarnation.

One of the greatest of the teachers who sought and taught such liberation was Prince Siddartha Gautama, roughly a contemporary of Confucius, who perceived the transience and sorrow behind the comfort and happiness of his own life in a fine palace with a beautiful wife and child. He thus became the Buddha, the "Enlightened One." Leaving behind all worldly pleasures, he gathered a band of disciples around him and taught them his Noble Fourfold Truth:

1. Life is inevitably sorrowful.
2. Sorrow is due to craving and clinging.
3. Sorrow can only be stopped by the stopping of craving and clinging.
4. This can be accomplished by a life of discipline, meditation, and moral behavior that can be fully followed only by a monk or wandering ascetic.

Almost as important was a line of argument, not without similarities to the arguments of the Buddha's Greek contemporaries, that sorrow was the result of the transience and instability of all things, and that, since there could only be certain knowledge of unchanging realities, everything one usually takes to be real and knowable is an illusion. It is because one is deceived by these illusions and cannot cease clinging to the objects of one's desires that one is caught in the endless cycles of rebirths. The life of discipline and meditation prescribed by the Buddha for himself and his followers was a process of breaking the ties of illusion and desire that could lead, usually after many lives of growing spiritual power, to a moment when at death the flame no longer is transmitted to a new life, but is extinguished. "Blowing out" is the literal meaning of *Nirvana*, the ultimate goal of all Buddhist meditation and spiritual discipline. The Buddha achieved it at the end of his life; in very early Buddhist art, there was an empty place at the center of a composition representing the final stage of the Buddha's progress toward this goal.

One need not accept all these teachings to recognize in them a core of calm, clarity, and psychological acuity that provides sound counsel for at least some times in all of our lives. In this earliest version, Buddhism had not developed its full potential as a guide for the lives of people who have families and have to earn a living; all but its most elementary moral disciplines required the full-time concentration of the monastic life. Indeed, Buddhism has never lost its sense of the importance to the integrity of Buddhist teaching of the disciplined lives and meditative practices of monks and nuns. Nor did this early version offer any guidance as to how one might see caring for other people as anything but deluded clinging. Its compassion was strictly that of the therapist trying to free the patient from his delusions, and the Buddhist adept aspired to leave forever the insane asylum that was the world of rebirth. Moreover, it was not at all clear how the wisdom and power of the Buddhist teaching could ever have arisen in a world that was not just deluded but delusion itself.

For many, solutions to these dreadful puzzles were found in the emergence of the immensely rich and many-sided new form of Buddhism that called itself the "Mahayana," the "Greater Vehicle," and that in its openness to varied forms of thought, worship, and spiritual discipline claimed to provide a Greater Vehicle that could carry far more people toward liberation from the cycle of rebirth. In the Mahayana vision, the deepest realities were the enlightenment and compassion manifested in the life of the Buddha. Nirvana, even the Buddha's Nirvana, was an illusion. The Buddha was one of many bodhisattvas, great spiritual beings who appeared at cosmic intervals in past, present, and future and manifested the purity of their enlightenment and compassion by vowing not to pass into final liberation until they could take all other sentient beings with them. If Buddhism was in a way a therapy, a dispeller of delusions and compulsions, if the enlightened seeker saw the world of ordinary men as full of insanity, here it was as if the psychiatrist on his way out of the locked ward turned and vowed not to leave until all the patients were cured and could go with him.

Over the centuries, in India, Tibet, China, Korea, and Japan, the Mahayana became a very large vehicle indeed. Bodhisattvas, with their immense compassion and spiritual powers, became objects of worship only theoretically distinguishable from gods and goddesses. Millions still pray for the mercy of the Amida Bodhisattva and the blessing of being reborn in his company in the Western Paradise. Bodhisattvas and lesser spiritual powers were exuberantly portrayed in some of the world's finest sculpture and painting. Mahayana thinkers showed, sometimes in extremely abstruse and technical writings, how even the basic Buddhist insistence on the illusory nature of the world of the senses could become a delusion, a false splitting of the world into illusion and reality. Looked at in an enlightened and undivided way, everything had some form of reality, and if one's vision was really unified and penetrating one saw in everything the deepest reality, the undivided Buddha Body of enlightenment and compassion. Other thinkers showed how apparently contradictory teachings could be understood as parts of the Greater Vehicle, differing in emphasis and level of sophistication. Modes of devotion were developed that made possible more serious Buddhist piety for the laity. Meditation in groups, meditation before images, questions and answers between masters and disciples all had their places in the spiritual progresses of monks and laity.

The first signs of the arrival of Buddhism in China date from the 100s C.E. and are associated with foreign merchants coming from Buddhist areas in Central Asia. It began to take root among the Chinese roughly in the 300s, as a faith offering consolations and magic powers, much as some Daoist faiths did, and as a world of ideas and images offering Chinese artists and intellectuals dazzling new forms of imagination and speculation. Emperors and aristocrats seeking religious merit endowed great temples and monasteries. Monks with good educations in Chinese literature and philosophy adapted their teachings to a Chinese world of Daoist speculation and refined conversation. The story of the growing sophistication of the Chinese in understanding Buddhism, so different in basic assumptions and forms of expression from earlier Chinese traditions, and of the growth of distinctively Chinese forms of Buddhism is a long and fascinating one; China was in fact one of the most important centers of many of the Mahayana trends discussed earlier. Of all the new developments, the most distinctively Chinese in style and expression, and it seems to me the one that preserves most clearly the psychological-therapeutic style and the focused, disciplined mindfulness of early Buddhism, was Chan.

The word *chan* is derived from the Sanskrit *dhyana*, meaning meditation. It is important that this teaching was named after a *practice*, while other Mahayana teachings were named after a key text or after the bodhisattva that was the main object of devotion. In Chan the goal of meditation and of all other forms of Buddhist teaching and practice is Enlightenment, in which the individual becomes fully conscious of the Buddha Mind of compassion and undivided wisdom that has always been present in the individual's own mind but has been obscured by the illusions and clingings of ordinary life. Scriptures, worship of bodhisattvas, philosophical analysis, good deeds, structured mental disciplines might help along the road to it, but the only reliable guide is an already enlightened human mind. The transmission of the teaching cannot be through a text, as in most forms of Buddhism and most other religions, but only mind to mind. An enlightened individual can transmit enlightenment to the next generation not by writing but by identifying disciples of unusual spiritual penetration and leading them on toward enlightenment, prescribing modes of meditation, asking questions, testing their progress, and always choosing the next step appropriate to each individual's difficulties and needs. An unquestioning concentration on any one text, idea, bodhisattva, or mode of meditation can itself become a form of clinging that will block progress toward enlightenment.

Chan Buddhism is grounded in a set of basic attitudes toward the world and human nature very different from those of the Confucian tradition, but it is easy to see how its emphasis on teacher–student relations would appeal to people raised on stories of Confucius and his disciples and on the whole heritage of emphasis on these relations. Gurus and their disciples also are prominent features of the Indian tradition, and occasionally still are in the news today. In the final, fully developed version of the transmission of the Chan teaching, it was supposed to have begun when the Buddha himself silently held up a flower. Only one disciple smiled, and it was that disciple who transmitted this knowledge beyond words to his disciple, and so on through more than twenty generations until a monk named Bodhidharma brought the teaching to China in the early 500s. He obtained an audience with Emperor Wu of the Liang dynasty, a deeply committed Buddhist believer and a great supporter of Buddhist monasteries. The emperor asked Bodhidharma what merit he had gained by all his magnificent donations and good deeds. "None whatever." "What is the most important principle of Buddhism?" "Vast emptiness." "Who are you, anyway?" "I have no idea." Bodhidharma went on to the Shao-lin Monastery near Luoyang on the Yellow River and spent many years facing a wall in silent meditation. The fragments we have of his teaching do not seem very different from other Mahayana teachings of his time, but less reliable stories were told in which he nicely summarized some key Chan ideas. When a disciple told him he had not found peace of mind, Bodhidharma told him to bring him his mind and he would pacify it for him. The disciple thought for a long time and then admitted that he could not find his mind. "There," said Bodhidharma, "I have pacified it for you." He summarized Chan teaching in this way: "A special transmission outside the scriptures; no reliance upon words and letters; direct pointing to the very mind; seeing into one's own nature." When he assembled his disciples to test their attainment and see which would succeed him as patriarch of Chan, he was much impressed by the wisdom of several replies but bestowed his robe, symbolic of the transmission of the true teaching, on a disciple who simply bowed to him silently.

These stories no doubt have been shaped by the continuing preoccupation of Chan teachers with lineages of masters and disciples, an interest both very Chinese and very closely linked to the doctrine of transmission from mind to mind. Disputes between two disciples and their followers as to which was the true heir of the teaching of a revered master occasionally led to the formation of distinct schools or sects. There have been many important masters with records of teachings of great originality and power who did not become the founders of schools, because they did not have the teacher's knack necessary to insure transmission of understanding, because no student came to them who could fully grasp their teachings, or because the transmission failed in succeeding generations. In Chan the transmission of a written record was no substitute for the essential transmission from mind to mind, and the risk of failure of transmission was very great.

In this traditional way of looking at Chan history, Hui Neng is seen as the founder of a Southern School emphasizing the possibility of sudden enlightenment and criticizing the focus of a rival Northern School on defined disciplines of meditation and gradual progress through them toward enlightenment. Modern scholarship has shown that the questions of sudden and gradual enlightenment are by no means this simple, but the contrast, the prejudice in favor of sudden enlightenment, and the idea of Northern and Southern schools have remained very influential in Chan and even in art and literature.

Hui Neng's importance in the history of Chan was consolidated by the transmission and widespread study of a remarkable text, the only work by a Chinese called a sutra, a Buddhist canonical book. (The Chinese for sutra is *jing*, the same word translated as "classic" in the names of the revered ancient texts supposed to date from early Zhou or earlier.) The *Platform Sutra of the Sixth Patriarch* is an extraordinary document, recording his teachings and experiences in roughly chronological order, in the form sometimes of poetry, sometimes of connected exposition of an idea or problem, sometimes of conversation with a disciple. The basic values and ideas are quite un-Confucian, but the form occasionally reminds one of the *Analects*.

The *Platform Sutra* opens with a famous sermon to a large audience of monks and lay disciples, including some local officials, in which Hui Neng describes the beginnings of his Buddhist career. Autobiography would not seem to have much place in a teaching that insists that the individual self is illusion and counsels its annihilation, but here it is put to profoundly Buddhist uses. He recalls that his father was dismissed from office and exiled to

7. Hui Neng, working and meditating

the half-civilized wilds of the far south, in what is now the province of Guangdong, and then died. He and his mother lived at Nanhai, the modern city of Guangzhou. "We suffered extreme poverty and here I sold firewood in the market place. By chance a certain man bought some firewood and then took me with him to the lodging house for officials. He took the firewood and left. Having received my money and turning toward the front gate, I happened to see another man who was reciting the Diamond Sutra. Upon hearing it my mind became clear and I was awakened."[1] From him he learned that it was the Fifth Patriarch of Chan, Hong Ren, who had urged all his students to study the *Diamond Sutra*, saying that "simply by

---

[1] Translations follow Philip B. Yampolsky, tr., *The Platform Sutra of the Sixth Patriarch* (New York, 1967), with a few modifications.

reciting it they could see into their own natures and with direct apprehension become Buddhas." Hearing this, he says, he realized that he had been predestined to hear Hong Ren's teaching and took leave of his mother—later followers of his tradition would offer elaborate explanations of how he had provided for her care and thus was not being unfilial—and set out to become a student of Hong Ren.

At his first interview, the Fifth Patriarch asked how a "barbarian" from the far south could expect to become enlightened. He replied, "Although people from the south and people from the north differ, there is no north and south in Buddha nature. Although my barbarian's body and your body are not the same, what difference is there in our Buddha nature?" The patriarch seems to have recognized the extraordinary penetration of this answer, but he did not want to expose the new disciple too quickly to the extraordinary tensions and jealousies among his followers, so he said nothing more and put the young man to work in the monastery's threshing room for the next eight months.

One day the Fifth Patriarch assembled his disciples and told them, "You disciples make offerings all day long and seek only blessings in the next life, but you do not seek to escape from the bitter sea of birth and death. Your own self-nature obscures the gateway to blessings; how can you be saved? All of you return to your rooms and look into yourselves. Men of wisdom will of themselves grasp the original nature of their spiritual insight. Each of you write a verse and bring it to me. I will read your verses, and if there is one who is awakened to the cardinal meaning, I will give him the robe and the Teaching and make him the Sixth Patriarch. Hurry! Hurry!" This threw the disciples into a most unenlightened dither. Most of them deferred to their teacher, the head monk Shen Xiu. Shen Xiu worried that it would not be justifiable to offer a verse in order to seek the succession, but felt he had to do something in order to get the patriarch's assessment of his progress. Finally he decided to write a poem secretly on a corridor wall:

> The body is the tree of enlightenment,
> The mind is like a clear mirror.
> At all times we must strive to polish it,
> And must not let the dust collect.

When the patriarch saw the verse he praised it to the other monks but then summoned Shen Xiu and questioned him in private. Shen Xiu admitted that he had written the poem, and the patriarch told him, "This verse you wrote shows that you still have not reached true understanding. You have merely arrived at the front of the gate but have yet to be able to enter it. If common people practice according to your verse they will not fall. But in seeking enlightenment one will not succeed with such an understanding.

You must enter the gate and see your own original nature. Go and think about it for a day or two and then make another verse and present it to me. If you have been able to enter the gate and see your own original nature, then I will give you the robe and the Teaching."

Hui Neng, still working in the threshing room, heard a monk chanting Shen Xiu's verse and learned of the patriarch's command to his disciples to write poems. He was not well educated, perhaps even illiterate, but as soon as he heard the poem he understood its meaning and its limitations and asked someone to write on another wall his own poem, which made some crucial alterations in Shen Xiu's:

> Enlightenment originally has no tree,
> The mirror also has no stand.
> Buddha Nature is always clean and pure;
> Where is there room for dust?

He added another verse:

> The mind is the tree of enlightenment,
> The body is the mirror stand.
> The mirror is originally clean and pure;
> Where can it be stained by dust?

The Fifth Patriarch saw that Hui Neng was worthy to carry on the teaching, but did not announce his decision to all the monks. Summoning Hui Neng at midnight, he preached the *Diamond Sutra* to him, so that he was immediately enlightened and received the Teaching and Bodhidharma's robe. "From ancient times the transmission of the Teaching has been as tenuous as dangling thread. If you stay here there are people who will harm you. You must leave at once."

After he left Hong Ren, Hui Neng, not yet ordained a monk, wandered in the southern mountains and eked out a living for some years, perhaps as many as seventeen. One day he overheard some monks who were watching a temple banner waving in the breeze and were arguing over whether it was the banner or the wind that was moving. Hui Neng joined the debate, saying that both these views were wrong, that it was the mind that moved. The monks' superior was startled by this strange answer. Questioning him more, the superior learned that Hui Neng had received the Teaching and the robe of Bodhidharma from the Fifth Patriarch.

At last Hui Neng was ordained and began his own career as a Chan master. He brought about sudden great awakenings or enlightenments in many of his students, sometimes after only a brief conversation. His major contribution to Chan was to insist that such sudden enlightenment was possible and that it did not depend on the adoption of any particular posture or discipline of meditation. He frequently referred to the undivided reality to which one could awaken by that protean Chinese word *dao*, "the Way." "The Way is realized through the mind. What should it have to do with a sitting posture?" No distinction should be made, in fact, between meditation and the enlightenment to which some thought it led. "Students, be careful not to say that meditation gives rise to wisdom, or that wisdom gives rise to meditation, or that meditation and wisdom are different from each other. . . . If mind and speech are both good, then the internal and external are the same and meditation and wisdom are alike. The practice of self-awakening does not lie in verbal arguments. If you argue which comes first, mediation or wisdom, you are deluded people."

Nor did he teach that enlightenment led to a state of complete blankness, of annihilation of thought and personality. Rather, it led to a state in which one no longer was swept along helplessly and automatically from one thought to another, clinging to thoughts and the illusory objects of desires.

Good friends, in this teaching of mine, from ancient times up to the present, all have set up no-thought as the main doctrine, non-form as the substance, and non-abiding as the basis. Non-form is to be separated from form even when associated with form. No-thought is not to think even when involved in thought. Non-abiding is the original nature of man.

Successive thoughts do not stop; prior thoughts, present thoughts, and future thoughts follow one after the other without cessation. If one instant of thought is cut off, the Body of Truth separates from the physical body, and in the midst of successive thoughts there will be no place for attachment to anything. If one instant of thought clings, then successive thoughts cling; this is known as being fettered. If in all things successive thoughts do not cling, then you are unfettered. Therefore, non-abiding is made the basis.

Good friends, being outwardly separated from all forms, this is non-form. When you are separated from form, the substance of your nature is pure. Therefore, non-form is made the substance.

To be unstained in all environments is called no-thought. If on the basis of your own thoughts you separate from environment, then, in regard to things, thoughts are not produced. If you stop thinking of the myriad things, and cast aside all thoughts, as soon as one instant of thought is cut off, you will be reborn in another realm. Students, take care! . . .

Men of this world, separate yourselves from fixed opinions; do not allow them to arise from thoughts. If there were no thinking, then no-thought would have no place to exist. "No" is the "no" of what? "Thought" means "thinking" of what? "No" is the separation from the dualism that produces the passions. "Thought" means thinking of the original nature of True Reality. If you give rise to thoughts from your self-nature, then, although you see, hear, perceive, and know, you are not stained by the manifold environments, and are always free.

If someone speaks of "viewing the mind," that "mind" is of itself delusion, and as delusions are just like fantasies, there is nothing to be seen. If someone speaks of "viewing purity," then although man's nature is of itself pure, because of false thoughts True Reality is obscured. If you exclude delusions then the original nature reveals its purity. If you activate your mind to view purity without realizing that your own nature is originally pure, delusions of purity will be produced. Since this delusion has no place to exist, then you know that whatever you see is nothing but delusion. Purity has no form, but, nonetheless, some people try to postulate the form of purity and consider this to be Chan practice. People who hold this view obstruct their own original natures and end up bound by purity.

The traditional interpretation of these teachings sees Hui Neng not only defining his own approach but criticizing that of Shen Xiu, the former chief disciple of the Fifth Patriarch who had lost out to him in the test of the poems painted on the monastery wall. It is said that, when Shen Xiu heard of Hui Neng's teachings, he sent a monk named Shen Hui to spy on him and bring back a report. When the spy monk heard Hui Neng's teaching, he "was at once enlightened and awakened to his original mind." When he asked to receive further teaching and explained where he had come from, Hui Neng said, "If you come from that place then you probably are a spy." The monk replied, "When as yet you hadn't preached your sermon to me I was a spy, but now that you have preached I am not." Hui Neng replied by quoting an apt bit of extreme Chan teaching, that "the very passions are enlightenment."

Chan teaching was not always so wordy, and in later generations it frequently was less so. An important step in this direction was taken by Hui Neng in his teaching of Shen Hui, whom he later recognized as his successor, the Seventh Patriarch. Shen Hui asked, "Master, when you are sitting in meditation, do you see or not?" Hui Neng got up and hit his student three times. "Did it hurt or not?" "It hurt and it also didn't hurt." The Master then said, "I see and I also do not see," and went on to explain, "My seeing is always to see my own errors; that's why I call it seeing. My non-seeing is not to see the evils of people in the world. That's why I see and also do not see." Shen Hui now got at least a bit of the idea and said, "If it did not hurt, I would be the same as an insentient tree or rock. If it did hurt, I would be the same as a common person, and resentments would arise." That was part of the way to understanding, but not enough for the Master:

> The seeing and non-seeing you asked about just now are dualistic; hurting and not hurting are birth and destruction. You don't even see your own nature; how dare you come and toy with me! . . . Your mind is deluded and you cannot see, so you go and ask a teacher to show you the way. You must awaken with your own mind and see for yourself, and you must practice with the Truth. Because you yourself are deluded and do not see your own mind, you come asking me whether I see or not. Even if I see for myself, I cannot take the place of your delusion; even if you see for yourself, you cannot take the place of my delusion.

As Hui Neng neared the end of his life, he taught his disciples that the robe of Bodhidharma no longer would be handed down as a symbol of the correct line of transmission. More important were the teachings themselves, as recorded in the *Platform Sutra* and in a set of verses recorded in it, from that of Bodhidharma:

> I originally came to China,
> To transmit the teachings and save deluded beings.
> One flower opens five petals,
> And the fruit ripens of itself.

to his own:

> The Mind-ground holds the seeds of life,
> And the rain of Holy Teaching makes the flowers bloom
> Yourself awakening to the flowers and seeds,
> The Fruit of Enlightenment ripens of itself.

Good-bye all of you. I shall depart from you now. After I am gone, do not weep worldly tears, nor accept condolences, money, and silks from people, nor wear mourning garments. If you did so it would not accord with the sacred Teaching, nor would you be true disciples of mine. Be the same as you would if I were here, and sit all together in meditation. If you are only peacefully calm and quiet, without motion, without stillness, without birth, without destruction, without coming, without going, without judgments of right and wrong, without staying and without leaving, this then is the Great Way. After I have gone just practice according to the Teaching in the same way that you did in the days when I was with you. Even though I were still to be in this world, if you went against the teaching, there would be no use in my having stayed here.

When he finished these words, Hui Neng quietly passed away. He was seventy-six years old; the traditionally accepted year of his death is 713.

There were many teachers and trends in the later history of Chan and of Zen in Japan, some of the most important of them shaped by Hui Neng's teaching of sudden enlightenment and his blows and insults to his favorite disciple. Looking back at the historical evidence, we can see that Hui Neng's importance was emphasized and his legend elaborated by Shen Hui and his disciples as they argued that theirs was the correct line of transmission of the teaching, and that large issues of power and imperial patronage as well as of truth and teaching were involved. Hui Neng would not have been surprised; the very passions, he believed, are enlightenment.

EMPRESS WU

IN 700 C.E., Chang'an, capital of the Chinese Empire, probably was the greatest city in the world. Its only conceivable rivals were Baghdad and Constantinople, at the other end of a great network of Eurasian land routes and cultural minglings. In its Western Market, Chinese jostled with and stared at Central Asian soldiers and horse-grooms in Chinese service, their heavy eyebrows and big noses striking to Chinese eyes, and occasionally a small brown Burmese from the palace orchestra, a Buddhist monk from India, or even an African slave. They bought the many fine fruits and melons that the Central Asian peoples so loved and that now were grown in orchards and farms near the great city, exclaimed over the exotic spices, incenses, animals, birds, and precious stones, and cursed the wiles of the Uighur money changers, masters of all the currencies of Asia. The pleasure quarters were full of Chinese and foreign women offering song, dance, and sex. The city was dotted with religious establishments, of which the most numerous and impressive were Daoist and Buddhist monasteries and nunneries, but which also included a Muslim mosque and some kind of church for the Nestorian Christians who came all the way from Syria. Its fine parks with their flowering trees and artificial lakes were especially beloved of the many poets and painters who frequented the city and often could not get away, since like most Chinese artists and intellectuals in any age they were pursuing careers in the bureaucracy as well as fame in art or literature. On the north edge of the great city were the precincts of the imperial palace, with its huge, beautifully proportioned audience halls on a raised earth terrace. Chang'an stood on the Wei River plain, not far from the site of the capital of Qin. The highest mountain in the range at the north edge of the plain, looming far above the artificial mounds of the Qin and Han tombs, held the tomb of the great Taizong, second emperor of the Tang dynasty.

The splendors of Chang'an rested on remarkably sound foundations of agricultural and commercial prosperity, thorough and reasonably effective taxation, and effective government. The city itself reflected not only a prosperous and cosmopolitan society but also a government with a systematic will to rule unequaled in all of Chinese history. Its outer walls formed a regular rectangle. From north to south and east to west it was crossed by great straight avenues that divided the city into residential and commercial quarters, each with its own walls and gates, which were closed at night and patrolled by watchmen. Various kinds of merchants and artisans each were assigned to a particular district, so that all the traders and workers in precious metals were in one area, all the sellers of silk goods in another, and so on. An intelligently organized central bureaucracy controlled a great military establishment, based largely on local militia that sent units on rotation to the capital for training and guard duty. Its armies extended Chinese power to the northeast and northwest beyond the twentieth-century frontiers of China. It claimed, and in many areas exercised, the right to control landholding throughout the empire, assigning so much land per adult male, so much per wife, child, or aged parent. The tax system, based on the assumption that families had such equitable land allotments, required of each family twenty days of labor or military service per year, probably the most important support of state power, and fixed levies of grain and cloth.

Modern Chinese look back to this era with awe because of the power and sophistication of its government and because of the greatness of its cultural achievements, above all the great poets—Li Bo, Du Fu, Wang Wei, and many more. The Chinese world of the 600s and 700s was a world of vivid appetites and impressions, expressed not only in the life of the great city and its delight in exotic people and possessions, but also in the rich colors of religious and secular painting and in the vivid images and personalities of its poets. It also was a world of greed and will to power expressed in foreign conquest but even more in the shaping of society down to the level of the individual street or farm.

The will to power was nowhere more directly seen than in the personality and career of the person who ruled the Chinese Empire in 700. Governing very effectively, strengthening the powers of the throne and of the central bureaucracy, this ruler was an astonishing anomaly, a living affront to some deeply rooted proprieties, for the simple reason that she was a woman, the only woman ever to occupy the position of emperor, *huangdi*, in her own name. She deserves her place in this collection of great exemplary stories because of all the wonderfully shocking stories about her that have made her one of the most fascinating in the Chinese tradition's rich gallery of bad examples, and because of what we can learn about traditional gender roles and palace sexual politics. At least as important, in her struggle to keep power in violation of tradition she contributed significantly to a long trend toward concentration of power in the hands of the ruler, to the perverse interdependence of scholar-bureaucrats and sovereigns of doubtful morality or legitimacy, which is encountered at a number of points later in Chinese history.

Empress Wu built on the great political achievements of the first rulers of the Tang dynasty, founded in 618, usurped the throne from the Tang imperial house, and ultimately was forced to hand power back to the Tang. The Tang in turn had built on a heritage of energetic state-building in the late 400s and 500s. Chang'an and all of northern China had been under the rule of non-Chinese peoples, and China had been divided into two or more states, from the early 300s to the late 500s. Many have noticed the parallel with the decline and fall of the Roman Empire in these centuries, and the nonparallel of China's reunification and regeneration while there were still only small patches of literate culture, political cohesion, or market economy in Europe. The sources of the organizing energy and political genius that created the greatness of Tang are to be sought not in the south, where native Chinese dynasties had survived since the 300s, but in the north. In the early 400s a Turkic tribal people united all of northern China under the Northern Wei dynasty and began to systematically coopt the great aristocratic Chinese families who traced their lineages back to the Later Han or the Three Kingdoms. This was an alliance of mutual need, the aristocrats needing a regular and peaceful relation with the power of the nomadic cavalry, the non-Chinese rulers needing the bureaucratic skills, legitimizing heritage, and erudition of the Chinese. Both needed support against the continuing threat of Daoist popular sects, descendants of the Yellow Scarves and the Five Pecks of Rice, which still were powerful in the countryside. Respectable, nonsubversive forms of Buddhism and Daoism were identified and supported. From the 480s on, and especially after the Northern Wei moved its capital from the borderlands to the Yellow River valley in 495, the land-allotment and militia systems were developed that would be the foundations of imperial revival. The revival of Chinese elite culture was stimulated by the interest of the rulers in Chinese statecraft and by much interchange of Buddhist and secular art and literature between the north and the Chinese regimes surviving in the Yangzi valley.

The growing strength of institutions and military power in the north underlay the conquest of the south in 589 by the first emperor of the Sui dynasty, reunifying China for the first time since the early 300s. This remarkable ruler drew on all the resources of Confucianism, Buddhism, and Daoism to strengthen the legitimation of his regime, promulgated a simplified legal code, and reformed and reinvigorated the bureaucracy and the land and tax system inherited from the Northern Wei and its successors. He instituted a set of regular imperial examinations to judge the qualifications of young men for office. In Sui and early Tang the numbers passing the examinations were small, and most of those who passed them also were qualified for office by their aristocratic family backgrounds, but this was a major step in the development of an institution of immense long-term importance for the traditional Chinese state. The second Sui emperor did much, including the completion of a canal link, to consolidate the reunification of the south, but burdens of tax and labor service for that and for his wars on the northern frontier contributed to rising popular unrest, and by 616 rebels were in control of many areas of the empire. In 618 a former Sui general proclaimed himself the first emperor of the new dynasty of Tang. By 624 he had defeated all his important rivals. His descendants would rule until 907.

The Tang dynasty is equaled only by the Han as a time of power and culture on which the Chinese people look back with pride, awe, and delight. It was especially to the reign of the second emperor of the Tang, Taizong, who reigned from 626 to 649, that later Chinese turned for examples of splendor, effective power, and high principle. Unlike many earlier and later emperors, Taizong used a single reign period (*nian hao*) to number all the years of his reign, which may suggest in itself that he and his ministers were more concerned about the actualities of ruling and less obsessed with symbol-mongering than many others. That reign period, Zhen'guan, became for many later Chinese a symbol of effective and morally proper government, in particular for a nearly ideal realization of the Confucian "Way of the Ruler and Minister." All major issues were debated among a large group of high ministers meeting in the emperor's presence. The best of them did not fear to speak out in opposition to the emperor's wishes, and although he was a great warrior with a towering temper he sometimes listened and backed down in the face of principled ministerial opposition. The emperor also was a generous patron of classical and historical scholarship and made great efforts to control corruption in the bureaucracy and to encourage officials to take the less popular provincial posts. This conscientious pursuit of good government was all the more amazing because everyone knew that Taizong had come to power in 626 in a bloody coup, the famous "Incident at the Xuanwu Gate," in which he and his supporters killed two of his brothers, one of them the heir apparent, as they approached one of the gates of the palace. The shocked father almost at once relinquished control of the government to the victor, and he abdicated before the end of the year.

The reunification of China under the Sui and Tang kept some of the descendants of earlier invaders of north China in key roles in the evolution of the Chinese state. Their love of war, horses, falcons, and the hunt still was very conspicuous in early Tang elite culture. The revived imperial state thrust some other non-Chinese peoples into a more clearly external and antagonistic relation to the Chinese state. Empire-building processes among these various peoples made them more formidable adversaries, while the Tang rulers tended to assume that they had a right to interfere and to control events over at least as broad an area as the Han had at its height. The result was vigorous and intricate diplomatic interaction and Tang aggression, frequently encountering very effective resistance, toward the emerging states in Korea, especially Koguryo on both sides of the present Chinese-Korean border; toward the Turks in what is now Mongolia and the Chinese province of Xinjiang; and toward the Tibetan Empire. The foreign campaigns were the subjects of many of the most heated debates in Taizong's court, the desire of the emperor and his generals for conquest and glory clashing with traditional Confucian misgivings about military solutions to political and moral problems and about war's waste of resources and human lives.

In the last decade of his reign Taizong's interventions in Korea were particularly unpopular and ineffective. His ministers also criticized his abandonment of the restrained spending of his early years, particularly for some lavish palace-building. For a few years the imperial family itself was a center of conflict, as factions formed around the heir apparent and his rivals and several princes seemed about to revolt. These tense years ended in 643 with the appointment as heir apparent of a mediocre and relatively meek prince who was favored by the senior high officials, especially Zhangsun Wuji, the emperor's brother-in-law, perhaps in part because he would be easier to control. It was this prince, known to history as Gaozong, who succeeded Taizong upon his death in 649 and reigned until 683.

Thus it would seem that the ideal government of the Zhen'guan period had been much less ideal in the second half of the reign. In longer perspective, one might argue that the balance of ruler and minister that seemed so perfect was fundamentally unstable, bound to shift in one direction or another. The great ministers of Taizong were almost all members of great aristocratic families that had produced high officials for generations. When they confronted the emperor in court they were supported not only by the prestige of their offices and by their own abilities and convictions, but also by the prestige, wealth, and connections of their families. In the sixth century in both north and south China, the courts were dominated by these great families, which supported or overthrew imperial families whom they regarded as simply first among equals among the aristocracy. No dynasty lasted longer than about three generations. In the Tang it seemed likely that the great families would be able to maintain their power either by obtaining the selection of a weak heir apparent or by backing the various rival princes in factional strife over the succession. Few emperors would have the intelligence and force of personality to keep the ruler side of the ruler–minister equation as strong as it had been under Taizong. On the other hand, the basic theory and rhetoric of Chinese monarchy ever since the Qin had recognized no limits on imperial authority. The continued strengthening of systems of law, bureaucratic control, taxation, and military power under the Sui and early Tang, and the new sources of manpower available in a united, peaceful, and prosperous empire, produced a stable and largely self-regulating state structure that could isolate itself to a degree from palace irregularities and intrigues short of civil war, and had immense potential anytime a strong ruler appeared at its head.

In the early years of the reign of Gaozong, the dominance of the great high ministers was reinforced by the fact that they had served the great Taizong and could remind the weaker Gaozong of the deeds and teachings of his father, thus adding the imperatives of filial piety to their power over him. From about 652, however, their dominance was challenged by the rise of a young concubine named Wu Zhao. Everything we know about her is clouded by male prejudice against active female participation in government and by an all-too-human delight in the details of other people's sexual depravities, especially of those of whom we already disapprove on other grounds. Careful historians from the 1000s on have found that the terrible stories about her can be traced back to the earliest and most reliable sources. This does not prove that all of them are true, but simply that in her own time people already were ready to believe the worst about a woman who did not know her place. Still, it seems at least plausible that her efforts to satisfy her own taste for power in the face of these prejudices and in an age when the quest for power frequently took forms like the Incident at Xuanwu Gate did lead her to commit at least some of the monstrous deeds of which she was accused.

Chinese tradition is by no means as extreme in its fear and loathing of female sexuality as the traditions of Buddhism or of medieval Christianity. *Yin* and *yang* were thought of as complementary forces; the harmony of the cosmos and of human life required their balanced and complementary interaction, and there was no strong sense that *yin* was evil and *yang* good. The power of female sexuality was widely recognized, and in the Daoist tradition some of the most powerful metaphors of the unchanging Way were feminine metaphors of accepting passivity, taking the lower part, and the "gate of all mysteries." But even in this nearly balanced version the correspondences showed that the female should be passive, and that her role should be "inside" the household, while the male dealt with the outside world. In other aspects of the tradition there were important asymmetries. The elite male, especially the ruler, might well have access to more than one woman, above all if that was necessary to insure the birth of a male heir. In late Zhou texts there were elaborate ideal pictures of the Son of Heaven's hierarchy of household ladies and of the cycles and frequencies with which he was to have sexual relations with each of them. Later, *not* in Tang times, the elite ideal was that women should not remarry under any circumstances, and the subjected and housebound position of women was enforced by the bizarre custom of foot-binding. The ladies of the Sui and early Tang elite were relatively independent, riding horses astride, henpecking their husbands, somewhat influenced by the traditions of the steppe peoples, where long absences of male herdsmen and warriors frequently left women in charge. But the fundamentals of Chinese ideas of relations between the sexes were still very powerful.

Wu Zhao had come into the palace of Taizong about 640, in her early teens. Her father had been one of the first supporters of the rebellion of the future Tang founder against the Sui. Stories were told of her sexual involvement with the heir apparent, the future Gaozong, while she still was a member of Taizong's household. Even though it is not certain that she ever shared Taizong's bed, he had exclusive right to her, and accusations of his son's involvement with her were accusations of incest.

After Taizong's death in 649, all the women of his household were expected to spend the rest of their lives in nunneries praying for the repose of his soul. It was said that when Gaozong visited a Buddhist nunnery on the anniversary of his father's death he saw Wu Zhao, and her brown robe and shaved head did not keep the flame from leaping up again. Gaozong's determination to bring her into his household was supported by his leading consort, Empress Wang, who was childless and was losing his affections to another palace lady, Xiao Shufei, and wanted to distract him from her. She got much more than she bargained for. Soon Gaozong was ignoring both Empress Wang and Xiao Shufei, and by the end of 652 Wu Zhao had borne him a son and had been promoted in the hierarchy of palace ladies. Gaozong still was not ready to talk of deposing Empress Wang and naming Wu empress. Empress Wang was the daughter of one of the greatest aristocratic families of the empire and had the full support of the senior statesmen. Wu got her chance late in 654, not long after she had given birth to a daughter. The childless empress often came to her quarters to play with the baby. One day Wu smothered her own infant, and when the emperor came to see the child she went to the cradle, "found" the baby dead, and explained amid mock hysterics that the empress had just been playing with it and must have killed it. The emperor believed the story and now wanted to depose Empress Wang, but the senior statesmen still supported her, even when the emperor and Wu Zhao went in person to the mansion of Zhangsun Wuji to give him gifts and honors. Some argued that the Wu family was not of high enough social standing to provide an empress. But now other officials, less highly placed and more in need of support to advance their careers, began to argue in favor of a change. All of them are portrayed in the traditional histories as worthless opportunists, but at least one, Xu Jingzong, was a man of great literary talent and administrative ability. In the winter of 655–56, Empress Wang and Xiao Shufei were accused of plotting to poison Gaozong. The empress was deposed, Wu Zhao was named empress, and Wu's son was named heir apparent. The former empress and Xiao Shufei were confined in miserable quarters. Gaozong visited them and pitied them, and Empress Wu in a rage ordered that their hands and feet be cut off and that they be thrown in a wine vat. "Let those witches get drunk to the bone!" They died after several days, and their corpses were decapitated. Or so the story went; but a somewhat similar story had been told of the savage vengeance of the Empress Lü, widow of Emperor Gao of the Han, on her late husband's favorite concubine in 194 B.C.E.

Now more and more of Empress Wu's opponents were sent into exile in distant southern provinces, until in 659 even the redoubtable Zhangsun Wuji suffered this fate. Late in 660 Gaozong suffered the first of many strokes or seizures that left him dizzy, partially blind, and unable to deal with the affairs of the empire. Soon Empress Wu was making all the decisions for him, and even the hostile traditional histories acknowledge that she did so with great intelligence. The proprieties of female nonparticipation in public affairs were preserved, as they had been in many periods when empresses or empresses dowager were politically powerful, by having the lady "listen to government affairs from behind a screen," where officials could at least pretend not to see her and she could hear everything and tell her husband what to say or have a eunuch transmit her decisions to the officials.

From the first years when she dominated the court, Empress Wu showed an interest in symbols and omens of all kinds that was in marked contrast to the rather pragmatic political and military orientation of Taizong's court. If the story of the killing of the former empress and Xiao Shufei is anything more than legend, it would seem to reflect a desire to utterly humiliate and symbolically annihilate her rivals. Taizong had used one reign title from 626 to 649; twelve were used between 661 and 683. In 662 every office in the central bureaucracy was given a new title, taken from or inspired by the *Ceremonies of Zhou*, which had so fascinated Wang Mang. (The earlier Tang titles were restored in 670.) In 664 it was discovered that Empress Wu was permitting a Daoist sorcerer to visit her in the palace. Involvement in sorcery was an extremely grave offense, and Gaozong almost worked up the courage to dismiss her, but backed down when she confronted him.

The most interesting of all Empress Wu's efforts at symbolic innovation was that of the *feng shan* ceremonies at Mount Tai in 666. These were the ceremonies that had been so much discussed at the court of Emperor Wu of the Han, and which Sima Tan had hoped to witness. They had been performed not more than six times in all of China's previous history, the last time in 56 C.E. In Qin and Early Han times the imperial ceremonies there probably had a good deal to do with the emperor's quest for immortality, but beginning with the Later Han they were taken more as a particularly awesome assertion of the moral and spiritual power of a dynasty, of its establishment of peace, prosperity, and unity, and the unique position of the emperor as intermediary between Heaven and Earth. Scholars tended to argue interminably about the exact precedents for their performance, and both officials and rulers approached them with trepidation because of the vast expenses involved and because of a fear that they might imply excessive pride, too close an approach to Heaven. Officials may also have feared that these ceremonies placed the rulers too far above their ministers. The ceremonies had been discussed and planned repeatedly since the Sui reunification, but not yet performed.

According to the regulations that had been worked out on Han precedents, the *feng* ceremony took place in two phases, the second on the peak of Mount Tai. An elaborate prayer and announcement by the emperor to Sovereign Heaven of the achievements of the dynasty and its current sovereign was prepared on strips of jade bound by gold cords and at the end of the ceremony was buried on the summit in a great stone coffer secured by more gold cords and sealing materials. The *shan* was a similar ceremony to Sovereign Earth on a lower hill to the south of Mount Tai. The *feng* ceremony was *yang*, on a mountain, to Heaven, on a round altar. The *shan* was *yin*, in a lower place, to Earth, on a square altar. Here Empress Wu found a perfect opportunity to glorify herself and the whole women's world of the inner palace by exploiting the contradiction between the theoretical equality and complementarity of *yin* and *yang* and the actual monopolization of the public and ceremonial spheres by males. She convinced Gaozong that while he should offer the primary homage to the Earth, it was not appropriate for male princes and officials to perform the later phases of the ceremony; these should be done by the empress and her palace ladies. In 665 all the princes of the imperial house and high officials were ordered to proceed to Mount Tai. Envoys from a number of foreign countries also joined them. The procession of the court was well over a hundred kilometers long. Early in 666, at the Chinese New Year, the splendid ceremonies were performed. At the *shan*, the empress and her ladies did follow the emperor onto the square platform, setting out the offerings of food and drink and singing the sacred texts. The ceremonies were followed by a great banquet that went on all day and by the granting of promotions in honorary ranks and a general amnesty to the empire, as was done on all auspicious occasions.

In the 670s the empress began to strengthen her own resources for involvement in politics outside the palace. She gathered around her a private brain trust of scholars who would advise her on policy and draft state papers for her. Because their offices were outside the north gate of the palace, the gate closest to the women's quarters, they became known as the North Gate Scholars (*beimen xueshi*). They wrote and compiled a number of important books, including a series of biographies of famous women and the *Chen gui* or "Model for Ministers," expressing the empress's views on the ruler–minister relation, which emphasized the need for absolute commitment of the minister: "Although the father–son relationship is extremely close, it still cannot compare with the ruler and minister forming part of the same organism." Thus the empress, like Wang Mang in his ascent to power, presented herself as a patron of learning. At the same time she built up a store of erudite arguments for the dignity of women and the supremacy of sovereigns. She also had in the North Gate Scholars a group of learned men completely dependent on her, with none of the standing and independence of the great ministers of state, who soon were processing for her state papers that had not gone through regular bureaucratic channels.

In the Confucian conception of good government, ceremonies and patronage of scholarship mattered a good deal, but not as much as the practical foundations of rule, especially the choice of good ministers and compassion for the common people. In 674 Empress Wu sought to demonstrate her qualifications in these areas as well, presenting to her husband a famous "Twelve-Point Memorial," calling among other things for the encouragement of agriculture, the reduction of government expenses and the burdens of taxes and labor service, the promotion of "all long-serving officials whose talent was greater than their rank," the encouragement of the expression of opinion to the throne, and requiring that the full three-year mourning be observed for a mother even if the father still was alive. The emperor issued an edict approving most of her proposals, but it is not clear how much effect they had.

Thus by 674 the empress was building a substantial power base for herself and presenting herself effectively as a capable and principled participant in imperial politics. But it was not clear just in what role she was casting herself. Clearly she was much more than a conventional empress, much more than even a high minister of state. The role of a regent-minister, like Wang Mang during his rise, or that of an empress dowager in charge of the government was plausible and respectable only when a child sat on the throne. The ambiguity thickened in 674 when the emperor and empress adopted new titles that seemed to place them beside each other on a level above all their predecessors: heavenly sovereign (*tian huang*) and heavenly empress (*tian hou*). Moreover, if someone had to hold the reins of government when the emperor was incapacitated by illness, if the heir apparent was a capable adult it was thought more fitting to order him to "administer the realm" (*jian guo*) than to leave affairs in the hands of a woman. The heir apparent, Li Hong, was thought to be intelligent and capable and had filled this role effectively during several of Gaozong's illnesses. He frequently opposed the empress's wishes, and in 675, not long after he had argued with her publicly about her savage treatment of two daughters of Xiao Shufei who still were locked in the palace, he died suddenly under mysterious circumstances. Many at the time, and many later historians, thought that his mother had had him poisoned.

The new heir apparent, Li Xian, was not as promising or widely admired as his late brother. A more substantial counterweight to Empress Wu's power was the emergence in the high bureaucracy of a number of able and independent-minded officials. Some came from distant southern areas and had risen by passing examinations rather than by relying on aristocratic family connections. Some were given positions as advisers of the heir apparent, which probably helps to account for the good impression he made when he functioned as administrator of the realm during his father's illness in 679. Empress Wu now seems to have seen him as as great a threat to her power as his brother had been. She had her North Gate Scholars compile a set of *Biographies of Filial Sons* for his instruction. She accused him of ordering the murder of a physiognomist who had said he did not have the face of a future emperor. Finally in 680 she accused him of plotting to rebel against his father and mother, and after several hundred sets of armor were discovered in his palace he was degraded to commoner status, banished to a distant province, and later forced to commit suicide.

Between 675 and 680 the empress had four other princes exiled to distant provinces. There still were some senior princes who might serve as centers of opposition in the capital. Also, many descendants of the first Tang emperors remained in the provinces, living on their estates or serving as provincial governors and local magistrates. But for the time being she had the situation well under control.

Among all the crimes of which she was accused, the ordering of the death of two of her own sons may be the most shocking to us, but it was not so to the Chinese historians who elaborated her black legend. They made less of this than of her brutal suppression of opposition in the 680s or the interference of her favorites in government. It is almost as if brutality within the imperial household was expected, and not too much made of it unless it interfered with orderly government. To a remarkable degree the great, intricately regulated machine of the Tang bureaucracy *did* continue to function, and its stability limited the effects on the whole empire of the melodramas at court. In less obvious ways, Empress Wu was having an effect on politics, at least in exploiting and reinforcing broader trends. As the decades of peace and unity passed, more people outside the aristocracy had the wealth and leisure to study and to aspire to office. From the 660s on, the empress already had favored recruiting larger numbers of men into the bureaucracy, frequently ordering provincial officials to recommend virtuous and competent men for appointment. She apparently supported reforms in 669 that, among other things, reduced the influence of family connections on the examination process by concealing the names of paper-writers from the examiners. Another set of reforms in 681 increased the difficulty and prestige of the examination called *jinshi*, "presented scholar," which became a challenging test of ability to write coherently about political and moral problems and to write exacting formal styles of prose and poetry. Very gradually, this examination would become the main route to high office in imperial China. Empress Wu sometimes has been given more credit for this shift than she deserves. But she rose to power in a time when the bureaucracy was expanding, consistently presented herself as anxious to find and promote deserving officials, and continued to tinker with the content and practices of the examinations through most of her years in power. High officials tended to oppose the expansion of the bureaucracy because Confucian principles counseled a government that kept its burdens on the people as light as possible and because of aristocratic prejudice against the appointment of men of lower-class backgrounds. But the gradual rise of an elite selected by examination continued and was accelerated by the decline of the old aristocracy; the empress contributed to that side of the change by her savage repression of her opponents during the 680s.

Gaozong died on December 27, 683. The seventeen-year-old heir apparent, known posthumously as Zhongzong, was enthroned three days later. The late emperor's will had ordered that Wu Zhao, now the dowager empress, be consulted on matters of war and other basic decisions. On the recommendation of Pei Yan, the senior minister who had been entrusted with the will, she actually retained broad decision-making powers. But the young emperor was not completely under her control, and his wife, of the Wei family, wanted to enjoy the rewards of her position. The emperor repeatedly proposed his father-in-law for very high posts in the bureaucracy, but was opposed by Empress Wu and Pei Yan. Finally he burst out to Pei Yan, "If We wished to hand over the empire itself to Our father-in-law, could We not do so? How much more may We make him President of the Chancellery!" Pei Yan was horrified and promptly reported the emperor's words to the empress.

Savage as she was in dealing with her sons and anyone else who threatened her power, Empress Wu had administered the empire conscien-
tiously and effectively for most of the preceding twenty years. Now she
could present herself as defender of the integrity of the imperial administration and of the Tang dynasty itself against an irresponsible teenager
who was threatening to give away his entire patrimony. The next day,
about six weeks after the emperor ascended the throne, Pei Yan and other
high officials, acting on the empress's orders, ordered Zhongzong to descend from the throne and proclaimed his deposition. "What is my crime?"
he asked. The empress replied, "You wanted to give the empire away to
your father-in-law. Can you call that no crime?" He was led away to
prison.

The next day another son of the late Gaozong and Empress Wu was
proclaimed emperor. Known posthumously as Ruizong, he was kept out of
the way in a separate palace and allowed to play no part in government.
The empress now moved closer to playing the full imperial role, no longer
staying behind a screen at audiences, and using the imperial "We." An Act
of Grace, releasing many from prison and conferring other benefits on the
common people, was commonly used to mark a new reign or an especially
splendid achievement. Empress Wu's Act of Grace on this occasion was a
striking mix of vigorous attention to political problems and obsessive symbol-mongering. She ordered strict enforcement of military regulations and
tried to deal with the steady shift of population toward the south by ordering the creation of new units of administration in areas where population
was growing. Reiterating her determination to appoint men of virtue, she
ordered each high official to recommend one qualified man. She bestowed
awards on aged commoners, allowed border soldiers to return home to
carry out their ancestral sacrifices, and promised reductions of taxes. She
changed the color of banners to gold, gave new names both to Chang'an
and to the city of Luoyang farther east where she usually resided, and
renamed most organs of the bureaucracy, using some names from the early
Zhou and others, such as "Phoenix Court," that suggested some kind of
supernatural realm.

All this was very much in the style of an emperor ascending the throne,
or even of the founder of a new dynasty. Her intentions seemed even
clearer when she ordered the establishment of seven ancestral temples,
appropriate only for the imperial family, for her Wu ancestors. Pei Yan
warned her bluntly against following the path of Empress Lü, who had
dominated the Han court after the death of Emperor Gao and might have
established a new dynasty if she had lived longer. He may have plotted to
have her seized on a trip outside the city and Ruizong restored to power,
only to be frustrated by bad weather.

Another plot was hatched among princes and other members of the imperial family in the Yangzi valley. The city of Yangzhou was seized and a proclamation issued listing all her real and rumored crimes: "With a heart like a serpent and a nature like that of a wolf, she favored evil sycophants. . . . She has killed her own children. . . . She is hated by the gods and by men alike; neither heaven nor earth can bear her." The empress is said to have admired its style and to have regretted that a writer of such talent had not been promoted to high office. The rebels assembled a substantial army and might have really threatened the court if they had marched north immediately, menacing the capital and drawing on separatist sentiment in the northeast. But they turned south toward Jiankang (modern Nanjing), perhaps intending to establish a new dynasty there. Divided among themselves, arousing no response in the capital or in the northern provinces, they were crushed within about two months by armies sent from the capital. Pei Yan was executed and his family exterminated, as was common in the punishment of "traitors."

If the empress had found the opposition to her growing power effective, she probably would have moved slowly and carefully, keeping Ruizong as nominal sovereign. Seeing it divided and incompetent, she now sensed that the way was clear for her to crush the remaining resistance. She began offering generous rewards and appointments or promotions to anyone who would inform the authorities of anyone who spoke or plotted action against her power. Soon a vast system of informers sprang up, as all kinds of people from all levels of society took the opportunity to advance themselves and do in their enemies. Anyone who became an informer, even a farmer or woodsman, was summoned to the capital, entertained at official expense, and granted an interview with the empress. Two men, Zhou Xing and Lai Junchen, rose to great power and high office as they developed whole networks of informers. They even had a special prison where confessions were extracted by torture: metal bands tightened around the head, vinegar poured in the nose, the spine bent sharply backward, and so on. The instruments of torture were displayed for the prisoners to see, and many confessed their real and imagined crimes on the first sight of them.

Some old families were ruined by this reign of terror. If they were not wiped out as relatives of traitors, they were exiled to remote regions or entirely excluded from office until after the empress's death. Surely others learned to keep quiet and to forget the ideal ministerial fearlessness of the Zhen'guan period. The rise to office of village intriguers who informed on their neighbors was a horrible business, but it brought a great many men into government who would have had no such opportunity in the rigid class system of Sui and early Tang. Some of them proved useful and capable. The legal system was sorely tried but not destroyed; when officials worked up the courage to protest some particularly outrageous frame-up, justice often was done. A great urn that stood in a public area near the palace had four openings. One was for the deposit of reports of omens and secret plots; another for complaints of injustice; a third for criticisms of the government; and a fourth for recommendations of policies that would benefit the common people and self-recommendations by would-be officials.

Of all the new people who rose by attaching themselves to Empress Wu's drive to power, none was stranger or more powerful than a peddler of cosmetics and medicines, probably including aphrodisiacs, named Xue Huaiyi. First introduced to the palace by the empress's daughter and other great ladies, he soon was summoned by the empress. Every nasty story heard about the empress had been told and retold in the previous decades, but nothing has come down to us to suggest that she ever had been unfaithful to her husband. Now he was gone, and something happened. Soon the empress's intimacy with Xue was an open scandal. Men were not supposed to be present in the inner quarters of the palace, but sometimes exceptions could be made for relatives of palace ladies and for monks. The empress ordered her son-in-law Xue Shao to adopt her lover, and also ordered that he be made a monk and installed as abbot of the famous and venerable White Horse Monastery outside Luoyang. She made a large donation to the restoration of the monastery's buildings, but that can hardly have assuaged the insult of the installation of such an unqualified, unmonastic, and arrogant abbot. Soon Xue had gathered an entourage of ruffians who beat up priests of Daoism, the great rival of the Buddhism with which he now was associated, and anyone who did not get out of his way in the streets. He expected even high nobles to hold his horse while he mounted.

Xue encouraged the empress in one of the most lavish building projects in all of Chinese history, the Bright Hall (Ming tang). He even is credited with the design, or at least the conception, of this remarkable building. To build a Bright Hall, as Wang Mang had done, was to identify strongly with the perfection of early Zhou and to emphasize, as strongly as the *feng* and *shan* sacrifices, the position of the sovereign as the pivot of the cosmos. Empress Wu's Bright Hall had a square lower level about ninety meters on a side, surmounted by a square second level and a round third, the tower at the center reaching about ninety meters above the ground, topped by a huge figure of a phoenix, emblematic of the empress. The four sides of the first level were decorated to symbolize the four seasons, the upper levels the divisions of the day and the year. A Heavenly Hall (Tian tang) containing a huge Buddhist image was built just north of the Bright Hall. Thus the image was facing south, like a sovereign, superior by its position to the Bright Hall with its hallowed aura of early Zhou. Construction of the Bright Hall went on through most of 688.

Informing and sex appeal were not the only ways that outsiders could take advantage of Empress Wu's quest for power. Others sought to report omens or present strange natural objects that could be taken as signs of heaven's favor toward the empress. By far the most spectacular example of this was the "discovery" in the Luo River in the summer of 688 of a white stone that, when cracked open, revealed the inscription "A Sage Mother shall come to rule mankind; her rule shall bring eternal prosperity." It is believed that this object was faked at the direction of the empress's nephew Wu Chengsi. The empress named the stone the "Precious Chart," led her whole court to give thanks to Heaven in a dazzling ceremony on the banks of the Luo, and took for herself the title "sage mother, holy sovereign" (*sheng mu shen huang*). Containing neither the word *di* (lord, emperor) nor the word *hou* (empress), this novel title came very close to announcing the empress's full assumption of sovereign power without flaunting the violation of sex roles by a woman occupying the imperial position.

The Bright Hall, the Precious Chart, and the new title all clearly indicated that the empress was moving toward full assumption of imperial powers. In the fall of 688 princes of the Tang imperial family who held provincial offices in the east and southeast were summoned by the empress to appear in the capital for the ceremonies marking the completion of the Bright Hall. Convinced that she was planning to take full power and fearful that she might have them massacred if they came to the capital, the princes once again plotted to rebel against her. Their risings were poorly coordinated, few officials or troops in other areas responded to them, and some of their own officers and men fled at the first opportunity. One local official who held out against them declared, "When the Prince of Langye [one of the rebels] fights against the state, that is rebellion." The word here translated "state" is *guojia*, which means just that in modern Chinese; not at all common in this period, it suggests some kind of loyalty to the centralized, bureaucratic order that was stronger than loyalty to any particular imperial family. This kind of loyalty here worked to the benefit of Empress Wu so long as she presided over the center of that bureaucracy in reasonably acceptable fashion.

The rebellions collapsed in a few weeks. The empress now proceeded with unbridled savagery, wiping out almost all branches of the Tang imperial house. Zhou Xing and Lai Junchen rose to new heights of power as false accusations, rigged convictions, exiles, executions, and suicides followed one after another, continuing into 690. At the beginning of 689 the empress appeared for the first time in imperial robes, holding the imperial jade scepter. Xue Huaiyi added another strand to the complex of symbolism surrounding her rise to power with his commentary on a Buddhist work called the *Great Cloud Sutra*. This sutra prophesied the reincarnation of the bodhisattva Maitreya as a woman, ushering in an era of peace and plenty. "At that time all her subjects will give their allegiance to this woman as the successor to the imperial throne. Once she has taken the Right Way, the world will be awed into submission." It was obvious, wrote Xue, that this was a prophecy of the rise of Empress Wu. In 690 the empress ordered the establishment and rich endowment of a Great Cloud Temple in every prefecture of the empire.

Late in 690 the high ministers repeatedly requested the empress to assume full imperial powers. The captive Ruizong joined the chorus, seeking to abdicate in her favor. Finally the ministers reported that a phoenix had been seen flying from the Bright Hall into the palace, and thousands of red birds had perched on the audience hall. Finally she agreed, naming her new dynasty Zhou (the same character as the ancient Zhou) and taking for herself the title sage and divine emperor (*sheng shen huangdi*). Ruizong abdicated and was named her successor.

Empress Wu's Zhou dynasty lasted until 705. The coup that brought her down in that year was as narrowly based as the palace coup by which she had deposed Zhongzong. The sources, which report everything negative they can about her, give no indication that there was any broad opposition to her rule among the officials or the common people. To be sure, she had made it clear that terrible things would happen to anyone who did seek to oppose her. But she also turned out to be quite an effective ruler. Ever since her Twelve-Point Memorial she had made a point of seeking out men of talent and giving them office. Few officials avoided service under her out of loyalty to the Tang. Many capable men served her, and some of them occasionally argued successfully against a policy or a sentence. The most important of them, as an adviser, administrator, and general, was Di Renjie, around whom many stories grew up in later centuries of his intelligence and justice in settling criminal cases. His death in 700 may have been an important cause of the final decline of the empress's regime.

The relation of these men to the empress was quite different, however, from that of the great ministers of the Zhen'guan period to Taizong. Some of them were "new men" with no aristocratic family behind them. Even the aristocrats knew that they could not go too far in opposing her, and no one questioned the right of the emperor to appoint and dismiss officials at will. She used that right to keep more chief ministers in office at a time than there had been early in the century, and to keep individuals in particular offices for shorter terms; the average term of a chief minister was seven years in Zhen'guan, but only two years between 684 and 705. This subtle shift in the management of the upper bureaucracy made the individual chief ministers much more dependent on her favor, much less able to build up a power base in the offices or ministries they supervised. No new precedents or forms of government were established, and there was a partial reversion to longer tenures in office and greater ministerial power early in the 700s. But her practices, simply by increasing the number of men who served for a time in the most powerful and prestigious posts of the bureaucracy, fit well with the long trends toward the decline of aristocratic privilege, the ability of more provincial families to prepare their sons for office-seeking, and the access of these new men to the bureaucracy.

The other "new men," the informers and torturers, were more dispensable now that the opposition was decimated and the legitimacy of the empress's rule generally accepted. Also, she could win favor by punishing some of these monsters, insisting that she only now had learned of their crimes. In 691 Lai Junchen told Zhou Xing that he had to confess to some of his recent crimes, and if not he would be the victim of some of the tortures he had inflicted on others. Zhou confessed, was exiled to the frontier, and was murdered on the way by relatives of one of his victims. Within the next year 850 of Zhou's men were tried and punished. But Lai remained in power.

Lai now made an important alliance with Wu Chengsi, the empress's nephew, who had made several contributions to her rise to power. In 692 Wu instigated requests from his allies that he be named successor to the throne, replacing Ruizong. Li Zhaode, a high-principled and highly competent official of modest background who had risen through the examinations, warned the empress against letting her Wu relatives have too much power, and she dismissed Wu Chengsi and two others from all their posts. Lai remained powerful and feared until 697–98.

Xue Huaiyi still was the empress's lover, a powerful and feared figure in the capital, with a guard of one thousand strong-arm men whom he had had ordained as monks. He even was sent as a general on border campaigns, with results that were mixed but not disastrous. Early in 695 he overreached himself badly in a number of bizarre "No Bounds Gatherings" at the Bright Hall. At one, his men threw ten cartloads of coins to the crowd; people were trampled to death in the rush to pick them up. At another, a big Buddhist figure was raised from a pit as if it was rising from the earth. The empress could not tolerate these wild public displays. She had found a new lover, one of the imperial physicians. Shunned by the empress, Xue Huaiyi set fire to the Heavenly Hall; the fire spread, and the Bright Hall was destroyed as well. The empress ordered one of her Wu relatives to ambush and murder Xue.

The last gross evil to be cleansed was Lai Junchen. In 697–98, after he accused members of both the Wu family and the Tang imperial family of conspiracy, he was executed. The people of the capital celebrated, tearing his corpse apart. The empress insisted she had not known about Lai's reign of terror, and she took serious steps to end the informing and torture.

The Chinese state no doubt was better off without the sources of disorder and corruption that now had been cleared up, but even when they were active the bureaucracy had operated fairly effectively. Not much was done, however, to deal with problems that required firm direction and innovation, such as building up new administrative units in the south to register and tax the new migrants there. Neither the empress, confronting one court melodrama after another, nor the frequently appointed and dismissed chief ministers had enough time or attention to give to real policy making; this was a recurring, but not universal, difficulty in Chinese imperial politics.

One set of policy challenges that could not be ignored was in foreign relations. In the northeast part of the empire, to the north and east of the location of modern Beijing, the non-Chinese Khitan people were settled more or less under Chinese control. In the summer of 695 they revolted against the Zhou officials in the area, who treated them harshly and had not supplied sufficient aid in a famine year. On the west and north of the empire, the Tibetans and the Western Turks (Tujue) took advantage of the situation to encroach on territory under Chinese control and to make new demands. Empress Wu and her officials did not panic, and they manipulated the difficult situation effectively. They sought to placate the Turks, with the result that the Turks attacked the Khitan bases in 696. The Khitan rebellion never was entirely defeated, but it collapsed of internal dissension in 697. The Turks remained extremely powerful and threatening.

Since a female ruler was not part of the grammar of the Chinese monarchical tradition, it was not entirely clear who would succeed Empress Wu on the throne. Ruizong was her designated heir, but from time to time she had treated her Wu relatives, sons of her brothers and cousins, as if they might be designated in his place. As long as she did not conclusively decide, partisans both of a Wu and of a Tang succession would hope to keep in her favor so that the decision would go their way. Thus the anomaly of her position and the uncertainty of the succession was at least in the short run one source of her political strength. In 697–98, however, the continuing Turkish danger interacted with the urgings of Di Renjie and other elder statesmen and the empress's determination to weed out the informer networks after the execution of Lai Junchen. She recalled Zhongzong from his provincial exile and prepared to make him her heir. The sources do not explain her decision to favor him over Ruizong; perhaps the strength of will that had seemed a liability in the young emperor of 684 seemed an asset in her successor. In the fall of 698 there was another Turkish invasion, the leaders of which sought Chinese support by declaring their intention to support the restoration of the Tang. Huge levies of troops were ordered, but few responded. Zhongzong now was formally declared successor, and recruiting abruptly became easier.

Empress Wu now was about seventy, and she might have been able to spend the last years of her life in dignified semiretirement, watching her capable officials administer the empire, or might even have abdicated voluntarily in Zhongzong's favor. But power is addictive. And she already was involved in a final episode of sex, symbolism, and corruption that marred her last years and finally led to her forced deposition. Two brothers, Zhang Yizhi and Zhang Changzong, entered her service about 697. They were young and very handsome, and one was an excellent singer. Soon they both became the empress's lovers. The historians assert this tersely, without undue expressions of horror or gamy details like those of Lao Ai and the dowager queen of Qin; presumably for them the bare assertion was horrible enough. For an aging male ruler to enjoy himself as far as he was able with the young women of his household was normal, even admirable; a lascivious old woman was another matter. Dressed in rich silks, their faces painted and powdered, the Zhangs demanded deferential treatment even from high officials and the empress's Wu relatives. They staged endless banquets and theatricals, drinking, gambling, and mocking each other in the empress's presence. In one performance Zhang Changzong was dressed in feather garments and raised mechanically to the ceiling on the back of a wooden crane. Feeling her own mortality, the empress was entranced by this spectacle of youthful vitality and by the acting out of the ancient belief in immortals riding away on the backs of cranes. More handsome young men were summoned to serve in the palace, which to outsiders began to look more and more like a male harem for the empress. A new office, established to give them bureaucratic positions, was ordered to engage in literary compilation work. It was called the Crane Court.

The bureaucracy had managed to keep its equilibrium through the rise and fall of Xue Huaiyi, and even to insulate itself somewhat from the horrors of the Zhou Xing–Lai Junchen tyrannies. The Zhangs, less capable and less cruel than Xue, Zhou, or Lai, turned out to be more of a threat to the state. In the first place, the empress was aging, and no longer so actively involved in limiting the excesses of her favorites and staying in control of decision-making. Also, the Zhangs had a large number of brothers and cousins who obtained office through them. Many of them turned out to be harsh or corrupt officials. Zhang Yizhi and Zhang Changzong were quite ready to arrange official appointments in return for payment.

The death of Di Renjie in 700 removed one of the most important forces for good government in the empress's court, but there was no lack of other principled officials who spoke out against the Zhangs and their various corruptions and who urged the empress to yield the throne to

Zhongzong. She treated the givers of the latter kind of advice gently, but usually was very harsh toward anyone who attacked the Zhangs. She was in steadily declining health, and when she did not or could not rise from her bed and appear for formal audiences the Zhangs still waited on her, filtering communication from the bureaucracy much as eunuchs did in some other periods. They also allied themselves with the empress's Wu relatives, excluded from the succession but still very powerful.

In 704 various Zhang brothers and cousins were accused of corruption. Some were demoted and exiled to the provinces. The investigation of Zhang Yizhi was halted by the transfer of the official in charge to the provinces. The empress simply pardoned Zhang Changzong. The Zhangs had been spared for the moment, but they would be in great danger if the empress died. They now very foolishly tried to form their own clique, independent of both the Wu family and the Tang interests. There were many rumors that they were plotting to seize power for themselves. On January 19, 705, Zhang Changzong was accused of treason. The empress tried to dispose of the charges by sending one accusing official to the provinces, but he refused to go and continued to demand the execution of Zhang. Having exhausted all her legal dodges, the empress again pardoned her favorite.

A group of high officials now decided that direct action must be taken to eliminate the Zhangs and to remove empress Wu from power. Zhongzong's consent was secured. On February 20, 705, the conspirators accompanied Zhongzong to his mother's palace residence. Encountering the Zhangs, they beheaded them on the spot. The empress rose from her bed, berated her son and the conspirators, and went back to bed. Two days later she abdicated in favor of Zhongzong. She was removed to a separate palace, where she continued to be treated with imperial honors until her death at the end of 705. The tomb mountain in which she was buried beside Gaozong still can be visited. The figures of animals, warriors, and officials that line the road leading to it are evocative of the forcefulness and symbolic obsessions of her reign.

Tang politics for the next few years reenacted the corruption and female political power of her reign with greater viciousness and less competence. One of her Wu relatives, Wu Sansi, became very powerful, in part because of a sexual liaison with Empress Wei, Zhongzong's wife. Empress Wei, the Taiping Princess (Empress Wu's daughter), and other palace ladies became wealthy and corrupt. Zhongzong died in 710, apparently poisoned by his wife. Soon Ruizong was placed on the throne, with the Taiping Princess holding the real power. He was forced to abdicate in 712, and his successor was strong enough to quash a coup attempt by the Taiping Princess and to go on to a long reign of revived political competence and great cultural brilliance that ended in 755 in yet another upheaval brought about in part by the influence of a palace woman and her relatives.

Many modern readers will not share the Confucian historians' horror at the sexual appetites of the Empress Wu and some of the women who surrounded her and followed her example. Few will be horrified by the idea of a woman involved in government. But most will be appalled by (and reasonably skeptical of) the stories of her smothering of her infant daughter and causing the deaths of her two crown prince sons. Many people who seek great power have a little bit of monster in their makeup. Those who are drawn to power and believe themselves competent to wield it but are excluded by custom and prejudice, as all women were in traditional China, sometimes will become more monstrous as they thrust themselves forward.

Empress Wu's efforts to seize and hold power had important effects on long trends in the Chinese political tradition. Holding on to power in the face of widespread prejudice, she broke the old aristocracy, promoted many men from modest provincial backgrounds, and managed the upper bureaucracy in such a way that no high minister could develop a secure base of power from which to oppose her. Her contribution to the rise of an elite chosen by examination sometimes has been exaggerated, but clearly she was interested in examination and other aspects of personnel recruitment. Others rose from nowhere by informing on their neighbors and torturing suspects. In our modern prejudices social mobility and careers open to talent are good things; despotic power a bad thing. The study of Empress Wu's reign can remind us of the distressing compatibility of these good and bad things: new people depend on their superiors for their careers and may be less able to resist arbitrary power than people with their own resources of family and wealth. Moreover, in a regime balanced between rulers of doubtful legitimacy concentrating on suppressing opposition and holding on to power, on the one hand, and officials insecurely seeking survival and promotion, on the other, it is not likely that anyone will have either the power or the time and mental energy to deal coherently with the real problems of state and society.

10

SU DONGPO

• • • • • •

SU DONGPO's life is the earliest of this set that can be explored in great detail from reliable sources. Volumes of his poems, essays, and state papers and of those of many of his friends and enemies have been printed. We have a few samples of his calligraphy and perhaps a few paintings by him. So we are not so much at the mercy of one biography or one collection of sayings or a few chronicles compiled long after the events as was the case in earlier chapters. It would be easy to spend a lifetime, and an altogether stimulating and agreeable one, reading the writings of the great men of the eleventh century and trying to understand their complex and energetic world. Sometimes reading them is like sitting at one of their great dinner parties, probably seeing a friend off on a long journey to a new official post, with learned gentlemen discussing the great personalities of the past, the nature of fossils, the difficult criminal cases they have judged, the quantity theory of money, the sayings of Chan masters, the real meaning of Mencius's teaching of the goodness of human nature, and Su Dongpo at the head of the table, making everyone laugh, holding forth on the fine points of herbal medicine, suddenly turning angry at the government's disastrous policies, getting drunk and falling asleep, rousing himself to dash off a brilliant poem of friendship and parting that brings tears to everyone's eyes.

Su Dongpo's world was quite different from that of the Empress Wu and Hui Neng. Politically, in 700 China had been a world of immense imperial power and competence, of total control (in policy if not always in fact) of residence and landholding, of a great capital-area aristocracy only beginning to feel the challenge of new men qualifying for office by their literary and bureaucratic competence, of conquests and trade routes reaching far into Central Asia. By 1050 it had become a world of new men from all the provinces rising through examinations and a carefully worked out system of bureaucratic advancement, of emperors ceremonially farther above their officials than the great Tang rulers but in fact somewhat less the focus of political power and mystique. The bureaucracy was much less in control of society and economy than the early Tang had been, full of ad hoc arrangements and special adjustments to regional interests, debating reform proposals, playing an intricate politics of networks of personal connection and common conviction. Culturally the world of bright colors, high passions, great spiritual powers had not disappeared, but now it was supplemented and for some people superseded by a less colorful, more earnest, more studious culture of historical and classical scholarship, political debate, and observant fascination with the intricate interrelations and harmonies of the natural world. The other-worldly glories of Buddhist art and the vivid colors of earlier painting now were joined by monochromatic landscape paintings of the finest detail and the most uncanny atmosphere, products of the sharp eyes, subtle minds, and disciplined brushes of scholar-officials.

It is easy to see the culture, society, and politics of about 700 as one interrelated whole and those of 1050 as quite a different one, but it is not at all easy to pick out the key strands of change from one to the other. The easiest place to start is with a great shift of the geographic center of gravity of the Chinese world, from the Yellow River watershed with its wide dry fields, uncertain rainfall, and openness to storms and nomad raids from the north, to Su Dongpo's Yangzi valley, with its many waterways and mild, moist climate. Already in Empress Wu's time people from the north were moving south and opening up new lands. The early Tang tax system depended on people staying where they were registered, and occasional reregistration efforts could not keep up with the movements of population. Moreover, the reassignment of fields in the equal-field system would not work in the south, where farmers might have to put years of work into preparing rice paddies and their dikes and ditches, and would do so only if they and their descendants had secure rights to the fields.

The Tang land system was under great strain in the early 700s, but its sudden and irreparable collapse at midcentury was the result of a massive rebellion of the Tang armies, led by the Central Asian general An Lushan and supported by the northeastern aristocrats who always had held themselves aloof from the Tang. The rebellion was put down and the dynasty saved only by the assistance of the Uighurs and of Tang provincial military commanders who were rewarded with much greater autonomy in control of their provinces. The Tang survived until 907, a ramshackle affair of eunuch power and factional strife at court, of financial improvisation that drew much revenue from tea and salt monopolies and did not try to distribute land but simply levied taxes on it without regard to who owned it. New men found new opportunities in the monopoly commissions and on the staffs of military men, and the instability of politics and policies led to a revival of interest in basic political and moral principles. Some scholars were sympathetic to Legalist present-mindedness, while others were literal-minded Confucian fundamentalists who wanted to restore the early Zhou feudal order and even chariot warfare. More influential thinkers, especially the great ninth-century writer Han Yu, deplored the florid literary style of recent centuries and the great influence of Buddhism, and called for a return to the pure literary style of the ancients, a struggle against Buddhist influence, and a revival of the long-neglected moral continuity of the Confucian Way. These ideas probably helped to stimulate a great confiscation of monastery lands and forced return of monks and nuns to lay life in 845, but otherwise they had little effect in the disorderly century that began with a great rebellion in 873 and ended with the reunification of the empire under the Song just over a hundred years later.

The years 907 to 960 are called the "Five Dynasties and Ten Kingdoms"; five short dynasties succeeded each other in the north China plain, while as many as ten kingdoms ruled separate areas in the northwest, in the Yangzi valley, and in the far south. As in the Warring States before Qin, disorder was not incompatible with prosperity, and trade and rivalry among the multiple states of the south may even have stimulated economic growth. There was a broadening of the political elite, as former bandits, rebels, and local leaders found themselves with major political responsibilities in the various southern states. There also were important changes in technology and economic organization that had begun in late Tang and continued in these years: advances in metals, porcelain, and water transport, but above all in food production, with the steady improvement and spread of wet-rice cultivation, by far the highest-yielding grain agriculture in the premodern world. New strains of early ripening rice were introduced from Southeast Asia, making two crops a year possible in some areas. The use of various types of coinage and instruments of credit expanded rapidly. These changes, aptly described by a modern author as "economic revolutions," laid the foundations for the immense prosperity of the early Song and especially for the emergence in the Yangzi valley and the far south of a new elite of prosperous provincials whose sons had leisure to study and prepare for official careers. Another great technical advance in these years, of immense importance for that studious provincial elite, was the printing of books.

The five dynasties of the north succeeded one another through a succession of military coups, with considerable involvement of the Turkic Shato people and later of the Khitan of the northeast, within a relatively stable structure of central administration and regional military power. Talented ministers provided a measure of good government and continuity by serving several dynasties in succession. The founding of the Song in 960 seemed no more than another military coup in the capital, but in just fifteen years the new dynasty managed to reunify the entire empire, bringing all the separate southern kingdoms under its control. This reunification turned out to be permanent: the southern areas were more and more thoroughly integrated into the centralized empire, and never again did China have a stable system of more than two competing states.

The immensely important political process of the Song founding and unification has been little studied and less thought about. Economic and commercial growth, especially in the south, probably made peace and unity attractive to many influential people. Internal disorders in the Khitan Liao state to the northeast probably freed the Song armies for southern campaigns. The Song rulers astutely exploited the rivalries among the southern states, always finding allies as they subdued them one by one. In the longer run, the loyalties of the southern elites were secured by a great expansion of opportunities for bureaucratic advancement. The annual average numbers passing the civil service examinations were the highest of any time in Chinese history, and there also was a generous but less prestigious system by which each high official was entitled to recommend one son or other relative for a beginning official position. The new armies were brought under effective central control, the great generals transferred to the capital, producing a military system that was expensive and cumbersome but no longer a threat to the stability of the dynasty. The central bureaucratic structure was less clearly focused, less under the control of a single powerful prime minister, than that of the Tang had been. Many variations in taxation and monopoly structures were left over from the late Tang improvisations and the century of disunion, and were only gradually brought into some kind of uniform administrative pattern. Song administration had considerable deficiencies, but the real glue of the new unity lay not in bureaucratic uniformity but in the attractions of bureaucratic employment to the provincial elites and the openness of the system to ambitious new men from the provinces, rising through the examination system and the system for recommending relatives.

In the 990s the Song armies confronted a revived and threatening Liao state, fought it to a standstill, but could not regain Chinese territory around the modern cities of Beijing and Tianjin. In 1005 the Song and Liao signed a peace treaty that made excellent practical sense to the Song officials. Annual payments to the Liao were far less than the vast costs of the annual military campaigns. But many scholars and officials bitterly resented the gifts to buy peace, the acknowledgment of near-equality of the Song and Liao rulers, and the nonrecovery of some Chinese territory. A new flare-up of tension and intermittent warfare on the northeastern and northwestern frontiers in the late 1030s increased anxieties and stimulated proposals for the strengthening and reform of the Song state.

There were three major episodes of reform proposals and debate about them in the course of the eleventh century; they stimulated the most searching and intelligent discussion of political and economic issues in all of Chinese history. Visions of systematic reform and institution-building emerged and were put into practice in the last and greatest of the reform episodes, but then were rejected and the new institutions dismantled. The long-run consequences of these debates and political struggles can scarcely be overestimated. Never again until the desperate days of the late nineteenth century would the enrichment of the state and the strengthening of its armies seem respectable goals for Confucian statesmen. Talk of sweeping institutional innovation, of increased intervention of the state in the economy, was permanently discredited. This was in part because of the defects of the actual reforms of the eleventh century, but more because of the emergence in the opposition to them of an intensely moralistic style of politics that esteemed purity more than practicality and was more at home in attack on others' policies than in proposing concrete modes of dealing with real problems. It dominated Chinese politics at least until the early 1700s, and echoes of it can be found as recently as the Cultural Revolution of the 1960s and the Korean opposition movements of the 1980s.

The first reform episode was in 1042–43, when Fan Zhongyan dominated the court. He proposed reductions in labor service levies, organization of militias, and measures to stimulate agricultural production. But more important to him than efforts to directly strengthen the state and improve the lot of its people were his proposals for changes in examinations and bureaucratic recruitment. Examinations should place less emphasis on literary form and more on correct understanding of the Classics and application of their basic principles to contemporary problems. Examiners should take into account information on the moral character of the examinees. The number of officials entering the bureaucracy through the nomination of relatives by high officials should be reduced. Instead, high officials should sponsor meritorious junior officials for promotion and then be held responsible for their conduct in office. All this fit the Confucian emphasis on finding the best men, but might well have had the effect of increasing political partisanship by making it easier for high officials to favor in examinations and sponsor for promotion their political allies. Despite widespread admiration for Fan as a man of high principle, little of his reform program outlasted his brief period in power. The next important reform effort, led by Ouyang Xiu in 1057, concentrated entirely on issues of style and content in the examinations. Su Dongpo's career began with a great boost from this reform, and his life in turn brings it and the politics of the rest of the century into sharper focus.

Of all the brilliant men of the eleventh century, Su Shi or Su Dongpo is the best known to the Chinese people of later centuries. (Su Dongpo, a literary name he took in midlife, is the name by which he is best known.) A major scholar, intellectual, painter, and politician, he owes his fame much less to those excellences than to his place among that small number of poets whose name will elicit a smile of recognition, and usually a recitation of some favorite lines, from any well-educated Chinese. Like much Chinese poetry, his work reaches some of its heights when it makes something strange and wonderful of the sights and sounds of an ordinary moment:

> ON A BOAT, AWAKE AT NIGHT
> Faint wind rustles reeds and cattails;
> I open the hatch, expecting rain—moon floods the lake.
> Boatmen and water birds dream the same dream;
> A big fish splashes off like a frightened fox.
> It's late—men and creatures forget each other
> While my shadow and I amuse ourselves alone.
> Dark tides creep over the flats—I pity the cold mud-worms;
> The setting moon, caught in a willow, lights a dangling spider.
> Life passes swiftly, hedged by sorrow;
> How long before you've lost it—a scene like this?
> Cocks crow, bells ring, a hundred birds scatter;
> Drums pound from the bow, shout answers shout.[1]

Su was representative of his age not only in the brilliance and variety of his accomplishments but also in his modest provincial background, his rise in the bureaucracy solely on the basis of his political, administrative, and literary talents, and the ups and downs of his career. He was born in 1037 in Meishan, not far south of the ancient city of Chengdu in Sichuan, since Qin times an area of considerable population and productivity, important to any unifying regime but far from the capital and hard to control. Shu in Sichuan had been one of the Ten Kingdoms of the 900s, and there had been a serious rebellion in the area after it came under the Song. The Song court did not trust Sichuan men, and few made it to high office in the early decades of the dynasty. Su's uncle had passed the *jinshi* examination, the most important regular examination given in the capital, but had an undistinguished career. Su's father, Su Xun, was a writer and thinker of originality and power, but never managed to pass the *jinshi* exam or to obtain any position of real power or prestige. Su Xun's wife supported the family by running a clothing business; there was enough money for the sons to continue their studies, but no settled wealth, no security. Su Xun probably

---

[1] Translations of Su's poetry follow Burton Watson, tr., *Su Tung-p'o* (New York and London, 1965), unless otherwise noted. For other excellent translations and sophisticated critical comment, see Michael A. Fuller, *The Road to East Slope* (Stanford, 1990).

gave his sons much of their education. He seems to have transmitted to them his own ambition, taste for wide reading, and an attitude toward history that was wary of reliance on classical models or moral absolutes derived from an idealized past, and very much interested in how circumstances changed and causes interacted. He was more sympathetic to the role of the intimate adviser of a ruler showing him how to gauge trends of change and survive in difficult circumstances than to that of the scholar-critic keeping his distance from power and preserving his purity.

In 1056 Su Xun led his sons Shi and Che on the long journey across the mountains to the capital at Kaifeng on the north China plain, believing that the rising influence of Ouyang Xiu and other reformers would improve his sons' chances of passing the examinations and might even rescue his own career from mediocrity and frustration. He was received by all the great men, his writings were widely admired, but he found only marginal scholarly employment. The real winners were his brilliant sons, who may have had some inside information on Ouyang Xiu's plans, not publicly announced in advance, to switch the examinations to a format giving more emphasis to classical learning and policy discussion; both Su Shi and Su Che placed near the top of the new class of *jinshi*.

The young men now should have been ready for their first official appointments. But their mother died, and they had to return to Meishan for the obligatory twenty-seven months of mourning. Late in 1059 they set off again, this time by boat through the great gorges of the Yangzi:

> From the boat watching the hills—swift horses:
> A hundred herds race by in a flash.
> Ragged peaks before us suddenly change shape,
> Ranges behind us start and rush away.
> I look up: a narrow trail angles back and forth,
> A man walking it, high in the distance.
> I wave from the deck, trying to call,
> But the sail takes us south like a soaring bird.

In the capital the brothers sat for an extraordinary examination; the few who passed it could expect very rapid promotion and brilliant careers. A sponsor was needed for this examination; Su Che's was the great historian Sima Guang, and Su Shi's was Ouyang Xiu himself. Both brothers passed, Shi with unusual distinction.

The essays Su Shi wrote for the examinations of 1057 and 1061 have been preserved in his collected works. They include essays both on the classical sources of political values and on contemporary problems of administration. The Confucian Way (*Dao*), he insisted, arose from what people could put into practice and was not an external standard that could be applied to change people into what they were not. The sage rejoiced

in it. Codes of law should be evenly applied to all, as had been recommended by Han Fei Zi, but administered with more tact and subtlety
than the Qin regime had. Su thought the Song state of his own time
was strangling itself in rigid bureaucratic regulation and losing the necessary capacity to respond to changing circumstances. Supple and tactful
dealing with human nature, human feeling, human relations was fundamental to sound politics. These apparently academic exercises, done when
he was just twenty, show signs of approaches to life and politics from which
he would never waver: the importance of feelings and joy, a realistic and
flexible conception of politics partly derived from his father's ideas, and a
suspicion of ahistorical conceptions of the Way that sought to use the past
to produce major changes in the present or impose unity on the marvelous
diversity of human experience and action. Already he may have been reacting against two currents of cultural change just beginning to appear
that sought to impose ahistorical uniformities on human nature and
human society: the moral absolutism of Confucian revivalists like Cheng
Yi and Wang Anshi's advocacy of new, uniform, and systematic political
institutions.

Su Shi and his brother Su Che now parted ways to pursue their official
careers, and they rarely were together again. Although Su Shi wrote en-
gagingly about his children and hauntingly about his dead first wife, some
of his deepest expressions of personal feeling were in poems to the absent
brother. He loved to recall the days when they studied together and talked
half the night. On the festival of the midautumn full moon he wrote:

> Six years the moon shone at mid autumn;
> Five years it saw us parted.
> I sing your farewell song,
> Bringing sobs from those who sit with me.
> . . . .
> I wanted to write a verse to your last year's song,
> But I was afraid my heart would break.

Su Shi now was appointed an assistant magistrate at Fengxiang, west of
Chang'an in the ancient Wei River valley. His papers reveal him getting
varied experience, organizing militia, directing the transportation of logs
for an imperial tomb, deciding legal cases, praying for rain. He also turned
his poetic talents for the first time to portraying the misery of the common
people:

> IT SNOWED IN SOUTH VALLEY
> It snowed in South Valley—a priceless sight.
> I raced my horse to get there before it could melt,
> Pushing back branches, following the trail alone,

Ahead of dawn, first to cross the ocher bridge—
To find roofs caved in, nowhere to spend the night,
Villagers starving: their listless voices show it.
Only the twilight crow knows how I feel—
He flies up and the cold limb sheds a thousand flakes.

In these years Su's intellectual and artistic energies seemed almost limitless. His poems, like the one above, reflected in more and more complex ways the world he experienced and his political and social place in it. He had a growing reputation as a calligrapher and as a commentator on that most Chinese of arts. Especially after his return to the capital in 1068 he was close to a number of distinguished painters and probably did some painting himself, but he was most influential as an articulator of new ideas about painting that made its practice much more a part of the life-style of the scholar-official than it had been previously. In painting, Su wrote, what was important was not the exactness with which external forms were represented but the way in which the painter caught and expressed the vital force, the dynamic pattern of a landscape or the character of the subject of a portrait. Painting that sought verisimilitude was the work of "artisan painters"; intellectuals and scholar-officials sought the spirit of the subject and expressed their own characters. We may have a faint reflection of his own practice of his ideas in a painting of a twisted tree and a rock, which may be a copy of a Su painting or a copy of a copy, but cannot be from the brush of the same person who composed some of his masterworks of calligraphy. Even at this remove the tree twists with natural energy and the rock has a lurking power.

Su returned to the capital in 1065 and seemed to be high in imperial favor and to have a brilliant career ahead of him. But Su Xun died in 1066, and the brothers accompanied their father's coffin home for the long mourning. By the time Shi returned to court late in 1068, great changes there had turned the Song court toward decades of debate and partisan struggle, in which Su's chance to advance himself and show what he could do in a coherent and congenial setting vanished. A new emperor, Shenzong, came to the throne in 1067. Trouble on the northern frontiers increased military expenses, and the Song state began to experience large budget deficits. Shenzong was interested in pursuing a more active foreign policy instead of just waiting for the northern powers to attack, and in finding new sources of revenue that would overcome the budget deficits and make possible the new foreign policy initiatives. He soon came under the influence of Wang Anshi, who previously had been associated with Ouyang Xiu's reform forces. Wang, drawing on ideas that had been in the air ever since Fan Zhongyan's proposals, developed an ambitious, comprehensive, and controversial reform program.

8. From a painting attributed to Su Dongpo

Over the first five years of Shenzong's reign, Wang Anshi proposed and the emperor approved a set of reforms each of which was a response to a specific problem or opportunity but that were held together by a special vision of the relations between state and society sanctioned by a particular way of drawing on the authority of the classical past. Both had something in common with Wang Mang's visions and proposals, but they may seem to us more plausible and less strained than those of the Han usurper. The state was to confront the reality of a growing commercial economy, intervening in it much more energetically, mitigating some kinds of commercial exploitation of the common people and at the same time increasing the revenues of the state. Although Wang Anshi had no plans to revive the well-field system, the *Ceremonies of Zhou* again provided the ultimate classical sanction for an ideal of a systematic bureaucracy energetically managing society and economy. Young men seeking office would be educated with more emphasis on the Classics and on statecraft and would get practical experience and find opportunities for advancement in the expanding bureaucracy, especially in its organs of financial management.

Later historians have tended to concentrate on Wang's new fiscal policies, which were subject to abuse and had some unintended consequences. But both he and his opponents, good Confucians and thoroughly aware of the real sources of cohesion and stress in the Song state, focused on the politics of examinations, recruitment, and bureaucratic organization. One

of Wang's first steps was to establish a separate Financial Commission reporting directly to the emperor. Later the examinations were changed,
pushing the classical and practical emphases begun by Ouyang Xiu to the
complete exclusion of literary exercises. Su Shi wrote vigorously in opposition, arguing that the rapid advancement of young men in the Financial
Commission would alienate other officials who were advancing their careers through more normal channels, and that the changes in the examinations would make them less objectively open to all talented men, more
subject to partisan distortion as examining officials favored examinees
whose classical interpretations and policy proposals matched their own
convictions. Su's career had begun, of course, with Ouyang Xiu's similar
shift in examination content and partisan use of the examinations, but that
did not keep him from taking a broad and realistic view of the situation.
And while he and his friends had deeply admired Ouyang Xiu, they did not
trust Wang Anshi.

Wang's most important schemes for economic intervention were his
state trading system and his crop loan program. In both, the state was to
get into competition with private business, offering better terms to con-
sumers but at the same time earning some additional money for itself. The
crop loans program, called the Green Sprouts Law (*qing miao fa*), grew out
of the need of many farmers for loans of grain to keep their families from
starving in the spring, while they watched the beautiful green sprouts grow
in their fields and their stores of grain run out as they waited for the new
crop to ripen. The state set up crop loan bureaus all over the empire, loan-
ing grain or cash to farmers at lower rates of interest than the commercial
lenders charged, thus benefiting the farmers and finding in the interest
charged a new source of revenue for the government. This plan made the
most sense for the areas of the empire with the most commercial development, and even there was most advantageous to those farmers who were
the best money-managers; others might get the loans, spend the money
unwisely, and still have principal and interest to repay. Some opponents
alleged that the Financial Commission was setting quotas of loans that its
officers had to make even if they had to force them on the farmers; even if
there were no such explicit quotas, it is very likely that ambitious young
men sought to make good impressions on their superiors by making as
many loans and producing as much interest as possible, and used every fair
and foul means to persuade the farmers to borrow. And there were stories
of commission underlings who opened wine shops down the road from
loan offices, where some farmers spent a good deal of the money they had
just received.

The State Trading System also sought to undercut the profiteering of
private merchants, in this case the guilds that controlled various lines of

interregional trade, by putting the state into direct competition with them. One minor branch of it, criticized by Su Shi in a famous memorial, involved state purchases in Zhejiang and sale in the capital of the special ornamental lanterns used in the New Year festivities. The trading bureaus also dealt in foodstuffs, coal, cloth, and so on, and promoted border trade with peoples to the northwest. Su argued that in both the State Trading System and the Green Sprouts Program the state was seeking to increase its revenue. Any increase in the revenues of the state could only come from a loss of wealth and well-being of the common people. It was shocking to find the emperor interested in personal profit, high ministers concerned with controlling wealth. While referring obsequiously to the lowliness of his position and the deficiencies of his understanding and to the emperor's extraordinary wisdom that would enable him to become a Yao or a Shun, he also reminded him that the people's allegiance "is as necessary to the ruler as the roots to the tree." "A state depends for its survival not upon the measure of its power but upon the loftiness of its ethical standards, and for length of life not upon the degree of its prosperity but upon the soundness of its national character." The First Emperor of Qin was a perfect example of what happened to a state that adopted "remorseless legislation."[2]

So Su was very much at odds with the Wang Anshi regime, and his criticisms did not seem to be accomplishing anything. Perhaps he also began to think that in such a vast empire the real work of adjusting government policies to circumstances and human feelings was best done by good men in provincial office; in 1071 he resigned his court positions and requested assignment elsewhere. His first assignment was at Hangzhou, southwest of modern Shanghai, famous for its fine location by the Qiantang River and the lovely West Lake. The economy of the area was highly commercial, and he found it possible to administer the Green Sprouts Program for the benefit of some of the people. His basic focus on the variety of human nature and experience and his suspicion of all efforts to impose uniformity on it made him less doctrinaire in his opposition to Wang's policies than many others, and inclined to use them when they could be used and even to argue for the preservation of some of them. From Wang Mang to Deng Xiaoping, Chinese policymakers all too often have lacked Su's suspicion of uniformity and have made great trouble for themselves and their people by trying to impose on all of China policies that make sense for some important part of it.

But Su also turned his poetic genius to portrayal of the misery of the

---

[2] Cyril Birch, ed., *Anthology of Chinese Literature from Early Times to the Fourteenth Century* (New York, 1965), pp. 370–80.

rural people in the springtime (with an ironic reference to Confucius forgetting the taste of meat) and the way in which the farmers had been snared by the Green Sprouts Program into a strange urban world:

> MOUNTAIN VILLAGE
> Old man of seventy, sickle at his waist:
> Thankful for spring hills—their sprouts and ferns are sweet.
> Is it Shao music's made me forget how things should taste?
> For three months now no salt for my food!
> . . . .
> With goosefoot staff, boiled rice for the road, he hurries off;
> Copper coins in no time will be lost to other hands.
> "What's left to show? My son speaks fancy language—
> Over half the year we spend in town!"

Su struggled without much success with the problems of irrigation and flood control in the lowlands around West Lake, and he presided unhappily over many trials of poor people who had been caught trying to make a living by smuggling salt in violation of the state monopoly. He found solace in long weekends of quiet in the lovely monasteries in the green valleys around West Lake, in parties with his friends on the lake, and in a steady growth of quantity and quality of his poetry. There had been some Buddhist practice in his family from the beginning, but it seems to have been in the Hangzhou years, and especially in the long, tranquil weekends in the hill monasteries, that Buddhism came to affect him more deeply. There is a clear note of Buddhist compassion in his descriptions of his public and private efforts to help the poor. Chan ways of being in the world without clinging to it deepened his own understanding of how he could respond to humanity in all its variety and not impose his own fixed ideas on it.

Transferred to Mizhou in Shandong in 1074, Su was in charge of a poorer area where there always were bandits and where new government efforts to extract revenues by imposing a salt monopoly were driving many more people into smuggling and banditry, causing military expenses that consumed at least half of the new revenues. The court ignored Su's protests against these misguided policies, and he spent a good deal of this time building a pavilion on the city wall where he and his junior colleagues and friends could relax, drink, and exchange poems. He did not have much money, but "there is something to be seen in everything, and all pleasurable; things need not be especially strange or beautiful. One can get high on the dregs of wine, and full with nuts and vegetables. On this principle, where should I not be happy?"

In 1078 Su was transferred to the important city of Xuzhou, and he soon found himself supervising the struggle against a terrible flood; for weeks he lived in a shack on the city walls and did not go to his regular quarters. Finally the flood was turned into an old abandoned course of the Yellow River, and the city could begin to recover. He also took an unusual interest in the welfare of prisoners in his jurisdiction, visiting the prisons and appointing a physician to look after them. His literary life also was at full tide, as he wrote many poems in which a wide variety of human emotions and reactions to sights and situations were vividly expressed. Later he would say that his writing was like the outflow of a great spring, flowing here and there, conforming to the objects it meets, always rushing on. Again he built a tower on the city wall, where he and his friends could gather to drink and exchange poems. He recalled how two of his friends went boating on some nearby rapids with three singing girls; he had to stay at the office, but got away late in the afternoon to watch the jolly sight as his friends returned, drinking and playing flutes. Later he went with a monk friend through the same rapids:

> See there, on the face of the green rock bank,
> Holes like hornets' nests where ancient boatmen
>   braced their poles!
> Only make sure the mind never clings!
> The Creator may hurry us, but what can we do?
> Turn the boat around, mount horse, and go home.
> Master Canliao complains I talk too much!

Friends came and went on their way to and from official posts, and Su sent off a steady stream of letters and poems in all directions. He no longer was in the forefront of attacks on Wang Anshi's policies, thinking that the vehemence of the opposition had done a good deal of harm, but he still did not hesitate to criticize abuses and puncture pomposities wherever he found them. Shenzong had had to give in a bit to the opposition, and Wang had resigned in 1076, but his policies remained in force until the death of Shenzong in 1085, maintained by younger men of far lesser stature than Wang who had risen under his patronage.

As their position weakened, these younger Wangites had every reason to fear that they might be ousted altogether, and if an antireform government emerged, surely one of its most important figures would be the widely respected and loved poet and statesman Su Shi. The Wangites had been keeping files on every indiscreet joke or barbed phrase Su wrote, and when he wrote in a memorial of thanks to the emperor about "those unqualified young men who have been suddenly promoted" they were personally insulted, felt their careers threatened, and decided they had enough material on file to initiate proceedings to bring Su to trial on charges of defaming the emperor and his ministers. Su was brought to the capital and thrown into prison. The legal structure was so stacked with his enemies that he expected a death sentence. He gave the prison warden a poem to be delivered to Su Che:

> Our Sage Ruler, like Heaven, makes spring for all things.
> This lowly minister, stupid and benighted, has caused
>   his own death.
> I pay my debt before I have completed the full span of years.
> Ten mouths with no home will burden you all the more.
> Bury my bones anywhere there are green mountains.
> In later times you will grieve alone on rainy nights.
> We shall be brothers through many lives,
> Completing the destiny cut off in this life.[3]

Su was not executed, but he was demoted to a very low rank and exiled to the backward and impoverished region of Huangzhou on the middle course of the Yangzi from 1080 to 1084. He had very little money, only a few menial duties, and was not allowed to leave the area or to comment on government affairs. He turned these years of exile into a triumph of creativity and character, doing some of his most important poetic and scholarly work, practicing Buddhism more seriously than before, and still enjoying himself. He managed to buy a small farm at a place called Eastern Slope (Dongpo) and began to sign himself "The Recluse of the Eastern Slope." We recognize the importance of this time in his life every time we call him Su Dongpo.

Deeply shaken by his brush with death, Su spent some time in serious Buddhist devotions and also followed Daoist practices for the prolonging of life. He took on some of the greatest challenges of Confucian scholarship, writing about the *Analects*, the *Yi jing*, and the *Shu jing*. He was not destitute; his household probably included about twenty people. But he very much enjoyed playing the gentleman farmer, noting each small step toward making something of his little Eastern Slope farm: finding a well, watching rain water flow into a cleared irrigation channel, watching the first rice crop ripen and anticipating its fresh taste. He visited nearby officials and other cultured men, and he watched the light and clouds change over the great river and the mountains beyond it. Above all, he found time for long thoughts on what it meant to be passionately committed to the literary life and at the same time to the improvement of public morals and the life of the common people. He grappled with this especially in his

---

[3] Following and modifying Fuller, *The Road to East Slope*, pp. 246–47.

commentary on the *Yi jing*, which he took very seriously: "Even if on reading you find nothing of value in it, it will still be enough to show that when forlorn I did not forget the Way, and when old I was able to learn." The immense variety and changeability of human situations and of appropriate responses to them could be seen clearly in the *Yi*, and this was precisely what made literature so important: its ability to portray vividly the infinite variety of things. The literary man thus exemplifies the ability of the sage to let everything develop and flourish in its particular way; this was precisely, he said, where Wang Anshi went wrong, in his determination to make all men think and act alike.

His most famous achievement of the Eastern Slope years is a pair of prose-poems (*fu*) describing boat trips with friends to a place called Red Cliff. This was not the same Red Cliff as the site of the famous Three Kingdoms battle, but apparently Su thought it was. The first of the pieces evokes the carefree, otherworldly feelings of two friends drifting and drinking in a small boat on the vast river on a moonlit night. The friend's flute-playing darkens the atmosphere: "The flute made a wailing sound, as though the player were filled with resentment or longing, or were lamenting or protesting. Long notes trailed through the night like endless threads of silk, a sound to make dragons dance in hidden caves, or to set the widow weeping in her lonely boat." When Su asks his friend why he plays this way, the friend replies:

> "'The moon is bright, stars grow few,
> Crows and magpies fly to the south.'

"That's how Cao Cao's poem goes, doesn't it? . . . Surely he was the greatest hero of his time, yet where is he now?" Su replies by quoting Confucius: "The water flows on and on like this." That is how it is with the river and the moon; they change and yet they remain the same. "If we look at things through the eyes of change, then there's not an instant of stillness in all creation. But if we observe the changelessness of things, then we and all beings alike have no end. What is there to be envious about?" The breeze over the river, the moon, are things that belong to no one, for all to enjoy. The first piece ends with the two friends sprawled in the bottom of the boat among the empty cups and bowls, not even noticing that dawn is coming.

In the second piece, another drinking trip on the river opens up a harsher and more uncanny world. The river level has fallen, and rocks stick out along the banks. Su scrambles up the cliff ahead of his friends. "I gave a long, shrill whoop. Trees and grass shook and swayed, the mountains rang, the valley echoed. A wind came up, roiling the water, and I felt a chill of sadness, a shrinking fear. I knew that I couldn't stay there any longer." Back out on the river they are startled by a single crane swooping low over their boat with its huge wings like cartwheels. Later Su dreams that he sees

a Daoist immortal in his feather cloak who asks him if he enjoyed his out-
ing, and realizes that the crane flying low over the boat had been this immortal. The richness of language, the evocation of changing atmospheres,
the delight in a floating life of wine and friendship, the fascination with
Cao Cao and the allusion to the Daoist side of Zhuge Liang, the sense of
being perilously at home in the ceaseless flow of a world of change and risk
and danger, seizing joys where they can be found, make the prose-poems
on Red Cliff widely beloved as among the richest evocations of the spirit
of this wonderful man, his great age, and his great people.

Shenzong died in 1085, and the dowager empress holding power for a
boy emperor immediately moved to dismiss the surviving Wangites to provincial offices and to bring all their opponents, Su Dongpo among them,
back to the capital. There were many differences among these opponents,
however, some traceable to their ties to different native places, some to
differences of temperament and conviction. The philosopher brothers
Cheng Hao and Cheng Yi and the great historian Sima Guang did not
share Su Dongpo's appreciation of the benefits of some of the Wang reforms; all were based, they said, in fundamental moral errors, in departure
from the classical primacy of moral teaching and self-cultivation and in
officials' love of profit and clever schemes, and all must be abolished. Su
disagreed, in particular wanting to maintain parts of a very useful scheme
to convert commoners' assigned duties at the local government offices into
a tax that paid for people hired to perform these duties. Su lost. When
Sima Guang died, Su and Cheng Yi fell into a nasty personal quarrel over
the proprieties for his funeral, which Cheng insisted on conducting according to the ancient ceremonial texts without any consideration for contemporary customs. Highly respected but not very influential, constantly
at odds with his narrow-minded classical-moralist colleagues, Su requested
and finally was given a provincial assignment.

From 1089 to 1091 Su again was magistrate of Hangzhou. He worked
hard to relieve the plight of refugees displaced from nearby areas by floods,
annoying people in the capital by his insistent and effective lobbying for
relief for his people. But his greatest achievement of these years was finally
to bring the complicated West Lake water system under control, providing
some new rice paddy lands on one side of the lake, protecting the lake from
sudden changes in level, and in the process making the whole thing much
more pleasing to the eye. Today West Lake (Xihu) is much admired by
Chinese and foreign tourists, who take boats to the little artificial island in
the middle of the lake that Su helped design and stroll along the Su Ti, Su's
Dike, which divides the paddy lands from the lake. The dike is a key part
of the water control system and was planned by Su not only as a practical
improvement but as a place of relaxation and outdoor enjoyment for the
people of Hangzhou. It is hard to imagine a finer monument.

Su was in and out of capital office from 1091 to 1093. Then the dowager empress died, and the young emperor began to recall partisans of the Wang reforms to capital offices. They renewed their old accusations against Su, and he was exiled to more and more distant and lower-ranked provincial posts. In the fall of 1094 he arrived at Huizhou in the beautiful East River valley in modern Guangdong. He renewed his interest in Buddhism and enjoyed the semitropical fruits, the exotic greenery, and the Tanka boat people, and he seems to have been a bit relieved to be far from the bitterness and danger of court politics:

> I'm a frightened monkey who's reached the forest,
> A tired horse unharnessed at last,
> My mind a void to fill with new thoughts;
> Surroundings are old to me—I see them in dreams.
> River gulls flock around, growing tamer;
> Old Tanka men drop in to visit.
> South pond lotus spreads green coins;
> North hill bamboo sends up purple shoots.
> What does the "bring-jug" bird know about wine?
> He inspires me with a fine idea.
> The spring river had a beautiful poem
> But, drunk, I dropped it somewhere far away.

Examining a local scholar's collection of calligraphy, he was moved to thought of the fragility of a worldly reputation, even one bolstered by literary fame; it might last longer than an inscription on bronze or iron, but still it would pass. The only thing for a man who understands fate to do is to do his duty, so that as he looks back he can be without regrets.

In 1097 the court authorities sent Su as far away as they could without exiling him from the entire empire, to the island of Hainan. The southern climate was hard on his health, no rice was grown on the island, and many of the people were non-Chinese Li tribesmen. But Su continued to study Buddhism and the great poets of the past, made friends with the local people, and learned to drink the local wine and to eat rats, bats, and taro root.

> Half-sober, half-drunk, I call on the Lis;
> Bamboo spikes, rattan creepers tangle every step.
> Following cow turds I find my way back—
> Home beyond the cattle pen, west and west again.

A new emperor came to the throne in 1100, and new efforts were made to overcome the partisan strife of the previous decades. Su was given an honorary post in the Yangzi valley and hoped to go home to Meishan, but he died on the way. When a monk urged him to pray for rebirth in the Pure Land, he replied, "Perhaps there is a Pure Land, but I shall not pray for it."

In the years that followed, Wangites, even more partisan and less competent than those who had prosecuted Su in 1080, dominated the court, banned from politics all the post-1085 antireformers and their descendants, and even banned their writings. The Wangites' reputation in turn was destroyed by the disaster of the Jin invasions of 1125 and 1127.

Su's fame, of course, never rested on his partisanship, and not much on his political opinions. In addition to all the accomplishments I have noted—poetry, prose, painting and calligraphy and critical theories of them, classical scholarship, Buddhist studies—he was an important student of herbal medicine, and very knowledgeable about the Daoist quest for physical immortality sometimes associated with it. His insistence on reverence for the variety of humanity and nature, his rejection of all efforts to conceive reality or shape society in conformity with any single set of ideas, was a profoundly humane kind of wisdom too often ignored by the Chinese of later centuries and indeed by almost all thinkers and leaders everywhere. Above all he is remembered as a great friend, a man of impulsive candor, an unsurpassed phrase-maker and image-catcher in his poetry, and one who lived by his own youthful admonition that the sage should rejoice in the Way. As Confucius said, "To have friends come from afar, is that not also a source of joy?"

11

YUE FEI

• • • • • •

Su Dongpo's life was not altogether free of anxiety and danger, but his world had a low level of organized and unorganized violence and was governed by regular bureaucratic procedures decided on by discussion that at least attempted to be rational. Culture and politics were dominated by scholar-officials, and military men were kept away from the centers of power as never before. But within forty years after his death China had experienced years of war and banditry that form the historical background for two very different sets of tales of violence and heroism, those of the righteous bandits of the great novel *Shui hu zhuan* (Water Margin) and those surrounding the loyal minister-general Yue Fei. Moreover, Yue Fei had sought to resist an invasion from the northeast, which in retrospect can be seen as the beginning of a phase of imperial history of almost eight hundred years, in well over half of which north China was ruled by ethnically alien dynasties, and alien dynasties twice conquered and ruled all of China.

The threat from the north confronted by the Song was one of the most basic justifications for the state-strengthening policies Wang Anshi had advocated. This threat was quite different from those of the Xiongnu of Han times or the Western Turks who made so much trouble for Empress Wu. Those nomadic peoples had been dangerous raiders but had shown little interest in holding Chinese territory and administering and exploiting its agricultural population. The northern neighbors of the Song all had Chinese ministers advising them, used some of the language and symbols of the Chinese imperial state, and adopted Chinese patterns of bureaucracy and taxation to administer any Chinese territories they conquered. This adaptation can be seen most clearly in the Khitan people, whose homeland was in what now is northeast China, some of whom already were settled under Tang authority in the area around modern Beijing and making trouble for Empress Wu around 700. They took advantage of the turmoil of the Five Dynasties (907–960) to proclaim their own Liao dynasty and to occupy the area around modern Beijing, which they made their southern capital, and parts of the north-central frontier around the modern city of Datong. In 946 they raided all the way to the Yellow River, overthrowing one of the short-lived north Chinese dynasties. Developing separate Khitan and Chinese bureaucracies and drawing some talented Chinese officials into their service, the Liao held on to their conquered territories and taxed and administered them in Chinese fashion.

After 960 the Song were preoccupied with reunifying south China, and the Liao with internal tensions. Neither gained much in major battles in the 990s, and in 1005 they signed a treaty recognizing the territorial status quo and requiring the Song to send annual gifts of silver and silk to the Liao court and to recognize the ceremonial equality of the Song and Liao emperors. In many ways this was a realistic balancing of interests. The gifts were a small fraction of the large state expenditures of the Song, much less than the costs of annual military campaigns like those of the 990s, and were very attractive to the less affluent Liao state. In addition, of course, the Liao got to hold on to their conquered territories. On the Song side, the loss of territories that had been culturally Chinese since they formed parts of the states of Yan and Zhao in Warring States times and the foothold of foreign power inside the northern frontier passes were unacceptable to many statesmen. So was the ceremonial equality of the Song and Liao emperors; the Song revival of seriousness about Confucian precedents and principles made many unwilling to tolerate any violation of the superiority of the Son of Heaven over all other monarchs. The result was that throughout the eleventh century Song statesmen from time to time tried out new strategies to push the Liao back and reassert Song superiority, and when these failed they still sought to avoid full ceremonial and terminological recognition of the equality of the Liao.

The situation was further complicated by the emergence on the northwest frontier of a vigorous multiethnic state with a Tangut ruling elite, which occupied some important trading centers in the 1030s and proclaimed itself the Xia, as in the name of the first dynasty; the Chinese called it the Western Xi Xia. This new threat stimulated discussion of reform in the Song bureaucracy and an effort to ally with the Liao against the Xia, which accomplished nothing except to increase the annual Song presents to the Liao. Another burst of diplomatic activity under Wang Anshi, including an effort to ally with the great Korean state of Koguryo against the Liao, accomplished no more.

All this was dramatically changed by the rebellion in 1102 of the king of the Jurchen people, inhabiting what is now the northern part of northeast China, against the Liao. In 1115 the Jurchen king proclaimed himself the first emperor of the Jin (Gold) dynasty. Jin power expanded rapidly in the face of the weakening Liao.

To many Song statesmen it seemed that the rise of Jin offered a golden opportunity to escape from the dangerous and demeaning relation with the Liao and recover some or all of the lost Chinese territory. So it might have been for a Song state with fewer internal difficulties and a more capable set of rulers. But Emperor Huizong (reigned 1101–1126) was a weak and indifferent ruler. His real passions were Daoist studies and painting; he was one of the greatest painters of birds and flowers in Chinese history. Administration was dominated by supporters of the Wang Anshi policies, led by Cai Jing, who were much more interested in maximizing their own power and wealth and much less committed to the well-being of the people than the original Wangites had been. Their extortions produced a great deal of discontent in the countryside and one brief but violent local rebellion in 1120. Cai Jing himself does not seem to have been much interested in foreign policy, but that simply left the field open for others to bungle. These ministers acted on a long-standing Chinese delusion that the Chinese, Zhuge Liangs one and all, could trick and persuade any foreigner to act in the Chinese interest. They also were guided by the maxim of "using barbarians to control barbarians," which occasionally had worked for the Tang but had accomplished nothing for the Song, and now led to disaster.

In 1120 the Jin occupied the northern capital of the Liao. The Song court hurriedly negotiated a treaty of alliance with the Jin against the Liao; after Liao was crushed, Song would recover the territories within China that Liao had occupied and would pay to Jin the subsidy formerly paid to Liao. The rulers of Koguryo warned that the Song would be better off supporting the weak Liao than encouraging the dynamic Jin, but they were ignored. In a planned joint campaign in 1122, the Song armies were not able to advance against the weakened Liao even enough to retake the Liao southern capital, and they had to stand idly by while the Jin took it. The Jin refused to honor fully the territorial division agreed on in 1120, since the Song had contributed so little to the defeat of Liao. The Jin went on to finish off the remnants of Liao, picked a quarrel with the Song, and in 1125 mounted a great two-pronged attack on the north China plain. Huizong abdicated in a vain attempt at appeasement. The capital fell at the end of 1126; in 1127 the Jin armies withdrew to their home bases, taking with them the abdicated Huizong and his successor.

Yue Fei entered public life in response to the crisis of 1122, joining a local militia in his home area on the north China plain, not far from the Liao frontier. Our sources for his life are not of very good quality or great quantity; many official documents on him probably were destroyed after he died in prison, while the most connected account we have was compiled by a grandson and presents a spotless heroic image. Elements of legend, from his birth on, must already have been accumulating around him in his lifetime. It cannot have been easy to arrive at a balanced assessment of him even upon personal acquaintance; he owed much of his power to his carefully cultivated image and, like many gifted actors, seems to have believed absolutely in the role he played and the cause for which he lived and died.

Yue Fei was born in 1103 to a family that apparently was literate but farmed the land and had only the most modest heritage of official rank. It was said that he was given his name, which means "to fly," because a strange great bird had circled calling over the house at the time of his birth. This was thought to be an omen of the birth of a child who would rise far above common consciousness and expectation, like the giant bird in a famous story in the *Zhuang zi*. According to one story a great flood had swept his home area when he was an infant, and his mother had saved herself and her son by climbing into a great jar that floated away and miraculously came to rest on a safe shore.

Yue Fei is said to have been an excellent and diligent student, sometimes reading and writing all night. His adult writings certainly are those of a well-educated man with a real talent for literary expression. But he also was very much interested in military pursuits, and the teacher to whom he formed the strongest personal attachment was Zhou Tong, who taught him archery and other military arts. Yue grew to be prodigiously strong and an excellent archer, splitting with his arrows the arrows his teacher had just shot into the bull's-eye. After Zhou died Yue Fei went to his grave every night to mourn, present offerings of meat and wine, and shoot arrows from a bow his teacher had left to him. His father remarked to him at the time that if he fulfilled all his obligations with such fervor he might well have to sacrifice his life in the service of the dynasty. It was as if this obscure young provincial already was casting himself as the realizer of all the Song moralists' exhortations to selfless public service and at the same time as the reintegrator of the civil and military virtues, of *wen* and *wu*, that had drifted so far apart in the eleventh century.

In 1122 a general call went out for brave men to volunteer to participate in the attack on Liao or defend the Song borders, and Yue hurried to the nearest headquarters, where he made an excellent impression and was immediately placed in charge of a three-man combat squad. His first combat successes were against Chinese bandits, not the Liao or Jin; he sent men to infiltrate the bandits' camp, lured them into an ambush, and shot an arrow down the throat of one bandit leader. In 1126 he served in the Taiyuan area under a leading opponent of appeasement of the Jin and won notice for his bravery in a cavalry charge and in spying on the enemy camp.

When the Jin took the Song capital in 1126 and withdrew to the north with their two hostage emperors, the best prospect for maintaining a Song succession and rallying loyal forces seemed to be Prince Kang, who was inexperienced, inclined to make peace, only twenty years old, and trapped behind enemy lines. Yue Fei was among those who met the prince and tried to organize forces to defend him. In 1127 the prince managed to withdraw to the southeast, where he was proclaimed emperor; he is usually referred to by the posthumous title Gaozong. Eventually he established his capital at Hangzhou, the lovely city that owed so much to Su Dongpo's periods of enlightened and energetic administration; it remained the Southern Song capital until the Mongol conquest of the 1270s and became one of the greatest cities of the world of that time.

Gaozong now sought to consolidate Song power in the Yangzi valley and the south. He and his advisers confronted a dangerous and unstable situation. There had been some local rebellions even before the collapse in the north; now bandits and rebels arose everywhere. Some of them proclaimed their loyalty to the Song and their determination to repel a Jin invasion, but their primary loyalties were to their own leaders and home territories. Forces that had been recruited in the north might be useful in consolidating power in the south, but even if they would aid Gaozong in this way they would do so impatiently and would be anxious to turn to a reconquest of their homelands. The Song dynasty had sought from the beginning to limit the power of military men. Gaozong almost had been overthrown by a coup of soldiers and officers in 1129.

Yue Fei was just the kind of northern military man on whom Gaozong's court was so uneasily dependent. In one incident, Yue rode straight into a bandit camp, made a rousing speech condemning the Jin as rebels and offering the bandits a chance to make good names for themselves, and recruited the whole bandit force into his army. Soon he was dismissed from Gaozong's entourage after impetuously urging an immediate counterattack on the Jin. After the Jin withdrawal he returned to the area of Kaifeng, the Northern Song capital, and remained with the forces trying to hold it. But these forces often fought with each other and were so independent that there was little to distinguish them from the "bandits" they fought. Then in 1129 Yue's warrior band was among those that fell back to try to hold the line at the Yangzi as the Jin advanced. The Jin got a beachhead on the south bank, and the Song forces started to disintegrate. But Yue, dripping with blood from the battle, rallied his troops with a fiery speech reminding them of their obligation to repay with loyalty the dynasty's benevolence to them, of their chance to gain undying fame if they stood fast, and of his own orders to behead anyone who fled. He was able to stabilize the situation around Jiankang (modern Nanjing). Recommended by the senior commander Zhang Jun, he began to receive modest honors and promotions from Gaozong. Although he was ready to participate in the pacification of the south and to give advice on how to do it, he made it clear that as soon as possible he wanted the Song forces to go on the offensive against the Jin and the Chinese puppet regimes it had set up in the north.

Until about 1137 Gaozong and his court at least had to appear to heed this advice, since they needed the aid of Yue and other northern generals. Advocates of peace with the Jin were not denied office, but their views was not acted on. One of the most conspicuous of them was one Qin Gui, who had been taken away to the north with the captive emperors but at the end of 1130 had found his way south, probably with Jin connivance, and immediately had been given high office.

Yue now steadily built up the forces under his command. He maintained rigid discipline, punishing anyone caught stealing from the common people or showing any slackness in battle or in training exercises. Once his officers had to talk him out of executing his own son for letting his horse stumble in training. He was equally theatrical in his rewards for good performance: once he unbuckled his gold belt and presented it to a private who had won merit in battle. He lived in the field with his troops and ate the same food they ate. He made good use of literary men in the administrative staff of his army, and also had them tell his troops stories of the great heroes of the past. Scholars who read his poems and his reports to the emperor were impressed with his erudition, style, and fine calligraphy. The most famous of his own poems expressed the spirit he sought to cultivate among his men:

> My hair stands on end in my helmet.
> I lean against the railing; the driving rain lets up.
> I lift my eyes, and roar long at Heaven.
> My breast is filled with violence.
> I am thirty but my deeds and name are as earth and dust.
> Eight thousand li of road—nothing but moon and clouds.
> Do not slacken! The hair of young men whitens with
>   useless sorrow.
> The shame of Jingkang [1126] is not yet made white as snow.
> When will the minister's hatred come to an end?
> Let us drive our chariots through the Helan Pass.
> My bold aim is to eat the flesh of the nomads.
> Laughing I thirst for the blood of the Xiongnu.
> Wait until we can begin again,
> Recovering our old rivers and mountains,
> And paying homage again in the imperial court.[1]

---

[1] Hu Yunyi, ed., *Song ci xuan*, Shanghai, 1982, p. 199.

An equally famous expression of the central cause of his life was a phrase of just four characters: *Huan wo he shan,* "give us back our rivers and mountains." It has echoed through all China's times of struggle against alien domination, right down to the 1937–45 war of resistance to Japan.

A key challenge to the consolidation of the new Song regime in the south emerged in the middle Yangzi valley, around the great Dongting Lake. The leaders of a popular religious group that used various forms of magic and promised their followers prosperity and good health long had been powerful in the area. Sometimes, like many teachers influenced by the great heritage of religious Daoism, they also held out hope of a more equal social order, without officials, scholars, or monks. Like many other local leaders, they took advantage of the collapse of Song power in the north to bring their military strength into the open, ostensibly defending their territory against bandits or a possible Jin invasion. They maintained their power after the new Song court ordered them to disband, and survived several attacks by government forces and by other "bandits." In the tricky world of marshes and shallow channels around the great lake they were the local guerrillas who knew the territory and frequently evaded or defeated the government troops. Both sides used big boats with multiple paddle-wheels powered by men on treadmills. Despite many government setbacks, it is possible that the lake bandits were beginning to lose strength by the time Yue Fei was sent to take command in the area at the beginning of 1135.

Before taking up his command, Yue participated in some important policy discussions at the court. The emperor seemed warlike, enthusiastic about moving ahead against the lake bandits. This did not mean, however, that he was fully on the side of those like Yue who wanted to reconquer the north. Consolidation in the middle Yangzi could be a step toward a thrust up the Han River into the north China plain, or it could be simply part of the pacification of a separate realm in the south. Qin Gui got a promotion at this time. The emperor ordered the building of an imperial ancestral temple at Hangzhou. Was he just being filial, or was he about to make it the permanent capital of a separate regime? In his conferences he declared that he could not rest until the north China plain had been reconquered and the two captive emperors freed. (Huizong died in captivity about this time, but Gaozong still would seek to bring his coffin back for proper burial.)

Yue moved quickly against the Dongting Lake rebels. Before his arrival efforts already had begun to split the rebel leadership and to induce individual leaders to accept government amnesty. From Song times on, Chinese statesmen, wary of the expense and risk of military campaigns and the power of generals, often preferred this kind of "pacification" to military action against rebels. They assumed, not without reason, that the imperial state could wait out the leaders of a rebellion, that leaders and followers eventually would prefer the rewards and full rice bowls of garrison life to the hardships of resistance in the mountains or marshes, and that the imperial bureaucracy could manage the surrendered rebels, move them around, and in the long run tame them. Yue Fei engaged in a great deal of hard bargaining and persuasion, which paid off in the surrender of many bandit leaders. The paddle-wheel boats of a final holdout were trapped by floating rush mats that tangled the wheels and then rammed by the Song boats; the last rebel fortress then was taken by storm. Yue pleaded with the court for amnesty for those who had been led astray by the rebel leaders. Over fifty thousand former rebels were enrolled in Yue's army. These new recruits cannot have been easy to turn into reliable soldiers, but there is little evidence that the unity and discipline of Yue's army suffered any long-term decline. His army remained popular with landowners and common people in the areas it occupied, an almost unprecedented situation that made it all the more dangerous to the authority of the court, which would find it hard to drive a wedge between such an army and the people of a region.

With these victories late in 1135 Yue's power and prestige reached new heights. He received new honors and titles and was granted wide powers to make official appointments in the area under his control. When his mother died early in 1136 he proclaimed his determination to retire for his full period of mourning, but the emperor insisted that he return to office after a brief period. Although he always had demonstrated the greatest filial piety toward her, in fact he sometimes had left her behind and put her in considerable danger as he rushed about the empire on military expeditions. She figures in one of the most potent of the legends that surrounded him: It was said that she had tattooed on his back four characters, *jin zhong bao guo*, "exhaust all your loyalty in repaying your debt to the ruling dynasty."

Circumstances looked reasonably favorable for Yue to accomplish something in his great cause and for the Song to regain its mountains and rivers. In 1136 Yue drove his forces almost up to the Yellow River but then withdrew. Gaozong still was making warlike statements but not acting on them very effectively. The regional military commanders and their court allies who favored war were not a unified or uniformly competent group. Yue was summoned to audience with the emperor. His intelligence and honesty made a good impression, but then he made what may have been a crucial mistake. Gaozong's older brother, who had been briefly enthroned in 1126 and then taken away by the Jin, still was alive in captivity, and if the Jin decided to set him up as a puppet, he might provide a dangerous alternative focus of power. Gaozong had no sons; a cousin of the next generation seemed to be the best candidate to be named as his adoptive heir, but there had been no formal decision. Even in more stable conditions it was well understood that the lack of a settled succession could affect the stability of the state, but emperors always had tended to resent official interference in family matters, and this was a question that had to be handled with extreme tact, by the most senior court officials, and certainly not by military men. But Yue brought it up in audience with Gaozong. He emerged ashen-faced, evidently realizing that he had gone too far. Gaozong professed to admire Yue's frankness, but it seems that from this time on he was wary of any measure that would give still more power to this impetuous soldier who did not know his place.

Gaozong now sought to improve the military command situation by dismissing the least competent of his high commanders and reassigning his troops. At first he seemed to plan to put these troops under Yue, for a great advance into the center of the north China plain. But then other generals convinced him that the shifting of these troops from their present stations farther east might open the way for a Jin counterattack that would endanger the lower Yangzi valley and the new capital. The troops were placed instead under Zhang Jun, who had been one of Yue's first supporters. But the troops would not accept the commanders he sent to them, and some units rebelled and deserted to the Jin puppet regime. Zhang was dismissed from office.

With the war faction in deep disarray, Qin Gui's influence at court grew rapidly. The war faction seemed to offer a choice between incompetents like Zhang Jun and the impetuous, idealistic, perhaps uncontrollable Yue Fei. Moreover, the Jin were finding it hard to keep control of the north China plain. They faced guerrilla resistance in several areas. The puppet regime that ruled Henan (the area around the old Northern Song capital, on the Yellow River) was barely holding on. In 1137 the Jin abolished it and made serious overtures to Gaozong's court for peace negotiations. (There were stories that Yue Fei had contributed to this welcome development by a double-agent trick worthy of Zhuge Liang that sowed suspicion between the Jin and their puppet ruler, but the story is told of at least three different Song generals.) Control of Henan would be handed back to the Song. The coffins of Huizong and a dowager empress who had died in captivity would be returned for proper mourning and burial. But the conditions would be humiliating: the Song would have to acknowledge the ceremonial superiority of the Jin and send substantial gifts of silk and silver every year. Gaozong insisted that he was ready to bear these humiliations for filial piety's sake, that is, so that the imperial coffins could be brought back. And of course peace would lessen his dependence on the generals. A humiliating peace, in which the Southern Song emperors were not even called emperors and their regime was simply called Jiangnan, south of the river, not Song, was concluded early in 1139.

These changing circumstances seemed to doom Yue to futility. Visiting the capital in the fall of 1138, he had an interview with the imperial cousin who still had not been named heir apparent, and he was heard to remark, "Now the dynasty has a man! Isn't the basis for its revival right here?" In 1139, as the Song sought to reestablish their jurisdiction in Henan, he led a lightly armed party to investigate the condition of the tombs of the Northern Song emperors. It was an excuse for a reconnaissance of the area and an important ceremonial errand for Gaozong, but no substitute for real planning and commitment of resources to holding the area. At the end of 1139 and the beginning of 1140, recalling the virtues and talents of Zhuge Liang and thinking of two leaders of the war faction who recently had died, he seemed to confront the likelihood of failure and the need to remain steadfast. Of one of the dead leaders he wrote, "With death before him, he was stern and did not change his countenance. To the end he was capable of complete purity, holding himself unbowed." Later in 1140 he went through a ceremonial purification and then wrote again to the emperor urging him to establish an heir apparent. His insistent return to this dangerous subject suggests that he had given up trying to be effective and was more and more playing out a script of noble failure, of demonstrating the purity of his selfless devotion to righteous principles even when, or perhaps especially when, those principles could not be realized.

But then circumstances gave him a last amazing chance for success. In 1140 the Jin broke the new treaty and invaded Song territory along several fronts, avoiding the sector where Yue's army was stationed. The other armies lost some cities but did not collapse, so that Yue did not have to withdraw and go to their rescue. Gaozong and his ministers, among whom Qin Gui now was the most influential, were wary of the consequences of advances in the north but approved Yue's plans for a campaign. With Yue and his son personally leading cavalry charges, the Jin forces were defeated in battle after battle and the Song occupied several of the great cities of Henan, approaching old capital of Kaifeng. Guerrilla forces raised their heads in several areas farther to the north and east. But if Yue's forces advanced to link up with these guerrillas they would be in a dangerously exposed position, where a defeat might open the way for the Jin to advance again and threaten the Yangzi valley. A victory might leave Gaozong's court at the mercy of this impetuous general with his alarming views on the question of imperial succession. Yue was ordered to withdraw from his conquests on the north China plain. He said, "My ten years of effort are destroyed in a single day! It is not that I have not been able to fulfill my

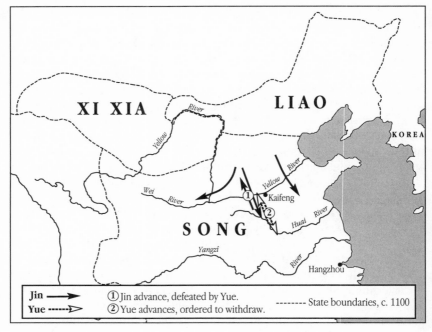

Map 3. Campaigns of 1140

responsibilities, but that the powerful official Qin Gui truly has deceived His Majesty!" But he was a loyal minister, and he did withdraw. He met popular protests in the cities that were being abandoned, saying to the protesters, "How can you think that what I am doing today is in accord with my own desires?"

By the summer of 1140 the Song forces were settling in on defense lines roughly along the Huai River. Yue was summoned to the capital. Early in 1141 the Jin invaded again, but moved forward only hesitantly, as if they were keeping pressure on for the negotiations that were about to begin. Qin Gui was determined to make peace. He also had Yue and two other powerful provincial generals kept at the capital, where they were given high-ranking posts in the military bureaucracy. Yue's request to retire from office was refused.

Qin was determined to get rid of Yue; some writers assert that the Jin were demanding his execution. After much investigation an officer was found who claimed that the best of Yue's generals had been plotting to use Yue's armies to force his release from the capital. It was easy enough to claim that Yue had been in on the plot and to imprison him. But Yue admitted to nothing. When first questioned, he tore off his shirt to reveal the four characters tattooed on his back. The judicial authorities would not convict him. According to one story, Qin's wife said to him, "Well, old man, are you so weak-willed after all? It's easy to catch a tiger, but hard to get rid of him!" Qin finally sent orders to the prison officials, and just before Chinese New Year Yue was murdered in prison, either by poison or by strangling. His son was executed, the family's property was confiscated, and many records of his career were destroyed.

In 1141 Qin Gui also managed to secure a peace treaty with the Jin, ceding more territory and promising ceremonial subordination and larger annual presents. Qin remained dominant in the court of Gaozong until he died in 1155. Beginning in 1161, after a new Jin invasion, Yue's honors were restored and there were new plans and abortive efforts to reconquer the north. Legends of Yue's heroism continued to grow. In some places, especially near Hangzhou, temples were erected to his memory. Outside these temples were statues of a kneeling Qin Gui; those who came to pay their respects to Yue were expected to spit on Qin as they passed. For some Yue became a warrior spirit who could be worshipped or summoned in trance, although far less widely venerated than Guan Yu.

The names of Su Dongpo and Yue Fei echo strongly in the Chinese historical consciousness down to our own time, but in very different ways: Su as poet, charming friend, wise and moderate statesman, maker of memorable phrases; Yue as single-minded, fierce warrior, noble in his pure loyalty and failure. But Yue patronized literary men and made a few fine phrases himself, and of course it is the literary phrase-makers and writers of history who have preserved his name and reputation. Both Su and Yue lived and died within the grammar of the Way of the Ruler and the Minister.

There are even better reasons for telling their two stories in succession in this book. They can be seen as two sides of the conclusive rejection in traditional Chinese political culture of the "rich state and strong military" sought by Wang Anshi and his allies. Su accused Wang of undermining the essentials of the Way of Ruler and Minister. The culture produced more moralistic critics than it did realistic alternatives to Wang's policies. And in Yue we see the far-reaching consequences of the Song separation of civil and military careers and virtues (*wen* and *wu*) and of the isolation of military men from the centers of power. Yue came to the very edge of using his military power to subvert the centralized order, but as a loyal minister he found no alternative to suicidal submission to that power, to the nobility of failure. Military values did not disappear; in the stories of Yue and other heroes and of the bandit heroes of *The Water Margin* they became ever more potent in the popular imagination. But it became harder to imagine morally approved forms of military effectiveness and success; all too often the only imaginable form of military nobility and loyalty was tenacity to the death in defeat and failure. This weakness of culturally approved forms of military success certainly was a major source of the nonmobilizing character of the Chinese state. This is not just a problem of the Chinese tradition; many in other cultures have had to acknowledge the difficulty of finding, in circumstances where war is less and less frequently a viable option, "moral equivalents" for the military values of courage, self-sacrifice, and victory.

A final factor in the long-run emergence of the nonmobilizing state in late imperial China also can be seen in its early stages in Yue Fei's lifetime, and we will look at it at greater length in relation to the eighteenth-century Qianlong emperor. Ethnically alien rulers of part or all of China, like Yue's Jin enemies, had to compromise with the Chinese elite but were not likely to trust them or to give them the larger measures of responsibility and power that a growing, resource-mobilizing state would have required. The last chapters of this book will follow the nonmobilizing state, and China's wrenching efforts to overcome its legacy, right into our own times.

A Yue Fei Temple is still to be seen near West Lake outside Hangzhou. Since China now claims to practice equality of the sexes, tourists entering now may spit on two kneeling statues, of Qin Gui and his wife. A few years ago a statue of Yue's mother tattooing the characters on his back was to be seen in a waxworks museum at the Kowloon end of the Hong Kong Star Ferry. And his name has reached some even stranger corners of the Chinese world: some years ago a student told me that she knew of a Chinese temple in Jakarta, Indonesia, where the spirit of Yue Fei was summoned regularly to give guidance to worshippers.

12

QIU CHUJI, THE DAOIST

• • • • • •

The spirit of the valley never dies.
It is called the mysterious female.
The gateway of the mysterious female
Is called the root of heaven and earth.
Gossamer it is, seemingly insubstantial,
Yet never consumed through use.

FOR THE Daoist master Qiu Chuji, Perfected Man of the Long Spring (Changchun zhenren), this was an exceptionally important passage in the great Daoist classic *Dao de jing*, stating beautifully the primacy of stillness, receptivity, *yin*, which he had sought to realize in long years of solitary meditation. For his particular school of Daoism, an early stage of meditation was described as that in which "the gods are in the valley," and when one hears them talking to each other it is as if they are talking a long way off, their voices heard echoing from one valley slope to another. For all Daoists and many others, the wisdom of the valley was that of letting things take their natural course, letting the streams run downhill to water the fields below. That was the kind of Daoist wisdom that was attributed even to Yu, and to many other statesmen who tried to use as far as possible the natural tendencies of human nature.

Nothing in these texts, this wisdom, or the landscapes of China could have prepared Qiu for the valley his party was descending in the autumn of 1221, in the mountainous heart of Asia, six months after they left north China. Great peaks that kept their snow all summer could be seen in the distance. The air was sharp and cold. The sides of the valley were thickly covered with the dark green of pines and the autumn gold of birches. Mountain streams poured down the slopes of the valley into the twisting, roaring river that ran through it. A road had been cut down the valley, with tunnels and cuts along the cliffsides and forty-eight timber bridges wide enough for two carts to meet.

Already Qiu Chuji and his party had seen the spring flowers on the endless grasslands, crossed at night a stretch of towering sand dunes, and visited a number of the great orderly camps of Mongol nobles. It was the rise of Mongol power that had brought Qiu so far from his Shandong retreat; he had been summoned by the great khaghan Chinggis, uniter of the peoples of the steppe and creator of an imperial military machine that under his sons and grandsons would reach from the Baltic to the Persian Gulf to the South China Sea. Already Qiu was seeing evidence that the Mongols, who certainly could be terrifying conquerors, also were statesmen: that spectacular mountain road with its rock-cuts and forty-eight bridges had been constructed under the orders of Chaghatai, second son of Chinggis. It was one of the beginnings of a great trans-Asian system of roads and post stations that the Mongols built to facilitate their own communications and troop movements but which also eased the way for trading caravans.

Already seventy-two years old when he set out, Qiu had protested that he was too old for this long and difficult journey. But the great khagan was no Liu Bei waiting respectfully for Zhuge Liang to wake up, and when he summoned you, you went. Also, it might be possible to win some favor for his Daoist teachings and to cast himself and his fellow-believers as defenders of Chinese culture under alien rule and as mediators protecting the people of north China from the worst excesses of Mongol conquest and exploitation. He believed that whatever fate brought it brought, like this journey and the possibility that he would die from its rigors. But he was more likely to survive it than many men twenty years his junior; years of severely disciplined meditation, staying awake for weeks at a time, special dietary practices, and sexual abstinence had produced a body that could "sit with the rigidity of a corpse, stand with the stiffness of a tree, move swiftly as lightning and walk like a whirlwind." After long years of solitude he sometimes complained of noise in the camps and lodgings of his long journey, but at other times he could be very convivial, exchanging poems, enjoying picnics and the scenic beauties along the way.

The great khagan's summons had been flattering enough, addressed to "the Perfected Man, Master Qiu," declaring that Qiu's merits were known all over the earth. "Now that your cloud-girt chariot has come forth from the Land of the Immortals, the cranes that draw it will carry it pleasantly through the realms of India. Bodhidharma, when he came to the East, by spiritual communication revealed the imprint on his heart. Lao Zi, when he traveled to the West, perfected his Way by converting the Central Asians. The way before you, both by land and by water, is indeed long; but I trust that the comforts I provide you will make it seem less long."

This edict may have been drafted by Chinggis's Chinese secretary Yelü

Chucai, who would become the great khagan's chief adviser on the adoption of Chinese ways of governing and a vehement critic of Qiu Chuji. Chinggis's reasons for summoning Qiu were complex. The Mongol rulers were products of a world of many religions and were interested in learning about all of them, for their insights, their magic powers, and their uses in ruling peoples who followed them. Chinggis was especially interested in hearing from a Daoist because one of the central features of Daoist teaching and practice was the postponement of aging and death and even, it was said, the achievement of physical immortality.

We have encountered this pursuit of immortality before, at the courts of the First Emperor of Qin and Emperor Wu of the Han and in the traditional image of Zhuge Liang. In the Daoism of the Later Han and after, the pursuit of immortality and of other forms of mastery of nature were linked to elaborate ceremonies, hierarchical organizations, the worship of many gods, and the use as basic scriptures of the great Warring States philosophical texts *Dao de jing* and *Zhuang zi*. These linkages were far from simple; none of the world's great religions is less simple, more baffling in its apparent heterogeneity and inconsistency, than Daoism.

There are no gods in the *Dao de jing* and *Zhuang zi*. There are some passages that can be read as promising bodily immortality:

> One who is good at preserving life does not avoid tigers and rhinoceroses when he walks in the hills, nor does he put on armor and take up weapons when he enters a battle. The rhinoceros has no place to jab his horn, the tiger no place to fasten its claws; weapons have no place to admit their blades.

> He who embodies the fullness of the Power of the Way is like a ruddy infant. Wasps, spiders, scorpions, and snakes will not sting or bite him; rapacious birds and fierce beasts will not seize him.

> The Perfected Man can walk under water without choking, can tread on fire without being burned.

But other passages express a lyrical *acceptance* of death: "The Great Clod burdens me with form, labors me with life, eases me in old age, and rests me in death. So if I think well of my life, for the same reason I must think well of my death." When Zhuang Zi's wife died, a friend found him pounding on a tub and singing. The friend scolded him, and he replied that he had mourned at first, but later understood how one change must lead to another. "Now she's going to lie down peacefully in a vast room. If I were to follow after her bawling and sobbing, it would show that I don't understand anything about fate. So I stopped."

There is, however, a consistent attitude expressed in these passages that can be traced on into the later developments of Daoism. This is one of the most physical and bodily of the world's great teachings. The early philosophical texts are full of evocations of the uncanny changes and wild splendors of nature, like a mountain wind storm; forests lash and sway, the wind "roars like waves, whistles like arrows." In later stages of Daoism its gods are the gods of mountains, directions, natural powers. Its visions and spiritual practices are organized in terms of the theory of the five powers and all the correspondences with them; for example, the meditator knows his vision is not authentic if it is the wrong color for the god of the direction he is trying to evoke. One of the most important forms of Daoist spiritual quest was the "alchemical" effort to follow the elaborate sequence of chemical and metallurgical processes that was supposed to lead, amid fasting, prayer, and meditation, to the production of a physical elixir of immortality. Another was a set of spiritual exercises focused entirely on the body of the meditator, in which a purified and immortal essence was supposed to be physically produced as a result of these exercises. Perhaps the most striking manifestation of this Daoist embodiedness was the transformation of Lao Zi, the legendary figure whose teachings supposedly are recorded in the *Dao de jing*, into a corporeal god whose body changes to form the world, much like the body of Pan-gu in the creation story told in chapter 1 of this book, and then gives birth to a new bodily Lao Zi.

This broader range of Daoist belief and practice seems to have come together under the Later Han. Already in the Earlier Han, the names of Huang-Lao, the Yellow Lord (*huangdi*) and Lao Zi, were associated with the doctrines of wise passivity and limited government that influenced the Han state between Emperor Gao and Emperor Wu. Other elements of the later Daoist synthesis that were important in the Earlier Han, but not yet identified with Huang-Lao, were the quest for immortality, aspects of the imperial ceremonies such as the worship of the Lords of the Five Directions and of the Great Unity, and the expectations of cosmic renewal that flourished around the time of Wang Mang. Excluded from the beliefs and practices of the state by the narrower Confucianism of the Later Han, these beliefs and practices now interacted in a wide range of developments that took on the new cohesion of religious Daoism. Individual seekers in their lonely retreats saw visions and wrote down texts revealed to them by the gods. Alchemists fasted and chanted spells as they worked over their retorts and furnaces. Prophets taught the common people elaborate ceremonies of healing illness and cleansing guilt, and eventually organized them in strictly governed communities that rose against the Han in the rebellions of the Yellow Scarves and the Five Pecks of Rice.

The leaders of these rebellions, all with the surname Zhang, are supposed to have taken the title heavenly teacher (*tian shi*). The initial suppression of the Yellow Scarves in 184 was only the beginning of the long struggle of the state and the elite against these Daoist communities. In the 400s the Northern Wei rulers attempted to bring them under control and to draw on their mystique to legitimize the dynasty by appointing one Kou Qianzhi as heavenly master and supporting his efforts to regularize and purify the ceremonies and beliefs of the Daoists. In Sui and Tang times we find more references to heavenly masters, and tradition has it that at some point in these centuries the office became hereditary in a family surnamed Zhang, claiming descent from the heavenly masters of the Later Han, who had their headquarters at Dragon and Tiger Mountain in Jiangxi and claimed jurisdiction over all Daoists in the empire.

These organizational changes were less important for the shape of Daoist belief than the quests of individual seekers for immortality, the elixir, and revelations from the gods in their heavens. In the 300s two massive sets of scriptures were presented by Daoist masters in the lower Yangzi valley as revelations from the Highest Pure Heaven where the unborn supreme powers dwelt and of ceremonies by which people could purify themselves, lengthen their lives, and maintain harmonious relations with the supernatural powers. Those in early stages of this progress, lightening their bodies, making them impervious to injury, and lengthening their lives, commonly were referred to as "perfected men" (*zhen ren*); the longer-range goal was to escape death entirely and become an "immortal" (*xian*).

These masters were the most serious and erudite pursuers of the elixir of immortality in Chinese history. One key operation was the heating of cinnabar (*dan*), mercuric sulfide, and the appearance out of the bright red mineral of that uncanny silvery liquid, mercury. Another common ingredient was realgar, arsenic sulfide. The results, after long heatings, repeated poundings and combinings, prayers, and spiritual preparation, were supposed to be elixirs of varying strength and purity that when swallowed contributed to the purification of the body, reversal of decay, and eventual physical immortality. Some believed that one of these elixirs also could change base metals into gold, but, unlike the alchemy of the European Middle Ages, this was a secondary goal. The manipulation of mercury was so crucial to Chinese alchemy that the word *dan*, originally meaning "cinnabar," came to be used to refer to the substance that would confer immortality, and here is translated as "elixir." Of course the mercury and arsenic made most of these compounds highly toxic. Neurological effects of first doses might include loss of appetite and thus of weight, visions, mental and spiritual exhilaration, and heightened sexual appetite. Of course heavy metal poisoning is cumulative, and less pleasant effects would follow. But some may have known of cases in which the heavy metal accumulation had retarded the decay of a corpse. And in any case when a Daoist seeker at the end of years of worship, meditation, purification, and gradually increasing doses of heavy metal compounds finally prepared to swallow a dose of elixir that was likely to end his ordinary life, he did so in faith that the elixir would complete the transmutation of part of his body into a new, subtle body that would escape the corpse and rise to join the immortals in one of the lower heavens.

Only a few wealthy adepts had the leisure and funds, and fewer still the courage, to pursue immortality by means of the preparation and ingestion of these chemical elixirs. From Tang times on we can find evidence of another tendency, equally bodily and physical, that taught that the elixir could be prepared by purification and concentration of essences already present in the body, without the preparation and ingestion of drugs. This teaching came to be known as the Inner Elixir (*nei dan*). By contrast to this the preparation and ingestion of chemical elixirs became known as the Outer Elixir (*wai dan*) school.

The basic concept of the Inner Elixir school is supported by passages in the *Dao de jing*, makes use of the ancient concepts of *yin* and *yang*, and expresses in a quite amazing way that basic optimism about the potentialities of human life in this world found so often in the Chinese tradition. Each of us is born as the result of a harmonious encounter and merging of *yin* and *yang*. As a result, each infant begins with a perfect endowment of physical, mental, and spiritual energy, true *yin* and true *yang*. Thus "He who embodies the fullness of the Power of the Way is like a ruddy infant. Wasps, spiders, scorpions, and snakes will not sting or bite him; rapacious birds and fierce beasts will not seize him. . . . His essence has reached a peak. He screams the whole day without becoming hoarse. His harmony has reached perfection." In the ordinary course of life, however, *yin* and *yang* become mixed with each other in complicated ways, and also gradually are lost through dispersal outside the organism, resulting in aging, decline, and death. The passage above about the baby concludes: "Something that grows old while still in its prime is said to be not in accord with the Way. Not being in accord with the Way will lead to an early demise." The next conceptual step taken by the Inner Elixir Daoists was a bold one, and in tension if not in contradiction with the lyrical acceptance of natural processes characteristic of the ancient Daoist masters. If one understood natural processes and learned how to pay close attention to them, one could use them to *reverse* their apparent natural tendencies. The natural flows of bodily fluids that ordinarily contributed to mixing of *yin* and *yang*, corruption, decay, and death could be brought to consciousness, controlled, and their directions *reversed*, until ultimately a repurified true *yin* and true *yang* met within the body to form an incorruptible, immortal embryo, which could be nurtured into growth until it was ready to leave the body and live an independent and eternal existence.

Daoism, in addition to its embodiedness and fascination with the phenomena of the physical world, always has been aware that the same realities can be talked about and experienced in many different ways. As the Daoist grows in wisdom and spiritual power he or she pays less attention to these differences and mixes vocabularies and forms of experience more easily. The Inner Elixir scriptures use several languages to describe these processes of reversal and reunion; all of them focus on the body of the meditator. The fluids produced by various organs are classified according to the five powers scheme, and their relations to each other are explained by its sequences. The *yin* and *yang* are referred to by the alchemical terms mercury and lead. The processes of smelting and purification that lead to the production of true mercury and true lead, true *yin* and true *yang*, take place primarily in three cinnabar fields (*dan tian*) in the lower and upper abdomen and in the head. There is an elaborate internal geography of paths, channels, and gates, all presided over by gods and their servants and gate-keepers.

There seem to be two ways in which *yin* and *yang* are purified and then brought together. In one of them the *yang* essence, still mixed with *yin*, retained by sexual abstinence or properly controlled sexual activity, is consciously moved up a channel in the spine—*reversing* its normal flow down and out—to the brain, where it is forced down by constant swallowing of the saliva to join with the *yin* in the middle cinnabar field. In the other, the true *yang* is prepared in the lower cinnabar field and the true *yin* in the middle. In their ordinary "natural" positions *yang* is above and *yin* below, and the dissipation of their perfect harmony is aggravated by the tendency of *yang* to rise and *yin* to sink. This *reversed* position, in harmony with the early Daoist wisdom that preferred the feminine virtues and characteristics summed up in the "valley spirit," places true *yin* and true *yang* in positions where their natural rising and sinking bring them together to form the Immortal Embryo, in triumphant *reversal* of the inevitable processes of decay and death.

There is yet another level of ambiguity and, to the noninitiate, confusion in the texts of the Inner Elixir school. In some versions of these teachings it seems that the production of the immortal substance within the body is the product not of a harmonious blending and mutual purification of *yin* and *yang*, both conceived of as essential to life at any level, but of the smelting out of all *yin*, leaving a pure *yang* immortal substance. In one sermon before the great khagan, Qiu Chuji seems to have been following this line of thinking.

This is a bare summary of a process that is thought to require years of total concentration. Each step is accompanied by sensations of warmth and light within the body. The signs must occur at the right times and in the right way. The meditator carefully raises and lowers the heat of each of the purification processes and guides the circulation of the gradually purifying essences.

Many readers will find these images and practices bizarre and baffling. We can never be sure how literally they were taken by some of the people who followed them. For some the body itself became a set of metaphors, the organs, essences, and internal gods giving focus and substance to their quests for spiritual insight and tranquility. Many aspects of the practices taught and the experiences reported are quite similar to those of Hindu Yoga and other mystical traditions. Modern students, especially Joseph Needham, the greatest Western historian of Chinese science, have pointed out the intuitive anticipations of modern concepts of circulation of bodily fluids and of the contributions of various organs to the complex chemistry of the bloodstream. Daoist-related practices of diet, exercise, and sexual moderation or abstinence have been followed in moderate forms by many Chinese down to the present, and probably do contribute to the long and healthy lives of many followers.

Qiu Chuji was a disciple of the founder of a particular branch of Daoism, one of a number of new schools or sects that arose in the 1100s and 1200s in North China. In these times there were thinkers and teachers who followed only Confucianism, or only Buddhism, or only Daoism and had nothing but contempt for the other two great teachings. But there also were many who, while centering their teachings in one of the three, had a good deal of interest in the others and in fact borrowed from them more or less consciously. Some even insisted that the three great teachings really all had a common origin, or a common goal, or a common set of basic principles. The new Daoist sects in north China inclined toward some measure of "Three Teachings" syncretism in part because they emerged in a period of foreign rule, as the Jurchen Jin dynasty ruled the north and then gave way to the rising power of the Mongols. In these circumstances, Han Chinese intellectuals tended to see themselves as guardians of all facets of the Chinese heritage in the face of the political power and cultural contamination of the foreign rulers. They also needed all the tools of moral persuasion, religious mystique, and magic arts they could lay their hands on if they wished to obtain from the foreign rulers a measure of toleration for themselves and their beleaguered people. The Jin actually made conscientious efforts to provide a stable Chinese-style government and to woo the Chinese elite, using many Chinese forms of government and even holding examinations, but never before had so much of China been ruled be a dynasty not of Han Chinese culture and language. Bitter memories of the disgraceful collapse of the 1120s made the situation even harder to accept. Then after 1210, as the Mongols began to take and hold Chinese territory, the people of north China learned that there were situations far worse than Jin rule.

Wang Zhe, the founder of the sect to which Qiu belonged, was a member of an elite family that had a good reputation in its home area for helping the poor in hard times. He was a restless young man with a classical education and a fascination with warfare, much like Yue Fei a few decades earlier. It was said that he once held military office under the Jin, but then resigned, abandoned his family, and lived the life of a drunken drop-out until, about 1159, he had a series of uncanny encounters with strangers who turned out to be Daoist immortals. He dug a grave and lived in it for three years, then lived in a nearby hut for four more years. In 1167 he went to Shandong, prime breeding ground for Daoist teachers and movements since Warring States times, and began to teach. The disciplines of the quest for the Inner Elixir were central to his teaching, but unlike most earlier Daoist masters he insisted that complete celibacy was essential for progress in the quest. This may have been one of a number of ways in which he was influenced by Buddhism; he also used Chan ideas in his disciplines of meditation and declared the Buddhist *Heart Sutra* and the Confucian *Xiao jing* (Classic of Filial Piety) to be works of spiritual teaching as great as the *Dao de jing*. His teachings on the importance of single-minded study and concentration, on the choice of the right companions for one's quest, on doing charitable good works, and on finally achieving the tranquility and insight of the Way of the Sage are full of echoes of and parallels to Confucian teachings. But he seems to have had none of the Confucian interest in improving politics or lecturing rulers, and there is no evidence that he had any relations with the Jin court. He also was much less interested than most great Daoists in the use of magical powers to control nature.

In several places in Shandong congregations of the followers of Wang Zhe were formed. All had the phrase *san jiao*, "three teachings," in their names. Soon, however, the name Quanzhen, "Completion [*Quan*] of [the teachings for becoming] the Perfected [Man; *zhen ren*,]" was used for his teachings, suggesting both their Inner Elixir core and their rounding out by elements of the other two great teachings.

Out of many who honored him and followed his teachings he judged only seven to be fit to be his disciples. Two of them, man and wife, separated as they began their pursuit of the Way. All became important teachers. It is not surprising to find a woman among the seven disciples; some of Daoism's most profound formulations preferred female virtues and attitudes to male. All seven followed Wang in complete celibacy and an extremely meager and harsh way of life, including a hundred days of retreat and meditation every winter during which the seekers were not supposed to sleep at all. One, it was said, sat on a bridge for three years, eating only when people brought him something. When someone pushed him off the bridge he sat under it for another three years, not moving even when the waters rose to his waist.

Qiu Chuji was one of the seven original disciples of Wang Zhe. He was said to have been from a poor family and little educated, but under Wang's influence he soon was learning a thousand characters a day and was put in charge of composing documents. Wang Zhe gave him the name Chuji, "Abiding in the Subtle Beginning." He gave himself the name Changchun, "Long Spring," with its wonderful evocation of the faith that the springtime of life could be greatly lengthened even for those who could not ultimately escape the autumn and winter of aging and death; "Perfected Man" was a respectful title used to address him by his followers and disciples and ultimately even by the great khaghan Chinggis. His surviving writings show him taking the subtleties of the teaching of the Inner Elixir very seriously. But when he was talking to someone of little intellectual or spiritual cultivation, like the great khaghan, he was capable of drawing on all of the Three Teachings and a great deal of common sense.

In 1187–88 Qiu was one of two Quanzhen leaders summoned to the Jin court. In an audience with the emperor, Qiu declared that he was willing to teach his sovereign the full meaning of the "Spirit of the Valley" passage from the *Dao de jing*, but first the emperor would have to observe the rules of the Quanzhen sect, including sexual abstinence. The emperor was unwilling to do this for even three days, and the matter was dropped. Still the emperor sent a plate of peaches to Qiu, and although Qiu had not taken fruit or tea for more than ten years he ate one in recognition of the honor.

Much later, in 1216, Qiu rejected another summons to the Jin court, as well as one from the Southern Song emperor in 1219. By that time Jin was fighting for survival, and Southern Song was looking no stronger. Chinese rebels against the Jin in Shandong might have made real progress against the Jin if they had been fully supported by the Southern Song, and even without that support they caused the northern regime a great deal of trouble. But the real threat came from the north, as Western Xia and Jin became the first sedentary states to experience the power of the Mongol cavalry, a power that would dominate the history of the Eurasian world for the next two hundred years.

Since the rise of the Xiongnu in Warring States times, the mounted archers of the steppe had been a constant challenge to Chinese diplomacy and military organization. In its purest form the life of the nomadic herdsman, living off the meat, milk, wool, and hides of his flocks, required no literacy and few products of agriculture or sophisticated handcrafts. Superb horsemen and archers, the men of the steppe might keep in practice by stealing horses or women or avenging old wrongs in attacks on their steppe neighbors. But they also could be brought together by a gifted leader into a vast, highly disciplined army that could move with astonishing speed and strike where they were least expected. The people of the steppe might know nothing of city life or of the ruling and exploitation of an agricultural population, but they all understood trade: the protection of and extortion from caravans, the devastation of a trading town by the disruption of its trade. Traders brought to the nomad camps news of political changes of the settled world and of its great religions: Buddhism, Islam, Christianity.

The unification and rise to power of the Mongols took place within the lifetime of Qiu Chuji and was largely the work of his younger contemporary, the great khaghan Chinggis. In the Mongol epics the future great khaghan is portrayed rising from dire poverty, including times as a hunted fugitive, by a long succession of hard-fought battles, enemies pursued and crushed, rivals eliminated, and loyal allies treated with great generosity. Chinese epics like *Three Kingdoms* and *Water Margin* have their share of blood, vengeance, loyalty, and betrayal, but rarely is the hunter's lust for the kill as close to the surface as in the Mongol tales. In the descriptions of individuals and the reports of their speeches we sense the raw power and eloquence of men who lived every day with hardship, danger, and the threat of violence. We also get a keen sense of the beauty and harshness of the steppe, of the physical stamina and courage needed to fight (or flee) across it. Chinggis, in his courage, tactical brilliance, flawless judgment of men, stunning impulsive generosity to the loyal, and wolflike savagery in hunting down his enemies, was as much a product of his harsh and dangerous external world as Qiu Chuji was of his years of intense cultivation of his internal landscape.

Chinggis made at least one short-term alliance with the Jin, but in the longer run he was determined to avenge the grisly death at their hands of some Mongol envoys. His long struggle to unify the Mongol peoples culminated in a great assembly of princes and chiefs in 1206 at which he was named the great khaghan, or king of kings. All the people under his rule were formed into a great hierarchy of military units, beginning with squads of ten soldiers each and rising by multiples of ten to commanders of ten thousand. A whole branch of this vast structure, with its families, flocks, wagons, and craftspeople, could move from place to place and set up a great, orderly camp, or the cavalry could be sent off, each rider with five mounts, changing mounts and living off the milk and blood of their horses, on campaigns that could cover more ground per day than any other striking force before the present century.

The first sedentary state to confront this frightening menace was the Tangut-ruled Western Xia kingdom in northwest China. Three Mongol campaigns were enough to persuade the Western Xia king to acknowledge Mongol overlordship. Jin was harder, especially because the Mongols had neither experience in nor equipment for sieges of frontier defenses or walled cities. But in 1214 the Mongol armies were before the Jin capital, on the site of modern Beijing, and withdrew only after the Jin gave them massive gifts. The Jin emperor then withdrew his court further south, to the old Northern Song capital at Kaifeng on the Yellow River. The Han Chinese people of Shandong revolted against a Jin regime that seemed to be on its last legs. But despite the superior striking power of the Mongol cavalry, the Jin regime clung to life. One reason for its survival was that the Song were extremely ambivalent about either allying with the Mongols or helping Shandong rebels they could not control.

Chinggis, leaving some very capable generals to pursue the frustrating war against the Jin, now turned his attention westward. There the advance of his armies had brought him to Kashgar, now on the western edge of China's province of Xinjiang, where the people were largely Muslim. Across the mountains, in what are now the Muslim republics of the former Soviet Union, the kings of Khwarezm ruled the magnificent ancient trading cities of Bokhara and Samarkand and most of what is now Afghanistan and Iran. Chinggis seems to have moved cautiously into this completely new world, with its different languages and religious and cultural allegiances of which the Mongols knew nothing. He apparently hoped to develop peaceful trade with Khwarezm, and sent ambassadors with a rich caravan. But after a Khwarezm official killed the ambassadors and plundered the caravan, Chinggis led his main armies west. The Mongol armies took both Bokhara and Samarkand in 1220, slaughtering their garrisons, sparing most of the people, looting and burning. The last king of Khwarezm was pursued across what now are Afghanistan and Iran, leading to the destruction of several fine desert cities and their fragile irrigation systems. He died near the Caspian Sea; one part of the pursuing armies then went on in an incredible reconnaissance expedition into the fringes of what is now the Ukraine and back east across the steppes.

Qiu Chuji probably spent most of the years of these astonishing dramas in silent and disciplined retreat, rarely sleeping, controlling his breathing, all his senses turned inward toward the circulation and purification of the *yin* and *yang* in his body. One record, however, says that in the fall of 1214 he intervened to secure the submission to the Jin of a group of "Red Coat Rebels" in Shandong; perhaps these rebels were in some way associated with the Quanzhen congregations in that area. The same name was used for the rebels who became much more powerful in that area a few years later. In the chaotic conditions of the next few years, every power-holder sought Qiu's favor; he refused invitations to the courts of Jin and of Southern Song and to the headquarters of the local "loyalist" forces who had revolted against the Jin and were holding most of Shandong in nominal allegiance to the Southern Song. But then at the end of 1219 one Liu Wen arrived at the head of a troop of twenty Mongol horsemen. Liu was a specialist in herbal medicine who served the great khaghan; he may have been the first to stimulate Chinggis's interest in Qiu by telling him that the Master was three hundred years old. Qiu promptly agreed to set out on the immense journey. In refusing invitations from other rulers he had said that his movements were controlled by Heaven; "When the time comes to go, I shall go." But we may also suspect that he had enough mental energy left over from his meditations to give a bit of thought to the political situation, and preferred to deal with the rising power, not the fading ones.

Qiu's party made its way northeast, stopping at Yanjing, the old Jin capital, where vast crowds came to ask him to give them a poem or a name or to accept them as his disciples. Qiu had thought he was setting out to visit the khaghan in the Mongol homeland, not too long a journey from the Chinese frontier. Now he found that the khaghan was far away in the heart of Asia. Worse still, because of unsettled conditions in and around Western Xia, his party would not be able to take the straight line out toward the Silk Road and the oases of Central Asia but would head north-northeast into the steppe before turning west. Qiu sent a message off to the great khaghan asking to be excused from the terrible journey because of his age. He spent the summer in the mountains northwest of Yanjing; by the time he received Chinggis's reply insisting that he come it was fall, and he remained there until the following spring. Although the Quanzhen masters in general were not excessively interested in magical powers, Qiu was said to have them in abundance. A ceremony he performed in the capital was followed immediately by rain ending a worrisome dry spell. When a huge crowd collected outside a temple where he was conducting ceremonies he took pity on it, and a cloud like an umbrella came and shielded the crowd from the sun for hours.

In the spring of 1221 Qiu and his escorts set out into the steppe. A detailed account of the long journey, written by one of the disciples who accompanied the master, is one of the most famous pieces of travel literature in Chinese. The party passed by the edge of a great salt lake and crossed a stretch of sandy desert. Finally they came to the great camp of a Mongol prince. Qiu's description of the Mongols is observant, respectful, and not devoid of a tendency to romanticize the simplicity of the people of the steppe that goes back to Sima Qian's account of the Xiongnu, with a bit of extra Daoist idealization of primeval simplicity. "They have no writing. . . . Whatever food they get is shared among them, and if anyone is in trouble the others hasten to his assistance. They are obedient to orders and unfailing in their performance of a promise. They have indeed preserved the simplicity of primeval times."

The party now turned west, across grasslands and sometimes across high country where there were thick, dark pine forests and where, in midsummer, there was ice on the ground in the morning. At one point their trail led along the edge of a cliff, with a terrifying view down to a lake thousands of feet below. In July they stopped at a great settled camp presided over by one of the wives of the great khaghan. "The palanquins, pavilions, and other splendors of this camp would certainly have astonished the rulers of the old Xiongnu." On they pushed, through a dust storm and across great sand dunes, like a ship climbing over one huge wave after another. Some of the wildest stretches were said to be the abodes of evil spirits, but the Master, not denying the reality of spirits but showing that the powers of the Daoist were superior to theirs, said "Do you not know that ghosts and evil spirits fly from the presence of honest men? . . . And if this is true of ordinary people, the followers of the Dao ought surely not to be afraid." Now they began to come to Uighur towns, where they were greeted with warm hospitality and presents of the wonderful grape wine, fruits, and melons produced in these oases. There were several more mountain ranges to cross, including the one with the great valley, road, and bridges described at the beginning of this chapter. Now they were in Muslim country, where there were no more Buddhist or Daoist temples and everyone "worshipped the western quarter" (bowed toward Mecca in prayer).

On December 3, 1221, the party entered Samarkand. The city had only about a quarter of the population it had had before the Mongol conquest and massacres, but was far from dead. The Mongol governor at first had lived in the old palace of the kings of Khwarezm, but there was so much disorder (or sporadic resistance) in the city that he now lived across the river. Qiu and his party, undaunted or less menaced by anti-Mongol feeling, found quarters in the palace. They were much impressed with the system of diversion canals that sent fresh water in channels down both sides of every street. Chinese craftspeople, taken in the conquest of various Chinese cities and brought here in service to the Mongols, were delighted to welcome Qiu and his party. The great khaghan was off to the south, commanding the pursuit of the last king of Khwarezm, and it would not be possible to get across the high passes to his camp until spring.

As spring came Qiu and his party took many walks in the country, admiring the blossoming almond trees and the rich promise of the irrigated fields. Qiu dropped his reserve and meditative austerity, chatting, enjoying picnics, and exchanging poems with anyone with a Chinese education. Prominent among them was Yelü Chucai, the great khaghan's Chinese secretary and leading adviser on understanding and governing the Chinese. In Yelü's collected works there are forty-four poems written in response to themes and meters set by Qiu in this pleasant interlude. Qiu's party also demonstrated the great Daoist tradition of compassion for those in need, providing food and other support for many destitute people in the city.

Then the snow was melting on the passes and Qiu was off, through great canyons and over snow-covered heights, to the camp of the great khaghan, somewhere in the region of modern Kabul, Afghanistan. The camp was reached in May. The great lord and the great teacher were a study in contrasts. Chinggis was at least ten years younger, but probably looked and felt older, with his many scars and broken bones, his high-protein and high-fat diet, and the endless pleasures of his harem. What did this amazingly light-footed and alert old man know? Was he really three hundred years old? Chinggis had faced death and escaped more times than he could remember. Did this strange man have a secret, a drug, that would allow him to escape death once and for all?

"What medicine of long life have you brought me from afar?"

"I have means of protecting life, but no elixir that will prolong it."

The great khaghan may have been impressed; people did not often tell him so plainly that he was not going to get what he wanted. He had a tent set up near his for Qiu and his party. More discussions were planned, but then Chinggis decided he had to deal in person with some local resistance in the mountains, and the discussions would have to be postponed. Qiu Chuji returned to Samarkand, where he dealt very sensibly with the heat of the desert summer, bathing in a cool lake and sleeping on the flat roof of his quarters. He and his party noted the daytime fast and nighttime feasting of the month of Ramadan, the calls to prayer from the minarets, and the huge numbers of worshippers who assembled for public prayers. But there is no evidence that they tried to learn about the teachings of Islam. Islam already had put down roots in a few places in China in the 1200s, notably in Quanzhou on the south coast, Xi'an, Kaifeng, and Yanjing, but very few non-Muslim Chinese have ever shown much interest in its history and teachings.

Qiu Chuji and his party rejoined the great khaghan in September 1222 and moved about with him until April 1223. He had many conversations with the great khaghan. Before the first of them he informed the khaghan's courtiers that Daoist masters did not kneel or prostrate themselves before emperors but simply made a slight bow; Chinggis agreed to this procedure. Chinggis was very cordial and asked Qiu to take all his meals with him, but Qiu declined, stating that he had spent so many years in solitude that he was at ease only by himself. Later he was allowed to travel a little ahead or behind the imperial party so that he would be less troubled by the noise.

Qiu Chuji must have had to draw on all his reserves of patience and mental discipline to continue his efforts to enlighten his awesome pupil. Chinggis was very intelligent but had absolutely no book-learning or experience with abstract religious discussion. As far as we know he was illiterate. Qiu was trying to present to him elements of the many-layered teachings of the Inner Elixir school and of their basic harmony with Buddhism and Confucianism. There is a full record of only one of their sessions, that of November 19, 1222. In it, Qiu explains that the Dao is the origin of all things.

> Most men know only the greatness of heaven; they do not understand the greatness of the Dao. My sole object in living all my life separated from my family and in the monastic state has been to study this question.
>
> When the Dao produced Heaven and Earth, they in turn opened up and produced Humanity. When man was first born he shone with a holy radiance of his own and his step was so light that it was as if he flew. The earth bore fungoids that were moist and sweet-tasting. Without waiting to roast or cook them, man ate them all raw; at this time nothing was cooked for eating. The fungoids were all sweet-tasting. Man with his nose smelt their smell and with his mouth tasted their taste. Gradually his body grew heavy and his holy light grew dim. This was because his appetite and longing were so keen. Those who study the Dao must learn not to desire the things other men desire, not to live in the places where other men live. . . . If there is any attachment [to concrete things] the follower of Dao will fail to understand it or its operations. If the eye sees pleasant sights or the ear hears pleasant sounds, if the mouth enjoys pleasant tastes or the natural state is perturbed by emotions, then the original spirit is scattered and lost . . . .
>
> The male we call *yang*; its element is fire. The female we call *yin*; its element is water. But *yin* can quench *yang*; water conquers fire. Therefore the Daoist must above all repress sexual desire.

Ordinary worries and pursuits lead to some loss of spiritual vitality, but nothing like the loss that results from unrestrained sexual activity. Since *yang* is akin to heaven and *yin* to earth, if man nurtures the *yang* in himself he can rise up to heaven and become an immortal, just as a flame rises. But if common people who have only one wife can ruin themselves by excessive indulgence, what must happen to monarchs whose palaces are filled with concubines? I learned recently that Liu Wen had been commissioned to search . . . for women to fill your harem. Now I have read in the *Dao de jing* that not to see things which arouse desire keeps the mind free from disorders. Once such things have been seen, it is hard indeed to exercise self-restraint. I would have you keep this in mind.

After explaining briefly the main lines of the history of the Daoist teaching and the Quanzhen school, Qiu returns to his main theme. All rulers, he explains, are supernatural beings who have been exiled from heaven. If they are virtuous on earth, when they return to heaven they will be given a higher rank than before. He urges Chinggis to try sleeping alone for a month, and assures him that there will be an amazing improvement in his physical and mental energy. There is an old saying that "to take medicine for a thousand days does less good than to lie alone for a single night." The great khaghan has many sons and does not need to worry about producing more.

This was not very welcome advice, and it seems that Chinggis never followed it. But at least it was relevant to the subject of long life, on which the Daoists were supposed to be experts. Chinggis may have been a bit surprised when his singular teacher, who had spent many years in minimal contact with other humans, now turned to politics. Qiu urged that an honest official with good knowledge of Chinese ways of governing be sent to Shandong and the other newly conquered areas with orders to work out a plan to remit the taxes from those provinces for three years. He reminded the khaghan that the Jin in the early years of their conquest of the north had made good use of a puppet regime under Liu Yu as a transitional stage to Jin rule. Reminding Chinggis that he also had been honored by the Jin court, he returned to his main theme, claiming that the Jin emperor to whom he advised sexual abstinence had taken the advice and had found his health much improved. (It is not at all clear, of course, that the Jin emperor took his advice; in any case, he died the year after his interview with Qiu.)

The imperial party paused for some weeks near Samarkand and then continued to the east. There are fragments of Qiu's discourses to the khaghan on Mongol customs that needed reforming and on filial piety. On March 11, 1223, the khaghan was seriously hurt when he fell from his horse while hunting. Qiu urged him to go hunting as little as possible, but Chinggis said that was impossible for a Mongol. Not long thereafter Qiu took his leave of the imperial party, receiving as a final splendid honor an imperial decree exempting all his followers from taxation.

Qiu did not repeat the wide swing through the steppes but headed straight east, reaching the northwest frontier of China in August. A Mongol official asked him to intercede to persuade the people of Shandong to give full allegiance to the Mongols, for if the khaghan sent a great army much life surely would be lost. After much hesitation Qiu sent one of his disciples with the official to transmit his advice not to resist the Mongols. He made his way slowly across north China, performing great ceremonies and received everywhere with respect. He accepted an invitation to take up residence in Yanjing and was greeted by a great crowd when he arrived there in January 1224. He received many messages from Chinggis inquiring if he was being well treated. "Since you went away, I have not forgotten you for a single day. I hope you do not forget me. If there is any place in all my realms where you would particularly like to be, you have only to say so, and you shall live there. I wish your disciples to recite the scriptures continually on my behalf and to pray for my longevity." In addition to the tax exemption granted to Qiu's followers, an edict soon arrived giving him authority over all who "had left the world" and taken up the monastic life, both Daoist and Buddhist. The great khagan had not been ready to follow his teachings, but still may have sensed something of his spiritual power, and also seems to have decided he would be a useful intermediary in dealing with the religious leaders of northern China.

These privileges, powers, and signs of imperial favor contributed to a great surge of interest in the Quanzhen teachings, many lay people joining congregations at Quanzhen temples. Qiu and his followers now began to take advantage of their privileged position. They took over and renovated abandoned Buddhist temples, then evicted Buddhist monks from others, and turned them all into Daoist temples. Refugees from the terrible wars and disruptions in the countryside were lodged and fed in the temples. The tax exemption for Quanzhen followers was very useful in protecting the poor, but also attracted many unprincipled and opportunistic followers. Sensing the possibility of final victory in their long struggle with the Buddhists, the Daoists began to use every weapon at their command. They particularly outraged the Buddhists by spreading the old story that Lao Zi had gone out beyond the western frontiers and taught a few barbarians, and that one of these barbarian pupils had become the Buddha!

Qiu Chuji certainly is not free of blame for this astonishing politicization of his apparently austere and apolitical teaching, but he saw only the first stages of the process, dying early in 1228. Quanzhen Daoism remained very powerful in the Mongol-ruled areas of China until the 1250s, when Buddhist counterattacks and protests at Daoist abuses of power led to their ascendancy and the gradual decline of Daoist power. Tibetan Lamaists, followers of a particularly vivid and powerful form of Mahayana

Buddhism, became very influential, beginning the influence of Lamaism among the Mongols that has continued down to the present.

In 1234 the Mongols, abetted by Song neutrality and grain supplies, finished off the last remnant of the Jin. Then their main forces swept west again, conquering Persia, modern Iraq and Syria, and the Russian principalities, and making a frightening foray into Poland and the German eastern frontier, where they seem to have found little worth occupying. Then they turned their attention back to Southern Song. Its fortified cities and fleets on the Yangzi and the south coast made it, perhaps the least militaristic in ethos of any thirteenth-century society, the toughest nut to crack in all Eurasia. The Mongols took the Southern Song capital at Hangzhou in 1276; the last resistance fleet was defeated near modern Hong Kong in 1279. The Mongols already had proclaimed a Chinese-style state, with the dynastic name Yuan. The Yuan ruled all of China from 1279 until 1368. It held examinations and made other gestures toward the Confucian tradition, but many non-Chinese assisted the Mongols in their rule, opportunities for Chinese literary men were meager, and taxes were unusually high.

Daoism has survived down to our own time in the form of various lines of authority and teaching passed down from master to master. The White Cloud Monastery in Beijing where a hall was built in Qiu's memory maintained a coherent and disciplined community down into the twentieth century. Today it houses the offices of the Chinese Daoist Association; I attended a splendid ceremony there on a cold winter day early in 1985. In Taiwan several branches of Daoism play vigorous and sophisticated roles in the intense popular religious life. After the collapse of Mongol rule in China Daoism entered court politics only on one occasion, when a sixteenth-century emperor became fascinated with its charms and spells.

This rather patchy picture of organizational coherence and influence is not an adequate measure of the continuing impact of Daoism in Chinese culture. The cryptic wisdom of the *Dao de jing* and the brilliance of the *Zhuang zi* have never ceased to attract readers and explainers, good Confucians, modernizers, and Communists as well as acknowledged Daoists. Daoist ideas of breath control, sexual control, and exercise have influenced the daily practices of immense numbers. They are fundamental to the widely practiced exercise systems like *tai ji quan* and *qi gong*. Daoist naturalism and the boldness of Daoist hopes for "reversing the flow" and overcoming the unwanted effects of natural processes may have contributed to the great interest in modern science and the high hopes for social transformation on scientific principles seen in twentieth-century China. Perhaps its compassion for the downtrodden and contempt for worldly prestige and authority have contributed in some degree to the social conscience and political dissent of our time. Qiu Chuji, Perfected Man of the Long

Spring, made his peace with political power in a big way in his last years. But it is best to remember him, with the face and movement of a younger man and a mind sharpened by years of mental discipline, refusing to kneel in the splendid tent of the fearsome conqueror, giving him lessons he did not want to hear, and trying to obtain some breathing room for the beleaguered people of north China.

13

WANG YANGMING

· · · · · ·

ALTHOUGH Wang Yangming lived over four hundred years after Su Dongpo, the patterns of their lives as scholar-officials seem remarkably similar. Both were students of the Confucian Classics, products of the examination system. Both owed much of their fame to their writings and their ideas, not to their political achievements. Both plunged into political controversy, were exiled as a result, but later returned to positions of considerable influence. Both were effective and innovative local officials.

As we look more closely, some striking differences appear. Su once feared execution, but few Song statesmen died for their convictions or misdeeds. Wang was beaten in court, may have been pursued by assassins, and was in some very dangerous situations late in his career. Where Su's learning had been many-sided, specific, perhaps a bit scattered, his language rich and exuberant, Wang pursued with single-minded simplicity and intensity a few of the central puzzles of the Confucian moral life.

These great differences were in part the results of changes in culture and politics that already had begun in the 1000s but reached full development only in the Ming dynasty (1368–1644). The power and status of the highest ministers had declined from Tang to Song, as aristocrats with military training and values were replaced by scholar-officials with no secure family prestige and no military skills. A mode of political discourse that insisted that every emperor ought to become a sage, and sometimes expressed itself as if he already was one, was linked to a style of political action in which one of the surest routes to fame was fearless criticism of the misguided policies or personal failings of the ruler that were keeping him from fulfilling his sagely potential. We have seen some of this in Su Dongpo's own writings, but it was much more central and insistent in the arguments of some of the more dogmatic Confucians with whom he could not get along in the "postreform" government of 1085–91. In the most famous of them, Cheng Yi, it was inseparable from new intellectual trends in which Su did not participate and which became basic to the elite culture of China down to the present century.

Our Western shorthand term for these trends is "Neo-Confucianism." The most common Chinese term is *lixue*, the study of principle. It began in the late Tang reaction against Buddhism and developed in Song times into an intellectually ambitious quest for Confucian answers to questions about the nature of reality and knowledge that had not been central in early Confucianism but had been insistently raised by Buddhism. Where Buddhism asserted that human life was a fabric of vain desires and delusions, Neo-Confucian philosophy of man focused on Mencius's teaching that human nature is fundamentally good. Where Buddhism saw impermanence and illusion in the world around us, Neo-Confucianism saw knowable and unchanging *li* (not the same character as the Confucian concept of "ceremony"), patterns or principles, in everything. Early Song scholars, with their great diversity of interests, discussed all kinds of *li*, but the ones that mattered most were the unchanging principles of human conduct and social organization. This can be seen especially clearly in the teachings of Cheng Yi, one of the towering figures of Neo-Confucian philosophy and a dogmatic opponent of the reforms of Wang Anshi.

Cheng's name usually is linked with that of the Southern Song master Zhu Xi, who brought Neo-Confucian thought to a new pitch of moral intensity and clarity of focus; Zhu's ideas were not widely accepted in his own time, but became recognized as the orthodox interpretation of the Confucian Way, mandatory for examination essays, under the Yuan and remained so until the abolition of the examination system in 1905. The Cheng–Zhu synthesis laid great stress on the "Four Books": the *Analects* of Confucius, the *Mencius*, and two works claiming to present parts of the teachings of Confucius, the *Doctrine of the Mean* and the *Great Learning*. One passage in the *Great Learning* was especially important, providing a set of problems and even a vocabulary fundamental to an understanding of Neo-Confucianism in general and Wang Yangming in particular. The ancients, it says, wishing to establish peace and virtuous government throughout the world, had to begin with the investigation of things (*ge wu*). Only on that foundation could knowledge be extended (*zhi*); only on that foundation could thoughts be made sincere, then in sequence minds rectified, persons cultivated, families regulated, states well governed, and the entire world brought to peace.

This insistence on the priority of moral purity and the setting of good examples over all considerations of profit, power, and practical policy is of course a genuine heritage of Confucius, even if it is not at all likely that the *Great Learning* is an authentic record of his words. We have seen how it took on new life in the politics of the broader elite in early Song, especially in the moralistic opposition to Wang Anshi of Cheng Yi and others. The reinforcement of this Confucian bias by political circumstance continued in the Southern Song, Yuan, and early Ming. The great causes of reconquest of the north and militant opposition to compromise with the Jin were vehemently maintained by many in the Southern Song elite, including Zhu Xi himself. Under the Yuan some high-principled scholars maintained their purity by living quietly with their students in isolated areas. Others found in the focus of Zhu Xi's teachings on a few texts and a few basic moral issues just what was needed to begin to spread a bit of Confucian teaching in the suspicious and multicultural atmosphere of the Yuan court.

The early Ming state was much farther from Confucian ideals of government than the Song had been, but in many ways it did not suppress but nourished Neo-Confucian moralism. It was born of reactions, both elite and popular, against the harshness and alienness of Mongol rule. In the early 1360s Chinese rebel warlords fought among themselves for control of the Yangzi valley. Then in 1368 the victor turned his armies north to drive the decrepit Yuan regime out of north China and to bring all of China back under a single Chinese sovereign for the first time since the fall of the Tang. This Taizu, first emperor of the Ming, had risen from beggardom in a peasant rebel army held together by Buddhist millennarian faith and hostility to the traditional elite, had been shrewd enough to realize that he could not govern the empire without the political support and expert advice of the scholar-officials, but remained wary of their ability to do things their own way through bureaucratic politics and had no use at all for their pretensions to moral autonomy and the right to criticize the ruler and his policies. The scholars found him alarming and dangerous to be around, but capable of imposing law and order after the chaos and the hostility to the elite that had been so widespread in the 1350s. They needed each other.

Moreover, the Ming founders, emperor and officials, shared in the general revulsion against foreign rule and the compensatory reassertion of the superiority of every Chinese value and institution. One important expression of this was the insistence that all foreign contact with China take the form of carefully managed embassies bearing "tribute" and acknowledging the supremacy of the Son of Heaven. Another was the comprehensive establishment of local directors of studies with students under them who had to pass an examination to gain the status of "official student" (shengyuan). The examination system thus gained the full three-tier form—local, provincial, capital—that it would retain until 1905. Shengyuan status carried a useful exemption from labor service but no right to office; it functioned to tie local elites to career-seeking through the examination system much more closely than they had been under the Song. And the orthodoxy of Zhu Xi's interpretations of the Classics for use in the examination system was reaffirmed.

The Ming dynasty carried much further the trend toward despotism—

concentration of power in the person of the ruler and limitation of the independent action of ministers—detected as far back as the reign of Empress Wu. Taizu executed one prime minister who he believed had been involved in a plot against him, and went on to abolish the office of prime minister, so that from that time on the bureaucracy functioned without a single senior minister at its head; the emperor had to keep up with much more administrative detail, assisted by middle-rank officials called grand secretaries who had no secure authority of their own. The third emperor came to power by a successful rebellion against his nephew the second emperor and continued the concentration of power in his own hands. It was he who, in violation of the founder's warnings, began to make extensive use of eunuchs as his private political agents outside the palace. Eunuchs, usually of lower-class origin and with few or no family ties, loathed by the scholar-officials, were the ideal tools of a despot. Scholar-official protest against their interference in government and eunuch suppression of such protest were regular features of Ming politics.

Confucius had taught that the gentleman is not a tool or ceremonial vessel but an independent moral agent and bearer of a great moral tradition. Ming history, however, shows a more complex and ambiguous relation between the Confucian heritage and despotism than that principle would suggest. Confucius's teaching had focused attention on the personal character and moral example of the ruler, and this tendency had been heightened by the moral absolutism of some of the opponents of Wang Anshi and by the insistent Neo-Confucian focus on the self-cultivation-first teaching of the *Great Learning*. It was a short step, which even Su Dongpo took sometimes, from telling the emperor he could be a sage to asserting that he already was one. "Sage" and "sagely" were regular epithets of the Ming emperors, in actuality a most unimpressive line of individuals. And this concentration on the morality of the ruler and of the minister deprived the protesting minister of any recourse to arguments of practicality, institutional stability and regularity, or the human needs and moral rights of individual ministers. The protesting minister stood before his all-powerful ruler and the ruler's ruthless agents knowing that his only hope of accomplishing anything was for his selfless, principled protest to arouse many similar protests by other scholars and officials. That could and did happen. It might be more likely to happen if he became a martyr, beaten bloody in public in the palace courtyards, tortured by the eunuch secret police, assassinated on his way to exile at a frontier post. But success or failure in mobilizing opinion and changing policy was not his central consideration. Above all he was acting out a moral drama, demonstrating his selflessness and purity of will. And as with Confucius's political frustrations, Sima Qian's bitterness, and Yue Fei's nobility of failure, the drama was heightened, the selflessness more perfect, when nothing else was accomplished except to demonstrate one's firmness in principle in the face of futility, humiliation, and death. Given all this, it is scarcely surprising that the intellectual life of the first century and a half of the Ming was dominated by a cautious and studious adherence to Zhu Xi Neo-Confucianism, that discussion of matters of practical statecraft was conspicuous by its absence, and that some of the greatest teachers of Neo-Confucian self-cultivation never went near an examination hall and had no desire to become officials.

The man best known as Wang Yangming was born in 1472 into a family that claimed a proud lineage of scholars and high officials reaching back to Han times but had produced in Ming times a succession of high-minded scholarly hermits. His father was the number one graduate of the *jinshi* examination in the capital in 1481, an honor that put him on the fast track for a brilliant career and no doubt intensified the ambivalence of the son about the examinations and the official life. Such a family inevitably had high hopes that its sons would perform brilliantly on the examinations, have successful careers, and thus cast glory on all their ancestors. Wang's first childhood name was Yun, "Cloud," after a dream of his grandmother's suggesting that the child was a gift from Heaven. But Heaven's gift did not learn to talk until he was four or five years old. About the time he began to speak his grandfather gave him the wonderfully Confucian name Shouren, "Preserve Benevolence." Once he started talking he made good progress in school, but still showed many signs of idiosyncratic interests not appropriate to a future scholar-official. He would make flags and order his friends around as if he were the general of an army. When he was fourteen, living in Beijing with his father, he spent a month at Juyong Pass northwest of Beijing, where a magnificently carved gateway dating from Yuan times still stands today, learning all he could about frontier affairs and learning archery and other military skills from the Mongols. These military interests were of course completely beneath the dignity of a scholar-official.

Wang Shouren was married at the age of sixteen to the daughter of another high official family. On the day of the wedding he could not be found; frantic servants scoured the city. Finally he was found at a Daoist temple, carrying on a long and intense discussion of methods of "nourishing life" with one of the priests. Perhaps he was simply fleeing from an adult role for which he was not ready, or rebelling against his family's planning his whole life for him. Perhaps he was getting a few tips from the priest for his wedding night, since "nourishing life" included some special sexual practices. But it was not a "normal" way for a promising young man to behave.

In 1489, the year after his marriage, his intellectual development turned from conventional preparation for the examinations to the intensely personal quest of the Neo-Confucian tradition. He met a scholar named Lou Liang who lived withdrawn from official life and learned from him about Zhu Xi's doctrine of the primacy of the investigation of things and the conviction of all the great Neo-Confucians that in self-cultivation everyone should aim at becoming a sage, and not settle for any lower goal.

It probably was in 1492 that Wang and some of his friends decided to make a serious effort in the investigation of things. Zhu Xi and his followers were more interested in history and moral problems than in nature, but these young men, perhaps tired of their classical studies, settled down to try to study a clump of bamboo. After seven days they were exhausted, did not seem to be making any progress, and gave up. If this was just the investigation of one not very important thing, and so much studying and learning had to come first in the *Great Learning* tradition, how was anyone ever going to get on to the stages of moral self-cultivation and action, which were the ones that really mattered? This was the naive and unsystematic beginning of one of Wang's great intellectual quests.

Knowledge first and action later also was the rule imposed on the scholar-official elite by the examination system; one could not begin the only really important form of action, that of the civil official, until one had proved in the examinations an exhaustive mastery of classical texts and literary forms. Wang passed the provincial examination in 1492 at the respectable but not brilliant age of twenty, but then failed the *jin shi* examinations in the capital in 1493 and 1496. He had grave reservations about the memorization and formalism of the examination life and the self-congratulation and mindless routine of the high officials, but could not really break with his own elite upbringing. One Daoist from whom he sought instruction laughed at him because he could not drop the formal and arrogant "demeanor of an official."

Wang finally passed the *jinshi* examination in 1499 and spent the next three years in a variety of assignments, including supervising the building of a tomb and checking over criminal cases in the provinces. The tomb was for Wang Yue, a great frontier general whom he very much admired, and Wang Yue's family gave Wang Shouren his sword. He also boldly submitted a memorial to the emperor on military affairs. His eccentric fascination with the arts of war was very much alive.

Wang had never enjoyed robust health or steady nerves, and he seems to have found bureaucratic work frustrating, exhausting, and far from the road to sagehood. He requested sick leave, returned to his native Zhejiang, and spent most of the time from 1502 to 1504 living in a place called Yangming Valley, wandering in the mountains, and practicing Daoist techniques of meditation and "nourishing life." Seeking to break his ties with the world, he found that he could not get rid of his concerns about his father and grandmother, and he came to realize that filial piety was simply a part of the basic structure of the human mind. Later in this period of retirement, visiting one of the beautiful monasteries near Su Dongpo's West Lake, he encountered a Chan monk who had been sitting in meditation for three years without looking at anything or talking to anyone. Wang shouted at him, "This monk with his lips moving talks all the time. What does he say? With his eyes open, he looks at things all the time. What does he see?" The monk opened his eyes and began to talk. Wang asked him about his family and learned that his mother still was alive. "Do you ever miss her?" "It is impossible to eliminate these thoughts." Wang then drew on his own recent experiences to show the monk that filial piety really was part of his mind. The monk was moved to tears. When Wang asked about him the next day, he already had left for home.

Much of Wang's teaching and many of his greatest insights start from the understanding that social values and commitments are not external but are parts of the structure of our minds. This period and these insights were so important to him that he began to call himself the Master of Yangming, and he is still called Wang Yangming.

Wang Yangming returned to official life in 1504 and began to teach his new insights to growing numbers of students. But his new stability and success now were shattered by a typical episode of Ming politics. An irresponsible young emperor came to the throne in 1505, and the eunuchs who catered to his whims and took him on wild tours outside the palace quickly gained control of the supreme power. The central figure was Liu Jin, one of the most powerful and most hated eunuchs of the entire Ming dynasty. Large numbers of civil officials high and low submitted memorials condemning the situation. Liu Jin had some of the high officials thrown into prison. Wang Yangming was a junior official with no bureaucratic obligation to speak out about the situation, but a Confucian inability to remain silent in the sight of bad government. When he submitted a memorial protesting the imprisonments, he was imprisoned, beaten forty strokes in the palace courtyard, and dispatched to run a small courier station at Longchang, far off in the malarial mountains of Guizhou. Many strange stories are told about his trip to his distant new post. One says that he feared that he was being pursued by assassins and left his clothes beside the Qiantang River, hoping his pursuers would think he had drowned himself. Certainly he was shaken by the time in prison and the beating and afraid of the long, hard road ahead. Finally, after visiting his father, he seems to have come to a new kind of calm bravery where "neither peace nor danger can make a mark on me."

Arriving at his remote post early in 1508, he quickly proved how much

he had grown. Once a pampered young man of fragile health and temperament, he now became the emotional and physical support of the three
servants who had accompanied him, helping with the farming and wood-
chopping, caring for them when they were sick, singing to them to keep up
their spirits. All around him were aborigines, outlaws, steep mountains,
and deep valleys. It was here at Longchang that Wang Yangming drew on
his newfound courage and utilized the terrible dangers of his situation to
push himself to his greatest insights.

He bought a coffin for himself, and night after night he sat in front of it
deep in meditation. One night he realized that he had been mistaken in
investigating external things and in looking outside himself for the principles of things. "My own nature is sufficient for me to attain sagehood."
"The ten thousand things are all complete within me." The next year he
achieved an equally important insight, that "knowledge and action are
one." What was so exciting about these sentences? Why did Wang sense
them as intellectual breakthroughs, and why did so many young scholars
flock to him to hear him explain them? Why did later generations develop
them in ways that made Wang's ideas crucial for Chinese intellectual life
for over a century after his death? Answers to these questions, however
tentative they must be, may bring us closer, at this last great summit of
Confucian thought, to some of its deepest strengths and problems.

The first breakthroughs were not so much changes in the Neo-Confucian vision as rephrasings of some of its deepest insights that rescued them
from excesses of intellectualism, self-consciousness, and explicit definition
and broke through the wall of things-to-be-studied that had seemed to the
young Wang to block the path to sagehood. The many patterns (*li*) of
things all were parts of one all-embracing pattern, and all were reflected in
human nature, in the structure of one's mind. To study things outside
oneself might be important, but fundamentally it was a means of clarifying
one's own nature. In the spirit of the Song masters lost in their landscapes,
at home amid unceasing flow and change, the boundary between self and
world faded away, and all the things in the world came to completion in
human consciousness, in joyful recognition of oneness with them.

The teaching on knowledge and action seems to have been more of an
innovation, and it contributed to a turning of many intellectuals away from
reclusive self-cultivation in the following generations. To Confucius,
human life was radically incomplete without social and political involvement and action. But the gentleman found his moral standards within himself and in the study of a literary heritage, and did not change them simply
because he was unable to make practical use of them in his own times.
Thus a teaching that laid greater emphasis on study and self-cultivation
than on effective action was a plausible, if incomplete, development of the

Master's principles. Zhu Xi's conception of the investigation of things was such a teaching, laying out detailed prescriptions for disciplining the mind through study, meditation, and ceremonial practice. Wang's objection was that it was very easy to drift from Zhu's undoubted seriousness into going through the motions of ceremonies, memorizing the texts of the classics, without their having any moral effect. It was especially easy in a social and political order that dictated study first and action later for the ambitious young man, that rewarded cleverness with literary forms and proficiency in memorization. Symptoms of the resulting nonseriousness included the hypocrisy and self-congratulation of the high official class in which Wang had grown up, and a tendency to explain moral lapses by saying "I know what's right; it's doing it that's hard." Wang rejected all such excuses, insisting that fundamentally people respond to good and evil as readily as they respond to a bad smell; they don't stop and say "Oh, a bad smell!" and then think about getting away from it; they move immediately to escape it. If they don't do this for good and evil, Wang said, it's because some selfishness, some calculation of personal advantage, has broken up the original unity of knowledge and action. The unity could be maintained if the individual had his mind constantly fixed on the goal of becoming a sage, for then he would not be inclined to make excuses for his own bad conduct. Also, the person who sought this goal would realize that the only real knowledge is knowledge that is engaged, is aware of its consequences in action:

> In all the world, nothing can be considered learning that does not involve action. Thus the very beginning of learning is already action. To be earnest in practice means to be genuine and sincere. This is already action. It is to make the action sincere and the effort continuous without stopping. In learning, one cannot help having doubts. Therefore one inquires. To inquire is to learn; it is to act. As there is still doubt, one thinks. To think is to learn; it is to act. As there is still doubt, one sifts. To sift is to learn; it is to act. As the sifting is clear, the thinking careful, the inquiry accurate, and the study competent, one goes further and continues his effort without stopping. This is what is meant by earnest practice. It does not mean that after study, inquiry, thinking, and sifting one then takes steps to act.[1]

Wang had come to these insights at a time when he had experienced terrible humiliations and dangers and confronted the possibility of his own death in the most literal sense as he meditated in front of his own coffin.

---

[1] Wei-ming Tu, *Neo-Confucian Thought in Action* (Berkeley, Los Angeles, and London, 1976), p. 152.

He was convinced that one of the most important forms of the selfishness that came between knowledge and action was that people "think too highly of their bodies and lives." The risk of moral failure also must be confronted: "If one had some success in his effort yesterday but fails today, he should not pretend that nothing has gone wrong. That would be making an artificial effort to help the mind grow, and any success previously achieved would be spoiled." But the only form of failure conceived of here was a failure of unrelenting and concentrated effort, a separation of knowledge and action. If that were achieved, there could be no failure: "All depends on making up the mind. If the student makes up his mind to have one thought to do good, his mind will be like the seed of a tree. If only he neither forces it to grow nor neglects it, but keeps on cultivating and nourishing it, it will naturally grow larger every day and night." The ideas that effort might be futile, that action following directly from knowledge of the good might have undesirable results, were nowhere within his mental horizon. Nor had his experience of knowledge and action up to this point in his life given him much reason to worry about these problems. He and his colleagues had smelled the stink of eunuch power and had not allowed concern for their own bodies and lives to keep them from reacting against it, taking action to try to cleanse the court.

In 1510 the eunuch Liu Jin fell from power, and Wang Yangming was released from his Guizhou exile and appointed to a local magistracy in Jiangxi. From then to 1516 he held several higher posts, largely in Nanjing, where a vestigial capital bureaucracy in the city that had been the first Ming capital provided low-pressure positions for many distinguished men. The political situation was less dangerous than before 1510 but still far from satisfactory, as the eccentric and impulsive emperor continued to maintain a court dominated by eunuchs, corrupt favorites, and even an exotic foreigner or two. Unqualified and fearless protest still seemed the only possible form of political action for the good man, and Wang's teachings, so clearly relevant to it, attracted more and more admirers and disciples. As he traveled about visiting other eminent scholars, crowds of several hundred scholars might gather to hear him discuss his ideas. But his disagreements with the Zhu Xi orthodoxy made him a heretic in the eyes of many.

Wang grew bored with his routine positions and requested permission to retire, but his requests were turned down, and in 1516 he was plunged into new spheres of action and danger where his straightforward and optimistic moralism offered only limited guidance. He was made governor of a large area centered in southern Jiangxi that had been dominated by bandits and rebels for several decades. (The area stretched across several provincial boundaries, making it easy for bandits and rebels to escape provincial troops by moving out of their territory; the same zone had been used in this way by rebels in Yue Fei's time and later was the base for Red Army resistance in the early 1930s.) Wang developed some policies he already had tried out in his first magistracy, publishing moral admonitions, having village elders lecture the people on moral topics, and establishing ten-family joint-responsibility groups. The fine Confucian flavor of the first two is somewhat undercut by the Qin antecedents of the third.

All of this was of some use in cutting the rebels off from clandestine trade and aid in well-settled areas, but it could do nothing against the many bandit strongholds in the mountains. For that side of his "pacification" effort Wang called on his long-suppressed military inclinations and became a trainer of troops, strategist, and trickster in the Zhuge Liang tradition. He raised local militias, clarified the command structure of government troops, and made excellent use of spies and double agents. Rebels who surrendered were called "new people" and either settled in civilian occupations or integrated in his forces. When one rebel leader waited too long to surrender, Wang first gave him a banquet, then found him guilty of "insincerity" and had him executed. In his first campaign, he sent small numbers of local mountaineers to the peaks around the bandit forts with flags and guns. When the bandits advanced to meet the main force of government troops, all at once they heard the thunder of guns and saw government flags on the peaks around them. Convinced that they were surrounded and that some of their posts were taken, they broke and fled, losing many of their men in the rout.

As areas were cleared of rebels and brought back under government control, Wang instituted his civilian control measures, established two new subprefectures, set up local schools, and elaborated his previous experiments in moral instruction by local elders into his famous "village compact" (xiangyue) system. This was an effort systematically to extend the Confucian culture of ceremoniousness and moral admonition to the common people, and at the same time to give a more Confucian twist to the "Legalist" practice of forming mutual responsibility groups. In every village the local people were to elect a whole group of compact officers, from a chief and two assistants to clerks and masters of ceremonies. On the fifteenth of every month, all the people assembled at the special hall built for the purpose, burned incense, and recited, "From now on, all of us compact members will reverently obey warnings and instructions. We will unite as one mind and join together in virtue, and will arrive at goodness together. If anyone should have any double-mindedness, outwardly doing good but secretly doing evil, let the gods and spirits destroy him." A special ceremony followed to honor those who had done good deeds in the previous month and to record them formally in the compact's book of good deeds. Then there was a similar ceremony recording bad deeds and admonishing those who had done them. The evil-doers replied, "How dare I not reform quickly but instead cause my elders to worry for me again?" The compact chiefs then said, "We have not been able to advise and instruct you in time so that you have fallen into this trouble. How can we be free from guilt?" The ceremonies concluded with a banquet.

Wang's policies seem to have been quite useful in restoring order in this long-troubled area and in settling conflicts between the residents and the ex-bandit "new people." But his state papers show few signs of interest in any other kind of statecraft than warfare and the Confucian complex of education, exhortation, and control; relief measures only in time of flood or famine, and nothing about irrigation, flood control, or stimulation of agricultural or craft production. There is little or no indication of the possibility that a government might be of any positive benefit to its people. The change from the statecraft of Su Dongpo's generation is striking.

This narrower range of interests is characteristic of mid-Ming scholar-officials. Wang was not an ordinary man, however, and he might have developed a wider range of interests in statecraft if he had served in a more tranquil age. He was still confronting one small local rebellion after another when in 1519 he turned to face the most difficult challenge of his career. Under the Ming, princes of the imperial house were given large estates in the provinces but were forbidden to participate in politics and were very closely watched. The only case in the whole history of the dynasty of a provincial prince rebelling against the emperor was that of the rebellion of the prince of Ning, which broke out in Jiangxi in 1519. Wang was the key organizer of the dynasty's efforts to defeat and capture the rebel prince. Wang advanced quickly to occupy the city of Nanchang, which the prince had left with a small garrison. In a little more than a month he had routed the prince's armies and captured him; his final blow was an attack by fire on the prince's river ships, which were moored and all chained together.

The real dangers for Wang came after the prince of Ning was captured. Wang's enemies at court had spread rumors that he had been in touch with the prince and had intended to join his rebellion. Worse, the irresponsible emperor already had decided to lead an expedition against the prince in person, to gain military glory for himself and his court favorites. Anything might happen if this silly man and his vicious entourage descended on an area that still was unstable and had suffered much from war and misgovernment. He did not stop even when Wang reported his victory, and some agents of the court wanted Wang to release the prince so that the emperor could capture him again. A eunuch was sent to take the captive prince to the emperor. Wang preferred to deliver him himself, but finally agreed to turn the prince over to a more reputable eunuch, one who had opposed the power of Liu Jin. Months later, the emperor's favorites still were demanding credit for the victory, and Wang finally had to give in and send in a report telling the court what it wanted to hear. He was kept in high provincial office until the middle of 1521, when he requested sick leave.

From 1521 to 1527, Wang was out of office. He attracted more and more disciples, but the volume of attacks on his deviations from Zhu Xi also grew. The dissolute emperor died without an heir early in 1521. The nephew who succeeded him set off a great controversy at court by his insistence on honoring his natural father with ceremonies appropriate only to an emperor; hundreds of scholars protested outside the palace gates, but some promoted their own careers by ingenious interpretations of classical texts that supported the emperor's intentions. Eunuch influence on government was sharply reduced. The political situation thus was much less clear-cut than in the previous reign, the smells of good and evil much harder to distinguish. Wang had tricked, betrayed, killed, compromised with eunuchs in order to get his jobs done and survive the last terrible years. Knowing and doing could not seem as straightforward and moral a unity in 1522 as they had before 1516. And surely the Buddhist and Daoist quests of Wang's early years continued to echo in his mind. His teachings of these years are recorded in a great collection of sayings and letters entitled *Chuan xi lu* (Instructions for Practical Living). Its discontinuous form and its emphasis on master-disciple relations are reminiscent of the *Analects* of Confucius and the *Platform Sutra* of the Sixth Patriarch. I am not sure that it equals the psychological, spiritual, and moral depth of those two great books, but it is not absurd to make such a comparison.

The central new concept of Wang Yangming's later teaching can be literally translated Good Knowledge (*liang zhi*). It was developed to explain the nature of the knowledge of morality that always is present within us and is the knowledge that is "extended" in our moral action as outlined in the *Great Learning* sequence. This was in a sense a rephrasing of his idea of the unity of knowledge and action: hard work, facing danger, improving one's character, and serious study all were ways to extend Good Knowledge. Introspection was not a very good way; "without experience and dealings with others, there will be no Good Knowledge to be extended." But Good Knowledge also could be sensed as part of the unity of the cosmos; "at bottom Heaven, Earth, the Ten Thousand Things, and Humanity all form one body. The point at which this unity is manifested in its most refined and excellent form is the clear intelligence of the human mind. . . . Plants, trees, tiles, and stones would not be what they are if it were not for the Good Knowledge of humanity." Extending Good Knowledge was a matter of not seeking certain results or effects of our actions but of unremitting moral effort, alive and alert, and at the same time cautious, even fearful of any beginnings of selfish or improper thoughts. Eventually Wang taught, in phrases strikingly like Hui Neng's on the unity of meditation and enlightenment, that the basic substance of the mind was unremitting moral effort, and unremitting moral effort was the basic substance of the mind. This teaching appealed strongly to scholars who were committed both to serious and principled involvement in politics, community life, and family affairs and to a quest for a vision of and unity with the deepest cosmic and spiritual realities. The two were entirely compatible, even inseparable; the essence of moral action was effort, not results, and that effort was the most direct revelation of the basic structure of the human mind and thus of the unity of all things.

There was one final step in the development of Wang's late thought that carried him to the outer bounds of, and some of his disciples beyond, the basic moralism of the Confucian tradition. It was summarized in his famous Four Sentences:

> In the basic structure of the mind there is neither good nor evil.
> When there is movement of the will, then there is good and evil.
> Knowing good and knowing evil is the Good Knowledge.
> Doing good and destroying evil is the Investigation of Things.

The shocker here for the Confucian, of course, is in the first line. Wang clearly had not forgotten all that he had learned from Buddhism and Daoism, with their understanding of the amoral and illusory aspects of mind and being. He now knew much more of how deeply rooted evil was in the minds of men, even his own. He had been in situations where not every action could be examined for any beginnings of selfish or improper thoughts, where one might act and then have one's Good Knowledge perceive the evil of the act. I suspect he had drawn, as many do under great stress, on kinds of detachment and tranquility-in-action that are indeed beyond good and evil. Wang later suggested that his teaching about the original nature of mind was only for the few who were so intelligent and perceptive that they could apprehend this level directly; others needed more positive and detailed moral teaching. One is reminded of Hui Neng's explanation that some teachings are for the quick and intuitive while others are for those who learn slowly, step by step. This seems to have encouraged some of his disciples to place themselves among the elect who could understand the level "beyond good and evil" and to develop Wang's teachings in the direction of a radical rejection of all conventional moral distinctions. Some of these radical followers drew far more on Chan Buddhism than Wang had, and their "wild Chan" teachings were pointed to by the orthodox as grim lessons in what would happen to tradition if deviations from the Zhu Xi orthodoxy were tolerated. On the other hand, his teachings encouraged in many a new moral earnestness and political commitment. The complex heritage of Wang's quest for moral engagement and personal authenticity also was transmitted to Japan, where his teachings have remained influential down to very recent times.

In 1527 Wang was given a high provincial post and sent to pacify a tribal rebellion in Guangxi and Guizhou provinces. He offered generous terms to the leaders and secured the surrender of most of them. To subdue a strong force that was holding out in eight forts in the mountains, he sent some of his troops away so that the chiefs thought he was not going to attack, then turned on them with the rest of his forces and took the forts in a month's fighting. He had been ill for some time and died on his way home from the campaign, in January 1529. His last words were "My heart is full of brightness; what more can I say?"

14

ZHENG CHENGGONG
(Coxinga)

• • • • • •

EVEN today in China it is possible to feel that the rest of the world is not really there, or does not matter very much. The Chinese people, it seems, have been working things out for themselves from the beginning, and rarely have had anything to learn from outsiders. Buddhism is an important exception, but reminders of its Indian origins became less striking as centuries passed. Chinese scholars were capable of great linguistic feats in mastering the huge vocabulary and various styles of their own language, but very few ever learned a foreign language. Chinese political skills have built a world apart, a single political order that includes seacoasts, deserts, rich plains, and some of the world's great mountains. From the 1500s on, the reality behind this sense of self-sufficiency has been gradually eroded, but at the same time the population of China and the size and geographical variety of the areas inhabited by Chinese-speaking people have continued to grow, so that China's scale and its immense economic and political difficulties have even reinforced to a degree the inward-turning of Chinese public life.

Partly because of these changes and partly because the historical record begins to shed much more light on life away from the court and capital, our view of the last centuries of imperial China is increasingly shaped by awareness of regional diversity and regional histories. The life of Zheng Chenggong is a piece of such a regional history. It takes us for the first time to adventures at sea, in a Chinese milieu fundamentally altered by the presence of foreigners. It also echoes themes of the Three Kingdoms and shows a would-be hero acting out a Yue Fei role and at the same time struggling to get beyond Yue's trap of the "nobility of failure." Zheng's struggles and eventual failure were parts of the failure of Chinese resistance to conquest by the Manchu Qing dynasty, which ruled China until 1911 and profoundly shaped its responses to its growing relations with the rest of the world. The Qing conquest, and the efforts of Zheng and others to resist it, were the first events in Chinese history to be described to European audiences within a few years after they happened. His short and bitter life offers an almost too neat turning point toward the story of China's involvement with the rest of the world.

Wang Yangming was a contemporary of Columbus, Vasco da Gama, and Martin Luther. The Portuguese already had arrived on the coast of China in his lifetime. A few intelligent officials noticed their excellent cannon and began to copy them; Wang himself may have used some against the rebels in Jiangxi. But no one in the Ming elite saw them as anything more than a minor complication in the Ming state's long-standing difficulties with Japanese pirates and with Chinese who dodged strict maritime controls to trade with the Japanese, engage in piracy, and make illicit voyages to Southeast Asian ports. After 1550 the Ming maritime controls broke down: the Portuguese were allowed to settle at Macao (near modern Hong Kong) by arrangement with local officials and became important carriers of trade between China and Japan; the Spanish settled at Manila and large numbers of Chinese traded with them there; and Chinese, Japanese, and European traders and pirates met in all the ports and seas of Southeast Asia. Japanese and Europeans bought Chinese silks and other fine manufactures, and paid for them with substantial parts of the growing silver production of Japan and of Spanish America. Some American silver came via Europe and the Indian Ocean, but more came, in the most improbable single commercial link of the age of sail, in annual galleons from Acapulco to Manila. Roman Catholic missionaries came with the Spanish and Portuguese traders and were especially successful in making converts in some areas of southern Japan and among native peoples and Chinese settlers in the Philippines. The great Jesuit Matteo Ricci aroused interest and admiration among Chinese who met him, and reached Beijing in 1601. For a very few Chinese scholar-officials, conversion to Roman Catholicism became a way of responding to a widespread sense of cultural crisis, of the moral inadequacy of received institutions and teachings (very much including the teachings of Wang Yangming), but most Chinese were totally unaware of the missionaries and the traders.

Chinese who lived along the south coast, especially those who participated in maritime trade, did understand and respond to the novel challenges of the European presence, but their activities were marginal to the concerns of the Chinese state and sometimes completely outside the law. It had not always been so; the Southern Song had recognized the importance of maritime trade as a source of revenue and had systematically encouraged it, but without any effort to extend Chinese sovereignty or administration beyond the oceans. The Yuan had continued to encourage trade and had made spectacular but unsuccessful attempts to conquer both

Japan and Java. The attitudes of the early Ming tyrants toward the coast were dominated by fear of the growth of Japanese piracy and Chinese collusion with it, leading to severe restrictions on Chinese navigation abroad and foreign trade in Chinese ports. Between 1403 and 1436, an effort to turn Chinese seafaring from uncontrolled private voyages into officially organized and controlled ones produced seven great expeditions into the Indian Ocean, some all the way to East Africa and the Red Sea, but after domestic political opposition stopped these expeditions, the Chinese state never again sought to assert itself beyond the seas. For the Ming state, centered in Beijing, even Japanese pirate raids in the Yangzi delta in the 1550s were less alarming than Mongol raids across the Great Wall in the same period. The novel European presence in Manila and Macao rarely was noticed by capital officials. And when greater dangers came in the form of Dutch fleets in the 1620s, the empire faced a set of internal and external challenges so grave that few paid attention to the dramas on the coast.

There was one very important way in which connections with Europeans had shaped the general crisis that developed in the 1600s: the inflow of American silver had contributed to a widespread commercialization of the economy and a steady inflation. Ming officials developed some intelligent methods of converting taxes in grain and labor service into payments in silver, but in general the impact of silver and commerce on the Chinese state was negative. Its officials were not supposed to profit from their posts in any way except a modest salary, but prices were rising, salaries were not, and the continuity and prosperity of his family were among a man's deepest commitments. The result, of course, was that many officials could be bribed. Money talked in late Ming China. The court also needed more income, and frequently employed court eunuchs to search for new sources of revenue or squeeze the maximum out of old ones, exacerbating the old eunuch–civil official conflict.

The prosperity of late Ming China, including steady growth in the quantity and variety of printed books in circulation, produced a superabundance of earnest and ambitious Confucian scholars. Some of them became involved in discussions of changes in government policy needed in order to adjust to the rising commercial economy. Their suggestions sometimes were detailed and grounded in deep knowledge of local conditions, but they always had the goal of restoring an impartial and equitable centrally administered order that was presumed to have existed in the early Ming. To these scholars, the commercial economy was a threat, not an opportunity; they had no interest in enriching the state and improving the livelihood of the common people by *encouraging* commercial growth, as many of their contemporaries in Europe and Japan were doing. By no means incompatible with these "statecraft" interests, and even more deeply rooted in the Confucian moral tradition, was an emphasis on individual moral renewal and on selfless resistance to evil authority. Scholars, especially those associated with the Donglin Academy in the lower Yangzi valley, agitated against the influence in government of eunuchs and the opportunistic officials who associated with them. In the 1620s some officials were tortured to death by the court eunuchs, proclaiming to the end their totally selfless devotion to their principles and their ruler. The Donglin movement was not all noble failure; at times it wielded great influence through the sophisticated manipulation of the examination system and bureaucratic promotion processes. Some of the Donglin moral revivalists were inclined to blame Wang Yangming's individualism and subjectivism for what they saw as the moral deterioration of their age. Certainly, in the commercial, sophisticated, frequently cynical culture of the great cities, some had developed Wang's ideas in deeply anticonventional directions, but for others, Wang's conviction of the goodness in each of us and his teaching of the union of knowledge and action were inspirations for moral revival and interest in statecraft.

By the 1620s the corruptions and distortions of the Ming tax system were such that many wealthy landowners were escaping taxation entirely, while tax burdens on their less powerful neighbors grew steadily heavier. In the midst of overheated private prosperity, the government faced huge arrears in tax collections and an empty treasury. It tried to economize by dismissing employees of the extensive government postal-relay system in the northwest, and some of the dismissed employees became leaders of forces of mounted rebels that swept back and forth across north China for years at a time. On the northeast frontier, the Manchu people, descendants of the Jurchen who had ruled north China as the Jin dynasty from 1125 to 1234, proclaimed an independent empire and began to take and hold Chinese border towns. In Beijing, dedicated officials were being dismissed or beaten to death for their opposition to the all-powerful eunuch Wei Zhongxian. Small wonder that capital records contain little about the dramas taking place on the south coast!

Eunuch power declined somewhat after 1627, and the Ming court staggered on, solving none of its problems. The Manchus advanced, and the northwestern rebels rampaged back and forth from the north China plain to the lower Yangzi. In 1642 the rebels began to take and hold whole provinces, and on April 27, 1644, Beijing fell to them; the last Ming emperor hanged himself on Prospect Hill north of the palaces. But the Manchus had added Chinese generals, troops, and cannon to their own forces, and had advanced all the way to the Great Wall. They were ready when a Ming general sought their assistance against the rebels, and on June 5, just six weeks after the rebel entry, a large force of Manchus entered the capital, proclaiming that their Qing dynasty had received the Mandate of Heaven and that they had come to chastise the rebels who had caused the death of the Ming emperor and given Beijing six weeks of nightmarish misrule.

There followed one of the swiftest and most astonishing changes in the history of China. A nation-in-arms of about two million people occupied the core areas of a nation of over one hundred million, all the way to Guangzhou, in just over three years after the fall of Beijing to the Qing. Some Chinese, especially in areas ravaged by the rebels, welcomed the Qing as restorers of law and order. Others tried to organize resistance, setting up a series of princes of the Ming imperial house as emperors claiming the legitimate succession. But all the conflicts and failings of late Ming politics were reproduced and magnified in these loyalist courts. Many of the finest heirs of the moral revivalism of the late Ming had little or no relation to the courts or any other organized center of resistance, but still felt compelled to prove their selflessness and play out their loyal minister roles by jumping into ponds, running into burning temples, or—just as suicidal—spitting in the faces of Qing captors who tried to persuade them to take office under the new regime. Here many who had been pulled this way and that by the ambiguities and intricacies of late Ming politics and intellectual life finally were able to be perfectly selfless ministers, to achieve a union of knowledge and action. It all was wonderfully Confucian, and even some people of the time thought it was an appalling waste.

The Yangzi valley and the north China plain remained under Qing control thereafter. A last Ming loyalist emperor was pushed back into the mountains of the southwest, chased into Burma in 1659, and finally brought back and executed in 1662. Chinese generals who had been early allies of the Qing revolted in the south and southwest in 1673 and posed a grave threat for a few years, but then they were turned back, and after 1681 there was no organized resistance to Qing power on the Chinese mainland.

Zheng Chenggong's life marked the peak of a trajectory of family power that covered three generations and a fraction, and matched almost exactly the span from Ming upheaval in the 1620s to final Qing consolidation in the 1680s. The founder, Zheng Zhilong, began his life as a maritime trader, spending parts of his young manhood in Macao, Taiwan (then inhabited by non-Chinese aborigines, with a few Chinese and Japanese trading outposts on the coast), and southern Japan. This maritime world was full of uncertainty and violence at sea and in its ports. Its most successful and powerful men were not the bravest or the best fighters but the most flexibly persuasive, multilingual Zhuge Liangs with no fixed principles, who could win the trust of Ming eunuchs, Japanese samurai, and Spanish hidalgos, linking them all in a network of trade that benefited all and made the indispensable middleman rich. Zheng Zhilong emerged as a subordinate of one of the most important men in this world, Li Dan, chief of the Chinese community at Hirado in southern Japan. In 1622 a fleet of the Dutch East India Company made an unsuccessful attack on Macao and then occupied the Pescadores (Penghu) Islands in the straits between Taiwan and Fujian. Li sent Zheng, who probably had been a leader in one of the Chinese settlements on Taiwan, to persuade the Dutch to withdraw from the Pescadores, which were part of the Ming Empire, to Taiwan, which was not. He was successful, and from 1624 to 1662 the Dutch base on Taiwan, near the modern city of Tainan, was one of the key commercial centers of the South China Sea. Buoyed by this success and by the aid of the Dutch, Zheng Zhilong emerged as one of the leading merchants in the South China Sea, using his wealth to build up fleets, trading legally when possible but always trading in any case, and using his fleets to protect his own trade and extort protection money from other traders. In 1628 the Ming government, bankrupt and completely unable to control violence along the coast, made him a naval commander and sought to use him against other "pirates" along the coast. His last major rival was defeated in 1635, his wealth and power continued to grow, and he bought great estates in Fujian and bribed officials all the way to Beijing.

By the fateful year of 1644, Zheng Zhilong had obtained important military commands for two of his brothers. When the first of the loyalist courts was established at Nanjing, the Zhengs were assigned to important defense commands along the Yangzi River, and it is by no means clear that they did all they could to resist the crossing of the river by Qing forces, which led to the rapid collapse of the Nanjing regime and the capture and execution of the fleeing loyalist emperor. Ming loyalists then scrambled to set up another court to legitimize their activities, and two courts emerged, one in Zhejiang and one in Fuzhou, the capital of Fujian.

Zheng Zhilong played a key role in setting up the Ming prince who claimed the succession in Fuzhou, and he was the most important military and financial supporter of this regime. The emperor himself was more able and energetic than any Ming ruler in over one hundred years, and he had in his service not only the formidable Zheng military power but some extraordinarily brave and competent civil officials in the late Ming reformist tradition. Zheng Zhilong soon found himself at odds with the emperor and court he supported in a number of ways. The civil officials suspected him of taking advantage of his political power to enhance his private fortune, while he insisted he was supporting fleets and troops from his own funds. Zheng did not always accept the traditional inferiority of military officials to civil in court ceremonies. Worst of all, the emperor and the civil officials insisted on acting as if they still were responsible for the entire empire. Thus they devoted much of their time and energy to making long-run

plans for recruiting good officials and otherwise correcting the accumulated abuses of late Ming government, to confirming the jurisdictions and
titles of Ming loyalists in other provinces, and to urgent and excited discussions of how they could link up with and give aid to other loyalist forces
that were in more immediate peril than they were. To Zheng Zhilong
these plans were useless at best, and at worst might lead to the dissipation
of the regime's strength in futile expeditions inland, or even to efforts to
force him to move his own forces inland, away from their vital sources of
naval power and commercial wealth.

Zheng's fears were quickly confirmed. One of the most eminent
scholar-officials of the Fuzhou regime was one Huang Daozhou, who had
been born in coastal Fujian, probably in greater poverty than Zheng, but
had taken the traditional route of ambitious young men, rising through the
examination system and distinguishing himself on the Donglin reformist
side in the factional struggles of the late Ming. In 1645 he avoided the
dangers of the loyalist court and Nanjing by having its emperor send him
to offer an imperial sacrifice at the reputed tomb of the sage emperor Yu.
He also was a distinguished philosopher in the tradition of Wang Yangming, determined to let nothing come between knowing what was right
and doing it. The emperor was enthroned at Fuzhou on August 18, 1645;
in less than a month Huang had set out inland, where he stopped to recruit
several thousand troops and then plunged on early in 1646 into Jiangxi
Province, where loyalist resistance was collapsing rapidly. He was captured
by the Qing, refused to take office under them, and was executed. By that
time the emperor himself was preparing to lead an expedition inland.

Somewhere near the center of the extraordinary tension between the
emperor and Zheng Zhilong was Zheng's oldest son, soon to be known as
Zheng Chenggong. Only twenty-one years old in 1645, he clearly was a
bright young man with great wealth and power at his disposal, who in more
normal times would have had a most promising future. He had been born
in Hirado to a Japanese woman of good family whom Zheng Zhilong had
married when he was working for Li Dan. The son had lived in Japan until
he was seven years old, when his father had summoned him to the family
base on the China coast. He passed his local examination at the very early
age of fourteen.

In 1644, when Zheng commanders were important military supporters
of the loyalist regime at Nanjing, the young man was enrolled in a prestigious imperial academy there. The atmosphere of the city was hectic and
morally ambiguous. It long had been famous as a center of literati culture
and of licentious pleasures. The loyalist court was increasingly dominated
by people who were at home in this lush atmosphere and were hated by the
Donglin reformers. Young Zheng studied with Qian Qianyi, one of the

great literary men of the age, who had been on the Donglin side in politics but had a strong esthetic and nonconformist bent. Qian wrote some poems especially for his promising and well-connected pupil. We can imagine the buffeting of the young man's emotions by the attractions of the city, the hyperrefined literary society (for which he may have been well suited but that must have seen him, the son of a pirate and a foreign woman, as a freak), the terrible quarrels in the court, the endless reports of the advancing conquerors. Then his relatives shared in the collapse of the Yangzi defenses, and while loyal scholars rushed to suicidal resistance Qian Qianyi was among the first to welcome the conquerors to Nanjing and to take office under them.

Perhaps it was out of these terrible disillusionments, where the options seemed to be incompetence, craven surrender, or noble failure, that young Zheng began to think of trying to embody another option, of effective resistance, of noble success. When he was presented to the new loyalist emperor supported by his relatives in Fuzhou, the emperor bestowed on him the imperial surname Zhu and a new personal name, Chenggong. The bestowal of the imperial surname was a rare but not unprecedented gesture of imperial favor, implying a sort of adoption into the imperial family, perhaps even the possibility of becoming a crown prince and a successor. No doubt it was in part a conciliatory gesture toward Zheng Zhilong, but many stories suggest that the emperor was deeply impressed by the young man and became very much attached to him. The young man in turn now was bound to his emperor not only by loyalty but also by filial piety. His prince also was his adoptive father. The personal name the emperor gave him is almost as interesting. "Chenggong" means "success." Zheng may have suggested it, or the emperor may simply have thought it appropriate to his character. In any case, he now was the Lord of the Dynastic Surname, "Guoxingye," and his very name proclaimed that he would never settle for noble failure.

In the winter of 1645–46 many reports reached Fuzhou of centers of loyalist resistance in Jiangxi, Hunan, and in the lower Yangzi region. The emperor and his advisers excitedly recognized all the leaders with splendid titles and discussed various plans to link up with them, to send troops to aid them, and even for the emperor to lead troops personally on an expedition inland to link up with other loyalist forces.

Zheng Zhilong opposed all these plans, urging the emperor to consolidate his base in Fujian, and when his advice was rejected he continued to make delays in sending his own troops inland and to send far fewer than his assigned quotas. His strategic logic was excellent; the Fuzhou regime did not have enough troops for a major inland expedition, and conditions inland were so unstable and information about them so unreliable that any plan agreed on was likely to be outrun by events. But his arguments were far from disinterested—he could not afford to endanger his own coastal power and bases, least of all when his great trading ships were expected to return from Japan on the winter monsoon—and his dodging of clear imperial orders left a bad taste in everyone's mouth. The emperor's determination personally to lead an expedition inland became more and more clearly a desire to flee the frustrating relationship with Zheng Zhilong. In January 1646 he set out inland from Fuzhou. Zheng Zhilong soon left Fuzhou in the opposite direction, withdrawing to his bases on and near the island of Xiamen (known to Westerners as Amoy) on the southern Fujian coast. Later in the spring the emperor announced his intention to continue his advance from inland Fujian over the passes into Jiangxi, but Zheng troops at his court rioted in protest, and the emperor had to stay where he was. Soon the loyalist centers in northern Jiangxi, which the emperor had hoped to join, collapsed, and Zheng units in the passes retreated to less exposed positions.

It is not clear just when Zheng Zhilong began to consider the possibility of defecting to the Qing side. He had ample experience of the impracticalities and military weaknesses of Ming loyalism, and he knew that some prominent Ming generals who had gone over to the Qing were being treated very well indeed. He also seems to have had a sublime faith in his own ability to persuade others, to manipulate them for his own ends. This overconfidence sometimes led him to trust others too much; it had gotten him in several very dangerous situations in the 1620s, and this time it would bring his career to an end.

At the end of September Qing forces advanced into Fujian unopposed; some sources say Zheng Zhilong, already negotiating with the conquerors, deliberately pulled his forces back from the passes, but even if he did, this was only part of a general collapse of resistance. The loyalist emperor was captured and executed by the Qing. Zheng Chenggong and other relatives pleaded with Zheng Zhilong not to surrender, but when he was promised the high office of governor-general of Fujian and Guangdong he agreed, and late in November he went to Fuzhou to greet the conquerors. There he was isolated from his loyal bodyguard and informed that he must go to Beijing to thank his new ruler for his clemency and generosity. He spent the rest of his life in comfortable confinement there, sometimes allowed to correspond with his relatives in Fujian, urging them to follow him in accepting Qing rule. If they all had done so, coastal resistance to the Qing conquest would have been crippled beyond hope of recovery. But at least four prominent relatives, each with his own following of troops and ships, chose to ignore his pleas. With Zheng Zhilong removed from the scene, each had a chance to claim all or part of his maritime empire, especially the rich ships that would be returning from so many ports. Zheng Chenggong might have the best claim to his father's inheritance; he is said to have seized two ships early in 1647.

Myth and reality are hopelessly entangled in stories of Zheng Chenggong's first years as an independent commander. This is not accidental; many of these stories were circulating in his own time and contributing to his fame and power. He himself was using mythic themes, acting out traditional roles. In the fullest melodramatic versions of the end of 1646, his Japanese mother was seized and violated by Qing troops who took his father's castle; she then committed *seppuku*. Hysterically trying to cleanse her spilled entrails of the pollution, he swore vengeance on the conquerors. He rejected his traitor father and opted for the heritage of his adoptive father the late emperor, calling himself the Lord of the Dynastic Surname. His banners chillingly revised Yue Fei's "Exhaust loyalty to repay the debt to the ruling house" (*jinzhong baoguo*) to "Kill the father to repay the debt to the ruling house" (*shafu baoguo*). He publicly burned his scholar's robes and put on armor, abandoning the scholar's life until the invader should be entirely driven out. Only ninety men joined him at first, in a hideout on Gulangyu Island in Xiamen Harbor, but soon his forces grew.

There is much in these stories that cannot be believed. Japanese ladies did not commit suicide by slitting their stomachs; they stabbed their throats. The "Kill the father" banner is psychologically plausible, but I doubt that it ever flew. On the other hand, Zheng did use the Dynastic Surname, and it became an important part of his popular mystique. The stories of his burning of his scholar's robes are linked to a specific temple in the area and are relatively convincing. If he did this, he was doing far more than turning his back on civilian pleasures and enlisting for the duration. He was rejecting the seductive literati life of Qian Qianyi, the earnest futility of Huang Daozhou. Even while rejecting his traitor father, he was continuing the family struggle against the traditional superiority of civil officials over military. The power structure he built up would be literate and intelligently run, but would be entirely mercantile and military, with almost no place for scholar-officials.

In his first years Zheng Chenggong campaigned in changing combinations with his relatives. Then late in 1650 he turned on two distant relatives—perhaps unrelated leaders who had been "adopted" when they accepted Zheng Zhilong's leadership—and killed one, drove the other away, and took over the family's key base at Xiamen. While he was away on campaign in 1651 Qing forces overran Xiamen; he returned to drive them out, execute one of his uncles for military incompetence, and drive another uncle into retirement.

Having eliminated his relatives, he could begin to build an organization in which there would be no limits to his own will. Although he was Lord of the Dynastic Surname, he could not give his will the ultimate legitimation of the imperial position as long as princes of the Ming imperial house survived and claimed the succession. There were two such princes in the 1650s; one was nearby, barely surviving on the Zhejiang and Fujian coasts, while the other was retreating into the southwestern mountains under the protection of various warlords. Zheng Chenggong chose to accept ranks and titles from the more distant ruler, thus ensuring that he would never be hampered by actual subordination to an emperor and a court full of civil officials as his father had been at Fuzhou. Nor did he tolerate independence among his own officers. Late in 1651 an officer named Shi Lang executed one of his own junior officers, although Zheng Chenggong had wanted to spare him. Zheng then ordered his men to kill Shi, but Shi managed to flee and surrender to the Qing. He was the first of several very capable officers who fled Zheng's ferocity and gave the Qing much-needed expert advice on maritime warfare in general and measures against the Zheng power in particular. Thirty-two years after his defection, Shi commanded the Qing expedition to Taiwan that finally put an end to the power of the Zheng family.

In 1652 Zheng Chenggong went on the offensive, taking Haicheng near Xiamen by surprise and advancing to a six-month siege of the great city of Zhangzhou. Apparently he was less interested in taking the city than in luring Qing armies into an open fight; while thousands of people starved to death in the city, he seems to have made no effort to find confederates who would open the gates to him. When Qing forces finally did advance, he broke off the siege, lost a battle in part because of a sudden shift in the wind, then had to be dissuaded from executing all his commanders who had played any role in the defeat.

At the end of 1652 the Qing court made suggestions for a negotiated settlement in which Zheng Chenggong would receive many of the honors and privileges his father had been promised in 1646, and Zheng showed enough interest to keep the discussions alive. Was he seriously interested in surrender? Not if I read him correctly, as reacting against his father's trusting and manipulative nature and against his final fate at the hands of the Qing. It is much more likely that he was using these negotiations to buy time to strengthen his own position. In the short run he gained a great deal, as his forces were allowed to spread out in coastal areas during the truce that accompanied the negotiations. But in the longer run time was not in his favor; the Qing government had been very much weakened by court upheavals in 1651, but by 1653 firm new leadership was emerging, both in Beijing and in the southern provinces. In 1654 the negotiations finally were broken off; at the end of that year, the officers of the Qing garrison in Zhangzhou opened the gates of the city to Zheng. Zheng now moved toward the establishment of a coherent and autonomous government of the areas under his control, with some bureaucratic specialization at the center and troops divided up for administrative purposes into seventy-two garrison units. The troops trained constantly and were extremely well-disciplined. But as big Qing armies advanced into Fujian in 1656 Zheng simply withdrew from some of his land conquests, keeping his headquarters and main commercial and naval base at Xiamen, where he had started out in 1646.

Zheng's ability to resist the Qing on land was limited, but they still could do nothing to stop him at sea. He moved north by sea to attack and hold coastal points near Fuzhou and even farther north. As he lost ground near Xiamen, he had to depend on grain supplies from more distant areas to feed the troops and a huge population of refugees there. This situation worsened sharply as a result of the loss of Haicheng, a great center of grain and military supplies, by the defection of its commander, Huang Wu, in 1656. Huang, who had feared that Zheng Chenggong might execute him for his role in some minor defeats, also gave his new masters some excellent advice. The Zheng regime depended, he said, on trade with areas under Qing control. If that trade could be cut off, Zheng Chenggong could not hold out for long. This led to increasingly strict Qing bans on maritime trade and finally, in the last two years of Zheng's life, to the evacuation and devastation of some of the coastal areas most involved in the trade.

Zheng Chenggong's increasingly far-reaching naval expeditions culminated in 1658 and 1659 in two great efforts to invade the Yangzi valley. He had to reach out in some direction, and if he could have gotten a firm foothold in that vital region his position would have been transformed. Also, he might have relieved Qing pressure on loyalist forces that now were on their last legs in the far southwest. The only obvious alternative was to wrest Taiwan from the Dutch as a source of grain and a refuge for his troops. Here the conflicts among his myths and inheritances came to a head. He could claim Taiwan through Zheng Zhilong's role in early settlement there, as an extension of the actual power base of fleets and trade connections he had claimed as his father's heir. But he had rejected *that* father as a traitor, ignored his urgings that he surrender to the Qing, and remained steadfast in his role as Lord of the Dynastic Surname, quasi-heir of the martyred loyalist emperor, last upholder of the Ming cause. If he invaded the Yangzi valley he might even take Nanjing. The city had enormous symbolic importance for the Ming cause, as the first Ming capital, the site of the tomb of the great first emperor of the Ming. It had additional personal meanings for Zheng, as the site of his seductive exposure to the literati life, of the fame and craven surrender of his teacher Qian Qianyi. To retake it would be a crowning vindication of his martial values, of bravery and single-minded will, over the literati values he had so firmly put behind him. It would carry him definitively beyond the nobility of failure to the splendor of success.

Many observers said from the beginning that it would not work. The 1658 expedition was broken up by a great windstorm, with much loss of ships and men. When Zheng tried again in 1659, his superbly trained and disciplined forces won some impressive victories at key points on the lower Yangzi. Zheng's generals urged him to leave strong garrisons at these points, but he ignored their advice and took most of his forces a hundred miles up the river to Nanjing. Many with loyalist sympathies came to offer their allegiance, but one independent loyalist commander was badly misused and sent far from his bases of power, and I think most of the literati loyalists soon would have been disillusioned with their prospects under a leader who employed so few literati and emphatically rejected their values. At Nanjing Zheng did not have enough men to besiege more than a fraction of the huge city walls and did not press his siege; probably he was waiting for a commander in the Qing garrison to defect to him. Then in a final act of arrogance he allowed his men to relax and get drunk to celebrate his birthday. Just at that time the Qing managed to bring in reinforcements and attack. Zheng was routed with great loss of men and ships. All Zheng outposts in the Yangzi valley were abandoned in the general flight back to Fujian.

Zheng defeated a big Qing attack on Xiamen in the summer of 1660, but the Qing efforts to cut off coastal trade were becoming very effective, and he now had to turn to the other solution that had been there all along: Taiwan. In the spring of 1661 he led a fleet of hundreds of ships and an army of over twenty thousand across the Straits and besieged the Dutch castle. It finally surrendered at the end of January 1662. Zheng already was moving energetically to take control of his rich new territory and to get his soldiers settled farming on its fertile plains. But his effectiveness as an organizer was offset by more and more severe mental stresses. His discipline, always harsh, had become insane; one commander was executed for dispensing grain with a small measure. His commanders at Xiamen were reluctant to cross to Taiwan, because of its unhealthy climate and the hazards of being near their master.

One independent loyalist commander wrote to berate Zheng for abandoning the loyalist cause, as in fact he had. Taiwan was part of his inheritance as son of his despised father, not as Lord of the Dynastic Surname. The Qing rulers in Beijing decided that Zheng Zhilong was of no more use to them, since Zheng Chenggong could not be induced to surrender, and executed him. The last Ming loyalist emperor was captured and executed by the Qing. Thus the way finally might have been open for the succession of the Lord of the Dynastic Surname, but it was too late. The last straw came when he learned that his own dissolute son had fathered the child of a wet-nurse of one of his younger children; incest, in the strict Chinese understanding. His son had betrayed him, he had failed his adoptive father the loyalist emperor, he had contributed to the death of his real father, and all he had left was a piece of the old pirate's legacy. He ordered the execution of his son's paramour, their baby, and even his own wife (for failing to keep order in her household). His commanders ignored his orders. Howling that he could not face his prince-father, he clawed at his face and died in June 1662. He was not yet thirty-eight, an age at which many literati still were struggling to pass examinations or were just getting started in their careers.

Zheng Chenggong's descendants fought among themselves for the right to succeed to his power, many of the losers defected to the Qing, and the Zheng forces soon lost their last footholds on the mainland. But they ruled Taiwan and contributed greatly to its development until Shi Lang conquered it for the Qing in 1683.

The development of Zheng Chenggong's reputation after his death is almost as strange a story as his life. The Qing emperors, faced by rebels against their rule, came to esteem his steadfast loyalty—even though it had been steadfast in opposition to their ancestors—and conferred honors on him. Stories of his heroism were most popular in Fujian and Taiwan until the late Qing, when he attracted some wider attention as a "nationalist" hero. He usually was made out to be a noble failure in the Yue Fei mold; only a few recognized that he had completely lacked that gift for interdependence and the giving and taking of advice that was so important to Zhuge Liang and the other Three Kingdoms heroes. No one wanted to think about the possibility that he had aspired to be something different from the Yue Fei noble failure ideal, had failed, and in his last days had become a monster of thwarted will and tangled family feelings. The Chinese settlers of Taiwan made him a half-deified founder, who had opened mountains and tapped springs on a great magical progress through the island. The Japanese were fascinated by him, attributing his bravery to his Japanese ancestry. There is a starkly melodramatic *jōruri* puppet play about him by the great Chikamatsu Monzaemon. Even seventeenth-century Europeans wrote about "Coxinga" (Guoxingye, the Lord of the Dynastic Surname), in at least six languages. In recent times the Republic of China on Taiwan has honored him as a local hero who never faltered in loyalty to his cause, while the People's Republic honors him for driving out the Dutch imperialists from Taiwan and assembles historians at Xiamen, his old base, to discuss his contributions to making Taiwan part of China. The man who sought only success and purity of will failed to accomplish his own goals, but in the process he became Taiwan's first Chinese ruler and everyone's misunderstood hero.

15

THE QIANLONG
EMPEROR

· · · · · ·

THE TOURIST in China today usually spends a good deal of time admiring old temples, palaces, and gardens, which are very nicely kept up and look as if the people who visited them and lived in them when they were new might come back at any time. Restoration work has been necessary, of course, but the curious visitor who reads pamphlets about historic sites and looks for stone tablets memorializing their construction or reconstruction will learn that many of the buildings he or she is admiring are not much more than two hundred years old—not very old either by the standards of Chinese history or by those of the Europe of Roman aqueducts and Gothic cathedrals—and that they were lived in and maintained for their original purposes into this century. The tourist is likely to be especially struck by the number of inscriptions that record a date of construction or reconstruction in "Qianlong xx year." "Qianlong" was a year-period designation like the "Zhen'guan" of Taizong of the Tang. In Ming and Qing times each emperor adopted such a designation at the beginning of his reign and kept it to the end, so that their subjects and later students often have used it as if it were the emperor's name; only the fussiest Sinologist will object if we sometimes say "Qianlong" instead of "the Qianlong emperor."

Buildings dating from the long Qianlong reign (1736–96) are frequently splendid, sometimes a little too richly ornamented, not as fine in proportions as the Tang palaces probably were, but all in all fitting reminders of China's last great era of prosperity and cultural self-confidence. With the wisdom of hindsight we can see in these years social and economic changes, political dilemmas not resolved, that did much to shape the following century in which these splendid buildings were the scenes of anxieties and horrors beyond the imagination of the Qianlong court and elite. In the fifty-eighth year of Qianlong (1793), the imperial court was visited by an embassy sent by George III of England, in itself a harbinger of the impatient new world that would batter down China's doors in the next century. The ambassador, Lord Macartney, a distinguished diplomat and a fine representative of his age of optimism, observation, and elegant style, wrote:

> The Empire of China is an old, crazy, first rate man-of-war, which a fortunate succession of able and vigilant officers has contrived to keep afloat for these one hundred and fifty years past, and to overawe their neighbors merely by her bulk and appearance, but whenever an insufficient man happens to have the command upon deck, adieu to the discipline and safety of the ship. She may perhaps not sink outright; she may drift some time as a wreck, and will then be dashed to pieces on the shore; but she can never be rebuilt on the old bottom.

From the beginning of this book, we frequently have had to remind ourselves that we get full value out of these "lives" only when we see them as "lives and times." Nowhere is this more important than in the case of the Qianlong emperor. In Macartney's nautical metaphor, we have to talk about the ship as well as the captain. China in the Qianlong period was being reshaped by economic and demographic forces of which the emperor and his court were aware but which were far beyond their control. Still, the ways in which the Qing state responded to these changes did much to limit its ability to deal with the great crises of the nineteenth century; and the political culture of the Qianlong court—conscientious, culturally conservative, preoccupied with forms, proprieties, and images, wary of its ministers and people—can be seen clearly in the actions and images of the Son of Heaven who presided over it.

Zheng Chenggong had sought a mode of effectiveness, of mobilization of individual wills, that went beyond the fragility and excessive balance of the Way of Ruler and Minister. The enemy he so gravely underestimated in the 1650s already had been showing signs of such effectiveness. The Manchu people had their own heritage, religion, language, writing system, and social and political organization. The entire Manchu people was registered and governed through military units, called the Eight Banners, from the different colors of the banners carried and the outer coats worn by their cavalry. By the time they began their conquest of China in 1644, they also had under them banner units for the Mongols who had joined their cause and for the Ming generals and armies who had surrendered to them, adding their expertise in firearms to the striking power of the Manchu cavalry. In the early Qing, less than two million Manchus ruled well over one hundred million Chinese. Outside the capital and a few garrisons in major provincial cities, Manchus were hardly ever seen. They remained in control because they stuck together, determined to preserve their identity against the attractive power of Chinese culture, aware that hostile Chinese would exploit any Manchu disunity to drive them out of China. Their rule also was facilitated by the ease with which Chinese elites fitted into the channeled ambitions of the examination system and the dependent roles of the Way of Ruler and Minister, accepted practical, administrative conceptions of political morality, and worked devotedly and intelligently to maintain order and prosperity in the Manchu-ruled empire. As a result, China in the eighteenth century enjoyed a kind of internal peace and competent government it had seen only rarely in the previous four hundred years.

The stability of the Qing government was enhanced by good luck in the longevity of its emperors. From 1662 to 1796 China had only three emperors, three reign periods: Kangxi, 1662–1722; Yongzheng, 1723–1735; and Qianlong, 1736–1796. Each of the first two made a distinctive contribution to the impressive political structure their son and grandson inherited in 1735. The great Kangxi defeated a dangerous rebellion of his Chinese generals; extinguished the Zheng regime and made Taiwan part of the Chinese Empire; drove back Russian frontiersmen and made peace with Peter the Great; and extended Qing control over most of the Mongols. He and his court were profoundly bicultural, speaking and writing both Manchu and Chinese. The emperor studied the Classics with the best scholars in the empire, but also went each summer out on the steppes beyond the Great Wall on vast imperial hunts, where he delighted in days of hard riding and in the taste of a bear's liver roasted over a camp fire. Politically, he learned how to make effective use of Chinese scholars and generals, but was deeply suspicious of the network politics of the scholar-officials and of their mystique of principled ministerial opposition. He also was thoroughly aware that many of his Manchu and Chinese bannermen took official assignments in the provinces primarily in order to get rich from bribes, presents, diverted tax revenues, and participation in the most profitable lines of trade. His strategy was to tolerate a great deal of corruption, but always to let the officials know that he knew what was going on and might punish any of them at any time. The most personal of his political worries, and one that contributed a great deal to the general political unease of the last years of his long reign, was the mental instability and moral unsuitability of the son whom he had originally chosen as his heir apparent. The heir apparent, accused of using witchcraft against his brothers, was deposed, restored, deposed again, and confined.

It is not at all clear that Kangxi had made a final determination who should succeed him before he died. The Yongzheng emperor claimed that he had been named in a secret will, but he came to power in something that looked very much like a coup d'état, in which he won because one of his supporters controlled the troops in the Beijing area. Several of his brothers who may have had as good or better claims to the succession were exiled, and their supporters were imprisoned or executed. Thus Yongzheng's desire to tighten administrative control was a result not only of the obvious slackness and abuse of power of the last years of Kangxi but also of his own political insecurity and need to deal harshly with any emerging opposition. He worked hard to tighten up administrative controls and to bring the finances of the state into better order. Long days of paper-shuffling, ruthless repression of dangerous factions, strong support of a narrowly defined Confucian orthodoxy of the Zhu Xi school, and a system of officials and others who sent the emperor secret reports on conditions and official conduct all over the empire produced one of the most effectively despotic state systems of the premodern world, in some ways a realization of the dreams of the First Emperor of Qin. Getting finances under control was much harder; all kinds of vested interests and technicalities were involved. The reform efforts dragged on into the Qianlong reign and were never more than a partial success.

The future Qianlong emperor was born in September 1711, the fourth son of the future Yongzheng emperor. According to one story, he had gone on the imperial hunt sometime in the last years of his grandfather's life and had calmly sat on his horse while his guards killed a charging bear. His grandfather, it was said, was very much impressed and left the throne to the future Yongzheng emperor in part so that this grandson would be the successor in the next generation. The latter part of this story does not seem plausible, but the incident with the bear may at least reflect a sense at the Court that this was a prince of special destiny, and it also serves as a reminder of just how important the Manchu heritage of the ruling house still was.

Although the prince was carefully sheltered in his father's palace, he must have been aware of the tensions and anxieties of the last years of Kangxi, and no doubt he had a great deal of inside knowledge of the way his father came to the throne. Although he was only the fourth son of the emperor, the Qing recognized no principle of primogeniture in succession, and he seems to have been far more talented than his brothers. He and one of his brothers received a careful and thorough education under some of the best scholars in the empire. In 1730, not yet twenty, the future emperor presented to his father a collection of his essays, poems, letters, and so on entitled *Literary Drafts from the Leshan Hall*. "Leshan," "Delighting in Goodness," was the name of the hall where he and his brother studied with their tutors. The phrase was taken from a passage in the *Mencius* on "the great Shun . . . *delighting* to learn from others to practice what was *good*." A second version of this collection, compiled after he came to the throne, added a collection of 260 of his notes and comments on various historical subjects. Here we can see in its purest form his early commitment to Confucian ideals. The ruler–minister relation is all-important. The ruler always must be ready to hear the opinions of his ministers and to learn from them, especially when their advice goes against his wishes. The ruler also must set an example of devoted filial piety. In his ruling he must be "cautious and circumspect, respectful of both Heaven and the people, constantly diligent, and never for a moment presumptuous enough to be lax." He must be especially diligent in searching out and employing the best ministerial talent. But "the difficulty in appreciating men's worth today is ten times greater than in ancient times. The reason is that official positions are daily increasing in number and human nature is becoming more devious."

The prince placed great emphasis on the influence on history of individuals and especially of rulers. He especially praised Taizong of the Tang for his employment of talented ministers and his willingness to listen to them, and he condemned Gaozong, the founder of the Southern Song, for dismissing talented ministers, allowing himself to be controlled by Qin Gui, and acquiescing in Qin's destruction of Yue Fei.

The prince was writing down these orthodox opinions in the very years when his father was seeking to perfect his autocracy, in which ministers were expected to keep their accounts straight, inform on each other, and not oppose the emperor's wishes. Thus it is not at all surprising that when he succeeded to the throne upon his father's death in 1735 some senior officials hoped that he would revert to the less autocratic policies of his grandfather. They had all the more reason to hope because the new emperor, although in his midtwenties, would have to accept for some years the advice and counsel of two great high ministers left over from his father's court. Their power was enhanced, as that of the high ministers in the first years of Gaozong of the Tang had been, by their ability to exploit filial piety, reminding the emperor of the teachings and policies of his sage father. They also took advantage of their positions to consolidate and regularize a new organ of informal administration called the "Office for Military Plans" (Junjichu). Ostensibly set up to coordinate the secret planning and communication necessary for the great military campaigns that already had begun and would continue all through the Qianlong reign, it soon became a small central body very close to the throne that coordinated most important kinds of decision-making by the emperor; thus scholars writing in English call it the Grand Council. Close to the emperor and careful to avoid even the appearance of any infringement on his decision-making powers, the grand councillors with their wide range of connections in the bureaucracy and their control of the emperor's paperwork had immense

9. Qianlong confronts his younger self

influence in shaping policy. The long continuity of this efficient and powerful central processing unit, as it might be called in the computer age, was of key importance to the bureaucratic stability and general peace of the long Qianlong reign.

The two great ministers represented the two principal sources of strength of the mid-Qing monarchy. One, Oertai, was a Manchu who had distinguished himself as an effective administrator of the rapidly developing southwest provinces of the empire. (Manchus did not have Chinese-style surnames passed on from generation to generation; their names normally are transliterated as a single word.) The other, Zhang Tingyu, was a notable classical scholar and literary stylist, the offspring of a great family in Tongcheng, Anhui, where the elite had steered clear of suicidal resistance to the Qing conquest and thereafter had devoted themselves to managing their estates and giving their sons the best possible preparation for the examinations. Oertai remained on active service until his death in 1745; Zhang retired in 1750 at the age of seventy-eight. As happens in all large bureaucracies, each built up a large structure of more junior officials who owed their careers to the great man's support. The bureaucratic infighting between these groups and the power each great man gained from his network of allies continued the emperor's education in the gap between the Confucian ideals of relations between ruler and minister and the realities of his position. After Zhang's retirement, the leading minister was the emperor's Manchu brother-in-law Fuheng, who devoted much of his attention to building the empire in Inner Asia and to trying to revive the traditions of the Manchu people. The emperor had more or less a free hand in ruling China, but did not make bold use of it.

A broader look at the ruling elite of this period would reveal that the Manchus were heirs of an Inner Asian political tradition that emphasized success in war and ruthless effectiveness in ruling. Conscious of their own traditions and of the need to hold together if they were to continue to rule the empire, they gave the Qing Empire a cohesive and intelligent suprabureaucratic elite. The Chinese imperial state required such an elite if it was to run efficiently, but the scholar-officials almost by definition could not produce it, and it had been notably absent under the late Ming, with its weak emperors and powerful eunuchs. The Chinese scholar-officials, on the other hand, disillusioned by the results of the moralistic opposition politics of the late Ming and the suicidal idealism of the Ming Loyalists, aware that the Qing rulers would not tolerate unofficial mobilization of elite opinion, turned their attention to practical problems of administration. (There also was a great deal of serious and sophisticated study of the texts of the classical tradition, which had important long-run effects on intellectual life but did nothing at this stage to encourage discussion of political issues.) The result was that China in the Yongzheng and Qianlong reigns had both rulers and ministers who were intelligent, vigorous, and devoted to effective administration, and that China was better governed than it had been at any time since the early 1400s, or perhaps since 1125. And, as we will see, the Manchus also were building their domination over the steppes of Inner Asia, so that the threat of mounted warriors marauding across the north China plain was less than it had been since Qin times.

Good government left the Chinese people free to till their fields, weave their cotton and silk fabrics, produce all their magnificent porcelains and other manufactures, and raise their children. To have many children, and especially to have living sons to care for their aged parents and then to maintain the ancestral sacrifices, was of course one of the blessings most universally desired by ordinary Chinese. A new sophistication of commercial organization and a growing silver supply, the latter partly the result of tea exports to Europe, made possible greater specialization and thus increased productivity in many areas. The spread of food crops from the Americas, especially corn and sweet potatoes, made possible the cultivation of upland slopes. The result was a doubling of the population of the empire, from about 150 million at the end of the Ming to about 300 million in 1800, and the spread of Han Chinese settlement into many upland areas where government control was thin and into the southwestern mountains and valleys where Han settlement met fierce resistance from the indigenous peoples.

All this prosperity and growth thus presented a host of new challenges and problems to the government. Law and order in the form of local magistrates and their staffs had to be extended into areas where until recently there had been little or no Han Chinese settlement. Land had to be registered, in those areas and where reclamation of lake and river shores produced new fields. Taxes had to be fairly collected from all landholders and from the new concentrations of commercial wealth. Flood-control works had to be maintained, and famine relief provided for years of flood or drought.

The Yongzheng and Qianlong courts were thoroughly aware of these problems, and sometimes took effective action to deal with them. The establishment of a full-scale bureaucratic administration in the southwestern province of Yunnan, to which Oertai contributed so much, is an excellent example of this. There were some very impressive famine relief and flood control projects. But to do all that was needed would have required a steady expansion of the bureaucracy, and an expansion of government revenues to support it. There were many reasons why the Qianlong emperor and his ministers were not willing to do this. Most fundamentally, they were heirs of a Confucian tradition of political thought that idealized low taxes and minimal government, since whatever the ruler took was a diminution of a fixed store of goods available to the people. The ruler's duties were to find and employ the most talented and unselfish ministers, to listen to them, and to set an example to ministers and people of virtuous conduct and moderate expenditure; to seek to increase revenues in order to "enrich the state and strengthen the military" was to be distracted from these fundamental duties and to go the route of Qin. The defeat of the Wang Anshi policies had been the last time that more dynamic and growth-oriented state policies had been seriously considered.

The political imperatives of the early Qing pointed in the same direction: the conquerors had begun by cracking down on tax arrears and other abuses of the landholding elite, but had not gone on to a comprehensive resurvey and registration of landownership, which would have uncovered a great deal of unregistered and thus untaxed land in the hands of powerful local landlords. The implicit bargain was that the landlords would be left unchallenged as long as some taxes came in, no matter how inequitably they were levied, and as long as the landholding elite channeled its political ambitions into passing examinations and rising in the bureaucracy, not into mobilization of elite opinion or other political activities that might challenge the supremacy of the dynasty. It was as a result of this implicit bargain and of the fundamental principles of Confucian statecraft that Kangxi, in 1711, decreed that the empirewide quota for the land tax, the state's most important source of revenue, would never be allowed to rise beyond its level for that year. Thus his son and grandson were bound by bureaucratic precedent and by reverence for ancestral teaching as well as by basic Confucian principles never to try to increase this tax.

One of the most important consequences of the freezing of the land-tax quota was that the regular salaried bureaucracy of the Qing Empire could expand only very slowly. This did not trouble an officialdom imbued with Confucian ideals of minimal government or a ruler who already as a prince had associated an increase in official positions with the growing deviousness of human nature. In the first half of Qianlong's long reign, facts seemed to bear them out: there were no internal rebellions, and tax revenues were more than adequate to support the great military campaigns that extended Qing power far into Central Asia and lavish expenditures on palace buildings and imperial tours. As late as 1781 the imperial treasury had a surplus of over seventy million ounces of silver.

Although there were no major political difficulties before about 1770, the emperor and his ministers from time to time worried about unhealthy social and cultural changes. Some pointed to rising rice prices (although in fact modern researchers still disagree as to whether there was any such trend), others to a harsher struggle for survival among farmers and urban workers, both clearly connected with the rapid growth of the population. Still others deplored the increasing concentration of landownership and other signs of a widening gulf between the bare survival (or nonsurvival) of the vast majority and the luxurious life-styles of the rich and famous.

Insecurity and polarization could be found in the elite as well. The examination system was producing so many *shengyuan* (local graduates) that their chances of ever passing the provincial examinations and beginning an official career were becoming very slight. It was well known that frustrated *shengyuan* were apt to engage in all kinds of disreputable activities, from illicit tax deals to involvement in subversive organizations. Even if they passed the provincial examination and became *juren*, there were so many of these that the average wait for a beginning appointment as a local magistrate was over twenty years. Not even the Manchus were immune. The emperor was very concerned about the poor scholarship of Manchus who sought to better themselves through the examination system. Many ordinary Manchu bannermen had mortgaged the lands assigned to them to Chinese, eventually had lost the lands, and had no steady income at all. They resisted resettlement to frontier areas, not being willing to forgo the pleasures of Chinese urban life. The emperor wrote a long poem in Manchu on the glories of Mukden, the Manchu capital before 1644. He also ordered a number of research and publication projects on Manchu history and seemed sympathetic to the efforts of many bannermen of mixed or uncertain origin to establish by genealogical research that they were real, full-blooded Manchus.

Confucian tradition taught that government ought to keep taxes low and functions few, but at the same time that rulers ought to be able to solve all the problems of society. The Qianlong emperor and his ministers confronted this paradox in an acute and highly specific form. A regular salaried bureaucracy of almost static size was governing an empire bursting at the seams with growing population, migration, and ever more sophisticated and specialized trade and production. Someone had to collect the taxes, settle the disputes, catch and punish the criminals, and keep order in the marketplaces. Two groups were readily available. One was the great pool of ambitious, educated, underemployed *shengyuan*. The other was the growing number of local commoners employed at every *yamen* (magistrate's office) as clerks, messengers, constables, jailers, tax collectors, and so on. Qing scholars wrote a great deal about the duties and problems of the local magistrate, and generally were very skeptical of the reliability and integrity of both groups. The *shengyuan*, it was believed, would use their legal privileges and direct access to the magistrate to avoid part or all of the taxes their families and friends should pay, or to aid commoners and elite in making special deals with the magistrate. "*Yamen* runners" were thought to be drawn from the less stable and reliable strata of local society. Their formal wages were very low; most of their income came from customary fees paid them by anyone who had to do business with the *yamen*, which easily turned into open-ended extortions and solicitation of bribes. They lacked the education that would have given them a chance to advance through the examination system, sometimes were so despised that they were formally barred from the examinations, and had no alternative channel of promotion on the basis of experience and good performance. In Ming and Qing fiction, *yamen* runners, whether they come to arrest or protect, to levy a tax or to notify a man that he has passed an examination, always have their hands out for a big tip.

It was in this context that the Qianlong emperor rejected one proposal after another for dealing with worrisome social problems. Tighten up examination standards or lower quotas to reduce the surplus of graduates? Set limits on landholdings? Prohibit emigration to Sichuan? Conduct a census of the non-Han peoples in the southwest? Send beggars back to their native places? In every case, the answer was the same: Nothing can be done. Any action will give the officials and their underlings opportunities to cause trouble for the ordinary people and will stir up resentment and conflict.

In any case, institutional innovation was less fundamental to Confucian conceptions of what rulers should do than the setting of good examples in ruler–minister relations, scholarship, and personal life. In 1771 the emperor wrote, "We have always been mindful of precedent, revered the writings of the past, relied on the brush to govern, and ruled in accordance with principle. We have been diligent from day to day in our study." I already have noted the careful classical education the future emperor received, and the high Confucian ideals he expressed in his early essays. Even while he ruled he continued his studies of the Classics and of historical texts, practiced his calligraphy constantly, and occasionally did some painting. Every journey, every major achievement, even many viewings of historic and scenic places or meetings with high officials or with foreign princes were immortalized in a poem or prose composition "from the imperial brush." When all these works were collected, Qianlong was credited with the writing of over 42,000 poems, which would make him the most prolific poet in Chinese history. The emperor does seem to have been a fairly accomplished but uninspired student of most of the major forms of Chinese poetry, but these huge collections obviously contain large amounts of "ghost writing" by his court academicians. Actual imperial authorship was not the point of these productions; rather, they represented the imperial self-presentation as a student and practitioner of Chinese literature, and frequently imperial favor to the individual for whom they were done. A poem or even a four-character phrase, ostensibly in the imperial hand, would be carefully preserved and displayed, or even engraved in wood or stone, by the recipient. Such gestures were especially important in the discussions and exchanges of compositions with Chinese scholars that took place on the emperor's great tours of the lower Yangzi valley.

Ever since the Han, emperors of China had been expected to provide state funding and guidance for projects aimed at preserving some part of the classical and literary heritage. The Kangxi emperor had maintained this tradition with the preparation of a splendid edition of the Tang poets, two great dictionaries, and a huge encyclopedia. Yongzheng's publication projects, apart from some products of a personal interest in Chan Buddhism, were more narrowly political, including a long essay stating his own highly authoritarian principles and an amplification of a set of basic teachings for the common people first proclaimed by Kangxi. Qianlong returned to his grandfather's style of more expansive and literary support of publication. The first major product, published in 1739, was the *Qinding sishu wen* (Imperially Authorized Anthology of Four Books Prose), a collection of essays on the classical "Four Books" central to Neo-Confucian intellectual life, rigorously correct in style and orthodox in thought, highly appropriate as models for scholars preparing for the examinations. It was followed by compilations on music, painting, and geography, by continuations for the dynasties after Song of some earlier great standard histories, and by collected commentaries on the Classics.

Actions were even more important than the written word. The emperor, like his father and grandfather, was a very actively involved ruler, giving audience to his high ministers early every morning, reading and commenting on huge numbers of official reports, nominations for appointment, and so on. At the triennial examinations in the capital for the highest degree, the *jinshi*, the emperor personally determined the questions for the final ranking examination, approved or modified his ministers' suggestions of ranking, and received the new *jinshi* in awesome audience. Officials being named to new posts were received in audience. Mongol princes and other foreigners more or less under the hegemony of the empire were received and banqueted, and presents were given them in return for those they brought. When the emperor went on the winter solstice to pay homage at the great open Altar of Heaven on the southern edge of Beijing, he presented himself as the Son of Heaven, the pivot of Heaven, Earth, and Humanity. When he went on tour to the lower Yangzi, he was supposed to be inspecting the flood control and canal works, but also was following in the footsteps of the Great Yu and the First Emperor of Qin, monarchs touring in order to demonstrate their sovereignty over their realms. Tours to pay homage at Confucius's home and tomb in Shandong presented him as a disciple of the First Teacher. When he announced some great victory at the Imperial Ancestral Temple or went to pay homage at the tombs of his father and grandfather, he reasserted the glories of his ancestors and at the same time was an exemplary filial son. He went regularly to visit his mother, the empress dowager, in her palace and to inquire after her health and comfort. He took her along on most of his great tours, at immense expense, since elaborate preparations had to be made for her comfort on the way and for the lodging of her large household at every stop. Son of his parents and Son of Heaven, active ruler and studious scholar, he strove to present in every aspect of his life the image of an exemplary ruler.

All this image-building seemed to call for some splendid new stage-sets. Beginning late in the 1740s, the emperor had constructed northwest of Beijing a new complex of palace buildings, gardens, lakes, and fountains called the Yuanmingyuan, where he spent more and more time and frequently received foreign princes and other visitors. The buildings were designed in European Rococo style by Italian artists associated with a small Jesuit mission in Beijing, a rather disconsolate relic of a missionary presence that Kangxi had first tolerated and then turned against. Several days' journey northeast of Beijing, beyond the Great Wall, at a place called Rehe, "Hot River," Qianlong added greatly to the complexes of gardens, temples, and palace buildings called the "Mountain Estate for Avoiding the Heat," where the court spent parts of every summer and autumn.

The stays at Rehe, and the great autumn imperial hunts that set out from there, were especially important in the Qing Empire's relations with its rapidly expanding territories in Mongolia, Central Asia, and Tibet. The Inner Asian conquests were the greatest achievement of the Qianlong reign; they transformed the map of Asia, spreading Qing power out to the present frontiers of the People's Republic, and even beyond them over the present Mongolian People's Republic and parts of the Russian Far East and the former Soviet republics of Central Asia. The fiscal health and internal peace of the Chinese part of the empire were essential to these conquests, but very few Han Chinese participated in them directly. The troops were the Manchu banners; the Qing rulers claimed suzerainty over one area after another less as emperors of China than as successors to the great khaghan of the Mongols and as patrons and controllers of Tibetan Lamaist Buddhism.

The Qing overcame immense geographic, political, and cultural challenges in Inner Asia. Their troops had to make their way up to and across the great Tibetan Plateau, most of it over five thousand meters above sea level and inhabited by a thinly scattered nomadic population, and garrison Lhasa, over four thousand meters in elevation. Farther north, they had to follow the ancient Silk Roads that led from one oasis to another around the edges of the uninhabitable Takla Makan desert, or cross mountains and grasslands that supported only nomadic herdsmen. Tibet was the homeland of Lamaism. This distinctive variation of Buddhism, with its intricate ceremonies, powerful music and art, fascination with occult powers and reincarnation, focused on the spiritual and worldly powers of human reincarnations of various bodhisattvas like the Dalai Lama. It shared basic Buddhist principles with Chan, but the two were about as different in modes of expression as two religions could be. It already was spreading among the Mongols and had some fervent believers at the Qing court.

The oasis cities farther north were Muslim, ethnically and culturally linked to other Muslim peoples further west, open to new currents in Islam brought by migrants from the west or by pilgrims returning from Mecca. The Qing rulers made great efforts to keep well informed about all the Inner Asian peoples. Their understanding of the Mongols and of Tibet was aided by a long heritage of political involvement and by the personal interest of many Manchus in Lamaism. For the Muslim peoples they had neither such long experience nor much cultural or religious sympathy.

Manchu claims to suzerainty over the Mongols began with the first Mongol submissions to them, before their conquest of Beijing. In the 1680s and 1690s conflicts on the steppes ended with the submission of some Mongols to the Qing, the crushing of Galdan of the Dzungars, the last Mongol leader who might have really threatened Qing power, and the establishment of a Qing garrison and resident at the most important town in the Mongol realms. At the end of the Kangxi reign Qing troops occupied Lhasa and installed a garrison there, to supervise the theocratic regime of the Dalai Lama and to ensure that no Mongol leader could use the Dalai Lama's prestige against the Qing. Yongzheng installed a Qing high official permanently resident in Lhasa. His generals carried on some inconclusive high-risk campaigns against the Tibetan peoples of the forested mountains west of Sichuan and conquered the frontier area around the great Qinghai Lake, bringing under control another zone where Mongol politics and Lamaism threatened to come together without Qing supervision. The Dzungars defeated a Qing army in 1731 but then agreed to withdraw far to the west.

Thus when Qianlong came to the throne in 1735, the advance of Qing power into Inner Asia already was well under way. He would continue the development, begun by his father and grandfather, of a set of bureaucratic controls in which Mongol groups who acknowledged Qing suzerainty were assigned fixed territories, had to have successions of rulers approved by the Qing court, were subjected to Qing criminal law, and received aid in famine years.

Qing policy toward the peoples of Inner Asia was intelligent and energetic, but it would not have been such a colossal success without two independent changes. One was the spread of Lamaism among the Mongols, which introduced new divisions into their already fragmented politics, attracted some intelligent men away from warfare into the monastic life, and stimulated whole groups to abandon nomadism and settle down near the monasteries. The other was the spread of Russian power and settlement through Siberia. The Russian and Qing elites had little understanding or sympathy for each other, but each dreaded an alliance of the other with the Mongol horsemen. Thus after the initial conflicts over Russian settlers on China's northeast frontier, the Qing and Russian empires generally stayed on good terms, negotiated settlements of border difficulties, maintained a large and peaceful trade, and each refused to ally with the Mongols against the other.

Early in the Qianlong reign remnants of the Dzungars who had threatened the Qing in the 1680s and 1690s and defeated them in 1731 had withdrawn far to the west and become divided among themselves, and various leaders and groups were defecting to the Qing. The next Qing moves against them were prompted not so much by a perception of a renewed Dzungar threat as by a Manchu impulse to prove anew the glory of the Manchu military tradition at a time when the emperor and many others were worrying about the effects on the Manchus of soft urban life and of efforts to adopt the Chinese scholar-official way of life. A key figure was the Manchu general Zhaohui, a second cousin of the Qianlong emperor. He had risen as a court bureaucrat and Imperial Guard general, then had served on a frustrating campaign in the west Sichuan mountains. In 1753 he was sent on a tour of inspection in Tibet, where a recent rebellion had been very easily suppressed; he found Qing control secure. When Amursana, a Dzungar leader, surrendered to the Qing in 1754, the Qing supported him in an easy advance to occupy the Dzungar home territories. But Amursana soon rebelled, and in 1756 a large Qing army was sent against him. Zhaohui volunteered to lead troops at the front, far out in the Ili valley, at the present northwest frontier of the People's Republic. The campaign did not go well, and he and his men had to fight their way back to their main supply base through the horrors of an Inner Asian winter. When the Qing sent a much larger army in 1757, Zhaohui led it in easy victories and then in massacres of many of the Dzungars. The former Dzungar base area in the fertile Ili valley was largely depopulated and became a base for a major Qing garrison and a sort of Qing Siberia where many prisoners were sent from China to pass the rest of their lives in servitude to the army.

The Muslims of the oasis cities formerly had been dominated by the Dzungars. When the Qing generals sent envoys to the cities of Kashgar and Yarkand, the local people killed them. In 1758 Zhaohui moved on from his slaughters of the Dzungars, took Aksu in October, then passed another terrible winter near Yarkand, over three thousand kilometers from Beijing as the crow flies, besieged by the local people for three months, his men reduced to cannibalism. But in 1759 Qing reinforcements arrived.

The oasis cities were brought under control and Qing garrisons installed, but for the most part the Muslim peoples were left to govern themselves. They attempted to revolt in 1781 and 1784 and remained restive in the early nineteenth century, partly because they were affected by currents of "fundamentalist" revivalism in the world of Islam.

When Zhaohui returned to Beijing the emperor greeted him outside the gates, an extraordinary honor. Portraits of him and other commanders and great paintings of battles and encampments were placed in a new commemorative hall. The French Jesuits at the court even arranged to have great copper engravings of these scenes made in France and sets of the prints sent back to China. A few sets are preserved in European and American libraries; they are big, complex compositions that show the order of a great Manchu camp, the sweep of the banner cavalry on a charge, the great ceremony in which captives were presented to the emperor.

That was not quite the end of the triumphs of Qing Inner Asian policy. Another Mongol group, the Torguts, had responded to the rise of their enemies the Dzungars by moving farther west, finally settling along the Volga. Remaining true to their Lamaist faith, they had been under great pressure from their Muslim neighbors and from the growing power and settlement of Russians in the area. After the Dzungars were crushed, a return to allegiance to the Qing seemed a very attractive option. In the winter of 1770–71, the Torguts set off on a terribly difficult migration to the east, losing many of their people and livestock to Russian and Muslim attacks and to the bitter cold, but finally reaching the Ili valley and settling under the protection of the Qing garrison there.

Today the magnitude and distinctiveness of the Qing achievement in Inner Asia can best be sensed among the great monuments at Rehe, now called Chengde. The imperial palaces are much more modest in scale than those in Beijing, with elegant, clear-varnished wood columns and walls and pine trees in the courtyards. The memory of Qing domination over the riches and sophistication of the lower Yangzi is kept alive by pavilions around an artificial lake, in the fashion of Suzhou or Hangzhou. In the great imperial park with its pine trees and refreshing mountain breezes, the emperors might set up a tent to receive a Mongol, Tibetan, or Muslim envoy, to watch a horse race or some Mongol wrestlers. The great autumn hunts, in which many Mongol and other dignitaries joined and troops surrounded a huge area and beat all the game toward the imperial party, set out from here. Outside the palace walls are a series of great temples built to celebrate the Inner Asian triumphs and to awe the Lamaist subjects who came to Rehe to pay homage. One temple, begun to celebrate the final subjugation of the Dzungars, contains a fine wooden statue over twenty meters high of a "thousand-armed Guanyin" bodhisattva. The hall does not extend very far in front of the statue; one sees only the feet and the hem of the robe from the entrance, and has to walk almost up to it before the full figure can be seen looming in the half light. It must have been truly overwhelming to the parched and dusty believer who had just ridden over two thousand kilometers from the Ili valley. There also are two huge, square, multistoried lamaseries in Tibetan style. One was completed at the time of the return of the Torguts. Built as a replica of the Potala in Lhasa, it was supposed to house the Dalai Lama on a visit that never took place. The other was built for the Panchen Lama, who did come in 1779. Qianlong had a serious personal interest in Lamaism, took instruction from this great monk, and had throne halls built for himself and for the lama that are equal in size, splendor, and placement. There are many Chinese Muslims in the area today, but there is no mosque among its great monuments of the Qianlong period.

The spread of Russian settlement across Siberia and of Qing power into Inner Asia were the most important ways, but not the only ones, in which China was affected by an eighteenth-century world of growing population and commercial connections. Another was the result of the steadily growing demand in Europe and especially in England, Scotland, and British North America for tea, of which China was at this time the world's only exporter. By the end of the Qianlong reign China was exporting tea and other goods worth over six million ounces of silver per year, of which only about half was balanced by Chinese imports of goods, resulting in a large inflow of silver. The trade with maritime Europeans was restricted to the one port of Guangzhou, which the Europeans called Canton, and was kept under close official supervision there. By the end of the Qianlong reign the English and others were restive under these restrictions, but in fact the trade functioned quite smoothly, providing huge quantities of tea, porcelain, and other goods with excellent quality control despite the fact that no European could visit the centers of production. The Qing authorities drew a large revenue from the trade, much of which went not to the public treasury of the Qing state but to the Imperial Household Department. Upon their return to Beijing, the Imperial Household officials who supervised the trade were expected to present to the emperor and other high dignitaries elaborate clocks and clockwork showpieces made in Europe, wonderful examples of European ingenuity in the use of clockwork and of Rococo taste in enamel and metalwork; a big collection of them still can be seen in the Beijing palaces. Thus the "Canton trade" was a triumph of Chinese defensive foreign policy and of the Qing state's benign attitude toward trade, and even allowed the court to indulge a taste for a luxury import that gave evidence of the high technical and artistic achievements of the Europeans. But unlike Qing involvement in Inner Asia, it did not lead to any systematic collection of information about the foreigners. There were schools in Beijing in which Qing officials learned Mongol, Tibetan, Uighur, and even Russian, but not English or French.

Near the end of the Qianlong reign, in 1793, Lord Macartney came to the capital as ambassador from George III of England. His mission was to seek relief from the restrictions under which the English traded at Guangzhou, and to propose the establishment of a resident English minister or ambassador at Beijing. The court went to great lengths to ensure that he would not be put off by unfamiliar procedures or ceremonies, explaining everything to him very carefully, even excusing him from the usual *kotou*, three kneelings and nine prostrations, and allowing him to simply kneel when presented to the emperor. He was received at a great tent in the imperial park at Rehe. He left a fascinating description of Rehe and of the ceremonies of his reception. The emperor, he wrote, was "naturally of a healthy constitution and of great bodily strength . . . a very fine old gentleman, still healthy and vigorous, not having the appearance of a man of more than sixty." Macartney was informed that a resident minister was not permitted under the dynasty's regulations, and that China had no need for more open trade with Great Britain. The English scarcely noticed the officials' courtesies; to them it was the substance of negotiation that mattered, not the manner. They saw the Qing refusal of trade and diplomatic interchange as symptoms of an irrational arrogance that they someday would have to break down.

There were more anomalies and contradictions in the relations of the Qianlong court with the wider world. The computational and predictive superiority of European astronomy had been recognized since the late Ming and had led to the employment of Catholic missionaries as imperial court astronomers. This continued through the Qianlong reign, despite the prohibition of the preaching of Christianity in the Empire or its practice by Qing subjects. Early in the Qianlong reign there were a number of Jesuit priests and brothers who served the emperor as artists and musicians. The most famous of these was the Italian Giuseppe Castiglione (Chinese name Lang Shining), who designed the Rococo buildings of the Yuanmingyuan and developed a style of painting that combined Chinese technique and sensibility with Western perspective and rounded figures. His most famous work is a great scroll, now in the Palace Museum in Taipei, that shows a hundred horses racing, relaxing, feeding, and being groomed in an open landscape, as if they have just been turned loose to rest after a day on the great imperial hunt. Another is a portrait of the Qianlong emperor in his first year on the throne. His face is unlined and intelligent, his gaze calm and direct, perhaps already a bit masked and unexpressive from too much study of the awesome role he has just taken on. Another portrays him as a connoisseur of the Chinese arts, seated beside a palace lake, perhaps at Rehe, as servants bring him fine paintings to study.

Portraits of the emperor by other artists are remarkably varied. One shows him a bit older, and much more relaxed and lively in his gaze. In two others he appears as a scholar, seated at his desk surrounded by books and writing implements. In one we can read the poem he has been writing, a celebration of the abundant crops and good government of his reign and a conventional exclamation at the rapid passage of the years. One of the most startling is an elaborate Tibetan-style religious painting in which the emperor is the central figure, depicted as a reincarnation of the bodhisattva Manjusri.

Strangest of all is another portrait by Castiglione in which a very young man with the emperor's features and the dress of an apprentice Daoist priest encounters an older self; in the inscription the emperor wrote on it in 1782, he implies that it represents his inability to recognize that he eventually would be such a white-haired person (see page 236).

All this might be seen as a matter of images, of facades behind which something must be hidden. Can we ever catch the emperor off guard, get a glimpse of the private man? People have always wanted to know about the private lives of their rulers. For Chinese, this curiosity has been reinforced by the Confucian sense that rulers must set a good example in their personal conduct, and by more than two millennia of stories of those who did not, from the dowager queen of Qin to Empress Wu to the Zhengde emperor who so afflicted Wang Yangming's career. Beijing was (and is) a vast rumor-mill. In it, information on the private lives of the rulers may be of actual value in political maneuvering and at least gives the teller a reputation as someone "in the know."

What is reliably known of the private life of the Qianlong emperor is neither very extensive nor very interesting. His mother the dowager empress lived until the forty-second year of his reign. The emperor was ostentatiously devoted to her, and she must have been a great power in the palace, but no pattern of her influence on the politics of the empire can be detected. The emperor was devoted to his first empress, who died in 1748; her brother Fuheng and his sons were among the emperor's most trusted advisers, not always with good results. A second empress fled the palace to become a nun in 1765, amid lurid rumors of jealousies and sexual politics. Among the most persistent rumors from this period were those of a Muslim beauty brought back from the harem of the ruler of Yarkand who resisted all the emperor's advances. The dowager empress, it was said, fearing that the Muslim lady would use a concealed knife to kill the emperor, ordered her to commit suicide, and the emperor was prostrate with grief. There were even more bizarre tales in circulation among the common people, in which the emperor went out incognito on his tours of the south and used his martial arts to right private wrongs. Others claimed to have procedural and anatomical details on his sex life.

The sexual politics of an emperor's household, even if they can be reliably known, may be found not to have had much effect on the public actions of the ruler. Qianlong's special favor to his brother-in-law Fuheng and his sons may be the only case where he allowed his relations with women to affect his ruling. The portraits discussed above may in fact tell more about him than any exposé would. The variety of roles in which they present the emperor are reminders that in any political order, and very self-consciously in the Chinese tradition, the ruler is a player of roles, a shaper of symbols and images, as well as an administrator and a maker of "practical" decisions. An emperor also is very conscious of the glory of the dynastic line, of the imperative to maintain its fame or name (*ming*) and to establish his own. The Qianlong emperor, like every other Ming and Qing emperor, heard his own acts and words, even his face, referred to as the Sage Glance, the Sage Decrees, the Sage Visage, and so on. He was surrounded by people who called every one of his modest efforts in art, literature, and scholarship a work of genius. He could not help coming to believe it to a degree, but at the same time he was intelligent and well-informed enough to know the limits of his abilities and of his power to change things in his realm.

The result was that the emperor was exceedingly conscious of his public image and reacted defensively when he perceived any threat to it. As early as 1740, he became aware that some people recognized that Oertai and Zhang Tingyu had a great deal of influence over appointments. He stated:

> Since We have occupied the throne, We have never laid aside the appointive power. During the past several years, what persons have been appointed as a result of being recommended by these two ministers? What men have been degraded as a result of criticism by them? But as men generally imagine the matter, these two ministers are men of great power, who are able at will to effect the appointment or dismissal of others. What sort of ruler, then, do people regard Us to be?

The emperor's immense ghost-written literary production and the portraits of him as a literary man and a connoisseur of the arts clearly were meant to reinforce his image as a scholar and a patron of scholarship and the arts, and thus to appeal to the Chinese scholar-official elite. The Daoist portrait is more puzzling and perhaps more personal. Qianlong's inscription refers directly to his own aging, in the context of a teaching that sought physical immortality. To live to the age of sixty or seventy was less common then than it is in our own time, and would provoke even more self-conscious reflection in one who was daily called the Lord of Ten Thousand Years (*wan sui*).

And what of that Tibetan-style painting portraying the emperor as a reincarnation of a bodhisattva? We know that many Mongol and Tibetan Lamaists regarded the Qing emperors as reincarnated bodhisattvas. The Qing court did not deny the claim, but did not assert it publicly. As early as the Kangxi reign, the emperor was referred to colloquially within the palace as "the Buddha."[1] The Qianlong emperor's interest in Lamaism was serious and personal, not just a function of its usefulness in Mongolian and Tibetan politics. He received instruction from the Panchen Lama and from another high lama who resided in Beijing. Further striking confirmation of his personal interest is provided by a set of magnificent stone reliefs of Lamaist themes in the inner chambers of Qianlong's tomb, where they would be shut up after his death and it was hoped that they would never be seen again. (The tomb has been excavated in modern times and is open to tourists.) We might speculate that even if the emperor believed that he was in some sense a reincarnate bodhisattva, that became another role to fulfill, another set of disciplines to master. Godhood might be a source of power in Mongolia and Tibet, but certainly gave him no extra power or sanction to take initiatives in the ruling of China.

In 1792, near the end of his long reign, the emperor polished another image. He summarized the achievements of his armies in an essay entitled *Shi quan ji* (A Record of Ten Completions) and occasionally signed a poem "The Old Man of Ten Completions" (Shi quan laoren). The very real extension of Qing power into Inner Asia summarized above accounted for only three of the ten; the rest were not nearly such splendid "completions." Two were long and inconclusive campaigns against Tibetan peoples in the mountains of western Sichuan resisting the encroachment of Han settlers (the Jinchuan campaigns, 1747–49, 1771–76). One was the messy and expensive suppression of a rebellion on Taiwan (1787–88). One was a war on the Kingdom of Burma (1766–70), resulting from conflicts over the allegiance of border peoples, complicated by China–Burma trade interests and the migration of Chinese miners to northern Burma; many Qing troops were lost to disease and Burmese arms, and it ended with no real change in the frontier situation. Another (1788–89) was a very expensive and ill-advised intervention to support the ruling dynasty in Vietnam against a rebellion, which ended with the Qing acceptance of the rebel leader as the founder of the new Nguyen dynasty in Vietnam. In yet another, Qing

---

[1] Matteo Ripa, *Storia della Fondazione della Congregazione e del Collegio de' Cinesi* (Naples, 1852; recent reprint, Naples), 1: 461.

forces reacted to raids from Nepal into Tibet by sending forces to invade Nepal (1790–92), fighting most of the way to Katmandu against the Gurkhas, some of the best soldiers in the world, before withdrawing when Nepal agreed to send tribute embassies to Beijing. Of these seven campaigns, only the suppression of the Taiwan rebellion was a complete success, and all of them were much more expensive than they should have been, but in every case the commanders managed to report some victories and to bring matters to something that looked like a successful conclusion.

From Beijing or from most of the other great cities of China, all these campaigns seemed far away, and the imperial peace seemed secure. In 1771 the court celebrated the emperor's sixtieth birthday and the dowager empress's eightieth with great ceremony. The emperor, to be sure, was regularly reminded of the lower depths of chaos and crime in his great realm, since he had to review and approve every capital sentence handed down anywhere in the empire. In 1768 he was exasperated by an epidemic of reports of sorcerers who caused people's deaths by "stealing their souls," clipping the ends off men's queues or nailing papers on which their names were written to bridge pilings. He kept his officials looking for the masterminds of a plot, but there was no plot, just a shadowy world of fear and desperation. In the 1770s there was only one small outbreak of open opposition to Qing rule in the core areas of the empire. This was a local uprising of White Lotus religious sectarians in Shandong Province, near the Grand Canal, in the fall of 1774. Qing mobilization was cumbersome, and the emperor was outraged by reports that even some Manchu soldiers had fled before fierce rebel assaults, but still the rebellion was suppressed in about a month.

So despite continuing worries about various signs of social tension and corruption, the dynasty did not seem to be in any danger. The times seemed to call not for desperate measures of reorganization and innovation but for a stronger dose of traditional ruling strategies, in the form of a project that would exalt the names of the emperor and his dynasty to later generations; reinvigorate the role of the state as a definer of orthodox teaching; and give ambitious and talented scholars new opportunities to serve the state. In February 1772 the emperor ordered the first stages in what would become the largest project in Chinese history to collect, preserve, and evaluate old books, the *Siku quanshu* (Complete Collection of the Four Treasuries).

The aim of this project was to find rare books, either manuscripts or printed editions, that might exist in the hands of private individuals or local academies throughout the Empire, and to have the rarest of them copied so that reliable manuscript copies would be available to court scholars. As the project developed, copies also were prepared for several major scholarly centers in the provinces, critical studies were done of reliability and other merits of various works and various editions of the same work, and a comprehensive catalogue of all the books located and studied, with extensive bibliographic remarks, was published. This catalogue, 4,490 pages long in its modern reprint, lists over 10,000 titles. A total of 3,593 works were copied into the manuscript collections. Other less extensive collections of especially valuable items also were prepared. This really is a monument of officially supported scholarship. Everyone who studies pre-eighteenth-century China sooner or later relies on the great catalogue for guidance on sources or texts, or consults a work available only in one of the modern reprints of parts of the manuscript *Four Treasuries*. The organization of the collection is far more convenient to use than a huge collection done at the court of the third Ming emperor had been; this achievement of surpassing the Ming as a patron of Chinese scholarship was one that Qianlong had particularly in mind in his direction of the project. Scholars of the time responded eagerly to the imperial initiative, suggesting more investigation and preservation projects than the dynasty could fund, serving on the staffs of provincial Book Bureaus that sought out, checked, and reported on rare books, and arguing rather discreetly among themselves about issues of classical scholarship and Confucian philosophy that came up in the cataloguing work.

There was another side to this project, which seems not to have been part of the emperor's original plan and which emerged only gradually. Officials were aware from the beginning that such a project was likely to turn up pieces of the extensive private literature that recorded aspects of the Qing conquest of China in ways very unflattering to the dynasty. The emperor at first seemed inclined to be tolerant of divergent views, but by late 1774 he clearly expected all his officials and Book Bureaus to be on the lookout for books "defamatory to Our dynasty," which must be destroyed whenever found. In 1776 the Manchu governor of Jiangxi Province conducted a particularly vigorous and effective search and forwarded to the court for destruction over eight thousand volumes of books containing derogatory references to the Manchus. The emperor praised him and scolded the other provincial officials who had been less energetic in their searches. Of course, every official took the hint, and the books began to pour in. By the time the campaign wound down in 1781–82, over 780 books had been destroyed in whole or in part. Since Chinese books were printed with wooden printing blocks, the printing blocks were burned as well as all the copies found. Late in 1781 a court official reported that since 36,500 *jin* (roughly pounds) of printing blocks had been broken up for firewood, the court had saved almost a hundred ounces of silver on its heating expenses.

The destruction was human as well as literary. Scholars awaiting appointment as educational officials, like so many in an empire with more aspiring bureaucrats than positions, were sent to their native districts to search for subversive books. Some of them used their new powers to settle old scores in their home towns. As in the days of Empress Wu's informers, the contagion spread to commoners. One local troublemaker reported that a scholar in his area had written a dictionary in which he made critical comments about the great *Kangxi Dictionary*, compiled under the direction of the Kangxi emperor and one of the great monuments of Qing support of Chinese scholarship. The unfortunate lexicographer was executed and twenty-one of his relatives were condemned to slavery. The emperor was not always so savage in dealing with such reports, but this was not the only execution.

The *Four Treasuries* project was one of the stepping-stones to power of the man who dominated the politics of the empire from about 1780 to the death of the retired Qianlong emperor in 1799. This was Heshen, an imperial guardsman who caught the emperor's eye about 1775. By the end of 1777 he had been named a grand councillor and minister of the imperial household, among the highest offices in the government, and granted the extremely rare privilege of being allowed to ride horseback within the palace precincts. Although he was not without political ability and later performed some real services to the dynasty, he had accomplished nothing to deserve these honors at this time, and clearly owed everything to his personal relation with the emperor. This, of course, set the Beijing rumor-mill to working overtime. According to one story, the emperor became convinced that Heshen was the reincarnation of a concubine of the Yongzheng emperor who had hung herself to escape the prince's illicit advances; to some, this story implied a homosexual connection between the handsome young guardsman and the aging emperor.

Perhaps, however, it is enough to remember that in 1775 the emperor had sat on the Dragon Throne for forty years. It could be very lonely there. Most days were spent reading documents, discussing government problems, and performing exacting ceremonies. Everyone wanted something from the Lord of Ten Thousand Years, everyone flattered him, and no one ever spoke his or her mind. Qianlong's beloved first empress was long dead and a second was in a nunnery. Finally, we might recall that in 1782 he wrote on a Daoist portrait of himself an expression of inability to come to grips with the fact of growing old. In Heshen, perhaps, Qianlong found someone with whom he could relax and speak frankly, and recovered a bit of his youth.

It also is important to note that Heshen's mother was the daughter of a Manchu who served as grand secretary from 1776 to 1783. Among

Heshen's closest allies in his years in power were two sons of Fuheng, Fuchangan and the very able general Fukangan; it may be that his connection with this powerful family preceded and facilitated his rise to power. Soon he began to serve the emperor as an investigator of trouble spots in the bureaucracy. He became vice president, then president of the Board of Revenue. He uncovered inefficient and sloppy work in the copying and editing of the *Four Treasuries*. He was sent to Yunnan to investigate corruption and inefficiency under the Han Chinese governor-general there. He also was granted eight years in charge of the toll collection at one of the gates of Beijing, a post in which the usual one-year term was thought enough to make the holder rich. Both in his investigative work and in his mode of self-enrichment he was reviving roles played by Manchus in the early history of the dynasty, when they went out to the provinces to provide reliable supervision of the Han Chinese governors or to get rich by exploiting some toll-collection post. He was sent out once as a general, against a local Muslim rebellion in Gansu in 1781, proved to have no military talent, and never was so employed again. A member of a Korean embassy in 1780 thought him "elegant in looks, sprucely handsome in a dandified way that suggested a lack of virtue." Thirteen years later, however, a member of the Macartney embassy found that his "manners were not less pleasing than his understanding was penetrating and acute. He seemed, indeed, to possess the qualities of a consummate statesman."

High officials always sent rich New Year's presents to the Imperial Household. Heshen seems to have urged them to send ever more lavish gifts, and took many of them for himself. That was nothing more than the aggravation of a long-standing practice, and it is not clear that the sums spent in this way, always ultimately derived from diverted tax revenue or from presents from private individuals, noticeably increased the state's burden on ordinary people. Nor was it unusual or necessarily evidence of corruption that many of the top positions in the bureaucracy came to be occupied by Heshen's allies. What was distinctive about his years in power was the way he and his allies exploited the late Qianlong combination of a flourishing commercial economy with large-scale military campaigns on the peripheries of the empire; four of the "Ten Great Completions" were after 1780. What might be called a "campaign racket" pattern was clearly visible in the 1790s, and probably earlier. Generals took a cut from the military supplies and padded the muster rolls, keeping for themselves the pay for nonexistent soldiers. They exaggerated victories, covered up defeats and stalemates, and prolonged the campaigns and thus their own profit-taking. As costs of campaigns increased, officials put enormous pressure on big merchants who depended on state licensing and monopoly privilege to make huge "voluntary contributions" to the military budget. In the 1780s there were many bankruptcies among the salt monopoly merchants of Yangzhou, the tea exporters of Guangzhou, and the overseas shipping merchants at Xiamen.

Of course there was much resentment of the excesses of Heshen and his associates, but no official seems to have dared to speak out directly against him. Some tried indirect attacks, criticizing or arresting some particularly heavy-handed or corrupt associate of his. Even this was risky, since Heshen usually found out about such charges in time to help his ally arrange a cover-up. Moreover, the emperor always had been very sensitive to any challenge to or limitation of his ruling prerogatives. His defensive overreaction to any hint of criticism and Heshen's control of many of the levers of power at court made effective protest impossible. It was a long way from the Zhen'guan ideal of the Tang and a sad end for the high ideals of frank exchange between ruler and minister, of toleration of a variety of opinions, expressed in the essays of Qianlong's youth.

The situation got worse in the 1790s. A war against Miao tribespeople in the southern mountains dragged on and on. White Lotus sectarians rebelled in newly settled mountain areas of north China, and the campaign against them was the least effective, the most corrupt, and the most prolonged of all; not until after Qianlong's death did his successor bring in an effective commander and complete the suppression. But all that reached the palace were reports of great victories.

In the palace the deepening air of unreality culminated in a unique ceremony, splendid but hollow, of abdication. The emperor had vowed long before that he would not stay on the throne longer than his revered grandfather, the Kangxi emperor. Now he made plans to abdicate at the end of his sixtieth year on the throne. A fine set of buildings on the east side of the palace compound was prepared as his retirement palace. It was called the Palace of Tranquil Old Age (Ning shou gong). It is today one of the most elegant and evocative parts of the palace, with its dark woodwork inset with tens and tens of small panels containing paintings, poetry, and calligraphy given the retiring emperor by his high ministers. One also can see there some of the treasures that surrounded him and reminded him of the apparent excellences and achievements of his reign and of the great tradition of virtuous rule he claimed to follow. There is a pagoda-shaped gold case, containing about 100 kilograms of gold, fashioned to contain a hank of his mother's hair after her death. There is a huge piece of jade from the Muslim conquests, over two meters high, elaborately carved with figures representing the digging of canals under the direction of the Great Yu.

The abdication ceremony took place on February 9, 1796, New Year's Day in the Chinese calendar. The grand secretaries went to the Inner Palaces, brought forth the Imperial Seal, and placed it on a special table in the

Hall of Supreme Harmony, the main throne hall. Then both the Qianlong emperor and the heir apparent entered the throne hall in full court dress, while a court orchestra played the "music of Shun" and the great bells and drums sounded far to the south at the Meridian Gate. The Qianlong emperor took his place on the Dragon Throne for the last time. The heralds cracked their great whips, and all the princes and high officials took their places by rank, from the upper terraces down to the lesser officials a hundred meters away, at the back of the great courtyard. The heir apparent advanced and knelt before his father, the whole throng of nobles and officials kneeling in their rows. The declarations and memorials of congratulation were read out. The Qianlong emperor now handed his son the Imperial Seal. The new emperor then led the throng in the full three kneelings and nine prostrations before the retiring emperor. After Qianlong withdrew, the new Jiaqing emperor retired to another hall, changed into imperial audience robes, and returned to take his seat on the throne for the first time and to receive the homage and congratulations of his officials.

Emperors had retired from the throne in earlier dynasties, but always, it was thought, when they were forced to do so by overwhelming power or by their own incompetence. Qianlong, however, seemed to be abdicating in triumph, motivated only by filial deference to his grandfather. He even ventured to compare his abdication to those of Yao and Shun, noting that Shun had been eighty-six years old when he abdicated, just as he had. But he relinquished very little. He made it clear that although the new Jiaqing emperor could fulfill some of the routine administrative and ceremonial functions, he himself would make final decisions on major policies and appointments. He now was the grand supreme emperor (*tai shang huangdi*). The Jiaqing reign period would be used in public documents, but Qianlong still would be used within the court. The final proof that he was still in charge was that Heshen still was alive and more powerful than ever. In 1797 the Korean envoys recorded that Qianlong was becoming very forgetful. He died on February 7, 1799, in the Hall for Nourishing the Mind (Yang Xin Dian), with its great imperial desk and bookshelves, very much the right place for a sovereign who always had claimed to be completely in control. The Jiaqing emperor now moved promptly to arrest Heshen and confiscate his fortune and his property, including a magnificent estate where Beijing University now stands. His fortune was estimated at eighty million ounces of silver, the equivalent of almost two years of land-tax revenue for the entire empire. He was permitted to commit suicide.

The Jiaqing emperor struggled hard for over twenty years to revive the dynasty. He was assisted by many highly capable officials. Intellectuals tended to turn from studies of classical texts to questions of administration and statecraft. But, especially in the outlying provinces and the recently settled areas, central control never again was secure, and outbreaks of local rebellion were more and more frequent. Despite the capable hand on the deck, to return to Lord Macartney's nautical metaphor, the great ship was drifting toward the rocks.

16

HONG XIUQUAN,
THE HEAVENLY KING

• • • • • •

FOR ABOUT a week in the spring of 1837, an obscure local scholar in Guangdong named Hong Xiuquan lay ill, intermittently lost in visions in which he was transported to the heavens and received from various deities magic powers, special knowledge, and a mission on earth. Around 1850 he and his followers proclaimed on the basis of those visions the founding of the Heavenly Kingdom of Great Peace (Taiping Tianguo), with Hong as heavenly king (*tian wang*). By the time Hong died in the final collapse of his kingdom in the summer of 1864, over twenty million Chinese had died as a consequence of the rebellion he led and its savage suppression.

In his own time Hong was seen by many as a raving madman and his kingdom as a threat to everything proper and sensible. More recently, the Chinese Communists have seen in the "Taiping Revolutionary Movement" a confused but authentic precursor of their own cause, and many others have found in it rich evidence for visionary and egalitarian strains in Chinese culture that too often are overlooked in sweeping surveys like the present book. No one, however sympathetic or unsympathetic, denies the impact of the Taiping on Chinese history; the Qing dynasty never entirely recovered from it and was further shaken by internal stresses and foreign aggression. The end of the Qing in 1911 was the end of the 2,200-year-long imperial order that had begun with the unification under the First Emperor of Qin.

The inclusion of the story of Hong Xiuquan in this book is as obvious a choice as that of Confucius or Mao Zedong. Students' reactions to it set me on the path to this approach to Chinese history. It is historically important and luridly dramatic. Also, it gives an opportunity to correct for two biases of this selection of lives, toward the lives and values of the elite and toward historical developments in the capital and the most developed parts of the empire. This is the story of a movement that started in and was shaped by a remote and underdeveloped mountainous area. Although it was led by a man who had aspired to pass examinations and rise in the bureaucracy, it appealed to marginal and poverty-stricken groups that rarely left a trace in the historical record, and it drew on continuities in Chinese popular culture that I have noted only in passing.

This look into the world of popular culture will reveal much that seems very un-Confucian: violence, antihierarchical attitudes, a people frequently obsessed with ghosts and spirits and certainly not keeping them at a distance. Scholars used to describe the religious life of the Chinese common people as made up of Daoism, Buddhism, and various degenerate and superstitious cults and practices that might claim connection to either of these great traditions, both, or neither. Today many scholars (though by no means all modern Chinese) are more respectful of "Chinese popular religion," finding in its immense and unsystematic variety certain common themes: quests for harmony with the natural order; close interaction of the human and supernatural worlds, with ghosts everywhere, great men becoming gods, and gods possessing men; and a practical tendency to seek aid of particular gods in the pursuit of important worldly benefits, such as good crops, good health, the birth of sons, and passing examinations. If we recall the Han people awaiting the arrival of the Queen Mother of the West or joining the rebellion of the Yellow Scarves, or the Song religion-based revolt that Yue Fei helped to crush, we may suspect that this world of popular religion is as old and powerful as the Confucian or Daoist worlds of thought and action. Then it may not be so surprising to see it involved in the origins of the visionary and revolutionary side of modern Chinese political life.

Much of this religious life was quite supportive of the values of the imperial state and its quest for order and control. Every city had a temple of the Sovereign of the City Walls (*Cheng huang*), a sort of spiritual counterpart of the magistrate. These and other local deities were recognized by the state, and officials paid homage to them. Pilgrimages to famous Buddhist or Daoist temples, sacred mountains, and so on had some potential for disorder but usually were tolerated. If many Buddhist believers prayed to be reborn in a Western Paradise where all served and worshipped the bodhisattva Amitabha without distinction of rank or sex, that was certainly not in accord with the Confucian worldview but hardly threatening to the actual Confucian social order. When the deified men who were objects of worship included Guan Yu of the Three Kingdoms and (in a few regions) Yue Fei and Zheng Chenggong, the authorities tended to view these cults as supportive of the ideal of loyalty.

Also very important for the Chinese religious consciousness, and usually without political danger, was the vivid imagery of gods and goddesses, heavens and hells, that was found in popular prints of gods, images in temples and paintings on their walls, and the many stories and novels of the supernatural. In the greatest of these, *Xi you ji* (The Journey to the West), the beloved monkey hero Sun Wukong uses his magical powers to fight off all kinds of demons and assist a pilgrim monk on his way to India, rides the cosmos on his own magic cloud, and visits many dazzling heavenly palaces and their resident gods. This kind of religious imagination and imagery can be clearly seen in the visions of Hong Xiuquan.

The cautious authoritarians of the Qianlong bureaucracy had known that they could not hope to control all of the expressions of religious feeling in their vast and thinly ruled population, even if many of them were offensive to Confucian principles. They had to concentrate on identifying and suppressing those that were politically dangerous. For convenience these can be divided into two main types; in actuality, there was much variation and mixing.

The first type was based in some form of millennarian prophecy, usually a Mahayana Buddhist one of the end of an epoch of cosmic time, the destruction of the present world, and the coming to earth of Maitreya (Mi Le), the bodhisattva who was yet to come, to inaugurate a new and glorious order for the surviving believers. These would be those who had been initiated into the right secret knowledge and had taken the right vows, and joined in overthrowing the decadent authorities of the last days and welcoming Maitreya to earth. Prophecies of this kind were at the heart of the White Lotus teaching that was spread by networks of teachers, many of whom used martial arts and healing to establish personal relations that could lead to religious discussion and conversion. An important deity in this tradition was the Old Mother Beyond Birth (Wusheng Laomu), and many of the teachers were women. It usually was peacefully transmitted, but had produced major rebellions in late Yuan, late Ming, and late Qianlong. It was especially prevalent in Shandong and Hebei, and in 1813 an uprising of this type had briefly attacked one of the gates of the Beijing palaces before it was crushed.

A second type of subversive popular organization was connected less with clearly developed religious ideas and more with resistance to political authority. This was the loose network of "secret societies" that called themselves Triads, Heaven and Earth Society (Tian Di Hui), and many other names. Sometimes they claimed, not very plausibly, to trace their origins to Zheng Chenggong's Ming Loyalist resistance. Elaborate initiation ceremonies, owing much to the Peach Orchard Oath mystique of voluntary association in a noble cause, included oaths to overthrow the Qing and restore the Ming. Lodges of the society provided a bit of rough law and order in many remote settlements in the southern and western mountains, or aid and protection in a foreign port, growing in influence in the early 1800s.

Traditional ideas of the rise and fall of dynasties sometimes described an interaction of internal disorder and foreign aggression. In fact, the fall of the Ming was one of the few dynastic transitions to which this idea is fully applicable. In the early 1800s, the Qing rulers achieved a modest revival of order and administration after the stresses and corruptions of late Qianlong. But outlying areas, filling with migrants as the population grew, slipped farther and farther out of control. Foreign relations showed a similarly mixed picture. The great tea trade at Guangzhou remained under tight control and continued to grow, but in fact already in 1800 it was producing a great new social evil, the import of opium, and in 1839 led to the disaster of the Opium War.

The export of tea remained profitable to the English, and now to the Americans who joined in the trade, but there was no import the Chinese would buy in sufficient quantity to balance the trade, so there was a steady flow of silver into China. The English continually sought new imports that would balance the trade. Medicinal uses of opium had been known in China for centuries. Its recreational/addictive use depended on absorption through the lungs. In the 1600s, it seems, opium was mixed with tobacco and smoked. Later, a pure extract was vaporized and inhaled through a small pipe. The first Chinese to acquire an opium habit probably were immigrant traders and sugar plantation workers in Java. It already was spreading to the south China coast in the Qianlong reign, when its import and use repeatedly were forbidden. By 1800 a substantial share of English tea exports was paid for by imports of opium, smuggled along the coast in channels deliberately kept separate from the legal tea trade. Opium addiction spread among transport workers, government clerks, underemployed and disillusioned scholars, and even into the Manchu garrisons. The bribery necessary to keep the illegal trade moving became a factor in the general cynicism and fragility of order and morale, which in turn increased the demand for opium and other forms of escape. By the 1830s the rapid growth of opium imports had reversed China's balance of trade, producing an outflow of silver and severe currency problems.

Aware both of the currency problems and of the severe social and moral consequences of the spread of opium addiction, the Qing authorities stepped up their enforcement of the laws against the trade in and use of opium, but were unable to cut off its flow into the country. Finally in 1839 a vigorous and incorruptible imperial commissioner, Lin Zexu, had troops surround the foreign "factories" (residences and warehouses), cutting off all trade and supplies and threatening harsher action if the British did not surrender all the opium on their offshore supply ships. The British diplomatic representative made sure that he was in the factories at the start of the blockade. The opium was surrendered after the diplomat assured the opium firms that Her Majesty's Government would make sure they were compensated. The coercion of a diplomat and interference with his freedom of movement, a violation of the international law of which neither Lin Zexu nor any other Qing official had any knowledge, gave the British the cause for war they wanted. After some small naval battles and a British bombardment of a city farther north, an agreement was signed in January 1841 ceding Hong Kong Island to the British and meeting some of their other demands. But it was rejected both in London and in Beijing, and in May British troops surrounded Guangzhou city, arousing a great deal of popular hostility out in the country north of the city and withdrawing after an indemnity was paid. The Qing authorities were not at all interested in exploiting popular anti-British feeling, knowing how easily any popular mobilization could get out of hand and challenge their thin network of control.

British forces now were assembled, largely from India, including some very up-to-date steam-powered, iron-hulled gunboats. The British occupied the major city of Ningbo in Zhejiang and in March 1842 slaughtered a Qing attacking force. They then attacked other coastal points and proceeded up the Yangzi to Nanjing. Some Qing forces fled at the first sound of gunfire, but several of the Manchu banner garrisons fought to the last man. In addition to seeing no way to match the superior British arms and to not being at all inclined to arm the Chinese people against them, the Qing authorities noted the arrival in association with the English of Chinese from Guangzhou and Singapore with Heaven and Earth Society connections, whose activities in the Yangzi valley were not likely to be in the Qing interest.

The resulting Treaty of Nanjing was virtually dictated by the British. It ceded Hong Kong Island outright, opened four new ports, and abolished the old restrictions at Guangzhou. The Qing rulers thought they had gotten off easily, buying off a dangerous aggressor with trade concessions and the ceding of a barren and worthless island, buying the peace they needed for the stability of their own rule. Only after twenty years had passed and another war had been fought did they begin to understand how the Treaty of Nanjing had begun to enmesh them in commitment to a system of international law of which they knew nothing. In addition, the treaty had granted the foreign powers extraterritorial jurisdiction over their own nationals in Chinese ports and the most-favored nation principle by which a privilege granted to any foreign power could be claimed by all of them; these two principles were the keys to an intricate structure of foreign privilege and infringement of Chinese sovereignty that would grow steadily until the 1920s. In the short run, however, peace had been bought, and the Opium War had not led to a threat to the survival of the dynasty.

The Chinese common people around Guangzhou were no more aware of the long-run implications of the settlement than their rulers, but they intensely resented one provision of the treaty, the right of foreigners to reside within the city walls of Guangzhou, and organized enough agitation and low-scale violence that it was unenforceable. To them, it was clear that the Qing had sold out to the foreigners in order to save itself.

Guangzhou lies in the center of a rich lowland region, with fine rice land in several directions and good river connections (including one canal dating from the Qin) leading to the Yangzi valley. It had been a major port for China's trade connections with the Indian Ocean at least since Tang times. But mountainous country was not far away, and in it could be found a complex and violent frontier society. Closest to Guangzhou were hill areas settled by Hakka (Kejia), a group that is Han but culturally and linguistically distinct from the Cantonese. Migrating from farther north, the objects of prejudice from the settled local population, they were kept out of the fertile plains, farmed hill land, formed large clans that frequently feuded with each other, and sometimes built big fortified communal houses. Their women did not bind their feet. Hong Xiuquan was a Hakka. His vision of a society of equality and brotherhood clearly owes something to his people's experience of prejudice and of struggle for economic survival.

Farther west in Guangxi the frontier society was wilder and more diverse. There were ethnic minorities, the Miao, Yao, and Zhuang. The Heaven and Earth Society was strong among the Han settlers. Even the local religious cults were strange, including one to a man whose luck became very good after he murdered his mother and buried her in a lucky site, and many to a dog who was supposed to be the ancestor of the Yao minority. Pirates fled inland as British squadrons chased them from coastal waters. Soon all sides were armed to defend themselves against all others, and regular bureaucratic control was waning rapidly. This was the world where Hong Xiuquan's teachings would find an audience, and from which most of the leaders of his movement would emerge.

Hong Xiuquan was born in 1813 about thirty kilometers north of Guangzhou, the son of a Hakka farm family that had a bit of land but no pretensions at all to elite status. The boy's scholarly talent was recognized, and somehow the money was found to give him a few years of schooling. At the age of fourteen he went to Guangzhou for a first try at the examination for *shengyuan*, the first degree. Students frequently took the exam once before they were really ready in order to find out what it was like, and it is not surprising that he did not pass. Thereafter it seems that he had to earn his living as a schoolteacher, as many poor men did in their long years of studying for the examinations and taking them over and over. When he came to take the exam again in 1836, he saw one of the first Protestant missionaries to China preaching in a city street near the examination halls, while a Chinese assistant handed out copies of a religious pamphlet. He listened for a while and took a copy; later he would claim that he did not read it until years later. He failed the exam.

He failed it again in 1837. Exhausted and distraught, he was taken home in a sedan chair and lay for several days in a state of deep mental disturbance, sometimes talking wildly, sometimes lost in his own visions. In his visions he was taken up to Heaven. In the dazzling light he was received by beautiful maidens, but "cast no sidelong glances at them." He was washed to cleanse him of the filth of the world. His belly was cut open and his internal organs replaced by new, clean ones. Then he was led before a magnificent divine figure with a long golden beard, who lamented that the people of the world had lost their "original hearts" and were deluded by malicious demons. They no longer worshipped him, and they drank wine, smoked opium, and lived lives of debauchery and worldly vanity. Hong was eager to assist in chastising the demons and soon was allowed to do so, driving from Heaven the Dragon Demon of the Eastern Sea. Hong *belonged* in Heaven and had his own beautiful palace. It now was clear that the gold-bearded figure was his heavenly father, and he had a heavenly elder brother who assisted him in some of his battles. His heavenly mother and heavenly younger sisters brought him beautiful fruit to eat, and the younger sisters sometimes chanted sacred texts with him or joined him in his attacks on the demons. He was given a demon-slaying sword and a golden seal that forced demons to flee. Once he watched his father and elder brother chastise Confucius as one who had done the most to delude the people of the world.

Hong's heavenly father now ordered him to return to the world and assist in cleansing it of demon-worship and evil living. He went, most unwillingly. As he recovered from his trances and visions, his relatives and neighbors found him very strange and confused, but also much more dignified and forceful than he had been before. He now seems to have had some sense that he was a man with a mission, but could not yet see what his next step ought to be. He went back to teaching school.

Six years later, in 1843, Hong failed the *shengyuan* exam again. This time he was not devastated but angry at the system that had caused him to expend so much effort for nothing and that failed to recognize his talent. No doubt he was affected by his own vague sense of mission, but also by the general climate of opinion in Guangzhou, where anger was running high at the Qing sellout settlement in the Treaty of Nanjing. Soon thereafter he read or reread the Christian pamphlet he had obtained in 1837 and found the key to his visions. His heavenly father was Jehovah, the Lord on High

(Shang Di), the universal god of the Jews and Christians; his heavenly elder brother was Jesus Christ. He was the younger brother, sent to restore God's Kingdom on Earth. The pamphlet also helped to shape his understanding of his mission, by its scathing denunciations of the moral rot of the China of his time and by its repeated references to the Kingdom of Heaven (Tian Guo), which sometimes meant the heavenly reward of the believer after death and sometimes the community of believers on earth.

All the accounts we have of Hong's visions are more or less affected by his later Christian understanding of them. The summary given above tries to edit out the most obvious Christian elements and to emphasize facets that probably came from Chinese folk religion: the magic weapons and battles with demons, the sweetness and light of life in Heaven. The punishment of Confucius may be an echo of Christian hostility, or evidence that already in 1837 Hong was alienated from the orthodox tradition. God's golden beard may reflect a blond beard on the missionary heard on the street in 1836. The prominence of female deities, serving, reciting, even fighting, is striking and will remind us of the female deities and leaders of popular religion and rebellion and of the relative emancipation of Hakka women. It may also have been a private echo of a lost rural childhood, with a protective older brother, beloved mother and younger sisters, before the dreadful day when the boy's talent was recognized and he was committed to a life of discipline, memorization, and the dreaded examinations.

Hong's first converts included two cousins, Feng Yunshan, who was to be the movement's first real organizer, and Hong Ren'gan, who would be, seventeen years later, the last leader to offer any prospect of revival and intelligent leadership for the Heavenly Kingdom. Hong Ren'gan promptly got himself in trouble by removing the tablet of Confucius from the village school where he taught. Feng and Hong Xiuquan set out to spread their message in Hakka areas of Guangxi. Hong soon returned to Guangzhou, where he read, wrote, and spent several months studying the Bible with an American missionary.

Returning to Guangxi in 1847, Hong found that Feng Yunshan had made many converts and built up an impressive organization, centered at a place called Jintian with branches in other settlements, which was called the God Worshippers Society (Bai Shang Di Hui). It was founded on uncompromising worship of the One True God who had revealed himself to Hong, on rejection of the worship of all idols and "demons," and on puritanical standards of personal conduct. We might suppose that it gave the Hakka convert a remarkably clear new sense of the meaning of his or her life, and of the difference between this purified mode of life and worship and the religious weirdness and frontier disorder all around. It also produced a tightly centralized organizational structure, more effective for self-defense than anything the Hakka had had before. Self-defense became more necessary as the God Worshippers aroused the hostility of their neighbors by idol-smashing rampages in local temples. Thus the God Worshippers Society became an important factor in the general militariza- tion and rebelliousness of Guangxi, and soon attracted the attention of the Qing authorities.

Feng Yunshan and Hong Xiuquan both were away from their organiza- tion from the end of 1848 to the summer of 1849, and in their absence some new leaders emerged. Two of them, Yang Xiuqing and Xiao Chaogui, began to present themselves as channels for revelations from God or Jesus, who possessed their bodies and used their voices. Idol- smashing and conflicts with non–God Worshippers continued to grow, and the leadership seems to have decided it would have to leave the area and move ahead to a full-scale rebellion. In July 1850 the faithful aban- doned their home villages and assembled at Jintian. After some clashes with ineffective Qing forces, they proclaimed on January 11, 1851, the inauguration of the Heavenly Kingdom of Great Peace (Taiping Tian Guo) and called upon the people of China to purify their morals and over- throw the Manchu "demons." Starting north, they were besieged from September 1851 to January 1852 at Yongan in northern Guangxi. Then failures of coordination among the besiegers allowed them to break out and head north into Hunan and down to the Yangzi.

By the time they reached the great river, and probably sooner, a heady mix of military organization of rebellion, appeal to the poor and despised, and Taiping religion had produced distinctive ideals and actualities of or- ganization that were crucial to the rise and fall of the heavenly kingdom. At Yongan, all the major leaders were named kings (*wang*). Hong Xiuquan was first among equals, the heavenly king (*tian wang*); the word Lord (*Di*) was reserved for God (*Shang Di*), and the title emperor (*huang di*) was not used. This was one of a number of ways in which the Taipings expressed a sense of the brotherhood of believers, but politically a very dangerous one. Yang Xiuqing as eastern king had great influence both as a field com- mander and as a mouthpiece of God. Below the kings the entire population of the Heavenly Kingdom was supposed to be organized in a strict military hierarchy down to units of twenty-five families, each under a sergeant. Imperatives of military organization here interacted with theocratic poli- tics; unlike Confucian political ethics of the Way of Ruler and Minister, where orders came from human beings and could be questioned in the name of principles that ruler and ministers shared, Taiping edicts came from God, straight down the chain of command.

When they had assembled at Jintian, the Taiping faithful had left farms and homes behind and had become completely dependent on the distribution of captured supplies. At Yongan or on the first sweep through Hunan, the Taiping leadership turned this rough and ready expeditionary collectivism into a blueprint for an ideal new society that may have attracted many of the dispossessed but also must have convinced every property-owning Chinese who heard of it that there could be no compromise with the Taipings. The Taiping land system was the product of the intersection of this expeditionary collectivism, New Testament humanitarianism, and the ancient bureaucratic idealism associated with the *Ceremonies of Zhou*. At the local level, Taiping society was to consist of perfect little commonwealths, each with a sergeant who lived at a church where the youth were taught Holy Scripture. There was to be no private property. The sergeants were to classify land according to its productivity, and manage its distribution to their twenty-five families so that each received some good land and some bad, and all enjoyed an equal harvest. If there was not enough land in one place, people should be moved elsewhere. Mulberry trees for silkworms were to be planted everywhere. Every family was to keep five hens and two sows and make sure they were bred every year. At harvest time, after enough was set aside to provide for each family, the remainder was to be deposited in a common storehouse. "Thus all the people in the empire may together enjoy the abundant happiness of the heavenly father, Supreme Lord, and Great God. There being fields, let all cultivate them; there being food, let all eat; there being clothes, let all be dressed; there being money, let all use it, so that nowhere does inequality exist, and no man is not well fed and clothed."

In the rich and densely settled valleys of Hunan the Taipings seem to have found many people receptive to their message; by the time they reached the Yangzi and set out downstream in a great fleet of boats they probably had half a million people with them. Gathered at Wuchang on the Yangzi in February 1853, the Taiping leaders decided not to march straight for Beijing but to head down the river and capture Nanjing. This decision probably was a fatal error, giving the Qing time to improve its defenses. The Taiping leaders were drawn to the great riches of the lower Yangzi. Based at Nanjing they could move on to cut off the supply of lower Yangzi grain to Beijing. And almost two hundred years earlier Zheng Chenggong had understood the symbolic importance of Nanjing, capital of many southern dynasties and first capital of the Ming, for any anti-Qing effort. Sailing down the great river, bypassing the cities on both banks, the Taiping forces appeared before the great walls of Nanjing on March 6. The Qing garrison was small and incompetently led. The Taipings entered the city on March 19 and soon proclaimed it their heavenly capital.

The dilemma the Taipings had faced in this campaign was almost exactly the same as that Zheng Chenggong had faced in *his* Nanjing campaign. An invader or insurgent, unless the government in place was near collapse, could not afford to besiege, take, and garrison every city he passed by en route to his most important goal, but had to run the risk that defending forces would use these cities to mount a counterattack. The Taipings failed to take or took and then abandoned the major cities along their route through Hunan, and Wuchang on the Yangzi. Thus they left the way open for a revival of Qing power on their western flank.

Hunan was the home of some eminent scholar-officials who had made important contributions to efforts to revive traditional statecraft and Confucian morale in the preceding decades. Much of its rice land was held by tough, independent small landholders. Both scholars and farmers were threatened by Taiping principles and practices. Almost as soon as the Taiping wave had passed, they began to form militia units, with scholar-official officers and small-farmer soldiers, that would gradually build into the great Hunan Army that played a key role in the final defeat of the Taipings. These defenders of the Qing order would have to face other rebellions, north of the Yangzi, in the coastal cities, and among the Muslims of the southwest and northwest. Their ultimate success against these many challenges would be the result not only of their determination and organizing skill but of the failure of the various rebel groups to cooperate with each other.

Early in May 1853 a major Taiping expeditionary force set out to the north. From July to September it was tied up besieging the city of Huaiqing, a serious loss of summer campaigning time that again gave the Qing a chance to improve its defenses. At Cangzhou in October, over ten thousand Qing soldiers and civilians died as the Taipings took the city; banner soldiers and some others probably committed suicide, but many were killed in cold blood. Early in November the invaders were turned back near Tianjin and settled down in winter camp. They were very badly prepared for the northern winter; Guangxi had never been like this. They were hoping for reinforcements and supplies from the base area around Nanjing. Their supplies were dwindling. No help came, and in February 1854 they began to head back south. One rescue expedition that summer failed to reach them, and a dwindling remnant of the great northern expedition staggered on south, as the Qing brought in more competent forces and commanders. The last remnant of the northern expeditionary force surrendered in May 1855.

The Taipings were more successful in pushing back to the west into areas they had passed by on their run down the Yangzi to Nanjing. They advanced through Anhui in 1853 and were turned back in Hunan in April

1854. They occupied Wuchang in June 1854 and held it until the end of 1856. The pro-Qing Hunan militia forces were gradually building strength, but still had only very uneven success in battle.

But the Heavenly Kingdom was not just another warlord regime. Its success and failure depended in large measure on the extent to which its radical new vision of government and society produced a degree of individual commitment, military discipline, and coherent direction at least equal to that of the Qing. The few Western visitors, including missionaries, who visited Nanjing under the Taipings were impressed by the difference between what they saw there and the normal state of Chinese society. Indulgence in wine, opium, and tobacco was strictly forbidden. The whole population was under strict military discipline, men and women living in separate barracks; until about 1855, sexual relations were forbidden even between husbands and wives. Visitors were impressed by the ubiquity of serious commitment to Taiping religious beliefs and attendance at religious services. Women had their own military units and were eligible for many offices. Many women did heavy manual work, to which the Hakka farm women were thoroughly accustomed but which was very hard on some of the more recent recruits. In Ming and Qing China women were kept more or less secluded, and their mobility was restricted by the custom of footbinding. The Taipings followed Hakka custom in forbidding footbinding, and visitors noted with surprise the relaxed mingling of men and women on the streets of Nanjing. The kings might have more than one wife, but they all had roughly equal status, and the women's quarters of the palaces were managed by bureaucracies of women, not eunuchs.

There is little evidence, however, that the ideal picture of local control and land distribution was ever put into practice in the countryside, even in the areas most securely held. The Taiping leaders were more concerned to support their military efforts by drawing regular tax revenues from established rural power structures than to realize their revolutionary vision in the villages.

It is not particularly surprising that the rigid equality of the Taiping rank and file did not preclude a life of luxury for the kings and high officials. More serious were some problems among them that revealed flaws at the heart of Taiping political culture. The heavenly king rarely was an actively involved leader. Most of the time he was secluded in his palace, praying for the victory of his armies. Yang Xiuqing was one of the most talented and dynamic leaders and had gained great authority by the many occasions on which God spoke through him. In August 1856 he seems to have been moving toward deposing Hong Xiuquan and making himself the supreme ruler. Hong ordered three other kings to kill Yang and his followers; about twenty thousand were massacred. Then Hong ordered another king to attack the one who had led the massacre. A third king, one of the most talented, turned away from the bloody streets of Nanjing and led his troops on a series of expeditions through distant provinces, never to return. The chaos at the center contributed to the collapse of the Taiping thrust to the west, and soon Qing forces were camped not far from Nanjing itself, though not in sufficient strength to attempt an assault.

For several years thereafter there was a near vacuum of leadership in Nanjing. Then a few new talented field generals emerged, and at the center Hong Ren'gan, cousin of the heavenly king and one of his first converts, returned from long years of study with foreign missionaries in Hong Kong. Perhaps the first Chinese convert to Victorian optimism about technology and progress, he had ambitious plans to strengthen central control, cultivate friendship with the Western powers, build railroads and steamships, and so on. He never was able to realize these plans, but did provide a degree of rational decision making at the center.

In 1860 the Taiping armies, under new vigorous generals, moved down into the rich Yangzi delta, occupying Suzhou against minimal resistance. They moved on toward Shanghai, one of the ports open to foreigners. Other Taiping forces reached the coast farther south, occupying the port of Ningbo and then turning toward Shanghai. Foreigners had been intrigued by what they heard and saw of the Taipings, but now were inclined to think them unable to provide the stability necessary for the expansion of trade. Missionaries had come to understand just how unorthodox Taiping Christianity was. Also, a second round of warfare in 1856–60 had led to a new set of treaties between the Qing and the foreign powers, opening more ports and opening the interior to trade and missionary activity. The foreign powers now found it more attractive to support the government that was committed to these treaties. Previously they had sold arms to both sides. Now they supported the Qing, and Chinese merchants at Shanghai helped to finance and supply the Qing armies. Chinese military units enlisted, trained, and led by foreigners helped to defend the Shanghai area.

Old Western accounts exaggerated the contribution of these Western-led forces in the defeat of the Taiping. Most basic, however, were the Hunan Army and the other militia forces modeled on it, especially one from Anhui. Now they inexorably closed in on Nanjing from east and west. By the summer of 1863 Qing forces had blocked access to Nanjing from all directions, and the foreign powers had agreed to stop all shipments up the river to the Taiping capital. The heavenly king rejected proposals that the leadership try to break out of the encirclement and withdraw to carry on the fight elsewhere. No one with a mission from God should fear the "demons." "You are afraid of death," he told his best general, "and so you will die." As food supplies dwindled, he ordered the official and people to live on "sweet dew," meaning grass and weeds but seeming to recall both Han dynasty hopes for heavenly blessings and the Old Testament manna from Heaven. On May 30, 1864, a decree was issued that the time had come for the heavenly king to go to Heaven to plead with the heavenly father and heavenly elder brother to preserve the heavenly capital. On the next day, Hong Xiuquan died.

On July 19, 1864, a huge explosion breached the walls of Nanjing, and the Qing forces poured into the city. They killed anyone they could find except the young women whom they carried off, and they set fires everywhere. The Qing generals who took control of the palace treasuries seem to have kept the contents for themselves. Qing officials already were at work on the long and hard task of restoring outlying areas to normal life. The immense loss of life had come not only from the slaughter by both sides but also from the huge numbers of farm families who had fled before the armies, leaving their fields uncultivated and dying of hunger or disease along the roads. There were some fine agricultural plains where not a person was to be seen for miles. Qing campaigns continued against another rebellion north of the Yangzi until 1868, and Muslim resistance in outlying provinces persisted into the 1870s.

It took over two more years for the Qing armies to find and disperse Taiping armies that had been on campaign away from Nanjing in 1864. They did their work very thoroughly; no record has been found of any rebellious activity or private military organization in the late nineteenth century that was organizationally descended from the Taipings or was influenced by Taiping ideas. It is worth noting, however, that the revolutionary leader Sun Yat-sen, who grew up in the Canton delta in the 1870s, heard many tales of Taiping heroes. No one, as far as I know, has really tried to find out how widespread such tales of a great Taiping "lost cause" may have been in various areas.

There was in any case no recurrence in China's modern century of the Taiping combination of otherworldly religion and quest for an egalitarian utopia on earth. But several times in this book the utopian strain has turned up in different combinations—Wang Mang and the well-field scheme, the Daoist collectivism of the Later Han rebellions—and we will see it again in the career of Mao Zedong. In none of the earlier combinations, nor in the Taiping, did anything come of it for very long. Maoist collectivism certainly changed a great deal for thirty years or so, but its future at present is far from certain. A more substantial Taiping moral achievement, it seems to me, was the equality of the sexes and the humane relations between them that seem to have prevailed at Nanjing. This did not survive the fall of the heavenly kingdom, and it would be hard to argue that it had any effect on modern China's halting progress toward the elimination of gender bias and male chauvinism. But in thinking about the sources of moral vision for any modern society, we would do well to remember that this Taiping achievement was the work of uneducated, back-country farmers and their tough, big-footed women, and that it already was anticipated in their unhinged cousin's visions of heavenly little sisters fighting demons at his side and joining him in singing hymns in praise of their Heavenly Father.

LIANG QICHAO

For the people we have studied so far and their Chinese contemporaries, China was very much the center of the world, and Chinese culture was the only true high culture. The world that mattered was the *tian xia*, "All Under Heaven," and the emperor as *tian zi*, "Son of Heaven," was at least ceremonially the superior of all other rulers. The commercial connections with the world of Islam and the coming of European traders and missionaries remained marginal. Consciousness of the Indian origins of Buddhism, for a long time an important reason for the hostility to it of some Chinese intellectuals, faded as names, texts, and images became more thoroughly Chinese in style. Mongol and Manchu conquerors, while by no means abandoning their original cultures, represented themselves to their Chinese subjects as Chinese emperors and defenders of the Chinese tradition. The Taipings had believed in a God of all humankind whose relation to human beings previously had focused on the Jews, not the Chinese, but their vision had been rejected and their movement crushed.

Liang Qichao was an eminent member of the first generation of the Chinese elite who came to see China as one country, *guo*, among many, not as the center of All Under Heaven. In a stream of clear, powerful writings he articulated to the Chinese people the immense consequences of China's membership in a society of competitive nation-states and the new moral and organizational demands this placed on them. Beginning life with ambitions and a curriculum of study not basically different from Su Dongpo's, he spent much of his adult life struggling to interpret non-Chinese ideas of history and government in ways that would make it possible for Chinese to draw on them, and integrate them with the best of their own tradition, in building a new China. In the process he experimented with new roles, new ways of life, suitable for that new nation. His efforts in building parties and engaging in parliamentary politics were not very successful. His great contribution was in his writing, which took the new form of editing and writing for periodical reviews. He turned the great tradition of the politically committed literary man into the powerful modern form of political and cultural journalism.

The rulers and generals who crushed the Taiping Heavenly Kingdom in 1864 were just beginning to confront the reality of an intrusive outside world that would make the decline of the Qing not just a dynastic crisis but the end of a world. The Qing rulers and almost all their ministers had thought that they had ended the Opium War of 1839–42 by successfully managing and buying off the foreigners. It was much harder to take that view of conflicts with Britain and France between 1856 and 1860. The incidents that provoked these attacks were not major; the real cause was the refusal of the Western powers to accept Chinese rejection of Western forms of diplomacy and restrictions of foreign trade and missionary activity. In 1860 British and French troops occupied Beijing, burned and looted the Summer Palaces, and insisted that the court, which had fled to the summer estate at Rehe, accept the presence in Beijing of resident envoys of foreign nations and deal with them according to Western diplomatic norms. For the next ten years or so, Qing officials learned to make good use of the rules of diplomacy and international law. They sought to acquire and learn to use some of the modern weapons they would need if diplomacy failed, and much more tentatively to develop some of the modern means of production and transportation that modern warfare and arms production required. The same officials and others, as they finished the long, brutal suppression of the Taipings and the other rebellions, sought to restore the agrarian economy, revive traditional education, eliminate corruption, and in general revive the morale and effectiveness of traditional Chinese statecraft. There were some very intelligent and dedicated statesmen involved in these efforts, but they could not undo the effects of the civil wars and of the failure of the state to keep pace with growth of the society and economy since Qianlong times. Also, the efforts in foreign relations and modern arms clearly were viewed even by their advocates as disagreeable necessities, peripheral to the main concerns of statesmen, requiring no fundamental reorientation of politics, and there were many who bitterly opposed even these modest changes.

The result was that the modernizing efforts of the "self-strengthening" statesmen of the 1860s and 1870s were halting at best, often undercut by corruption, by transfers of key officials, and by inadequate coordination among provinces. Conflicts over Vietnam led to humiliating defeats in a brief war with France, 1884–85. A far greater shock was the result of the rise of Japan, building a new and dynamic political order as China strove to patch the old one together. Japan's long confrontation with China over hegemony in Korea led to open war in 1894–95, disaster for Chinese arms, and a peace treaty dictated by Japan. The Qing was forced to open China to foreign-owned manufacturing, to recognize a Japanese sphere of interest and investment in Fujian, and to cede Taiwan outright to the Japanese. This was shock enough; the Chinese had had little official contact with Japan or reason to think much about it since the days of Zheng Chenggong, and they tended to view it as some kind of crude and distorted reflection of China, certainly not a rival. And after 1895 Britain, France, Germany, and Russia, impressed by what Japan had gained by bullying the Qing Empire and anxious to get their own leased ports and zones for trade and investment, took turns in extorting concessions from China. It was in these desperate days, when it finally was clear to every thinking Chinese that the Qing Empire could not go on doing business as usual, that Liang Qichao appeared on the national political scene as a member of a powerless but prestigious and deeply engaged movement of young scholars.

Liang Qichao was born in 1873 in Xinhui, Guangdong, not far from Guangzhou, where foreign merchants had bought tea in Qianlong's time and where Hong Xiuquan had failed the examinations. This area had been deeply involved in foreign trade for hundreds of years and now was sending thousands of emigrants to settle in Southeast Asia, Australia, California, and so on. Liang's family had been farmers for many generations. His grandfather, who had received his *shengyuan* degree and had been a local director of studies, was the only member of the family even to begin the long climb toward officialdom. The grandfather was the boy's first teacher, and we can imagine his delight when the boy turned out to be a child prodigy, winning his *juren* degree at the age of sixteen, roughly comparable to getting a master's degree at that age today. The brilliant young man spent the next few years studying at an important academy in Guangzhou that combined Neo-Confucian studies with the detailed and critical research on classical texts that had flourished in the Qing but had no place in its curriculum for learning about the world outside China. In the spring of 1890 he went to Beijing, where he failed the *jinshi* examination, and on his way back south he stopped in Shanghai, where he acquired some Chinese books about the Western world and the sources of its daunting strength. Later in the same year he and a friend called on the older Cantonese scholar Kang Youwei. His first interview with Kang began early in the morning and lasted until evening. "It was like cold water poured down my back, like being hit on the head with a club. . . . I was both shocked and delighted, embittered and remorseful, frightened and uncertain." Their eyes opened to new worlds of ideas, the two young men talked all night and then went the next day to beg Kang Youwei to accept them as his pupils.

This drama of sudden intellectual awakening and ardent discipleship was not all that different from the experiences of Wang Yangming's disciples, or Hui Neng's, or Confucius's. The content of Kang's teachings was very Confucian, but they also were very much of their time. In the late 1880s and early 1890s there was a slow but effective spread of knowledge of the outside world in the Chinese elite, especially through the journals and translations of missionary-connected organizations. Several scholars had begun to write about the need for some kind of advisory assembly; here knowledge of Western parliamentary institutions fused with Confucian ideals of open consultation between ruler and ministers, but with little or no concept of citizens wielding power or defending their rights against the ruler.

Kang's position among these advanced thinkers was not a prominent one, but his ideas were unusual and adventurous, and many would come to regard them as dangerous. For him, reforms were not necessary adjustments of a fundamentally sound Confucian tradition, but part of an effort to recover the true teaching of Confucius, lost 1,900 years before in the days of Wang Mang. Kang taught that Confucius had been, despite his own insistence that he was "a transmitter and not a creator," the creator and founder of this teaching, an "uncrowned king." He drew on the New Text (*jinwen*) tradition of classical scholarship, which had its roots in early Han times. The New Text school had revived in Qing times partly because of the impact of textual scholars' criticisms of Old Text (*guwen*) versions of the Classics. It favored an activist, practical approach to the life of the scholar-official over the more moralistic, contemplative orientation of some representatives of the Neo-Confucian tradition. This in turn linked with the revival of interest in "statecraft" studies that had begun in the late Ming. Kang's New Text teaching went much further, claiming that all the Old Text versions had been forged to support Wang Mang's usurpation. Confucius had been the creator of a great new teaching that also had been lost in later times. One key element in that teaching was a vision of progressive change in human history, from disorder to "small order" to "great harmony" (*da tong*) or great peace (*tai ping*), in which all the usual barriers and differentiations of human society would be swept away. Theories of this kind had in fact been popular in the decades of Wang Mang's rise to power. Such a teaching depended for its transmission not on the teaching, administration, and exemplary personal behavior of the rulers but on the faith and determination of those who understood it and sought to "preserve the teaching." It is easy to understand how these amazing teachings could have such an impact on an impressionable young scholar; it also is easy to understand how thoroughly they would horrify many in the years to come.

Liang and Kang both went to Beijing in 1895 for the *jinshi* examinations. Kang passed; Liang did not. More important, they mobilized their fellow candidates to petition the Qing court to reject the peace treaty imposed by the Japanese and to begin the basic institutional reforms needed to save China from foreign aggression. The mobilization of the political convictions of students and scholars was in a tradition reaching back at least to the Han. Although the court paid no attention to their protests, the consequences of their collective action were immense. The scholars' sense of the urgency of their cause was sustained by one incident after another of imperialist bullying and Qing acquiescence. Kang, Liang, and their allies planned to arouse elite public opinion all over the empire by forming a network of study societies, which among other activities would publish journals to urge reform and to spread the knowledge of the modern world that it would require. The first of these societies and its newspaper, begun in Beijing in 1895, quickly withered in the face of government hostility. Liang and others had more success in Shanghai in 1896, founding the famous journal *Shiwu bao*, literally meaning "Reports on Contemporary Affairs," but carrying the English title *Chinese Progress* on its masthead. The publishing and wide distribution of a journal by a reform society was a strategic breakthrough, making possible regular transmission of new ideas to many centers in the provinces, and later the maintenance of influence from exile.

Liang's essays in *Chinese Progress* were very important and influential. He also managed to find time in 1897 to publish a book on "Western government." He now was arguing explicitly that China had to learn from the successes of Western (including Japanese) political life, not just Western technology. But he still adhered to Kang Youwei's desire to "protect the teaching" of Confucianism, and although his wide-ranging interests and fluent style made him a successful and influential journalist, he was not yet ready to identify himself completely with that novel vocation or to forsake his more traditional ambitions to be an advisor of rulers and a teacher of eager disciples.

In 1897 Liang turned down several invitations from prominent officials to join their personal staffs. The most notable of those who sought his services was Zhang Zhidong, governor-general of Hunan and Hubei, the most capable of the provincial officials who still were trying to realize the moderate "self-strengthening" reform programs. Zhang soon would be horrified by the radical ideas of Kang and Liang and become one of their most influential opponents.

Late in 1897, however, Liang accepted an invitation to move to Changsha, capital of Hunan, where a reform-minded provincial governor was encouraging the modernization of the city, the forming of reformist academies and societies, and the publication of a startling range of old and new opinions. In addition to advising the officials and contributing to provincial journals and other publishing projects, Liang became the head teacher at a new Academy of Current Affairs, where his intensely moral and personal style of teaching gave full expression to the millennial continuity of the master–disciple relation.

Shanghai was by far the best place in China to get news from the rest of the world and to talk to foreigners who were anxious to disseminate modern Western ideas and knowledge among the Chinese. Changsha in 1897 was a rare pocket of official commitment to learning from foreign experience in nontechnological ways. In these places, amid the unending reports of foreign designs on Chinese territory, it is not surprising that Liang's ideas developed rapidly, both in their political radicalism and in the depth of their criticisms of the moral foundations of Chinese civilization. He was not alone; his writing articulated changes with which many of his contemporaries were struggling. Already anticipated in his writings and actions of this period, and fully articulated in the essays of Liang and others in the next six or seven years, was the dissolution of the system of political roles and public morality followed in this book through so many changes since the time of Confucius. It no longer was enough for officials to rule over the common people with paternal kindness and to urge their rulers, selflessly and fearlessly, to rule with benevolence. It no longer was enough for local scholars to aspire to become officials. They had to go beyond the network of one-to-one relations implied by the Way of the Ruler and the Minister and the fundamental dependency of the minister's role. They had to take the fate of the nation in their own hands, discussing, organizing, mobilizing power, taking action. Even the common people, traditionally passive except in crises of the change of the Mandate of Heaven, had to become constantly involved citizens.

These basic transformations were necessary because China had been forced to recognize that it was part of a world of competitive nation-states. It had to mobilize its human and material resources not just to defend itself but to increase its wealth and power as other nation-states did. The Chinese had to conceive of themselves as one people among many, comparable and competing, if they were to learn the secrets of foreign wealth and power. The necessary transformations of politics and values were possible, or at least conceivable, because, although when taken together they represented a fundamental break with the past, they could be linked to many disparate elements in the theory and practice of traditional Chinese politics. The idea that people make their own history, sometimes by recognizing the necessity for fundamental change, was a recurring one in Chinese historical thought, and as early as the 1860s a few thinkers had begun to ask if China might be on the brink of a transformation comparable to the founding of dynastic rule after the death of Yu and to the bureaucratic unification under Qin. Despite the structural dependency of their role, officials were expected to be morally autonomous individuals and vigorous and effective administrators, like Su Dongpo or Wang Yangming; the stress on the moral autonomy and social effectiveness of the individual could easily become part of a new ideal of active citizenship.

Parliaments and other forms of expression of informed opinion made some sense in a tradition where channels of communication with the throne were supposed to remain open, and superior and inferior should be of one mind. In Ming times fearless criticism of abuses of government by officials had been supported by debates in academies and by the formation of politically active literary societies; this kind of organized private discussion of politics had been quickly suppressed in the first years of the Qing. But the increasing thinness of the formal bureaucracy had made the cooperation and informal organization of the local elite essential for orderly and effective government, so that in the nineteenth century it was more involved in something like local self-government but less involved in discussing imperial politics than the late Ming elite had been.

In his essays for *Chinese Progress* and in his teaching and writing in Hunan, Liang asked why China was having such difficulty making the reforms that were needed to defend itself against the aggressors, and he began to make really searching use of the contrasting case of Japan. The reason for Japan's great success, Liang said, was that it had reformed its political order first, instead of attempting to make technological changes within an inappropriate political order, as Qing China had. The new order in Japan was much more effective in exploiting the tendency of human beings toward *qun*, "grouping" or social solidarity, which has in its written form something of a link to the herd instinct of animals. Already in 1897 Liang was developing this concept, finding throughout the universe a tendency of beings to form into enduring groups. Beginning to absorb the "social Darwinist" ideas of a struggle among individuals for survival that were so influential in the West at this time, he saw that only those peoples who developed effective forms of social solidarity would survive in the modern world of competitive nation states. The consciousness and commitment Liang had in mind here were focused on the identity and common fate of all members of a group, and on their need to work together in competing with other groups. "It is not enough to have rulers, officials, students, farmers, laborers, merchants, and soldiers. We must have ten thousand eyes with one sight, ten thousand hands and feet with only one mind, ten thousand ears with one hearing, ten thousand powers with only one purpose of life; then the state is established ten-thousandfold strong. . . . When mind touches mind, when power is linked to power, cog to cog, strand around strand, and ten thousand roads meet in one center, this will be a nation-state."

The Japanese had been so successful in establishing a strong nation state, Liang said, because they had had such an abundance of energetic, determined, and unselfish "gentlemen with great goals" (*zhishi*). This phrase, pronounced *shishi* in Japanese, had been used in late nineteenth-century Japan to refer to men who had acted boldly, often at great personal risk, to seek to realize changes that they believed were vital for the future of the Japanese nation. In an essay commenting on Sima Qian's collective biography, "The Money-Makers," Liang already had shared the Han historian's admiration of those who became wealthy by cleverness and hard work and had moved away from the Confucian wariness of pleasure and human desire, finding in them sources of the energy needed to survive in the modern world. He was more and more suspicious of the ideals associated with the Confucian concept of benevolence and of a kind of "public spirit" that excluded any consideration of "private" gain; what was needed was a dynamic solidarity in which public and private goals were pursued at the same time. He now was on the brink of articulating a vision of a society of actively participating individuals, united in seeking personal benefit for each and strength and prosperity for the whole collectivity. He began to use phrases like "revolution" and "people's rights" in his writing and his teaching. Thus already in 1897 we can see very clearly the fundamentals of Liang's dramatic break with the Way of the Ruler and the Minister.

Liang and his friends printed thousands of copies of a banned account of the famous Manchu massacre of the people of Yangzhou in 1645. Intrigued by the way the great changes in Japan had begun with reforms in semi-independent outlying feudal domains, they suggested to the governor that he might consider declaring Hunan's independence from the Beijing government. Liang taught about forty young men at the Academy of Current Affairs. The content of his teaching was very radical, with much about people's rights, the solidarity of the nation, and even revolution. European, American, and Japanese ideas and institutions dominated students' reading. But in form and spirit, education at the academy owed a great deal to the Confucian tradition. The syllabus began with the need of each student to "establish his life goal," in a moral and political, not a careerist, sense. Very much in the spirit of Wang Yangming, students were urged to spend part of every day in "quiet sitting" and to "cultivate their minds." The students were not allowed to leave the school and were required to write voluminous notes on their reading and their responses to it. Liang sometimes stayed up all night to write long comments on the students' notes, which he discussed with each individual. Since students were not allowed to leave the academy, awareness of Liang's radical teachings was not widespread until the students went home on vacation for Chinese New Year of 1898 and showed their essays to their fathers.

Hunan had a very active and politically involved elite, but it also was the elite that had produced many of the leaders of the suppression of the Taipings and the revival of traditional government in the 1860s. The province had remained culturally conservative and strongly opposed to any foreign presence, and it is not surprising that the radical ideas of Liang and his friends aroused heated opposition. Moreover, many of the reformers were, like Liang, natives of other provinces. For all of them, despite occasional thoughts of the secession of a province, the relevant political unit was not a province but the whole empire. Regional allegiances were as unstable a foundation for politics as they had been in late Zhou times two thousand years before. Many local scholars and retired officials complained to the officials about the radical influences over the province's youth. A final blow to the reformers' hopes was the hostility of Governor-General Zhang Zhidong, who wrote and distributed widely a famous and powerful essay entitled "Exhortation to Study," which emphasized the need for thorough reforms in the self-strengthening mode but made it clear that reforms must never be allowed to undermine the basic relationships of husband and wife, father and son, and ruler and minister. The reform newspapers were shut down, the Academy of Current Affairs was closed, and most of the reformers left Hunan.

In 1898 attention again was focused on the capital. At the end of 1897 the Germans had occupied Jiaozhou Bay and the island of Qingdao on the south side of the Shandong peninsula. (Perhaps the most enduring consequence of this episode was the establishment of the brewery that still produces Qingdao beer.) Germany soon obtained concessions of railroad-building and mining rights in Shandong. Tsarist Russia, claiming that it sought to defend China against German aggression, occupied the ports of Dalian and Port Arthur (Lüshun) on the Liaodong peninsula, which the Chinese had paid a large indemnity to recover from the Japanese after the 1894–95 war. In March 1898 the Qing court agreed to a twenty-five-year lease of these ports and to extensive Russian railroad-building in "Manchuria," the usual Western name at that time for the northeast part of the Qing Empire. A great many Chinese were convinced that the empire was about to be "carved up like a melon."

In this crisis atmosphere, many officials recognized that major changes in policy were needed to strengthen the Qing state and insure its survival. The Guangxu emperor, twenty-six years old, was generally sympathetic to reform proposals. His aunt, the Dowager Empress Cixi (more familiar in the old Romanization: Tz'u-hsi), had ruled until he came of age. No longer involved in day-to-day decision making, she was kept informed of all court discussions and retained great prestige and formidable influence in the bureaucracy and the inner court. She was a highly astute political manipulator, and the descriptions of her as a corrupt enemy of effective government are very much overdrawn, but she was a creature of the traditional system, and her own survival in power was her most important goal. None of this made reform impossible, but in the Chinese tradition emperors did not normally take the initiative in policy making; in any case, this one was not experienced or talented enough to do so. No one minister had sufficient power to make things happen as Wang Anshi had; if one had emerged, he probably would have found his position undercut by the dowager empress.

The most widespread conceptions of the reforms needed were based on the "self-strengthening" ideas of the 1860s, which saw changes as defensive additions to a fundamentally sound system of morals and government. Moreover, even the reform measures that fit these preconceptions proved to be hard to put into practice. The huge bureaucracy was in many ways designed to keep things from happening, and it contained quite a few vehement opponents of reform and many more who regarded it as a disagreeable and difficult necessity.

The politics of reform in 1898 were very much complicated by the new assertiveness of elite opinion, first seen in the examination candidates' agitation in 1895. Kang and Liang were among the key organizers of a new wave of activity before and after the concessions to Russia. On March 17, 1898, in Beijing, Kang called the first meeting of a Protect the Country Society (Bao Guo Hui). He made a rousing patriotic speech, but there were things in his speech and in the statement of principles he had written that alarmed many people. The purpose of the society, he wrote, was to promote policies that would protect the rights of the nation (*guo quan*), the territory of the nation (*guo di*), and the teaching of the nation (*guo jiao*). "Teaching" here was in Kang's conception something very much like a religion, with Confucius as the founder, much less closely tied to the current state order than more conventional Confucianism. The use of the word *guo* in these phrases and in the name of the society was explosive. We will recall its use to refer to the pre-Qin Warring States (*zhan guo*); the ambiguous use of *guojia* by a general supporting Empress Wu against the Tang imperial house; and the phrase Yue Fei's mother carved on his back, where *bao guo* clearly meant "repay your debt to the ruling dynasty." The formal title of the Qing imperial state used in its communication with other states in the late nineteenth century was Da Qing Guo, Great Qing Dynasty; the nation had no identity apart from the legitimate dynastic succession of its rulers. But here the elite of the empire was being urged to take action to protect the *guo*, which was conceived of as having rights, land, and even a teaching quite distinguishable from, and more fundamental than, the power, territorial extent, and Confucian orthodoxy of its rulers. The *guo* here was something very close to the nation-state formed by the solidarity of its citizens conceived by Liang Qichao. To some critics it was clear that Kang intended to "protect China, not protect the Great Qing."

Several groups of fellow provincials formed their own societies in Beijing to "protect Zhejiang," "protect Sichuan," and so on, indicating that Kang's advocacy of protection of native soil would not always take an empirewide form. Censors took steps to inform the emperor of these alarming movements. Written attacks on the Protect the Country Society were circulated. Few now wanted to be associated with a movement of such dangerous reputation, and after about a month the society disbanded. More and more news reached Beijing of the condemnations of the reformers in Hunan, and Zhang Zhidong's "Exhortation to Study" was reprinted in the capital. Worst of all, it was just at this time, in the spring of 1898, that Kang Youwei published a book entitled *Kongzi gaizhi kao* (A Study of Confucius as a Reformer), the most comprehensive statement he had yet made of his New Text views and his radical reinterpretation of the Confucian tradition. Thus just when the need for reform was most widely accepted and when the court was taking more and more serious steps to make changes, Kang gave a perfect opportunity to any conservative who wanted to argue that reform would lead to perversion of the tradition. Many who had supported him now drew away, including a senior imperial tutor who had urged the emperor to read Kang's essays.

The reaction against Kang Youwei was not in itself crucial to the prospects for reform, for Kang, Liang, and their allies had only modest positions in the capital bureaucracy, where they prepared position papers for the emperor and the high officials to study. The real impetus for reform came from a broad revival of moderate reform programs in the spirit of the self-strengthening reforms of the 1860s. The emperor was determined that reforms be pushed through and that the channels of opinion be kept open so that all good ideas reached him. The result was that the court's apparatus of communication and decision making was completely overloaded, many proposals never received coherent consideration, little was done to implement or enforce those that were adopted, and in the provinces even capable supporters of moderate reform like Zhang Zhidong simply ignored most of the reform measures proclaimed in Beijing. The emperor became increasingly impatient and imposed harsh punishments on anyone he saw blocking channels of discussion or dragging his feet on implementation.

On June 11 the emperor approved an edict committing the court to basic changes, including an imperial college in the capital and the promotion of extensive borrowing of "Western learning." In the weeks that followed, the tests of prose and poetic style in the examinations were replaced by essays on practical affairs; an imperial college, translation bureau, and government gazette were established; modern schools with practical curricula were ordered set up in the provinces; associations to increase production and improve quality of Chinese export goods were encouraged; bureaucratic rules were simplified and many redundant posts and useless agencies abolished. The fate of these reforms was decided not by debate on their merits but by political infighting between those in favor of them and those opposed. On September 5 four young scholars, including Tan Sitong, a close ally of Kang and Liang, were appointed to serve in modest but potentially influential positions in the Grand Council. But the court also took steps to get Kang out of Beijing, ordering him to go to Shanghai and take over the *Chinese Progress* newspaper as a government gazette.

Kang clearly had been doing everything he could to increase his own influence and attack the conservatives. He and Liang tended to admire the accomplishments of Japan and portrayed Japan to their readers and to the emperor as an example of successful reform on a non-Western cultural base. They feared the growing power of Russia and looked to Japan and Great Britain as counterweights to it. All this was known and magnified in the Beijing rumor mill. It was just at this time that Prince Itō Hirobumi, the greatest architect of Japan's reforms, at the moment out of office as a result of the workings of the parliamentary system he had done so much to create, arrived in Beijing on a private visit. Kang sometimes dreamed of taking the role of a great Itō-like reforming minister, the Guangxu emperor taking the part of the Meiji emperor. In the overheated imaginations of their opponents, Itō's arrival at this time looked like a plot to turn the administration of the country over to him. The dowager empress returned from her usual residence at the Summer Palace outside the city to the inner palaces, and on September 21 she promulgated in the emperor's name his edict beseeching her to return to active supervision of government. The emperor was deprived of power and kept confined in a remote palace until he died in 1908. The "Hundred Days" of reform were over. Almost all the innovative measures were canceled, and orders were issued for the arrest of the leading reform agitators. Tan Sitong and five others were executed without trial a few days later. Kang Youwei managed to flee into exile with the help of the British. Liang turned up, ashen and trembling, at the Japanese Legation in Beijing, where he had an interview with Itō. He then somehow made his way to a Japanese warship off the coast and went into exile in the Tokyo–Yokohama area.

For China, the consequences of the collapse of these reform efforts were immense. Moderate reformers lost influence, and many of them were driven from office. The dowager empress and her high officials, stimulated by a rising tide of popular hostility to Christian missionaries in the northern provinces, shifted their attention away from the threats of economic and strategic penetration. Antimissionary feeling had been an important facet of Chinese foreign relations since missionaries gained access to the interior of China in the 1860s. It was fueled by memories of Taiping Christianity; by missionary interference in local affairs on behalf of their converts; and by local scholars' and commoners' resentment of Christian converts who did not participate in local festivals and who preferred the protection and education offered by the missionaries to those of the local elite. In Shandong, especially, these angers combined with traditions of subversive folk religion and of martial arts exercises and trances, supposed to confer immunity to gunfire, to produce the movement called the Righteous and Harmonious Fists, known to foreigners as the Boxers.

In 1899 the court and most of its high officials in the north actively supported the Boxers as their attacks on churches and massacres of missionaries and converts spread. In 1900 the dowager empress formally authorized the presence of Boxer units in Beijing. The "Legation Quarter," which contained the foreign diplomatic establishments, was besieged for fifty-five days in June and July, but then a foreign expeditionary force fought its way up from the coast and occupied the capital. The dowager empress and her captive emperor fled to Xi'an, once the glorious capital of the Tang but now the center of an impoverished and backward area. The foreign occupiers spread out to "pacify" north China and execute Boxers where they could catch them, and imposed a huge indemnity on the Qing court.

In January 1901, still in Xi'an, the dowager empress directed the emperor to issue an edict calling for thoroughgoing reforms of the government, including the military and educational systems. The most vehement opponents of the 1898 reforms were dead or discredited; the moderate reformers like Zhang Zhidong had kept their distance from the court and the Boxers. The dowager empress now saw that the opponents of reform had no answer to the foreign menace and was ready to give reform a chance. From 1902 to 1910 the Qing rulers presided over a host of serious and energetic efforts to convert their empire into a modern nation-state, adopting many of the basic principles and the specific reforms advocated by Liang Qichao and his fellow radicals in 1897–98. Liang and the other reformers of 1898, however, still were regarded as rebels with prices on their heads and had to keep track of these changes from foreign exile. The consequences of the Qing reform efforts in many ways marked the beginnings of a modern Chinese society and culture. But the energies they unleashed, as Liang had insisted they must be, turned out to be centrifugal, leading to the end in 1911 of the imperial order founded by the Qin 2,100 years before, and to a period of civil war and foreign encroachment. This, of course, was not at all what Liang had had in mind.

The first area in which the Qing undertook serious reforms was education. The heritages of Confucian teaching and of the examination system made Chinese statesmen more self-conscious about the political and cultural importance of education than those of any other civilization. The rigid forms prescribed for examination essays were abolished, the provincial governments were ordered to turn academies into schools with modern curricula, and young Chinese were encouraged to study abroad, particularly in Japan, where living was relatively cheap and the use of Chinese characters lowered the language barrier somewhat. Plans for modern primary and secondary schools followed in 1904. Many young men still preferred the modified classical examinations to the new forms of schooling, since everyone knew how to prepare for the examinations and they had the prestige of a millennial continuity behind them. The examinations always had been criticized by some of the most thoughtful Confucians as a routinization and perversion of the Master's teachings. Wang Yangming, for example, had found them extremely distasteful. In 1905 the government decided that young men would go to the modern schools in adequate numbers only if the examination system was completely abolished; this epochal measure took effect the next year.

I have suggested that since Song times the examination system had been the glue that held the enormous, single-centered empire together, channeling elite ambitions away from local mobilizations of power and into study and aspiration to bureaucratic service. Now all at once that glue dissolved. Moreover, in the old system young men had been able to continue memorizing the Classics and practicing writing model essays no matter where they lived. But modern schools were to be found only in the provincial capitals and other larger cities. In those modern schools, students discussed politics, passed around copies of Liang Qichao's latest magazine and other subversive literature, and discovered the power of the demonstration and the school boycott. Numbers of students abroad, especially in Japan, grew rapidly, and everywhere they started their own societies and periodicals and debated the merits of various forms of reform and revolution.

In 1901 the court also had taken the first steps to reform the military system, abolishing the old military examinations and ordering provincial governors to reform the military units in their provinces. Further measures for reform of the central military administration and the forming of "New Army" units with modern training and weapons throughout the empire were decreed in 1903. Some very promising units and commanders emerged. After the abolition of the examinations, army service and army schools attracted many ambitious poor youths. The trouble was that some of the greatest successes were in the provincial capitals, and central government control over these new forms of power was doubtful. In the Beijing area, the most prominent and effective builder of the New Army was one Yuan Shikai, who already had played an ambiguous role in the politics of the 1898 reforms. As the new-style military forces began to build up, the Manchu princes sought to keep control over them by instituting a highly centralized structure of Ministry of War and Imperial General Staff, modeled on the Japanese system which in turn was modeled on the Prussian. These changes accomplished little except to heighten mutual mistrust between Manchu princes and Chinese military men. In 1908 Yuan Shikai was dismissed from all his posts and retired to his native place, but he retained the loyalty of many younger officers who had risen under his patronage, and he would return as a central figure in the drama of the end of the empire in 1911.

In 1904–1905 Japan and Russia went to war as a result of long-simmering conflicts over the desire of each to dominate Korea and Manchuria. In the Straits of Tsushima Japan annihilated the Russian Baltic fleet, which had steamed all the way around Eurasia and Africa to its fate. Japan also won one land battle after another over Russian forces, on the territory of a Qing Empire that was a passive spectator. To the Chinese political elite, the lesson of this astonishing victory was clear: An East Asian monarchy with a modernized constitutional government could defeat a European one with an out-of-date autocratic system. In 1906–1907 the Qing court sent high ministers to Japan and Europe to study various constitutional forms of government. These missions clearly were most interested in constitutional models like those of Japan and of Germany, which limited parliamentary sovereignty and left large autonomous spheres for the military establishment and for the imperial house. But their interest in a constitutional order that would widen the sphere of consultation and discussion and would establish a firm legal foundation for the state was genuine. In 1908 the court announced a series of steps spread out over the next nine years that would lead to the adoption of a constitutional regime quite similar to that adopted by Japan under the Meiji Constitution of 1890.

The Japanese had taken nine years to implement their system, starting with an imperial grant in 1881. The Qing, however, did not have that much time. Provincial assemblies, a first step toward constitutional government, became hotbeds of agitation for a speedup of the constitutional timetable. Leaders of New Army units in the provinces, students returning from abroad or graduating from the new modern schools, and members of chambers of commerce and many other new voluntary associations joined in the clamor. There were many abortive attempts to start a revolution; when one finally had a local success in October 1911, coalitions of provincial assemblymen and military men took several provinces over to the revolutionary side. Yuan Shikai, summoned back to power in Beijing, told the Qing court it would have to abdicate. The old empire disappeared like snow on a sunny Beijing winter day.

Liang Qichao, of course, had to watch all this from a distance. He and other revolutionaries and radical reformers would return in 1912 to play important roles in the new Chinese Republic. Between 1898 and 1911 they argued among themselves over strategies and goals, articulated issues for the elements of the Chinese political elite that were looking beyond the Qing state's cautious nation-building efforts, and sought without much success some organizational leverage over events inside China. Liang's relations with Kang Youwei became more distant, as Liang lost interest in Kang's desire to "protect the teaching." But he and Kang distinguished themselves from the revolutionaries who sought to overthrow the Qing Empire, claiming that their goal was a constitutional monarchy under the Guangxu emperor. In 1898 and 1899 they elaborated a picture of themselves as loyal ministers of the Guangxu emperor, his key advisers in the Hundred Days of reform in the summer of 1898, now seeking ways to rescue him from oblivion, deposition, and death at the hands of the empress dowager. Their inflated account of their influence in 1898 has been generally accepted by scholars until recently, even though Liang himself wrote of his account of 1898 that "to claim what it contains to be all reliable history is a view I no longer dare entertain. Why is it so? It is because I became so emotionally involved and consequently exaggerated what had really happened." The traditional echoes of his emotional involvement should be obvious to anyone who has come this far in this book; the images of the beleaguered sovereign, the loyal ministers, the selfless martyrs to principle and loyalty must have done much to maintain his resolve in exile and to enhance his standing among the exiles and inside China.

From late in 1898 to early in 1912, Liang spent most of his time in Japan. Between 1899 and 1903 he made several trips to seek funds and support among the overseas Chinese for the Protect the Emperor Society that he and Kang had founded: to Hawaii in early 1900, to Singapore, Australia, and the Philippines in 1900–1901, and to the United States in 1903. In 1900 he drew very close to the revolutionary groups who were plotting to overthrow the Qing, and he encouraged an abortive revolt in the middle Yangzi. As numbers of Chinese students in Japan grew, organization efforts among them and journals published there became central in the struggles over China's political destiny, and Liang found himself very much on the front lines. In Japan he received financial support from local Chinese merchants and from Japanese politicians who combined a relative liberalism in Japanese domestic politics with a desire to spread enlightenment and modernization among their backward brethren in the Far East, very much including the Chinese. The support and example of the great Ōkuma Shigenobu, ardent patriot, founder of Waseda University, and leader of a loyal opposition in the Japanese Diet, who on one occasion had put together a majority and moved peacefully and legitimately from opposition to the prime minister's office, must have been especially important to Liang. If only such things could happen in China! If opposition intellectuals like Liang might be allowed to participate in building the nation, and even on occasion to direct its government!

Liang already had recognized the importance of the Japanese example in his writings of 1897. Now, in addition to seeing its political system in operation, he could travel widely by railroad, get around the cities of Tokyo and Yokohama by electric tram, admire the modern docks and shipping, shop in department stores, and gaze at a twelve-story tower of shops and exhibits, its floors glowing with electric lights. Policing was very thorough, and the legal system had been so completely transformed and codified that just at this time, in 1899, the foreign powers were content to abandon their extraterritorial rights and subject their nationals to Japanese jurisdiction; China would not gain the same right until the 1930s. An even more striking recognition of Japan's new membership in the modern world system was the signing in 1902 of a treaty of alliance and mutual assistance with Great Britain, the world's greatest maritime and colonial power.

Liang, always the scholar and writer, was especially impressed by Japan's universities, both public and private, and by its vigorous daily press and many journals of scholarship and controversy. In 1899 Liang wrote, "I have made several Japanese friends who are as close to me as my own brothers. . . . I have read Japanese newspapers daily, becoming so involved in Japanese political affairs that they seem to be those of my own country." Many of Liang's generation of political and intellectual leaders could have said the same thing, but not all of them were so frank about the effects of Japan on their ideas, and in retrospect, as Japan has been experienced as the great enemy and aggressor, the whole subject of Japanese influence on the reform and revolutionary movements has become a very sensitive one. Liang learned much from the Japanese example and quoted many Japanese books, but his balance and breadth of vision made him less susceptible than some others to Japanese ways of thinking that could not be naturalized in Chinese thought. For example, although he showed interest in the racist pseudo-biology that the Japanese adopted so readily from the European and American thought of the time, it was less important to him than to some of the revolutionaries, especially the famous scholar Zhang Binglin.

Liang used Japanese books and journals primarily as a mode of access to the ideas and institutions of the entire world. He made several attempts to learn European languages, but never read or spoke one with any ease. On the warship on which he escaped from China he had discovered that the Japanese use of Chinese characters made it possible for him to start reading with a tutor or helper. The Japanese had been hard at work for decades translating and summarizing the knowledge of the Western world; in the process they invented many new compounds of Chinese characters to translate Western concepts: science, civilization, society, socialism, anarchism, objectivity, subjectivity, self-government, constitution, and so on. Liang and his generation simply adopted most of these compounds for use in the modern intellectual Chinese they were creating.

Exile never is easy. But for Liang it made possible far greater productivity and influence than either his earlier or his later years in China. Even in exile he was drawn over and over again into futile political activity, but it did not consume his life as it did earlier and later in China, and there were intervals when he could spend all his time reading, writing, and talking with his Chinese and Japanese friends. He was in no personal danger. He had reasonably stable funding for his periodicals. The Japanese censors rarely paid attention to Chinese journals published in Japan. From 1899 to 1901 he edited the *Qing yi bao—qing yi*, "pure discussion," being a traditional term for the politics of moralistic opposition in China. From 1902 to 1907 he published his most famous and influential journal, the *Xin min congbao* (New People's Miscellany). *Xin min*, another profoundly Confucian expression, takes some explaining.

In his writings from 1899 on, Liang drew on his widening reading and experience to incessantly reexamine and refine basic ideas he had arrived at in 1896–97. The central ideas were those of *qun*, grouping or solidarity, and of the active individual *zhishi* "gentleman with a great goal," committed to the advancement of the group and identified with its fate. For the nature of the individual participant, Liang now frequently used the phrase *xin min*. *Min* is the word for the common people encountered from Confucius on; *xin*, "new," implies that now they must be something quite different from the usually passive people of the traditional conception. Well aware of how much Liang was learning from reading about Western politics and political thought in these years, some have translated the phrase as "new citizen." Certainly the activism and solidarity implied by the word "citizen" all the way from its Roman origins does convey a great deal of the new values Liang was promoting. But the expression *xin min* also carried strong Confucian echoes. It is found in the opening section of the *Great Learning*: "The Way of the Great Learning is to illuminate illustrious virtue; to renovate the people [*xin min*]; to rest in the highest good. . . ." (Classical Chinese has no parts of speech in the Western sense; the phrase can be read as a verb-object compound as well as an adjective and noun.) But some versions of the text read *qin min*, "to be parentally close to the people." Wang Yangming had preferred this version, in scholarship and more ambivalently in his work as a local official. Liang, a bookish aspirant to elite status now in exile, had little opportunity to be parentally close to the Chinese people. In his writings he had little to say about the terrible injustices and insecurities of livelihood experienced by ordinary Chinese. And although ordinary Chinese could and did respond to appeals for patriotic dedication and solidarity, the real thrust of Liang's exhortations was that the Chinese *elite* should renovate itself and guide the renovation of the common people.

Although the very idiom of moral appeal and self-renovation owed much to the Confucian tradition, Liang was more and more convinced that traditional Confucian ethics provided inadequate guidance for the renovation that now was needed. Traditional concepts of personal relationships were useful as far as they went; Liang was no critic of the traditional family system, and he sometimes thought that filial piety might help to reinforce wider political loyalties. But traditional political ethics, confined within the ruler–minister–common people concepts, were woefully inadequate. In his new writings on "public morality" in 1902, Liang became much clearer about the solidarity and activism that now was required of everyone if China was to survive as one among many competitive nation-states:

> The present-day international competitions among European and American countries are not like the imperialistic aggrandizements launched by the First Emperor of Qin or Alexander the Great or Chinggis Khan or Napoleon. . . . The motivating force stems from the citizenry's struggle for survival which is irrepressible according to the laws of natural selection and survival of the fittest. Therefore the current international competitions are not something which only concerns the state, they concern the entire population. In the present-day international struggles in which the whole citizenry participate [and compete] for their very lives and properties, people are united as if they have one mind. . . . How dangerous this is![1]

Most of Liang's examples of the kinds of public virtues the Chinese needed to cultivate were foreign. He was especially impressed with the Anglo-Saxon peoples:

> Those who excel at making compromises become a great people, such as the Anglo-Saxons, who, in a manner of speaking, make their way with one foot on the ground and one foot going forward, or who hold

[1] Hao Chang, *Liang Ch'i-ch'ao and Intellectual Transition in China*, 1890–1907 (Cambridge, Mass., 1971), p. 163.

fast to things with one hand and pick up things with another. Thus, what I mean by "a new people" is not those who are infatuated with Western ways and, in order to keep company with other, throw away our morals, learning, and customs of several thousand years' standing. Nor are they those who stick to old paper and say that merely embracing the morals, learning and customs of those thousands of years will be sufficient to enable us to stand upon the great earth.[2]

The point was, of course, that the Anglo-Saxon peoples, by their cultural and political moderation and continuity, had become the most dynamic and progressive peoples of the world of the turn of the century. Liang's faith in progress as an unqualified good, his conviction of the need for individual dynamism and struggle to advance, now were at their peak. Certainly this was a sharp break with the recent Confucian tradition, but Liang remained convinced that original Confucianism, with its optimism about human nature and its faith in the efficacy of moral exhortation, example, and action, was quite congruent with his new values. If we recall the great appeal of Wang Yangming's focus on the gap between moral knowledge and action, we can see Liang and others of his generation seizing on the new ideals, institutions, and examples of the Western tradition, and on the promise of abundance through science and technology, not to overthrow the Confucian heritage but to break out of the moral and political predicaments of the traditional order and to give new reality to the deepest hopes and promises of their own tradition.

Liang's new moralism glorified the human will, effort, and struggle. Sometimes he attacked head-on the fatalist elements in the Chinese tradition; sometimes he argued that they were the results of misunderstandings of Confucian or Buddhist teachings. Still, many of his examples of the kind of ceaseless struggle the Chinese people needed to engage in were Western, and his best biographer has commented that his concept of effort "is much closer to the modern Western concept of 'rational mastery over the world' than to the Confucian ideal of 'rational adjustment to the world.'" Certainly Liang sounds "Faustian" when he writes, "Human effort has been constantly battling against the course of nature, engaged in a process of struggle. The course of nature has often been at odds with the expectations of human beings. So its resistance to human effort is very great and intense. However, the admirable tendency of human beings to progress will never rest content with the status quo. So the whole life of a man is like sailing against the currents in a river for several decades without being able to rest for one day." But we might also hear echoes here of the Confucian disciple who knew that the gentleman's burden is heavy and his road is

---

[2] W. T. de Bary et al., eds., *Sources of Chinese Tradition* (New York, 1964), 2: 95.

long, for only with death does it come to an end. Certainly, we also will hear echoes of Liang in Mao Zedong's exhortations to effort and struggle.

Liang's writings from 1897 on had had a great deal to say in favor of Western concepts of freedom and of the rights of the people. Close examination of these writings has led many scholars to the conclusion that Liang never really accepted the idea of the fundamental and inviolable rights of the individual, that for him human rights were to be asserted and human freedom defended in order to overcome the passivity of the old order, that solidarity was more fundamental than individual rights. The same understanding of liberal ideas can be found in some of the Japanese writers who most influenced him and in some of his most distinguished Chinese contemporaries, such as the great translator Yan Fu. Liang also eventually drew on German theorists of the state as an entity above individual wills. Some have suggested that Liang and his generation, as a result of their preoccupations with the building and defense of a modern nation, did not so much distort classic liberalism as perceive and develop some latent "collectivist" tendencies in it. In any case, the issues Liang grappled with here are enduring ones. People in the West still are arguing about the limits of a negative conception of liberty, about the need for community and solidarity in postmodern society. And of course the future of liberty and human rights in China remains uncertain.

Liang's views of the process that would lead to the emergence of a modern Chinese nation were changeable, some would say confused or opportunistic. But surely it was sensible not to get locked into a particular program when trying to influence from exile the immense and many-sided transformation now beginning in China. Liang's broad reading and open mind kept him aware both of the dynamic energy that could be released by the quest for freedom, by the people taking power in their own hands, and of the advantages for nation-building and defense against aggression of a broad-based and orderly transition if one could be managed. In 1902, in a journal for new kinds of fiction he had started, he published several installments of a novel of his own entitled *Xin Zhonggao weilai ji* (A Record of the Future of the New China). Looking back from sixty years in the future, it records a series of discussions between an anti-Manchu revolutionary and a moderate who hoped to work out a peaceful transition guided by a "sage ruler" and a group of outstanding ministers. The moderate argues that the disorder of revolution would give the foreign powers an excuse to intervene again. But how, asks the revolutionary, can you trust the present rulers to relinquish their power? Both concede that the Chinese people are not ready to be effective citizens of either a republic or a constitutional monarchy. The moderate concedes that revolutionary energy at least will help to offset the dead weight of reaction, making constitutional monarchy a feasible compromise. Both the revolutionary firebrand and the careful statesman will be needed, as both Mazzini and Cavour were needed in the making of a united Italy a few decades before. Liang never finished the novel; it seems clear that the debate was one going on in his own mind in 1902, and that he was attracted both by radical activism and by the role of a cautious, constructive statesman.

Liang spent much of 1903 touring the United States, seeing most of its major cities, meeting important people (even if only five minutes with J. P. Morgan), and attempting to raise funds for the Protect the Emperor Society. He came to understand that American democracy was built on local representative institutions dating from before the American Revolution; this gradual building of democracy from the bottom up seemed far more workable than a sudden imposition from above. In any case, he was not much impressed with the present state of American politics, with its constant campaigns, its mediocre leaders, and its spoils system. He was awed by the sense of limitless economic potential, and he saw clearly how it could be mobilized to dominate other countries, especially under leaders like Theodore Roosevelt, then in the White House. The great trusts, he wrote, were far beyond the dreams of power of Napoleon or Alexander the Great. Visiting Chinese communities, he found them not very generous with donations and full of feuds between families and between natives of different places. San Francisco's Chinatown particularly depressed him; despite its high rate of literacy and its six newspapers and journals, factional fighting and corruption were endemic. If these Chinese could not govern themselves, how could the people of China be expected to cope with democracy?

Back in Japan, Liang found his pessimism about Chinese ability to create an effective democratic government turning his writings in two directions. One was away from revolution and toward an insistence on the supremacy of a state standing above individual wills. The other was a conviction that the Chinese could find important resources in the Confucian tradition for the moral revival they so badly needed. Individuals had to learn to look within themselves, to distinguish sincerity from hypocrisy, to demand of themselves the most perfect selflessness. He drew a great deal from the writings of Wang Yangming and his followers. The examples of heroic conduct in Liang's writings were more frequently drawn from Chinese history, less from Western.

Just as Liang was turning away from revolution, the young intellectuals in China and abroad who had been learning so much from him were drawn in the opposite direction. In 1903 agitation over the weakness of the Qing in the face of continuing foreign pressure was growing, and some were beginning to argue that the Qing must be overthrown if China was to survive. The fervent arguments and organizing efforts of these revolutionaries are described in the next chapter. In 1905 the revolutionaries met in Japan to form a united Revolutionary Alliance (Tongmeng Hui). The Qing pressed the Japanese government to bring the situation under control, and Tokyo issued a new set of regulations, requiring Qing approval of every application from a Chinese student and much closer supervision of all Chinese students. After the students called a strike, a Japanese newspaper commented on their "self-indulgence and boorishness." One of the young leaders of the Revolutionary Alliance drowned himself in the ocean to protest the insult to his people.

Liang responded to all this fervor with a confused and legalistic condemnation of the student strike. He went on, in 1906 and 1907, to engage in a long print duel with the *Min bao* (People's Report), the organ of the Revolutionary Alliance. He called revolutionary anti-Manchuism a diversion from the goals of nation-building. China needed a change of system, not an overthrow of dynasty. The Manchus were almost completely assimilated, in any case. The revolutionaries were advocating a "small China" just for the Han people, rather than a "large China" to be built by and for all the peoples of the Qing Empire. He condemned the proposals for social justice, equalization of wealth, "socialism" in a variety of senses, that were popular among the revolutionaries, saying they were unnecessary and divisive.

All this was not just an intellectual result of Liang's growing conservatism and authoritarianism since 1903. Serious discussions were under way in Beijing late in 1905 to explore the possibility of evolution toward a constitutional monarchy more or less on the model of Meiji Japan. Liang was in touch with the high Manchu official Duanfang and even drafted state papers for him to submit to the court. In September 1906 the court announced the dispatch of high commissioners to study the constitutional systems of various countries. Liang's vision of a gradualist, broad-based path toward the political transformation of China seemingly legitimized, he now sought to form a broad coalition of Qing statesmen and private opinion-leaders to arouse public opinion in favor of the rapid establishment of a constitutional order with representative institutions. Liang and his close associates, still viewed as traitors by the Qing court, would participate secretly. The resulting organization, with the neutral-sounding name Political Information Society (Zheng Wen She), was inaugurated in Tokyo in November 1907. Liang hoped to gain the support of the powerful general Yuan Shikai but was rebuffed. Thousands of signatures calling for rapid steps toward constitutional government were collected. Then in August 1908 the court banned the Political Information Society and ordered the arrest of its members.

The Society may have helped to stimulate growing political consciousness and organization in the provinces, but by 1908 the new politics had taken on a life of its own that did not depend on any single center of organization. Provincial associations for constitutional government, the new provincial assemblies, the leaders of the new army units, students in the new schools, chambers of commerce, and the publishers of an amazing number of new journals all joined in the agitation for rapid progress toward constitutional government. The revolutionaries under Sun Yat-sen mounted one abortive revolt after another. Finally it was revolutionary activity within the new army units that made possible the first successful revolt, at Wuchang on October 10, 1911, still celebrated by the Republic of China on Taiwan as its National Day. Various coalitions of revolutionaries, provincial assembly leaders, and army commanders declared the southern provinces for the revolution, and Sun Yat-sen was inaugurated as first president of the Republic of China. In the north, revolts to the east and west of Beijing made the court's situation untenable, and Yuan Shikai was recalled to office with full powers to manage the situation as best he could. He soon informed the court, now presided over by the six-year-old "last emperor," that there was no alternative to abdication. Yuan now made it brutally clear that he expected Sun to step aside and allow him to become president of the Republic in his place. Unable to match Yuan's military power and fearful of foreign intervention in the case of civil war, Sun did so.

Liang Qichao had watched this amazing drama from Japan, powerless. He had tried to build connections with some Manchu princes who he thought might be sympathetic to the constitutional cause, but he had been rebuffed. By March 1911 he was writing in favor of overthrow of the Qing. He seems to have had some influence, through personal connections with the officers involved and the kinds of changes they demanded, on the revolt east of the capital in November 1911 that led the court to recall Yuan. He now sought to participate in the practical work of building the kind of stable constitutional government he had witnessed in Japan and other countries and had so long dreamed of for China. He lingered for months in Dalian in the northeast. He could not bring himself to consider cooperating with the revolutionary forces; there were too many memories of old fights, too many differences of principle. Yuan Shikai had rejected the overtures of the Political Information Society, and later Liang had urged the Manchu princes to keep Yuan out of power, but now Liang turned to Yuan, addressing him as "enlightened ruler," presenting himself as a potentially valuable adviser.

In the confused politics of the first years of the Republic, the abstract question was that of the relation between the executive and the legislative power; it translated into a confrontation between Yuan Shikai and the provincial activists who had dominated the provincial assemblies and the provisional National Assembly, among whom the revolutionary forces, now called the Kuomintang (National People's party), were by far the strongest and best organized. In elections at the end of 1912, the Kuomintang emerged with a majority in the National Assembly, and its capable parliamentary leader, Song Jiaoren, began to talk as if his majority was going to take full charge, as in a parliamentary system, or have Yuan removed and a new president elected. On March 20, 1913, Song was assassinated by Yuan's agents. Military commanders loyal to the Kuomintang revolted in the southern provinces but were crushed.

In the parliamentary maneuvering of 1912–13, Liang experienced the consequences of his years of exile. He was a famous and popular political intellectual; everyone wanted to be associated with him, on good terms with him. But he was only one of several important politicians who had come out of the constitutionalist movement, and unlike the others he had no base of power in one of China's provinces. And he still could not stand the thought of cooperating with the "rowdy" radicals of the Kuomintang. After Yuan crushed the Kuomintang resistance, he turned to a coalition of constitutionalist politicians that called itself the Progressive party. Liang became minister of justice. Working to improve the administration of justice and seeking a measure of autonomy for the courts, he was overtaken by events in 1913–14, as Yuan banned the Kuomintang, dissolved the National Assembly, and took dictatorial powers for himself. Still Liang stayed on in Yuan's government, now as director of the Bureau of Currency. Liang, in his role of would-be scholarly statesman, had studied and written about China's complex currency problems for years, but the office had little power.

In 1915 it became more and more clear that Yuan intended to make himself emperor. Liang made his opposition clear, and by the end of the year he had resigned and was lending his support to a coalition of military and other forces opposing Yuan's monarchical plans, in which one of his students from the 1897 Academy of Current Affairs played a key role. Yuan backed away from his imperial pretensions and died early in 1916. But the real victors were neither the Kuomintang nor the old constitutionalists but the military men who had not wanted Yuan to concentrate so much power and legitimacy in his own person. The political influence of military men had been growing since the late Qing reforms, and now China was entering a decade when the only real power was that of the "warlords." For a year or two the generals restored and manipulated the National Assembly elected in 1913, but from then on to 1928 they simply allied with each other and fought each other for control of provinces or the capital.

In 1917 Liang participated in the first of these warlord-dominated governments, when the National Assembly still seemed to have a role to play, as minister of finance. But his efforts to stabilize the currency were doomed by the military expenses of the generals, and he resigned by the end of the year. That was the end of his political career. His early optimism about the merging of the best of Western political values with the best of China's moral traditions was mocked by the savagery and cynicism of the warlord era. He spent the rest of his life in scholarly pursuits. He was above all a reader and a writer, and the most enduring part of his inheritance from the Confucian past was his continuing faith that the scholar, the student and critic of culture, must somehow play a key role in creating a viable new China.

Liang had traveled widely in North America, Southeast Asia, and the Pacific, but he had never been to Europe. Now he went, arriving in London in February 1919. Here, amid memories of the senseless carnage of trench warfare, the collapse of the old order, the revolutions in Germany and Russia, the fear that nothing had been settled and Europe was simply between two wars, he encountered disillusion with progress, democracy, and science that at least matched his own. Still anxious to tap the latest currents in Western intellectual life, he met people who told him that Western thought was bankrupt, that it had ignored people's spiritual needs, that the West was now looking to the Eastern civilizations for revitalization. One French writer praised the profundity of the Chinese philosophers he had read in translation and urged that each people should develop the unique virtues of its own culture.

These encounters encouraged changes that already were under way in Liang's thinking, and they were very important for some of the younger intellectuals who accompanied him and interpreted for him. In the 1920s Liang taught at Nankai University in Tianjin, did a great deal of historical and literary research, and wrote several important books. As many of China's intellectuals were seized by new visions of progress through science, democracy, and radical social change, Liang and his younger associates were major contributors to the critique of excessive faith in science, insisting that the Chinese tradition had much to offer to a coherent philosophy of life. Trying to summarize the core of the tradition and to show how it combined social activism and inward self-cultivation, making a sort of middle way between Indian otherworldliness and Western materialism, he finally turned back to that core mystery and moral demand of the teachings of Confucius, the concept of benevolence. He died in 1929.

A failure in politics, bitterly disappointed in his early hopes for a rapid transition to a new China, Liang Qichao had contributed immensely to the long and still problematic struggle of the Chinese people for effective participation in the modern world by his translations and explanations of Western ideas and by his participation in the invention of modern Chinese intellectual journalism. Above all, his discovery, already in 1897, of the links among social solidarity, individual liberation, and nation-building had defined an epochal break with the Way of the Ruler and Minister and shaped the crucial first stages of modern China's search for a viable political form.

18

THE KUOMINTANG LEGACY

· · · · · ·

THE ONE-LIFE-per-chapter structure of this book has been a useful way of keeping discussion focused and of highlighting some of the types and individuals whose places in the Chinese historical consciousness are protean and enduring. But sometimes a bit of arbitrariness has been necessary. It was hard to choose one among the great scholar-officials of the Northern Song. Liang Qichao was much admired in his time and shared most of the key experiences and changes of his generation, but he was not its great hero or dominating political figure; I chose him because his *writings* show so clearly the immense challenges and stresses faced by his generation and the unraveling or transformation of the Way of the Ruler and the Minister. For twentieth-century lives the structure becomes even harder to maintain. We are too close to the events, see too many facets of them. In the consciousness of the Chinese people the lineups of heroes and villains keep changing. A few, we can be sure, will always be there, as heroes, villains, or complex mixtures. Mao Zedong dominated the first quarter-century of the People's Republic of China in such an extraordinary way that there is little question that his name will be preserved among those of the heroes and villains of Chinese history, and it makes fair sense to focus a chapter on him.

Not too long ago, most foreign scholars of China would have had little trouble writing a history of modern China that moved straight from Liang Qichao to Mao Zedong, arguing that the effective solidarity and national mobilization that Liang sought in vain were achieved, and could only have been achieved, by methods like Mao's. Now we are not so sure. The legacy of Mao seems less one of successful mobilization and solidarity, more one of national unity and tranquility bought at a fearsome price in suppression of initiative and discussion.

Some Chinese are not at all surprised. From the beginning they have rejected the appeals of Chinese communism in the name of another heritage or continuity, which many of its adherents would define simply as the legacy of the father of the country, the founder of the Republic, Dr. Sun Yat-sen. Until recently, foreign students of modern Chinese history have treated this strand in modern Chinese politics very dismissively. Now, as a government on Taiwan that reveres Sun as its founder moves on from economic miracle to an impressive transition to democracy, this strand in modern Chinese politics can no longer be ignored.

Still, it seems to me that to describe these developments simply in terms of the life and legacy of Sun Yat-sen would be to accept the myth-makers' inflation of his role in the 1911 Revolution and to downplay the distinctive contributions of his successors. Thus in this chapter I begin with two revolutionary extremists who carried a great deal of Confucian moral idealism into their search for a new politics and to their deaths in the noble failure tradition; then I do my best to explain the strange and many-sided life of Sun Yat-sen; and I end with his successors, Chiang Kai-shek and Chiang Ching-kuo, father and son, warrior and reconciler, sufferers of ignominious defeat and architects of China's most effective adaptation to the twentieth-century world. Winding its way from the days when Kang Youwei and Liang Qichao had their few weeks of hope for change led from within the imperial palace to the time of shattering of hopes beneath those walls in June 1989, this chapter echoes many themes of those that have gone before and provides a necessary counterpoint to the huge epic and tragedy of communism in China.

ZOU RONG

Zou Rong was just in his twentieth year when he died in the prison of the International Settlement of Shanghai in April 1905. His sole accomplishment was the publication of an essay, just forty-seven pages of Chinese text, entitled *Geming jun* (The Revolutionary Army). This remarkable work, in which the Yellow Lord, Yao, Shun, Yu, Washington, Napoleon, and Rousseau all are cited in Zou's effort to inspire the revolutionary ardor of China's youth, is one of the clearest pieces of evidence we have for the way in which traditional learning, literary skill, moral intensity, and optimism could be turned to radically antitraditional ends.

Political ferment between 1900 and 1911 had many centers. Hunan, Hubei, Sichuan, and many other provinces each produced its own leaders and organizations, but two of the most important centers of activity were in the great coastal cities of Guangzhou (Canton) and Shanghai. Sun Yat-sen was from the beginning one of the key leaders of the movements focused on Guangzhou. The Shanghai movements had many organizations and leaders. Shanghai, with its many foreign residents and foreign-connected publications in Chinese, was China's most important window on the world. The surrounding lower Yangzi provinces had rich traditions of scholarly activity and upper-class protest against bad government. Young scholars from all up and down the Yangzi valley came to Shanghai in search of modern education, political activity, and ship passage to Japan and other centers of study abroad. Shanghai offered, in addition to the gambling, drugs, and commercial sex available in any large Chinese city, opportunities to learn foreign languages and observe foreign ways. Young Chinese and old were humiliated by the sight of foreigners in power on Chinese soil—red-turbaned Sikh policemen directing traffic, clubs and parks where Chinese were not welcome. Some might "sell out" to the intruders, going to work for them or even becoming Christians. But Shanghai also was a relatively safe haven for political dissent. In the city's zones of foreign control, especially the International Settlement under largely British and American control, dissident Chinese could publish and hold public meetings freely as long as they did not threaten public order in the foreign zones themselves.

Zou Rong was born in 1885 in a well-to-do merchant family in or near Chongqing, Sichuan. A brilliant student in a traditional nonconformist style, he read widely in history and philology but refused to master the artificial styles necessary for the examinations. His impetuous condemnations of traditional values and interpretations led to his being expelled from school and denied a scholarship to study in Japan. His special intellectual hero was Tan Sitong, the most radical of the 1898 reformers. His views probably also were affected by Sichuanese resentment of missionary and other foreign presence in the province.

In the fall of 1901, Zou got some financial support from his father and set out down the river to Shanghai. By the fall of 1902 he was in Japan, enrolled in a school where young Chinese studied a wide variety of knowledge of the outside world and especially its political principles. Zou met some of Sun Yat-sen's associates. He made a fiery anti-Manchu speech at a big New Year gathering, which got him in trouble with the Japanese authorities. In April 1903 he returned to Shanghai.

In the spring of 1903 Chinese students and other political activists were alarmed by the possibility of French intervention in Guangxi just across the border from northern Vietnam. A larger and more basic threat was seen in growing Russian power in the northeastern territories of the empire, which foreigners then called Manchuria. In Shanghai a series of large public meetings united reformers, revolutionaries, and wealthy merchants in protest against the Qing court's apparent readiness to give the Russians what they wanted. The names of the steering committee of this movement—"Union of the Four Social Classes," then "Citizens' Union"—reflected its broadly patriotic and nonrevolutionary character, but many of the leaders were revolutionary students, including Zou Rong, just back from Japan.

Even in the International Settlement the students had to be somewhat discreet about their anti-Qing opinions if they wanted to avoid trouble with the police. The main organizing center of their activities was a Patriotic School, which ostensibly was devoted to giving young men modern education and some military and physical training so that they could help defend their country. Students and teachers did devote quite a bit of time to military drill, but beyond that their main activity was political debate, with radical anti-Qing opinions more and more openly expressed. The Patriotic School group also became closely linked to the *Su bao* (Jiangsu News) newspaper, which published increasingly radical articles. Zou was an energetic junior member of this group. He became very close to Zhang Binglin, an older scholar of immense erudition and vehement anti-Manchu sentiments which he had arrived at entirely out of his reading of Chinese history and political theory, with little or no Western influence. Zhang wrote a laudatory preface for Zou's *The Revolutionary Army*, and in May 1903 both Zou's essay and Zhang's scathing attack on Kang Youwei were on sale in pamphlet form.

The Revolutionary Army begins like this:

> Sweep away millennia of despotism in all its forms, throw off millennia of slavishness, annihilate the five million and more of the furry and horned Manchu race, cleanse ourselves of 260 years of harsh and unremitting pain, so that the soil of the Chinese subcontinent is made immaculate, and the descendants of the Yellow Lord will all become George Washingtons. . . .
>
> My voice re-echoes from heaven to earth, I crack my temples and split my throat in crying out to my fellow-countrymen: Revolution is inevitable for China today. It is inevitable if the Manchu yoke is to be thrown off; it is inevitable if China is to be independent; it is inevitable if China is to take its place as a powerful nation on the globe; it is inevitable if China is to survive for long in the new world of the twentieth century; it is inevitable if China is to be a great country in the world and play the leading role.[1]

Zou was blunt about his hatred of the Manchus and his conviction that they must be overthrown. In later sections of his essay he referred to the massacres of the 1640s and the forced adoption of the queue and gave a detailed account of the favoring of Manchus over Han Chinese in appointments to high office in the capital. The references to the descendants of the Yellow Lord were a rather new way, perhaps picked up from Zhang

---

[1] Translations are from Tsou Jung, John Lust, tr., *The Revolutionary Army* (The Hague and Paris, 1968).

Binglin, of emphasizing the racial identity of the Han Chinese, not their role as bearers of the great Chinese culture, in response both to China's longest period of rule by a non-Han people and to the pseudo-biological racism that was so prevalent in Western social thought at the turn of the century.

Zou also was responding to the Western thought of his time when he broadened his definition of revolution; it was "the universal principle of evolution . . . the essence of the struggle for survival in a time of transition." Citing Western works from the American *Declaration of Independence* to Rousseau's *Social Contract* to *Uncle Tom's Cabin*, he demonstrated that a basic revolution in attitudes and values was needed if the Chinese people were to make a successful revolution of any kind. The Chinese people *wanted* to be slaves. It was not just the household bondservants who cringed and flattered and hoped for a smile; the scholars were even worse, spending their lives in useless literary exercises hoping to gain a position serving the Manchu rulers, advising the rulers how to suppress Chinese rebels and revive the old order. The misery of the rural people and the bullying and discrimination faced by Chinese emigrants were results of the general Chinese slavishness and especially the servile submission of the upper classes to the Manchus.

In the days of Yao, Shun, and Yu, Zou wrote, the rulers were viewed simply as leaders, first among equals. But ever since the First Emperor of Qin, rulers had used all sorts of strange theories and superstitious portents (Zou referred to several of Wang Mang's omens) to establish despotic rule in which they treated the whole empire as their private possession to be passed on to their descendants. Now the Americans and the French were proving that in an enlightened modern age a great people could get along without hereditary rulers. The Chinese must create a new political order in accord with the universal principle that "all the inhabitants of a country together administer the government of that country." Filial piety would be preserved; it was simply a result of the fact that each person has ancestors and parents. But loyalty must be redefined as loyalty to the whole nation, not to the ruling house.

Near the end of his essay Zou included a sort of draft of a Chinese declaration of independence and a fairly vague statement of basic constitutional principles. It ended like an oath out of the Three Kingdoms: "Let High Heaven and the God of the Earth both scrutinize it." The whole essay ended by quoting a poem by one Liu Bowen:

> Ninety-nine of us will grasp our big swords
> And not put them down until we've killed all the
> 　　　Tartars [Manchus].

The pamphlets by Zou and Zhang electrified the Shanghai reformers and radicals; several thousand were sold within a month. The *Jiangsu News* published a review of Zou's work and Zhang Binglin's preface to it. Under great pressure from the Qing authorities, the administrators of the International Settlement raided the Patriotic School and the offices of the *Jiangsu News*. Zhang Binglin and several of the most important contributors to the *Jiangsu News* were arrested. Zou hid for a few days, then gave himself up. A long argument ensued between the Qing and foreign officials as to which court should try them; this gave the revolutionaries a good deal of free publicity. Finally they were tried in the International Settlement court. Neither Zou nor Zhang made good use of his day in court to make a bold statement for his cause, and Zou claimed that he had now abandoned the ideas in *The Revolutionary Army* and turned to socialism. Zhang was sentenced to three years' imprisonment, Zou to two, and the others received short sentences. Zou and Zhang spent their time in prison writing classical poetry; Zhang was surprised to find that Zou had real literary talent.

Zhang had remarked wryly that "We scholars don't have enough strength to tie up a chicken." The bad food and septic conditions in Chinese prisons had killed many stronger men. Zhang survived to continue his career as a leading revolutionary intellectual, but Zou died of some kind of a fever in April 1906. A memorial meeting was held in his memory. *The Revolutionary Army* was reprinted many times and remained an effective piece of revolutionary propaganda.

QIU JIN

Before 1911, making Shanghai a focal point of revolutionary consciousness and activity was all well and good, but nothing really was going to happen until revolutionary mobilization reached out into the provinces. Coordination among movements and actions in various provinces was difficult at best. Even within a province, the difficulties were very real. In Zhejiang, for example, parts of the province were prosperous, closely tied to Shanghai and to communications with north China, while other areas were divided into mountain valleys and coastal enclaves with many linguistic and cultural differences.

Zhang Binglin and several other important participants in the Shanghai agitation of 1903 were natives of Zhejiang, and in the following years they sought to build revolutionary organizations in the interior of their home province. They had to be very careful, since they had none of the foreign legal protection that had given them a degree of safety in Shanghai. Attempts to form a broad revolutionary movement in the lower Yangzi provinces were led from 1904 to 1907 largely by members of the Restoration Society (Guangfu Hui). There was some overlap of membership between it and the Revolutionary Alliance (Tongmeng Hui) founded in Tokyo in 1905, and some efforts were made to coordinate activities. The Restoration Society was secret; every member was introduced by someone already inside the organization and took a blood oath "to restore the Chinese race, recover our mountains and rivers, to devote myself to the country, and to retire after completing my task." Both in the Restoration Society and in the Revolutionary Alliance, the failures of earlier efforts led in these years to a growing interest in the assassination of Qing officials, seen less as a strategy to destabilize or demoralize the bureaucracy than as a way in which an isolated activist supported by little organization could publicize the revolutionary cause.

Revolutionaries spent much time in 1905 and 1906 traveling through Zhejiang and neighboring provinces trying to enlist the support of secret society leaders, with only modest success; the gulf between their modern nation-building goals and the societies' antimissionary and economic grievances and traditional social attitudes was very wide. They also tried to set up legal organizations that would serve as "fronts" for revolutionary agitation, as the Patriotic School had done in Shanghai. One of the most important of these was the Datong School, founded outside the prosperous, conservative city of Shaoxing in 1905.

In 1907 the leading figure at the Datong School was Qiu Jin. It is hard to imagine a less suitable emissary of revolution to the secret society leaders, prosperous wine merchants, and scholars of Shaoxing. Qiu Jin was a woman who loved swords and firearms, rode astride in Western men's suits, organized military drill for young women, and constantly proclaimed her belief in assassination and revolutionary violence.

Qiu Jin was born into a prosperous Zhejiang family in 1875 or 1877. She and her brother were educated in literature and the Classics. Very fond of popular stories of military heroes, she liked to think of herself as playing the part of a heavy-drinking, brawling martial hero. In a society where women of good family were not supposed to appear in public; where their lives were shaped by an extreme version of the ethic of modesty, meekness, and self-sacrifice already old in Ban Zhao's time; and where most women were half-crippled by their bound feet, Qiu Jin's itch to play the warrior still was not without cultural support. There were stories of women warriors in the popular tradition, some of them referring to specific figures who had tried to resist the Qing conquest. Plays and popular fiction contained several telling portrayals of wimpy male students and their strong-minded wives or fiancées. Further support was provided by new "Darwinist" worries about the future strength of the race. Campaigns against footbinding were a common and powerful feature of the modernizing movements from the turn of the century on.

Qiu Jin was married in 1896 to the son of a prosperous Hunan merchant family. She bore her husband a son and a daughter, wrote poetry, and was miserably bored in his conventional household. She found a few other educated women to talk to when her husband spent several years in Beijing. Stimulated by the post-1898 ferment, she already was talking of the need for reform to save the nation and of women's rights. Then, in 1904, she left her husband and children and went to Japan to study. She enrolled in a teacher-training college, but spent most of her time in political activity. She joined the associations of Hunan and of Zhejiang students, a society of reformist women, and even the Yokohama branch of the Heaven and Earth Society, which was an organization of student radicals, not traditional secret society men. She studied marksmanship and bomb-making and often carried a short sword. In 1905 she joined the Revolutionary Alliance and was appointed party chairman for Zhejiang.

Qiu Jin returned to Shanghai early in 1906 and soon joined the Restoration Society. She tried teaching, but her radical views angered both trustees and students, and she soon left. She experimented with explosives. She traveled around Zhejiang trying to organize an uprising, but nothing came of her plans. She founded a pioneer journal of opinion on women's issues. Many other revolutionaries were living similarly disjointed and distracted lives. To a degree this was to be expected as young people tried to invent new ways of organizing and acting for which their society offered few precedents. But it also is clear that these were very impatient people, seeking quick routes to successful action or at least to pure and morally glamorous failure. All around them bad weather was leading to distress and unrest in the countryside, but they seem hardly to have noticed, and never had the time for the hard, slow work of mobilizing this unrest or building up solid organizations among the common people.

Joining the group at the Datong School near Shaoxing early in 1907, Qiu soon found herself the sole leading figure, as her male colleagues took off in all directions in pursuit of their latest schemes, including military commissions that would facilitate subversion of the army. The general strategy of the Restoration Society revolutionaries in Zhejiang was to draw on the manpower, local connections, and anti-Qing traditions of the secret societies, to reorganize the forces thus recruited into a unified army, to give them some military training (which sometimes could be done in the open in the general vogue for training to defend China against foreign aggression), and to educate the secret society recruits in modern nationalist and revolutionary principles. This would have required great patience and attention to detail and personalities in organizing work, and attention to the economic grievances that were turning ordinary people toward revolt. Both were in short supply among the urban, educated revolutionaries. Qiu Jin worked out elaborate plans for the uniforms, ranks, and flags of a Restoration Army and made several trips to other cities to firm up relations with secret society leaders. At the Datong School a special military course already had begun, and many students were meeting in groups of five to swear to die together on the same day.

But Qiu would not hide her deep anticonformity. She ordered military drill for the students at the girls' school. She caused a riot when she rode into town, astride in her man's suit. Her dreams were not those of a canny female Zhuge Liang biding her time and marshalling her forces but of a heaven-storming hero:

> Ascending to heaven mounted on a white dragon,
> Crossing the hills astride a savage tiger,
> Angry shouts summon the winds and clouds
> And the spirit dances, flying in all directions.
> A great person in the world
> Must commune with heavenly spirits.
> And ignore those other sons of pigs and dogs
> Who aren't fit for her company.[2]

With such a view of the world and her place in it, it is not surprising to find Qiu Jin planning a coup in Shaoxing, set off by the assassination of the local magistrate, which would take place just six months after she became the central figure at the Datong School. Only one other Restoration Society leader was in a position to attempt a coup in coordination with her; that was to take place at a new police academy at Anqing, on the Yangzi in Anhui Province. A Restoration Society leader was in charge of the academy; the Manchu provincial governor was to be assassinated at the academy's commencement exercises. Both coups were to take place on July 8. After the assassinations the newly trained military forces under revolutionary leadership would take over their cities, and revolutionary forces all over the area would rise in spontaneous response. The Anhui governor asked that the commencement exercises be on July 6. Qiu Jin then postponed her planned coup until July 19; her reasons are not clear, and there is no clear evidence that word of the change ever got through to the Anqing conspirators. The Anhui coup was a farce. The conspirators could not shoot straight and did not have enough ammunition. They managed to fatally wound the governor, but were overpowered by local troops and soon executed.

[2] Mary Backus Rankin, *Early Chinese Revolutionaries: Radical Intellectuals in Shanghai and Chekiang*, 1902–1911 (Cambridge, Mass., 1971), pp. 45–46.

Trails of evidence and questioning led to Qiu Jin's plot. She learned of the Anqing disaster from the Shanghai newspapers. Government troops marched to Shaoxing. Ammunition was short because Qiu had ordered rifle practice with live rounds. She refused to flee. After brief resistance she and her coconspirators were taken prisoner. Arms and incriminating documents were found in abundance in the Datong School. Under torture, she refused to admit anything of her revolutionary plans. In prison, shortly before her execution, she wrote:

> The sun is setting with no road ahead.
> In vain I weep for loss of country.
> . . . .
> Although I die yet I still live.
> Through sacrifice I have fulfilled my duty.[3]

SUN YAT-SEN

Sun Yat-sen, the name by which the first president of the Republic of China is best recognized in the English-speaking world, is the Cantonese pronunciation of Sun Yixian. Many would say *Doctor* Sun, referring to his British colonial medical degree. Many Chinese would most easily recognize the name Sun Zhongshan, using a secondary name he began to use after he had, during his times of exile in Japan, sometimes used the Japanese name Nakayama, which is pronounced Zhongshan in Chinese. Thus even in deciding what to call him we confront the extraordinary range of his international associations and experiences.

Sun Yat-sen's first bases of recruitment and fund-raising were outside China, among emigrant students and merchants. He appealed to modern Chinese intellectuals partly as an expert on the outside world with some bold and fresh ideas about how China might draw on foreign ideals and institutions in its own nation-building process. He combined utter selflessness and frequent naiveté in power politics with an absolute faith in his own vision of China's future and his own central role in leading the country toward modern nationhood. With due allowance for huge differences of time and situation, his selfless idealism, fondness for vast visions of systematic reform, and faith in his own destiny can make one want to go back and think again about Wang Mang.

Sun was born in 1866 in a poor family in a village in Xiangshan County, Guangdong, the county in which Macao is located. Two of his father's brothers had lost their lives seeking gold in California. In 1871 Sun Yat-sen's elder brother emigrated to Hawaii, where he worked in the rice

[3] Rankin, *Early Chinese Revolutionaries*, p. 1.

fields, started a small store, and eventually became a prosperous merchant and landowner on Maui. In 1879 Sun Yat-sen joined him there. He had not had much Chinese education, but now found substantial opportunities in English-language schools founded by missionaries to educate Hawaiians and others. He won second prize for English grammar at Iolani School. His brother, afraid that Yat-sen was about to become a Christian, sent him back to Guangdong, where he smashed an idol in the village temple and told heroic tales of the Taipings. In 1884 he was baptized in Hong Kong and began to study the Chinese Classics under the tutelage of a learned Chinese Christian. He now sought an education in modern Western medicine, first in a missionary school in Guangzhou, then in a new medical college in Hong Kong. Graduating in 1892, Sun practiced medicine for a time in Macao, but found only limited demand among Chinese for Western medicine and many restrictions imposed on him by the Portuguese authorities. His concern for Chinese reform had continued to grow, and as his medical career became more frustrating he probed possibilities for a new career as an expert on things modern and foreign advising one of the more reform-minded Qing officials. He wrote a long statement of his views, not revolutionary and not far out of line with what many reformers were saying at that time, sent it to Li Hongzhang, governor-general of the capital area and the most powerful official in the empire, and sought an interview with him. Li had employed men with foreign knowledge and experience before, but at this time the Sino-Japanese War was imminent, and Sun never got to see him.

Sun returned to Hawaii, assembled his brother and some of his friends, and inaugurated an organization called the Revive China Society (Hua Xing Hui). The political goals of his first organizing efforts in Hawaii and then in Hong Kong are not entirely clear. What was clear was a focus on the menace of foreign expansion and on the weakness and corruption of the current political order. To organize merchants and other commoners to seek to remedy by their own actions such basic difficulties was, even without an open statement of revolutionary intent, a more radical challenge to the current political order than Liang Qichao's autonomous organizing of members of the elite in the Protect the Country Society four years later. Also, Sun's pronouncements and his organizing work were from the beginning more in tune with the economic difficulties and resentments of ordinary Chinese than either Liang Qichao's or those of later revolutionary intellectuals like Qiu Jin.

Japanese routs of Chinese forces on land and sea late in 1894 seemed to confirm Sun's picture of basic flaws in the existing order and to increase the probability that an assault on it would lead to radical political changes. Sun hurried back to Hong Kong and joined some of his own associates there with several like-minded groups in a second branch of the Revive China Society. An elaborate conspiracy to seize the city of Guangzhou was worked out. Several articles appeared in an English-language newspaper in Hong Kong praising the "reformers" and insisting that they were not at all antiforeign; this publicity may have helped to alert the Qing authorities that something was about to happen. Secret society members and other recruits gathered quietly around Guangzhou. A secret shipment of arms and about four hundred more soldiers arrived from Hong Kong on the day of the plot. But of course there had been a leak. The arms were seized and some of the leaders were arrested and executed; Sun barely escaped to Hong Kong. The British government there expelled him, and he sailed for Japan, not to return to Chinese soil until after the Revolution of 1911.

Arriving in Japan, Sun was startled to find himself mentioned in a Japanese newspaper as "the Chinese revolutionary Sun Yat-sen," using for "revolution" the Chinese character compound *ge ming*, which had taken on in Japanese all the connotations of the modern Western concept of revolution, but to Sun and other Chinese simply meant "change of the mandate." That's wrong, Sun thought, no one among us wants to be emperor. In the next few years he would absorb, often through Japanese translators and interpreters, a great deal of Western social thought and would become much more of a "revolutionary" in the sense implied by the Japanese report. Equally indicative of the immense changes he now was making were his decisions to adopt Western dress, grow a mustache, and cut off his queue. He also hoped that these steps would make him less easily recognized by spies and detectives in the pay of the Qing government.

In 1896 Sun stayed for a time in Hawaii, then went on across the United States and to London. In the next fifteen years he made about fourteen long ocean voyages, not counting trips to and from various ports in Southeast Asia. He had no secure source of funds and frequently had to obtain loans or contributions at one stop before he could pay his fare to the next. Often he faced serious competition from the constitutional monarchists for overseas Chinese support and donations. There were times when he was very discouraged, but as the years passed his vision of China's future grew. The Qing authorities pursued him by fair means and foul, seeming to take him much more seriously than the 1895 fiasco at Guangzhou warranted, and giving him one piece of wonderful free publicity and a sense that he had a great personal mission ahead of him.

In London in 1896 he was frequently in touch with Dr. James Cantlie, who had taught him medicine in Hong Kong. He spent many days in that great refuge of the self-teaching radical, the Reading Room of the British Museum. He got a deeper understanding of modern political order and industrial society, including their inequalities and injustices. Somehow he wound up in the clutches of the Chinese legation, which immediately began to make arrangements to sneak him out of the country and send him home to a most unpleasant death. He later insisted that he had simply walked past the legation and had been drawn into conversation and hustled inside. But it also is possible that some combination of curiosity, bravado, and homesickness led him to enter the legation on his own to inquire about other Cantonese in London. In any case, he was held prisoner in the legation. Eventually he managed to smuggle a note to Dr. Cantlie, who alerted the Foreign Office, Scotland Yard, and the newspapers. There was a great outcry over this flagrant abuse of diplomatic immunity. Sun was released. He wrote a little book in English, *Kidnapped in London*. He was famous. He was, in his own eyes, a man of destiny.

Sun now made his way back to Japan. In 1900 his Revive China Society organized a rebellion in Huizhou east of Canton, where Su Dongpo had spent part of his last exile, that was a much bigger and more serious business than the 1895 one but ultimately failed, partly because arms sent by Japanese backers did not arrive in time. As noted in the previous chapter, he and Liang Qichao took some tentative steps toward cooperation but then moved apart. Both Liang and revolutionary intellectuals like Zhang Binglin and Zou Rong were more effective than he was in showing educated Chinese the nature of the political and cultural transformation that was under way. But still he had advantages. Much less well-educated and a much less skillful writer than Liang, Zhang, or Zou, he knew the West far better. And his Japanese connections became very important in their support for of his efforts.

From 1896 on, Sun came under the wing of a shifting collection of Japanese supporters. These men were challengers of the oligarchy that had made and controlled the new Japan of the Meiji era. They cast themselves as providers of enlightenment and assistance to Asians who were having more difficulty coping with the modern world. That frequently implied open or covert intervention in the politics of another country, in support of elements favoring change and in opposition to the machinations of non-Asians. Some of these men were adventurers on the fringe of Japanese politics; others were outside the narrow inner circle of Meiji politics but eminently respectable, like Ōkuma Shigenobu, who served a brief term as prime minister in 1898. Another important politician, Inukai Tsuyoshi, was so impressed with Sun that he provided him with a place to live and substantial financial support. Throughout his career, Sun always was ready to accept help from anyone; he knew his own motives were pure and his ideas right for his country, and he had great confidence in his own ability to avoid being controlled by his foreign backers and advisers.

Sometimes it suited Sun and his Japanese friends to have him pass as a

Japanese. He chose at random the common Japanese surname Nakayama. The characters, meaning "central mountain," are read "Zhongshan" in Chinese. Eventually Zhongshan was treated simply as an alternate name, and a reference to him as "Sun Zhongshan" will be readily understood by many Chinese and taken as a sign of respect for him. After his death, many parks and streets were named Zhongshan. The important university at Guangzhou is Zhongshan University. Every city hall in Taiwan is called Zhongshan Hall.

Unlike Liang Qichao, Sun was not completely dependent on Japanese translations and interpretations of Western history and social thought. But he did continue his studies of them and was influenced by Japanese ideas and interests. The Japanese were beginning to grapple with the problems of modern industrial society that Sun had first witnessed and read about in London. Sun's friends were far from being socialists or revolutionaries, but they had no use for unbridled capitalism or for the accumulation of large amounts of frequently unearned wealth in private hands. Miyazaki Torazō, one of Sun's closest friends, was particularly attracted to the ideas of the English reformer Henry George. George saw unearned income from rises in land values, especially in growing cities, as an important source of the inequities of modern capitalist societies, and one that could be remedied without social or political upheaval by a confiscatory tax on increased values not resulting from improvements of property. Owners would be kept from underreporting the value of their holdings by a provision that the government could purchase a property for the value reported. This scheme appealed greatly to Sun and became a permanent feature of his approach to capitalism and economic equity. It did little to deal with the problems of rural China, and any student of real estate or of political economy will see the difficulties in its implementation, but it admirably represents his concern with economic justice, his rejection of unfettered capitalism, and his fondness for tidy, systematic solutions that avoid messy social conflict. In his various plans, it frequently was joined by other proposals for "equalizing land rights," especially limiting size of individual landholdings and rates of rent that could be charged to tenant farmers.

By 1905 Sun had come to the fundamentals of the political formula he would use and develop until the end of his life, the Three Principles of the People. A literal rendition of the Chinese *San min zhuyi* would be "Three People-ism"; it stands for three two-character phrases, each beginning with the character *min*, "people." *Min zu*, meaning "the people as a family/ tribe," usually has been translated as "nationalism." At this time it referred to the unity of the Han Chinese against the Manchus; later it would be recast in anti-imperialist form. *Min quan*, "people's rights," often translated as "democracy," refers to the right of the ordinary people to have ultimate control over their government. By 1905 Sun had begun to talk about a distinctive scheme, the "five-power constitution," in which to the American separation of powers were added the Chinese institutions of a censorate or inspectorate and a system of examinations to screen candidates for government positions. The people would have the rights not only of election of government leaders but of voting to recall them if necessary, and of legislation by initiative and referendum. These were of course innovations widely advocated in American progressive circles at the time. *Min sheng*, "people's livelihood," emphatically not socialism, embodied the Henry George scheme and other projects for regulated capitalism and economic growth and expressed a compassion for the sufferings of the Chinese people that was not common in elite reform and revolutionary circles.

In 1904–1905 the tide of student and intellectual opinion had begun to turn in favor of revolution, but there were many leaders and many centers of activity. Sun was out of the country, seeking support among Chinese in Europe and North America, as this revolutionary tide rose. In the same talks with Chinese students in Brussels in which he began to outline his five-power constitution, he agreed with them that the revolutionary movement needed to recruit modern students and to use them to infiltrate modern army units, as well as make alliances with secret societies. The students' letters about these conversations to their friends in Japan probably contributed to the enthusiastic reception Sun received when he arrived in Yokohama in July 1905.

Most of the revolutionary activity in Japan up to this time had been in groups from various provinces, of which those from Zhejiang, Guangdong, and Hunan were among the largest and most energetic. All of them now recognized the need for a unified movement. Not everyone was enthusiastic about Sun Yat-sen; some of the older scholar-radicals like Zhang Binglin were especially scornful of his limited Chinese education. But he had been among the leaders of the first modern revolutionary attempt; Qing pursuit of him enhanced his reputation; and he had a relatively coherent set of basic principles for a revolutionary movement and the government it would establish when it succeeded. Moreover, he had support and funds from Japanese sources and was in the process of building up some solid sources of funds among overseas Chinese, especially in Southeast Asia. In meetings at the homes of Sun's Japanese backers an agreement was worked out for the formation of a united Revolutionary Alliance. Sun inspired his new allies with a speech on August 13 in which he insisted that an enlightened China free of Manchu tyranny would modernize even faster than Meiji Japan had. At the inaugural meeting on August 20 over three hundred members of the new Revolutionary Alliance elected Sun director and swore an oath to uphold his Three Principles of the People.

Between 1905 and 1907 a number of articulate radicals writing in the revolutionary *Min bao* developed Sun's ideas and defended them against Liang Qichao's insistence that overthrowing the Manchus was unnecessary and would lead to disorder and increase the risk of foreign intervention. Thereafter, changes in China stimulated a rush of argument, innovation, and organization that were beyond the control of the exiled revolutionary and constitutional monarchist leaders. It was this growth of organizations that the Qing rulers could not control, followed by the disillusion of many politically active Chinese with the possibilities of energetic nation-building under the Qing, that led to the Revolution of 1911. Sun Yat-sen would emerge at the end of 1911 as the first president of the new republic, but his role in the events leading to it was geographically and organizationally marginal.

Japan expelled Sun in 1907. Thereafter he concentrated his organizing and fund-raising efforts among the Chinese in Southeast Asia, sought secret society allies in and around Guangdong, and from 1907 to 1909 organized seven local revolts, none of which lasted more than a few days. Another revolt at Guangzhou in March 1911 accomplished nothing except to give the revolutionary movement seventy-two revered martyrs. His only important contribution to the theory of revolution during these years was the idea that once a local revolutionary base was established it would be under military rule for several years while its people were educated in self-government; this theory of "tutelage" was applied to the entire country under Sun's ideological heirs in the 1930s.

In the summer of 1911 there was a widespread anti-Qing movement in Sichuan, set off by Beijing's efforts to take over a provincial railroad company, that owed little to Revolutionary Alliance organization. Organizing efforts in Hubei that fall were directed by a Central China Bureau of the Revolutionary Alliance that clearly was not under Sun's control and rejected his ideas of "equalization of land rights." Sun and many other revolutionary leaders had seen the potential of organizing within new army units. Now it paid off, in the army revolt at Wuhan on October 10, 1911, that set off a chain reaction of revolutionary seizures of power in the provincial capitals of the center and south.

In October 1911 Sun Yat-sen was traveling in the United States, seeking funds and support. In Denver he read in a newspaper that a revolution had broken out in China, led by Dr. Sun Yat-sen. He took the next train *east* and sailed for London, where he obtained a commitment from the government not to prop up the Qing regime with any more loans. Then he sailed for China, arriving triumphantly at Shanghai on December 25. January 1, 1912, was declared the first day of the first year of the Chinese Republic, and Sun was inaugurated as its provisional president. Nanjing, not Beijing, would be the capital of the new Republic.

His moment of glory was exceedingly brief. The Manchu court in Beijing had granted full powers to Yuan Shikai but still had not abdicated. Yuan's power in the north in any case owed far more to his patronage of younger military officers than to revolutionary organization and activity. He and his associates in Beijing would not accept Sun as president. Civil war and foreign intervention seemed real possibilities. Sun was immensely sure of the righteousness of his own cause and of its eventual triumph, but he had little interest in personal power and glory. He seems to have thought that an evolving constitutional order and assurances from Yuan that he would support it would be sufficient to keep the political evolution of the Republic on track. On January 22, 1912, he offered to resign and to recommend Yuan as his successor. The Qing abdication was announced on February 12, and Sun resigned the next day. Yuan now maneuvered and bullied to keep the capital in Beijing. Sun's Revolutionary Alliance joined with a number of smaller parties in a wider and more open party called the National People's party (Kuomintang). In elections for a new National Assembly a vigorous Kuomintang campaign was organized by Song Jiaoren, and the party won a majority of seats. Song talked of using that majority to establish a legislative power that could check the power of the president. In 1913 Yuan had Song assassinated, negotiated with the foreign powers for a huge loan that he used to prop up his military power, dismissed several provincial governors loyal to the Kuomintang, and easily crushed a "Second Revolution" of pro-Kuomintang military units in the south.

Sun's relation to all this was curiously distant. He left the political organizing to Song Jiaoren and devoted his time to elaborate plans to boost China's economic growth through railway development. One suspects that all those train trips across the vast spaces of the United States and Canada had left their mark on his mind. He also had noted new centers of prosperity along some of the rail lines that were beginning to be built in China. In his time railroads were almost universally thought of as one of the most powerful forces for an economic progress that would benefit everyone. Sun's plans would avoid the malignant concentrations of wealth and power produced by railroad-building in the United States; the Chinese government would retain ultimate control and ownership, as had been done in Japan and in Bismarck's Germany. Foreign investment, however, would be most welcome; Sun does not seem to have been much concerned by the many cases in his time, in China and elsewhere, in which foreign investment had led to foreign control.

Yuan Shikai, delighted to find that a potentially serious opposition leader could be so easily sidetracked, had named Sun director of railroad development. Sun now busied himself inspecting China's existing railways and those of Japan, soliciting Japanese investment, and laying out a magnificent, comprehensive scheme of east-west and north-south trunk railways. He denounced Song Jiaoren's assassination, but waited three months before he openly attacked Yuan and was fired from his railway position. He continued to try to organize military resistance to Yuan, but by the end of the year had fled to Japan.

Sun had not been happy with the broad coalition politics of the Kuomintang, which included many with whom he had no personal ties and who were not did not share his concerns with economic growth and social justice. In 1914 he reverted to a much more tightly controlled revolutionary movement, almost a secret society, called the Chinese Revolutionary party (Zhonghua Gemingdang). Each member took an oath of personal commitment to Sun and his principles. Some old revolutionaries refused to join under those conditions.

In 1915 Yuan Shikai took steps to declare himself first emperor of a new dynasty. He was opposed by old revolutionaries, old constitutional monarchists, and many military men; Sun's Revolutionary party played only a minor role. After Yuan's death in 1916 the Beijing warlords reconvened the 1913 Parliament, but they dissolved it in 1917 when it opposed their plans to enter World War I on the side of the Allies. Sun had been a minor player in these changes, but seized a new chance to legitimize a separate regime in Guangzhou by convening there a substantial number of members of the dismissed Parliament. The southern warlords who permitted these developments soon turned against them, and in 1918 Sun withdrew from Guangzhou politics. His follower Chen Jiongming had managed, however, to get some troops under his command, and in 1920 Chen conquered Guangzhou and invited Sun to return there. Sun now organized a full-fledged government in the south, claiming legitimacy through the continuity of the 1913 Parliament, and began to make plans to build up his military forces and reunite the country by force. Chen Jiongming, however, somewhat like Zheng Zhilong at Fuzhou in 1645–46, preferred to consolidate his own base in Guangdong and to work out loose coalition arrangements with warlords in other provinces. He turned against Sun; in 1922 his forces occupied Guangzhou, and Sun had to flee to Shanghai.

Through these years of turmoil and discouragement, Sun continued to make great plans for the future of China. He elaborated his five-power constitution scheme and plans for the process by which local areas would be instructed in the techniques of self-government. He prepared an ambitious set of plans for the development of water power, steel mills, railroads, ports, and modern cities, all with huge investments by the foreign powers. Many would worry that it would be very difficult to carry out these plans, he wrote. He blamed their doubts on the influence of Wang Yangming and other Confucian moralists, who had taught that "to know is easy, but to act is difficult," which of course often is true in personal morality. But actually, Sun insisted, "to know is difficult and to act is easy," and once the ordinary people understood that he and other advanced thinkers had done the hard part for them in figuring out what needed to be done, they would gain confidence and move ahead to carry out his great plans.

But in China in the 1920s it was indeed difficult to carry out a political program without internal military backing or large-scale foreign assistance, as Sun had learned over and over. But the foreign powers were less interested in adventures in China than they had been—even Japan was relatively cautious in the early 1920s—and saw no particular reason to back Sun. His first effort to build up a military power he could rely on had ended in disaster when Chen Jiongming turned against him. Now, however, he found a new source of foreign support and of guidance in the creation of a disciplined revolutionary movement, the Soviet Union.

Isolated in the world, especially concerned about Japanese hostility at the eastern end of their huge territory, the Soviets had their own reasons to find whatever friends they could in China. The ways in which they justified to themselves their willingness to deal with any Chinese who would deal with them will be discussed in the next chapter, in connection with the rise of Chinese communism. Their first contacts with Sun were in 1921. Lenin is said to have been delighted at reports of Sun's "virginal naiveté." In January 1923 Sun and the Soviet diplomat Adolf Joffe signed an agreement that acknowledged that communism was not right for China but pledged Soviet advice and assistance. Beginning late that year, after Sun had managed to return to Guangzhou, Mikhail Borodin advised Sun on the reorganization of the Kuomintang, the creation of a military force under its control, and the buildup of Sun's own position as an unquestioned leader and definer of revolutionary principles. All this was very Leninist in form. The Kuomintang was to become a party of "democratic centralist" organization, in which all members were bound to obey decisions reached at the center and party units were established in schools, factories, and so on. The nucleus of a reliable military force was to be provided by the training of young officers at a military academy under close party supervision, where they would acquire a strong dose of political convictions and commitments along with their professional skills. This academy was established at Huangpu (Whampoa) near Guangzhou; Chiang Kai-shek was its first commandant. Russian shipments of arms began to flow into Guangzhou. Members of the tiny Chinese Communist Party were allowed to join the Kuomintang and some came to occupy very responsible places in it.

Sun did not need much urging from Borodin to get to work on another set of sweeping plans and pronouncements for the guidance of his reformed party. He presented them in a series of lectures on the Three Principles of the People early in 1924. He told his audience that he already had been at work on a major set of statements of his principles when Chen Jiongming drove him out of Guangzhou in 1922, and that he had lost his drafts and many of his books in that attack. Be that as it may, these speeches offered little that could not be found in his earlier writings, and in their published form they contain enough strange ideas and misinformation to make readers shake their heads and wonder how they could be taken seriously: The population of Western countries, especially the United States, is growing much faster than that of China, which is in danger of being swamped by Western hordes. The human need for clothing, a basic part of the principle of people's livelihood, grew as mankind evolved and lost its body hair, which of course proves that the Chinese are the most advanced race. And so on.

Many of these oddities could be matched by passages in the writings of Western politicians and commentators of the time. In any case, the deficiencies of these lectures are not the most important point. At a time when Chinese politics seemed to be going from bad to worse, Sun Yat-sen held out hope for a future in which a coherent, capable government would be subject to the will of the people, in which economic growth would rescue the people from their desperate poverty, and the growing wealth would be distributed with reasonable equity. He was full of knowledge of a world about which even most educated Chinese still were badly informed, and he had a coherent picture of a political order that would learn from foreigners and still be distinctively Chinese. His sense of his own mission struck some observers as excessive, but to many young Chinese he seemed to offer a share in his vision of a bright future. He was utterly without ambition for private wealth or power. He could be very persuasive in private conversation, giving an impression of great interest in the person to whom he was talking.

None of that made him a ruthless or adept wielder of political power. Many thought he was naive to trust the Soviet advisers and the Chinese Communists. He still was looking for foreign backers wherever they could be found, even in Japan. And although preparations were under way for a military buildup and a northern expedition to reunify the country by force, he still was negotiating with some of the northern warlords to see if a reunification could be worked out without bloodshed. He was in Beijing for such negotiations when he died of cancer on March 12, 1925. In his will he charged his successors with the completion of the task of revolutionary unification to which he had devoted his life. Very soon his heirs began the process of raising him to the status of a heroic founder, burying him in a magnificent mountaintop tomb outside Nanjing, teaching every schoolchild his will, putting his picture on every public wall, making his lectures on the Three Principles the unchallengeable guidelines of the Kuomintang.

CHIANG KAI-SHEK

Sun Yat-sen had learned only very slowly that under the conditions of the early Republic his movement was condemned to futility unless it had relia-ble military power at its disposal. If the future of his movement and his ideas had been entirely in the hands of the civilian politicians who at first seemed his most likely successors, it is not at all probable that the Kuomin-tang flag he had designed would have been flying over all of China less than four years after his death. The nucleus of military power formed by the graduates of the Whampoa Academy and their commandant, Chiang Kai-shek, gave the Kuomintang a reliable armed force that could defeat many warlords and make the rest negotiate realistically. It also became the cen-tral force in the intricate internal politics of the Kuomintang, with results that sometimes seemed to be very much the long way around toward the emergence of the unified nation and effective democracy Sun Yat-sen had dreamed of.

Chiang Kai-shek's origins and early career were in the cultural ambiva-lences and dangerous political cross-currents of Zhejiang and Shanghai in the first decades of this century. His father and grandfather were mer-chants; his father died young, and he was brought up in very modest cir-cumstances. Born in 1887, he did not leave his home area until 1905, near the peak of the first wave of student revolutionary agitation. Amid the confusions that afflicted so many young people in those days, he was ex-traordinarily single-minded, pursing a military career from the beginning. He attended a military school in north China so that he could be sent as a government-endorsed student for military study in Japan. From 1908 to 1910 he attended a Japanese military school that prepared young Chinese for more advanced training, and he took field training with a Japanese artillery regiment. He seems to have thrived on the fierce Japanese disci-pline and later was quoted as saying that it represented the standard of discipline and selflessness to which all Chinese citizens should aspire. He also joined the Revolutionary Alliance and made a very important personal connection with the Shanghai revolutionary Chen Qimei.

Chiang and Chen hurried back to China as soon as they learned of the outbreak of revolution in October 1911. Chiang played only minor roles in Chen Qimei's revolutionary takeover in Shanghai and in the 1913 ef-

10. Sun Yat-sen and Chiang Kai-shek, 1924

forts to resist Yuan Shikai. In the latter, trying to organize an attack on the great Jiangnan Arsenal at Shanghai, he had to retreat into the International Settlement and allow his men to be disarmed by the foreign police. It was widely believed that he had personally shot and killed a rival revolutionary in his hospital bed. He confessed to living a very immoral life and to being unable to control his temper. In 1914 he joined Sun's Chinese Revolutionary party but played no very large or distinctive role in it. He edited a short-lived magazine, *Jun sheng zazhi* (Military Voice Magazine), in which his own articles strongly advocated national military strengthening, centralization of control of military forces at the national level, and energetic action to defend the country against foreign threats, especially those from Russia; all of these would be central themes of his later political career.

Chen Qimei, Chiang's first important political mentor, was assassinated by agents of Yuan Shikai in 1916. Chiang did not establish a really close personal relation to Sun Yat-sen until 1922. As Sun attempted to build a new power base in the south from 1917 on, Chiang tended to hold himself aloof, convinced that Sun should not be so heavily dependent on the military power of Chen Jiongming. In the meantime he spent most of his time in Shanghai or at home in Zhejiang. Sun had ordered some of his associates to engage in commodities speculation to raise funds for his party. Chiang was involved in these efforts. He must have been pursuing on his own some of the many possibilities Shanghai offered for making money, but there is little solid information about these years. It was rumored that he had ties to the Shanghai underworld. He learned much about money and power in Shanghai, but hated the place, calling it "a huge oven for the manufacture of evil men." Foreign power in the great city was particularly galling to this proud, angry soldier who once had had to surrender to the International Settlement police; in the 1930s and 1940s, after his rise to national power, he would argue that almost all of China's ills could be traced to foreign domination through the system of unequal treaties.

From childhood, Chiang had alternated periods of nearly ungovernable passion and bad temper with long efforts to discipline himself through meditation and moral self-examination. Japanese military discipline may have been a welcome aid in his struggle to control himself, but had been too external to be of any help in his years adrift after 1913. Sometimes he seems to have used his volcanic temper as an excuse to avoid getting into political positions where he could not control events. But still his temper made trouble for him, and he sought to control it by digging deeper into the Confucian tradition of self-cultivation; he learned the most from the writings of Wang Yangming and of Zeng Guofan, the great fighter against the Taipings and reviver of Qing power. Chiang's hot temper, his bouts of dissipation in a decadent commercial world, his attraction to military discipline, and later his drive for unshared political power may remind readers of another leader who sought to mobilize power amid chaos and wound up on Taiwan, Zheng Chenggong.

The hazards of depending on Chen Jiongming made Sun and his associates more and more interested in finding talented military men who did not have their own territorial bases or ambitions. From 1920 on they were hoping to draw Chiang into such a role, and by the end of 1921 Chiang had achieved a fair degree of personal stability and was ready to commit himself to Sun. He still held back somewhat, first because Sun was trying to conciliate Chen Jiongming and later because he had grave misgivings about the Kuomintang reorganization and Soviet alliance. But then he seems to have decided that it was just that Soviet alliance, in addition to his own rising reputation as a military expert, that could give him leverage to rise above the swirl of ambitious men around Sun. From August to December 1923 Chiang headed a high-level delegation to Moscow to consult with the Soviet leaders on aid to the Kuomintang and to study Soviet methods of party control of government and society, especially the training of reliably indoctrinated military officers.

Backed by the full confidence of the Soviet advisers and of Sun, Chiang now was named chief of staff of the armies of Sun's government and commandant of the new military academy at Huangpu (Whampoa) near Guangzhou. From the beginning he sometimes argued with the Soviet advisers to the academy and made it clear to Sun and others that he was not in sympathy with the Kuomintang's leftward trend. But he always managed to convince the Soviets that he really was on their side, and he accepted the participation of members of the Chinese Communist party in the Kuomintang and even in his academy, where a bright young man named Zhou Enlai was a political instructor.

In 1924 and 1925 three classes, totaling about two thousand cadets, entered the Military Academy. Chiang Kai-shek personally supervised their training and education and drew on the best civilian talents of the Kuomintang to give them a thorough political education. The result was a core of well-trained young officers who were thoroughly dedicated to the Three Principles of the People and personally loyal, as any good Chinese student would be to his old teacher, to their commandant. These "Whampoa men" would be the hard core of Chiang Kai-shek's strength in his long struggle for supremacy within the Kuomintang. Already in 1924 and 1925 they proved themselves in battle against dissident local forces in Guangzhou and against a renewed threat from Chen Jiongming.

Sun Yat-sen's death in March 1925 was followed by the assassination of a prominent left-wing Kuomintang leader; a senior right-wing leader was implicated in the killing and had to withdraw from politics temporarily. Chiang allied with the most prominent remaining civilian politician, Wang Jingwei, to dominate a government that still supported the alliance with the Soviets and the Chinese Communists. But then in March 1926 he began to turn against the Communists, alleging that there had been a plot to kidnap him, put him on board the Chinese gunboat *Zhongshan*, and take him away to Vladivostok. Step by step he removed Chinese Communists from important positions in the Kuomintang apparatus, all the time insisting to the Soviet advisers that he still was their true ally. The Soviets were slow to recognize the growing dangers of the situation; the advisers, and even more Stalin and the other bosses in Moscow, were unwilling to admit that their support of the Kuomintang might have been a mistake.

In July 1926 the Kuomintang launched its long-awaited Northern Expedition into the Yangzi valley. It was a stunning success; by October it had reached the Wuhan cities on the middle Yangzi. The armies drove on through Jiangxi and into Zhejiang, occupying Hangzhou in January,

Shanghai and Nanjing in March 1927. Chiang Kai-shek as supreme commander gained enormously in prestige and power. These great successes were the result of his achievements in military training and preparation; Kuomintang and Communist organizing efforts among peasants, workers, students, and others; and Chiang's readiness to negotiate with warlords who would give their allegiance to the Kuomintang. The result of such negotiations was that some important warlords left the way open for the advancing Northern Expedition or even joined it, so that the balance of forces shifted dramatically against those that remained to be defeated in open battle. Chiang had argued for some years that the Kuomintang government ought to be ready to give office to able people of all kinds even if they were not fully committed to the Three Principles of the People; the integrity of Sun's ideas and their eventual application would be assured by the commitment to them of the disciplined *party*, not government, elite. Thus he was working out ways to put Sun's quasi-Leninist party structure to thoroughly anti-Leninist uses.

The intertwined victories of Chiang's armies and of Communist and other radical mass movements brought to a boil the simmering conflict between military control and radical mass organization; it was clear to both sides that soon one would destroy the other. Chiang and his allies struck first. In April 1927 police, Kuomintang troops, and gangsters attacked the powerful labor unions and other radical organizations in Shanghai. Hundreds were killed and thousands fled or went into hiding. The warlords controlling the vital northern provinces of Shanxi and Shaanxi, and Guangxi in the southwest, declared their allegiance to the Kuomintang and their support for Chiang. Bloody repression of radical labor and peasant organizations, many with Communist leadership, spread throughout the Yangzi valley and to Guangzhou. The Chinese Communists, the Soviet advisers, and left-wing Kuomintang opponents of Chiang scrambled to form a rival center of power at Wuhan, but it rapidly disintegrated. In 1928 the Kuomintang forces and their warlord allies occupied all of north China, including Manchuria. A new national government was established in Nanjing, not Beijing, and Chiang clearly was one of the most powerful figures, probably the most powerful, in it.

In the "Nanjing Decade" from 1928 to 1937, the Kuomintang and its allies had their only chance to build a modern Chinese nation. Their efforts to build railways, industrialize, develop education, and extend administrative power into the countryside were energetic, dedicated, and often chaotic. Circumstances were extremely unfavorable. In the midst of a great depression, the advanced industrial world bought few exports and could offer no aid or investment. Japan was hostile to the Kuomintang from the beginning; it took over Manchuria beginning in 1931 and kept pressure up in the area around Beijing. The Communists, almost annihilated in 1927–28, had revived enough to form irritating guerrilla bases in the mountains of Jiangxi. The Nanjing government faced some kind of breakaway coalition of warlords and dissident civilian politicians, in Beijing, Guangzhou, or elsewhere, in every year of its short life.

Chiang Kai-shek's response to this daunting situation was to insist that effective national resistance to the Japanese menace could be expected only when the entire country was under the actual control of the central government and several years had been devoted to training and arming modern military forces. Sun Yat-sen had called for periods of military dictatorship and training of the common people in self-government. Advocates of immediate democracy and resistance to Japan, dissident politicians and warlords, and Communist guerrillas in Chiang's eyes all were alike in their opposition to the path of centrally directed modernization and political development that Sun had laid out and Chiang was trying to follow. He also took several measures to promote the moral revival of the Chinese people. Sun Yat-sen was memorialized as the great founder, teacher, father of the country. His picture was everywhere. School children learned to recite his will and to sing the stirring national anthem, "Three Principles of the People." In 1934 Chiang promoted a "New Life Movement" against corruption and sloppy personal conduct; ostensibly directed to the whole Chinese people, it was in fact largely relevant to the educated and office-holding elite. Many were surprised to see how "Confucian" the fiery radical general of 1925 had become. He also had become a Christian. He had married Soong (Song) Mei-ling, the intelligent and ambitious daughter of a very powerful Shanghai Christian family. His turn to Christianity seems to have been motivated among other things by his sense that it provided a strong supplement to Confucian moralism and character-building; it may also have been a way of finding something other than evil in Shanghai.

By 1937 Chiang had defeated his rivals in the Kuomintang and driven the Communists out of central China. But he had antagonized many patriots who thought he was appeasing the Japanese and many principled followers of the Three Principles of the People who found his government uninterested in rural rent reduction or other measures to improve the lives of the common people, wary of doing anything that might antagonize an entrenched local elite. The kind of centrally controlled authoritarian modernization he advocated sometimes has accomplished a great deal since World War II—in Singapore, in South Korea, and most ironically under Chiang and his son in Taiwan. Whatever small successes it managed in the unfavorable environment of the 1930s were wiped out by the war and civil war that followed. Some have argued that the Kuomintang would have done better to set aside temporarily its struggle for national political unification and to attempt to realize Sun Yat-sen's full vision of democracy and just, balanced economic development in one or two provinces, trusting that the strength thus developed would then make possible the spread of this revolution to the rest of China. But Chiang, like most Chinese, was the moral heir of Confucius but also the heir of the First Emperor of Qin in his assumption of the political unity of all of China and the preferability of centralized political control.

The tensions of these years came to a bizarre climax in December 1936 at Xi'an. Chiang had chased the Communists out of Jiangxi and now was pursuing them in northern Shaanxi. Many of the troops and commanders he was using were from Manchuria and were wondering why they were chasing Communists instead of trying to drive the Japanese out of their homeland. When Chiang went to Xi'an they placed him under house arrest and demanded that he stop the war on the Communists and unite with them against the Japanese. Chiang maintained his now steely self-control most of the time, but gave way to furious anger when his former subordinate Zhou Enlai appeared to negotiate with him on behalf of the Communists. Finally Chiang tacitly accepted the demands of his captors and was released, returning to Nanjing with his image as a national leader much enhanced.

The Japanese would not tolerate the emergence of even a tenuous united front against their advances. In July 1937 they shifted to full-scale invasion, beginning eight years of bitter war. Chiang Kai-shek was regarded, by most of his countrymen and most of the world, as the leader of the war of resistance. He and Madame Chiang were *Time* Magazine's "Man and Woman of the Year" for 1937. Chinese armies fought bravely, especially around Shanghai, but eventually had to retreat. The Japanese took Nanjing and turned their troops loose in an appalling orgy of looting and massacre. The capital was moved first to Wuhan and then to Chongqing in Sichuan, where it remained until 1945.

From 1937 to 1942 the Chinese fought on alone, eventually losing all the major cities and rail lines in eastern China. Chiang Kai-shek's rigid military bearing and singleness of purpose became for many a symbol of a beleaguered people refusing to give way to superior power. Chiang now was in unquestioned command of the apparatus of party and government. In 1940 his old colleague and political rival, Wang Jingwei, deserted him to organize a regime under Japanese control that never had wide support. The Chongqing government made some efforts to honor the tentative cooperative arrangements with the Communists worked out in 1937, but the two sides were deeply suspicious of each other, and after a major battle between them early in 1941 the "united front" was dead.

Wartime conditions took a terrible toll on the Kuomintang government and its supporters. The bases of China's budding industries and modern political elites, in the great cities of the Yangzi valley and along the coast, now were in Japanese hands. In Sichuan, Guizhou, and Yunnan, the Kuomintang government and its armies had to reach wary accommodations with old-fashioned local elites and warlords. With heroic effort, whole factories and universities were moved to the southwest, but their managers and professors found themselves in a strange and difficult land. Relatively democratic and egalitarian elements lost ground in the internal politics of the Kuomintang. Deprived of many of its most important revenue bases, the government tried to pay its troops and officials by issuing more and more paper money. The resulting inflation was one of the most important sources of the discouragement and cynicism that overcame many in Chongqing as the war wore on.

Pearl Harbor and the entry of the United States and Great Britain into the war against Japan brought major changes. China was recognized as one of the "Great Powers" directing the united effort to defeat the Axis. Chiang Kai-shek was included in a conference of heads of state at Cairo in 1943 but not in more important later meetings at Teheran and Yalta. By the end of 1943 it was clear that Japan would be defeated by American power in the Pacific, not by a grinding land war in China. Chiang got only moderate support for his continuing war effort, and he must have felt increasingly justified in his tendency to look beyond the anti-Japanese war toward the civil war with the Communists that inevitably would follow. The United States, however, still expected him to devote all the meager resources at his command to the war against Japan and to accept Allied training and supplying of Kuomintang generals whom he did not trust and even of the Communists. By VJ Day in 1945 Chiang's heroic image in the outside world was badly tarnished. A bright spot from his perspective had been the agreement of Great Britain and the United States in 1942–43 to abrogate the unequal treaties, which Chiang had seen as the key source of China's disgrace and weakness.

After VJ Day, the Kuomintang and the Communists rushed to occupy as much territory as possible as the Japanese armies surrendered. The United States sought to mediate and to avoid a civil war. Kuomintang political initiatives produced a new constitution and elections for a National Assembly in 1947, in which the Communists and their allies refused to join. The Kuomintang was not able to control the election process nearly as thoroughly as it had hoped. The National Assembly overwhelmingly elected Chiang president but rejected his chosen vice-presidential candidate, electing instead the Guangxi militarist Li Zongren. The Kuomintang reoccupation of the rich farmlands and cities of the lower Yangzi and northern China was chaotic and often corrupt. Inflation continued to spiral out of control. Kuomintang military forces badly overextended themselves in occupying the great cities of Manchuria and were surrounded and eventually forced to surrender in 1948. As the Communist forces occupied Beijing and advanced south, Chiang relinquished the presidency to Li Zongren and at the end of 1949 flew from Chongqing across wide areas already occupied by the Communists to Taiwan, where he resumed the presidency early in 1950 and sought to make the island his base for resistance and for the hoped-for reconquest of the mainland.

Taiwan had been a part of the Japanese Empire from 1895 to 1945. The Kuomintang officials who took control of it after VJ Day were exceptionally brutal and corrupt. The Taiwanese, the Chinese whose ancestors had been settling the island's plains since the days of Zheng Chenggong, rose in rebellion on February 28, 1947, and were suppressed with much loss of life. Chiang and the large numbers of soldiers, bureaucrats, and businesspeople who preceded and followed him to Taiwan had little interest in Taiwan for its own sake. They named most of Taipei's streets after mainland cities, built up a central Taipei business area that did its best to look like a lesser Shanghai, and continued to vow that they would return to the mainland. The Taiwanese were excluded from political power, and the social gulf between them and the "mainlanders" was very wide. Martial law remained in force, and the range of permitted political opinion was very narrow.

It was in these apparently unpromising conditions that the Kuomintang leadership managed to realize many aspects of Sun Yat-sen's dreams for a modern China. Sun had called for a long process of military dictatorship and political tutelage before democracy could emerge. The state would take an active role in directing economic development, investing in infrastructure and leading enterprises, limiting private economic power and ensuring a relatively equitable distribution of land and wealth. When Chiang Kai-shek died in 1975 his goal of returning to the mainland seemed more remote than ever, and the Kuomintang's control of politics and public opinion remained rigid, but Taiwan had changed enormously. It had a solid base of prosperous farmers owning the land they tilled, was industrializing rapidly, and had a far more equitable distribution of income than Mexico or many other developing countries. Taiwanese, excluded from political power, had amassed some of the largest industrial and commercial fortunes.

How was this possible? American support and advice played a role, encouraging a major land-distribution program, providing a crucial naval shield against Communist invasion after the outbreak of the Korean War, and supporting much of a large defense budget. The Taiwanese provided enormous amounts of entrepreneurial energy from commercial farms to great factories. The Japanese had left behind a better network of railroads and irrigation works than most parts of mainland China enjoyed. Even more vital, however, was the new freedom of the Kuomintang elite to pursue Sun's ideals. Some of the most corrupt and opportunistic Kuomintang leaders did not come to Taiwan but went to Hong Kong or the United States. The shock of the defeat propelled Chiang toward a serious and thorough reform and tightening of discipline within the Kuomintang. Confined to Taiwan, the Kuomintang did not spend all its effort and resources in pursuit of shaky national political unifications as it had done in the 1930s. Contemptuous of the Taiwanese landlord elite and not in need of its political support, it pushed through the kind of land reform many of them had dreamed of in the 1930s. Freed by disastrous defeat of the chimera of political unity that had been pursued by every victorious ruler since the First Emperor of Qin, Chiang and his colleagues were able to realize in their small realm the imperatives of effective political unity, universal education, and economic growth that had enticed and eluded Liang Qichao, Sun Yat-sen, and so many other thinkers and politicians on the mainland.

If one went to a movie in Taiwan in the last years of Chiang Kai-shek's life, before the movie began everyone stood while an impressive short film showed the military might of the Republic of China and Chiang Kai-shek as a quietly smiling, ramrod-straight old gentleman greeting visitors and practicing his calligraphy, while a chorus sang the stirring national anthem, "The Three Principles of the People." It was an image that combined the personal self-control, Confucian benevolence, and national strength that had eluded him for so much of his life. Chiang died on April 5, 1975. Huge crowds watched in grief as his coffin was borne through the streets of Taipei and to a suburban villa; he would not be formally buried, the government announced, until he could be buried beside Sun Yat-sen outside Nanjing.

CHIANG CHING-KUO

Leadership in nation-building requires vision, discipline, and an ability to pay attention to the common people and meet their needs. The leadership of the Kuomintang has provided a good measure of all three, but only in three successive generations. The third of these figures is the least known, and fully as important and intriguing as Sun Yat-sen and Chiang Kai-shek.

Chiang Ching-kuo (Jiang Jingguo), eldest son of Chiang Kai-shek, was in the last years of his life the highly respected president of the Republic of China on Taiwan. He presided over Taiwan's coming of age as a successful industrial society and guided its transition to democracy. He presented a shrewdly crafted image of an amiable and unassuming person with a winning smile, visiting farms and fishing villages, strolling in his windbreaker with his friends among the common people.

Chiang Ching-kuo's road to the eminence of his last years was as bizarre as anything encountered in this book. Raised in the strict traditional household of Chiang Kai-shek's mother, he experienced the turmoil and enthusiasm of the Nationalist–Communist united front of the 1920s; the despair of the gold mines of the Siberian Gulag; the challenges of reviving local administration in southern Jiangxi, very much in the footsteps of Wang Yangming; a ruthless and abortive crackdown on corruption in Shanghai in the late 1940s; and the creation and management of a ruthless and successful system of secret police control on Taiwan.

When Chiang Ching-kuo was born in 1909, his father was studying in Japan. The first major influence on him was the strict traditional Buddhist discipline of his father's mother. Until the death of his grandmother in 1921 he remained at the family home in Zhejiang, studying in some of the same schools and with some of the same teachers as his father had. Brought to Shanghai in 1921, he quickly became involved in anti-imperialist agitations and demonstrations. His father then sent him to a small school for the children of Kuomintang leaders in Beijing, where he again got in trouble for demonstrating against the warlord government.

In 1925 Chiang Ching-kuo told his father he wanted to go study in Moscow. Chiang Kai-shek was beginning to move against Soviet connections and influence in China but was not yet ready to show his intentions too openly, so he could not very well forbid Ching-kuo to go. In Moscow Ching-kuo enrolled in Sun Yat-sen University, established by the Soviets as a training school for Chinese revolutionaries. By the time Ching-kuo graduated in 1927, his father was engaged in full-scale repression of the Chinese Communists and their allies, and the Soviets did not allow Ching-kuo to go home. After attending another training institute he sought to go home in 1930, but again was turned down. He now served as a guide for visiting groups of Chinese students; was an apprentice in an electrical plant; argued with the heads of the Chinese Communist party and almost was sent to a gold mine in Siberia; was given a plot of land near Moscow and told to farm for a living; and was sent to the gold mine after all. Finally he was assigned to a heavy machinery plant at Sverdlovsk in the Urals where, despite being under occasional secret police surveillance, he rose to be assistant director and editor of the plant newspaper and married a young Russian woman. In the terrible years of the Stalin terror, on the edge of or within the Gulag, he had abundant experience of misery, despair, and of course the loneliness of an apparently hopeless exile. He also seems to have learned a good deal from his captors, and later did not hesitate to apply their techniques of party control and secret police work in the course of his rise in the Kuomintang.

In September 1936 Chiang was dismissed from his posts at the plant and his alternate membership in the Soviet Communist party was canceled. His father's adventures at Xi'an in December of that year and the subsequent shift toward an uneasy "united front" against Japan probably came just in time to save the son's life. In April 1937 he returned to China after an absence of almost twelve years. His Russian wife accompanied him and remained quietly at his side for the rest of his life. Making his peace with his father on terms of which little is known, he was assigned to a series of administrative posts in Jiangxi. In 1939 he was placed in charge of a district of eleven counties around Ganxian in southern Jiangxi, including the mountain areas that had been the main bases of the Communist party from 1930 to 1934. He was very much aware that this was the same area that Wang Yangming had sought to rehabilitate. He made improvements in public health and education; encouraged the development of local industry; established the control of the Nanjing government in an area where the local elite had ruled unchecked; and took stern measures against gambling, opium, and prostitution. These measures were in many ways rather close to what his father and his associates at Nanjing would have liked to do for the whole country if they had not felt compelled to spend all their time and energy seeking national unification, and in some ways anticipated the policies of the Kuomintang in Taiwan after 1949.

Between 1941 and 1945 Chiang Ching-kuo spent more and more time in Chongqing and was appointed to some responsible positions, but it does not seem that any very good use was found for his talents. His fluent Russian was a factor in his appointment to a mission to Moscow in 1945 and to positions in the northeast, where he could do nothing to slow the Russian looting of the area or the disintegration of the Kuomintang's strength. In 1948 he was part of a new team of officials sent into Shanghai to crack down on the rampant corruption and the currency speculation that had been fed by the hyperinflation. He arrested many merchants, bankers, and speculators, including a nephew of his stepmother Soong Mei-ling and the son of Shanghai's most powerful gangster. His father stepped in, and Chiang Ching-kuo had to issue a public apology. He had been guilty of taking his duties a little too seriously, or perhaps of thinking that desperate measures might yet save Kuomintang power at a time when many were giving up.

Chiang's role in the Kuomintang consolidation of power on Taiwan in the 1950s carried on the ruthless pursuit of law and order he had begun in Shanghai, but much more effectively. He developed a thorough system of

Kuomintang supervision within all military units, and he seems to have had his hand in several parts of the Taipei government's overlapping apparatuses for spying on its own citizens and suppressing dissent. He led the development of the Chinese Youth Anti-Communist National Salvation Corps, which helped to maintain political conformity in schools and colleges but may also have stimulated the interest in and affinity for young people Chiang showed later in his career. He also was appointed to direct the Vocational Assistance Commission for Retired Servicemen, which developed an amazing range of business ventures, including major construction projects, that turned the men of the overlarge armies that had followed the Kuomintang from the mainland into avid contributors to the development of Taiwan rather than underemployed and dangerous political intriguers.

From 1972 on Chiang Kai-shek was very infirm and no longer actively in charge; Chiang Ching-kuo as premier was coming into his own. He pushed through the adoption and completion of the Ten Great Projects, a set of ambitious dams, roads, and railroads. After his father's death he was recognized as head of the Kuomintang, and in 1978 he was elected president. A new approach to relations between the government and the common people, already faintly visible in his years as premier, became more pronounced. Every Sunday the national television news began with a segment showing the president strolling the streets in turtleneck and windbreaker, shaking hands, eating a bowl of noodles, talking to children and students, greeting workers on a dangerous mountain road. Photos in the newspapers showed him sitting on a stool in a fisherman's little house, throwing out the first ball at a Little League championship game.

None of this canny image-making implied any real relaxation of the Kuomintang grip on power. But ordinary people noticed that the radio weather reports now were in Taiwanese as well as in Mandarin and that, although open political opposition still was very risky, the range of subjects about which it was possible to argue and agitate was growing. The Taipei government rode out the shocks of the shifts of Washington, Tokyo, and many other capitals to recognition of Beijing in the 1970s, replacing formal diplomacy with a network of quasi-diplomatic "Coordinating Committees," trade centers, and so on. As the Taiwan economy became more complex and as trade and production became more central to its relations with other areas of the world, economists and engineers were given more and more high positions in the government. Quite a few of them were Taiwanese, and percentages of Taiwanese in the army, the Kuomintang, and the government rose steadily. These were the achievements of a broad and sophisticated elite, but it was Chiang Ching-kuo who set the tone and said yes to the reformers and no to those who wanted to turn the clock back to total control by the old mainlander elite and its obsessive anticommunism.

By 1985 Chiang Ching-kuo was in ill health, and the question of succession was on many people's minds. Chiang stated firmly and openly that no relative of his would have a special position in the government after his death. His choice as vice-presidential running mate in his 1984 reelection was Lee Teng-hui (Li Denghui), a Taiwanese Christian with a Ph.D. degree in agricultural economics from Cornell and no political base of his own. When opposition groups formed a Democratic Progressive party in 1986, Chiang did not move immediately to suppress it but instead laid down conditions for its legalization.

After Chiang's death in January 1988 Lee Teng-hui managed to consolidate power and win a great deal of public respect. Since then the Democratic Progressive party has been legalized, martial law has been lifted, and controls on the press and public opinion greatly relaxed. Early in 1992 Lee Teng-hui, the perfect representative of the highly educated technocracy that has guided Taiwan and also himself a Taiwanese, attended a solemn memorial concert with the families of the victims of the Kuomintang repression of February 1947. Contacts with the mainland, including visits and investment projects by Taiwan residents, now are permitted and even encouraged. Elections in 1989 and 1991, while far from perfectly clean, have given the Democratic Progressive party and other opponents of the Kuomintang opportunities to vie for power and sometimes win it in ways that still seem scarcely imaginable on the other side of the Taiwan Strait.

MAO ZEDONG

······

A QIN emperor breaking the mold and reshaping his society for the ages, a would-be Great Teacher, a Wang Mang promoting himself and ignoring realities, a Three Kingdoms hero rushing ahead and riding the chaos, condescending admirer of the Taipings, youthful reader of Liang Qichao, poet-politician, stroller by Su Dongpo's dike and the lakes of Qianlong's palaces, urging his people to always do without hesitation or selfishness what they know is right, to work as hard as Yu and sacrifice themselves as readily as Yue Fei, Mao Zedong echoes in his own experience and his exhortations to his people an amazing number of the themes of this book. To understand him and his times, we need to know a lot about Marxism-Leninism, economic development, world politics—and also a lot about a Chinese heritage that Mao found both precious and a dead weight on the forward march of his people.

As seen from the beginning of this book, China was too large to be held together by force alone; the attractiveness of the ideal of the good minister of the Son of Heaven, the possibility that any talented man could become such a minister through the examination system and the carefully regulated politics of the bureaucracy, the limitation of military power and the political roles of military men, all were essential to the unity of the vast empire. But the growth of effective military power was a basic aspect of survival in the modern world, and in China this growth and the disruption of the old civilian control structures set off an uncontrolled militarization that tore the country apart. By 1920 many were groping for new ways to control the military and reunite the country. Among the pieces of a solution were discipline of troops and their indoctrination in one form or another of nationalism and public spirit; mobilization of ordinary tradespeople, farmers, and workers as active participants in politics; and new ways of disciplining and indoctrinating a civil and bureaucratic elite. These developed in various forms and combinations. The famous Christian warlord Feng Yuxiang had real success in the first, little in the others. The reorganized Kuomintang of the 1920s and 1930s achieved much in the first and third, but had an ambiguous record on mass mobilization. Mao Zedong himself was led toward interest in mass mobilization by participation in efforts to protect his native Hunan against predatory military men. The Communist party eventually produced a powerful solution to all the pieces of this problem. The Chinese people still are grappling with the consequences of that solution.

These elements of effective resistance to military power might also be seen as practical corollaries of Liang Qichao's search for forms of solidarity of a "new people." The particular forms they took moved far beyond Liang's own ideas, propelled by the revolt of intellectuals against traditional culture, worldwide anti-imperialist ferment after World War I, and the impact of the Russian Revolution. After 1911 there was no emperor, after 1905 no examination system. Many young people in search of good educations and secure paths to elite careers—traditional Chinese values— were studying abroad and being exposed to the full range of twentieth-century ideas and movements. Even to those who stayed in China, Confucianism seemed irrelevant to a China with no emperor and a world full of new ideas and competing peoples, a humbug espoused by ruthless military men and by social conservatives seeking to deny young people and women full participation in the new Chinese nation. From 1915 on there was a rash of intellectual journals with the word "new" (*xin*) in their titles: *New Tide, New Literature*, and most famous of all *New Youth* (*Xin qingnian*), with its articles on literary revolution, on freedom for women, on the importance of physical education for strengthening the people of the Chinese nation, and one that proclaimed that all the works of "Confucius and sons" were just fit to be thrown into the privy. In 1919 this intensely nationalistic, intensely moralistic intellectual trend was politicized in the May Fourth Movement, beginning in demonstrations in Beijing on that date against the acquiescence of the warlord government in provisions of the Treaty of Versailles allowing Japan to retain some of the positions it had acquired in China during World War I.

Demonstrations by incensed literati were nothing new in China, and many of the people caught up in the May Fourth Movement went on to spend their lives in strictly intellectual pursuits, contributing to the development in China of modern science, a new colloquial language, a new literature, a new historical scholarship, and many other aspects of a vigorous modern academic culture. Liang Qichao did not share all their styles or convictions, but they were in many ways heirs to his approaches to China's problems. Other May Fourth participants, in the process of opposing warlords and organizing boycotts of Japanese goods, began to take more of an interest in the political mobilization of China's common people. Many of them became fascinated by one aspect or another of the great drama then unfolding in Russia. To some, the Russian Revolution provided assurance that Marxism was a scientific key to historical change that could be applied even to backward countries. Others saw in it proof that the moral energies of a backward and disorganized people could be tapped in a great volcanic eruption that would alter world history. Many saw in the Bolshevik pattern of organization of a party as an elite of disciplined professional revolutionaries a solution to China's failure of elite cohesion. This pattern had, especially in its organization into cells, echoes of China's secret society organizations and even of the voluntary commitment of the Peach Orchard Oath.

I already have noted Sun Yat-sen's interest in Soviet aid and models of organization. Soviet support for Sun was part of a wider effort to find ways in which "bourgeois revolutionaries" in Asia could be induced to ally with the Soviet Union in the struggle against the capitalist powers of the advanced industrial world and with the infant Communist parties that eventually would supersede them in the inevitable course of world revolution. The conviction that this balancing act was possible was one of the more astonishing of the many acts of Marxist faith this century has seen, but for a time Sun seemed the perfect bourgeois revolutionary ally. As has been seen, the turn away from the Kuomintang-Communist alliance began shortly after Sun's death in 1925, and by the end of 1927 the break was complete and the Communists had suffered a nearly fatal series of defeats.

Up to this point Mao Zedong was an inconspicuous participant in the turmoil of Chinese revolutionary nationalism, more interesting as an example of the wrenching transitions his generation passed through than for his influence or accomplishments. Born in 1893 in the family of a Hunan farmer and local grain trader who was among the more prosperous people in his village, strict with his sons and harsh and unbending in his business dealings with his neighbors, Mao early rebelled against the strict discipline and dull memory work of the local Confucian school. He was much happier reading the *Romance of the Three Kingdoms*, a biography of Yue Fei, and other stories of heroes, and exchanging tales from them with the old men of the village. In 1909 he was able to enroll in a "modern" school in a nearby county, where for the first time he got his hands on a copy of Liang Qichao's *New People's Miscellany* and read and reread it until he almost had it memorized. He had a teacher who had studied in Japan and who gave glowing accounts of that country's progress. In his reading Mao continued to be fascinated by Yao, Shun, Yu, the First Emperor of Qin, and Emperor Wu of the Han, but also learned about such sages and heroes as Washington, Napoleon, Peter the Great, Rousseau, and Lincoln. In 1910 he went on to a more advanced school in Changsha, capital of Hunan. Caught up in the excitement of approaching revolution, he posted an essay on the school wall calling for a new government with Sun Yat-sen as president, Kang Youwei as premier, and Liang Qichao as minister of foreign affairs. In 1911–12 he spent six months in the revolutionary army, apparently without ever seeing combat. Then he was adrift again in a world where the old paths to worldly success and political participation had disappeared. Reading the advertisements for schools in the newspapers, he considered a police academy and a soap-making school, then tried a commercial school but left after a month; some classes were in English, which he had scarcely begun to study, and he had hated keeping books for his father and never would have much use for accounts and statistics. After another brief stay in a school in Changsha he spent six valuable months reading on his own in the provincial library, concentrating on translations of Western political and social thought and studying a map of the world for the first time.

Then in 1913 Mao finally found a school that suited him, the Hunan First Normal School, full of alert and ambitious students and good teachers, low in cost because the provincial government subsidized it in order to produce schoolteachers for the province. He and his classmates were typical representatives of the radical youth of their generation, avid readers of the magazine *New Youth*, intensely nationalistic, interested in socialism, anarchism, and many other radical ideas of foreign origin. Mao and a group of friends were exceptionally devoted to physical fitness, taking long hikes in the country in all kinds of weather. One teacher became a key figure in his development: Yang Changji had studied in Japan, England, and Germany and had been profoundly impressed with German ethical idealism, which insisted that moral life was a matter of the realization of the moral nature of man, including his social obligations, not just of the pursuit of profit and pleasure for the self and others. It was not hard to harmonize elements of this Western philosophy with some basic Confucian teachings, and Yang, although he opposed the traditional Chinese family system, was a serious and respectful student of the Confucian moral tradition. Mao, deeply impressed, wrote for Yang an essay on "The Power of Mind," which Yang graded 105 on a scale of 100. Later Yang helped Mao get an assistant librarian's job at Beijing University, and Mao married his daughter, Yang Kaihui. (Mao's father had arranged a marriage for him when he was fourteen, but he claimed he had never lived with his village wife.)

The April 1917 number of *New Youth* carried an article by Mao Zedong; quite a coup for a normal-school student who had hardly been out of his home province. Entitled "A Study of Physical Education," it urged young Chinese to take more interest in their physical fitness so that they could take a more active role in defending China against the imperialists. The influence of moral idealism, exaltation of the will, and tales of ancient heroes also were apparent: "The principal aim of physical education is military heroism." He also became very much involved in two study societies, one called the "New People Study Society," with obvious echoes of Liang Qichao's ideas, the other focusing on the ideas and works of Wang Fuzhi, a Hunanese scholar who had refused to take office under the Qing conquerors in the seventeenth century and had used his long decades of withdrawal from public life to write some of the most brilliant and searching works of moral, social, and historical philosophy in the entire history of the Confucian tradition.

After he graduated from the normal school in 1918, Mao made his first long trip outside Hunan, to Beijing, where he lived a cramped, poor student's life and worked as an assistant in the university library, but also saw the great palaces and pleasure parks of the emperors in their chilly winter splendor and participated in the heady radical intellectual life of the city. Especially important to his growing radicalism and attraction to Marxism were his discussions with Chen Duxiu, editor of *New Youth*, and Li Dazhao, the head of the university library, whose responses to the Russian Revolution as a great eruption of moral energy and human will anticipated themes in Mao's approach to China's revolution. On his travels Mao also paced the walls of Xuzhou, a key city in the Three Kingdoms stories and scene of difficulties and pleasures for Su Dongpo, and of Nanjing; visited the shrines of Confucius at Qufu in Shandong; and climbed Mount Tai, where the First Emperor of Qin, Emperor Wu of Han, and Gaozong and Empress Wu had performed their great ceremonies. Revolution, nationalism, the heroic and precious legacy of China's past, all were and would remain vital to him.

Mao had been stimulated by the radical intellectual life of Beijing, but had found no way to contribute to it effectively. In 1919–22 he was in and out of Changsha. He was primarily concerned with the politics of Hunan, and on this stage he was much more effective. He founded the *Xiangjiang pinglun* (Xiang River Critical Review), a major provincial exponent of the "democracy and new culture" of the May Fourth Movement, wrote in it about the power of the aroused masses against warlords and imperialists, and experimented with various forms of agitation and organization, including labor unions and strikes, in attempting to oppose a particularly brutal warlord who controlled Hunan. In 1920 he visited Shanghai to coordinate the work of Hunan student groups there, and some long conversations with Chen Duxiu led him finally to firm Marxist convictions. In July 1921 he was among the founding members of the Chinese Communist party. In 1921–22 he was active in labor union organizing and other Communist activities in Hunan. From 1923 to 1926 he held a variety of posts both in the Communist party and in the much larger Kuomintang of Sun Yat-sen with which the Communists were allied. His own intense anti-imperialist nationalism made him an enthusiastic cooperator with the Kuomintang, with fewer reservations about the alliance than some of his fellow Communists. On a visit to Hunan in 1925 he experimented with the organization of rural people against their landlords and other oppressors, and in 1926 he directed the Peasant Movement Training Institute of the Kuomintang, housed in a former Confucian temple in Guangzhou, where relics of the spartan and highly militarized routine of the teachers and students of the institute still can be seen today.

Mao was not the only Communist who was becoming interested in the revolutionary potential of rural China in these years; another very important figure, Peng Pai, was building a considerable organization in eastern Guangdong. In Marxism the industrial worker is the best revolutionary, and peasants are thought to be too traditional, too individualistic, too easily satisfied with the ownership of the land they cultivate, to be good revolutionary material. But in a country where the vast majority of the people work the land, the chances of revolution would be very much improved if the rural population could be effectively mobilized. After surveying conditions in Hunan early in 1927, Mao wrote a famous "Report of an Investigation of the Peasant Movement in Hunan":

> When I first arrived in Changsha, I met people from various circles and picked up a good deal of street gossip. From the middle strata upwards to the right-wingers of the Kuomintang, there was not a single person who did not summarize the whole thing in one phrase: "An awful mess!" Even quite revolutionary people, carried away by the opinion of the "awful mess" school which prevailed like a storm over the whole city, became downhearted at the very thought of the conditions in the countryside, and could not deny the word "mess." Even very progressive people could only remark: "Indeed a mess, but inevitable in the course of the revolution." In a word, nobody could categorically deny the word "mess."

> But the fact is, as stated above, that the broad peasant masses have risen to fulfill their historic mission, that the democratic forces in the rural areas have risen to overthrow the rural feudal power. The patriarchal-feudal class of local bullies, bad gentry, and lawless landlords has formed the basis of autocratic government for thousands of years, the cornerstone of imperialism, warlordism, and corrupt officialdom. To overthrow this feudal power is the real objective of the national revolution. What Dr. Sun Yat-sen wanted to do in the forty years he devoted to the national revolution but failed to accomplish, the peas-

ants have accomplished in a few months. This is a marvelous feat which has never been achieved in the last forty or even thousands of years. . . . A revolution is not the same as inviting people to dinner, or writing an essay, or painting a picture, or doing fancy needlework; it cannot be anything so refined, so calm and gentle, or so mild, kind, courteous, restrained, and magnanimous. A revolution is an uprising, an act of violence whereby one class overthrows another. A rural revolution is a revolution by which the peasantry overthrows the authority of the feudal landlord class. If the peasants do not use the maximum of their strength, they can never overthrow the authority of the landlords which has been deeply rooted for thousands of years. In the rural areas, there must be a great fervent revolutionary upsurge, which alone can arouse hundreds and thousands of the people to form a great force.[1]

With its metaphors of storm and eruption, so like Li Dazhao's picture of the Russian Revolution and his hopes for China, with its sense of the dramas of rural life and emphasis on popular rage carrying all before it, the Hunan report was a remarkably individual document, rather casual in its attitude toward the usual Marxist forms of class analysis and policy debate. It also was horribly overoptimistic: very little of the activity Mao described survived the warlord and Kuomintang repressions of 1927. Wiped out or in hiding in the cities, barely surviving in the countryside, the surviving Communists were thrown back on learning how to fight guerrilla wars and how to win the support of the rural population. An army revolt in August 1927 at Nanchang under Zhu De and others led to the formation of the first small nucleus of independent Communist military power. In the fall Mao and other Hunan Communists led an uprising of peasants, miners, and soldiers that had no hope of success and was not approved by the party's Central Committee. Mao and other survivors took refuge in the Jinggang Mountains on the Hunan–Jiangxi border, where Zhu De's forces soon joined them. They began to organize "soviets," independent local governments completely under Communist control. Similar small bases appeared elsewhere in the mountains of south China, and a few north of the Yangzi. A Jiangxi provisional soviet government was proclaimed in 1930, and early in 1931 a central soviet government was established for the areas under Communist control, still largely in the mountains of Jiangxi. Mao was chairman of the soviet government, but did not control the Central Committee of the Communist party and frequently was in conflict with it.

[1] De Bary, *Sources of Chinese Tradition*, 2: 207–8.

In the Jiangxi Soviet years, 1930–34, the Communist party was struggling to keep alive a clandestine base in cities and rural areas under Kuomintang control, but it was dangerous work with meager results. Mao's recital a few years later of the early history of the movement was full of names of people shot by the Kuomintang in these years. Among them was his wife, Yang Kaihui. Over twenty years later, the spring drifts of seed-fluff from poplars on the streets of Beijing stirred him to send his most personal poem to a comrade who had lost a spouse named Liu (poplar and willow are *yang* and *liu*):

> I lost my proud poplar, and you your willow,
> Poplar and willow soar lightly to the heaven of heavens.
> The prisoner of the moon, Wu Gang, asked what he
>   has to offer,
> Offers them wine from the cassia tree.
> The lonely goddess in the moon spreads her ample sleeves
> To dance for these faithful souls in the endless sky.
> Down on earth a sudden report of the tiger's defeat,
> Tears rain down as if from an upturned bowl.[2]

Communist politics in the Jiangxi years were a tangle of urban-oriented Central Committee decisions, quarrels and power shifts among soviet leaders in various areas, and arguments over the redistribution of land, which secured the commitment of tenants and landless workers but might alienate cooperative small landlords if pressed too far. More important, the Communists accumulated a great deal of experience in rural organization and guerrilla warfare. True heirs of Zhuge Liang and of a millennium of banditry and bandit-chasing in these southern mountains, the Red Army delighted in luring Kuomintang units into traps, in attacking strong points and melting away into the mountains. They learned the importance of being polite and orderly in all their dealings with rural people and paying for everything taken from them. Nonmilitary organizers learned how to create mass organizations, such as peasant associations and women's associations, and to develop active local leadership by changing officers frequently and sending delegations from local groups to congresses at higher levels. The result of all this activity was a growing Communist base in Jiangxi, and a series of massive efforts by the Kuomintang armies under Chiang Kai-shek to encircle it, close in on it, and eventually eliminate the Communist cancer in China.

---

[2] Modified from Willis Barnstone, tr., *The Poems of Mao Tse-tung* (New York, 1972), pp. 88–89.

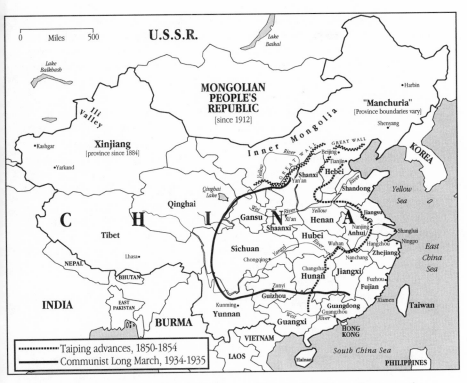

Map 4. China, 1800–1950. Political divisions and international boundaries as of 1955

In 1934 Chiang almost succeeded, but the Soviet leadership and key Red Army units managed to break out of the encirclement and begin a march of over eight thousand miles that would end in their joining with Communist groups from other endangered bases to form new bases areas in Shaanxi. This "Long March" was in fact a flight from nearly certain annihilation. Many comrades died on the way. Only by extraordinary courage, discipline, skillful leadership, and luck did any survive. The episodes of heroism and the sense of survivors that they must have been spared for some great purpose turned the Long March into a legend, a heroic epic, and a prime confirmation of Mao's conviction that human will can triumph over every obstacle. Early in the march, in January 1935, a conference at Zunyi in Guizhou ended in Mao's final victory over his urban-oriented rivals and his full control of the party apparatus. After a long feint south into Yunnan, the marchers crossed the upper Yangzi and then the Dadu River, shooting their way across the swaying chains of a suspension bridge high above the rushing mountain river. They moved north into ever higher and more dangerous country on the fringe of the Tibetan Plateau. Tribesmen shot at them from ambush, and the trail led through swampy grasslands. They had no firewood, so they ate their food raw. Carrying few tents, they got what rest they could huddled out of the incessant cold rain, two men under each umbrella.

The new base area in the mountains of northern Shaanxi, reached at the end of 1935, was far poorer and more remote than Jiangxi. But the rural mobilization strategies learned in Jiangxi could be put to work again here. And changes in national politics offered new opportunities. The Japanese had occupied "Manchuria," the northeastern provinces of China, in 1931 and continued to press for more power in the adjoining areas, down into the region around Beijing. To many patriotic Chinese, resistance to the invaders was clearly the first priority. The Jiangxi soviet government, safely out of reach of Japanese guns, played to this sentiment by declaring war on Japan. But Chiang Kai-shek ignored or suppressed calls for immediate resistance. Student demonstrations in Beijing in December 1935, which the Communists helped to organize, were suppressed. Growing numbers of students saw the Communists as the leading patriotic force in the country and sneaked away to join them in their base areas in the northwest.

In the summer of 1937 Japan responded to the threat of Chinese unity and determination to resist by striking first, beginning eight years of full-scale warfare. The armies of the Nanjing government bore the brunt of their assault. The Communists, far off in poor mountain country no one wanted, had a year or so to catch their breath and learn how to cope with the new situation. They had to modify their rural mobilization tactics to fit the united front pattern; land confiscation and redistribution was stopped, the soviet government became a special border region nominally under the national government, and the Red Army adopted numbers within the national system, of which the most famous was the Eighth Route Army. These were not superficial changes, but they left intact a hard core of Communist party discipline and of skills in rural popular mobilization and guerrilla warfare, developed in Jiangxi, that found new scope in the organization of resistance to the Japanese. The united front required at least the appearance of an end of class struggle, and thus sanctioned bringing into local resistance councils anyone who would cooperate with the Communists, regardless of class origins. The result was the spread of Communist-led resistance bases across north China, even behind Japanese lines, and in 1940 and 1941 a sudden increase in Japanese retaliation that strained resistance resources and led to some major changes of policy in the Communist capital, Yan'an in northern Shaanxi.

Communist experience in rural organization was cumulative, and experimentation and self-evaluation never ceased, but it was especially the changes of 1942–44 that produced the very distinctive organizational model we call "Yan'an communism," which has been a great source of strength to the Chinese Communists in later years but perhaps has contributed to some of their most serious mistakes. The border region government had become a fairly large and expensive operation, with conventional bureaucratic procedures and large-scale military organization. Now it tried to limit its expenses by encouraging everyone, including soldiers and bureaucrats, to grow some of their own food; by cutting back on numbers of soldiers and officials and trying to make them more efficient; and by carrying out policies less by passing down official directives and more by stationing individual cadres or activists in small settlements, typically as secretaries of local resistance councils, trying to adapt party policy to local circumstances and persuade the local leaders to adopt it, but fundamentally unable to order the local people to comply. This was the origin of the "mass line" mode of political life, oriented to imperfectly orderly mobilization of large numbers of people in great campaigns, that would remain characteristic of China until after Mao's death. To the degree that the system worked, in its early Yan'an version or the various later ones, it would make very effective use of a limited supply of intelligent, literate, committed people in dealing with the limitless problems and mobilizing the immense, dispersed energies of the Chinese people.

These policies would work, however, only if the individual cadres could be counted on to stick to party policy and promote it energetically in a situation where one person might be all alone in a remote settlement with no superior looking over his or her shoulder, subject to great social pressures from new friends and neighbors. Many of the educated young people available for such positions were former students who had come out from the universities in the great patriotic wave of the late 1930s, not hardened old revolutionaries, and sometimes they had too many ideas of their own. Thus the successful implementation of the Yan'an mass line required the simultaneous intensification of practices of ideological study, rectification, "thought reform," the origins of which can be traced back to the Jiangxi period and more remotely to the Confucian practice of friends banding together to criticize and exhort one another. Many cadres were brought in to Yan'an for short courses. Small study circles would focus on an important text of Marxist theory and exhortation to committed action. Members of a study circle would criticize each other and criticize themselves; frequently one member would be singled out for intensive pressure from the group, then readmitted to its good graces after he or she had made a sufficiently searching self-criticism and shown signs of changes in attitudes and behavior. The result in many cases was an intensification and internalization of commitment to the Communist cause, which was precisely what was needed if the cadre was to be effective and reliable in the difficult encounters of basic-level mass line leadership.

These policies were the work of a large collective leadership of great energy and intelligence, not just of Mao Zedong. But it is no mistake to call them Maoist. Anti-imperialist nationalism, the moral fervor of the educated young, the inchoate power of the Chinese masses, and the positive evaluation of the peasantry all were ground notes of Mao's approach to the Chinese revolution and of the Yan'an policies. Most of the texts read in study sessions were by Mao, and his position as leader and as articulator of basic principles was more secure than ever. It was a time of fruition in his life. Like most people in Yan'an, he lived in a cave dug in a vertical bank of the thick loess soil, an odd kind of dwelling but more comfortable than many he had seen in rural China. No longer on the move, his leadership unchallenged, he had time to do some connected thinking and writing, and he became a somewhat better-read, though still not very sophisticated, Marxist. A third wife had emerged from the Long March in poor physical and mental health. Mao, to the scandal of his puritanical colleagues, now established a liaison with a beautiful and willful film actress, recently arrived from Shanghai, named Jiang Qing. Foreign visitors found him sometimes disarmingly frank and earthy, apt to take his pants off before sitting down for a long chat on a hot summer afternoon, at other times a little distant and cool, but always a good listener, an assiduous learner and note-taker, a man of great intellect and will to power.

He wrote a great deal in the Yan'an years. Among the most important theoretical works were his essay on the "New Democracy," in which he claimed that the Communist party and the forces allied with it, not the Kuomintang, were the true heirs of Sun Yat-sen's revolution, and set down the principles for the building of a "new democratic" China in which leaders of various parties, representing various classes, would participate in the building of the new China under the firm guidance and hegemony of the Communist party. "On Practice" insisted at length that no amount of theoretical sophistication was worth anything if no practical application could be found for it. "On Contradiction" developed a broad view of conflict and contradiction as the most pervasive and most creative phenomena in human history:

> A great thing or event contains many contradictions in the process of its development. For instance, in the process of China's bourgeois-democratic revolution there are the contradiction between the various oppressed classes in Chinese society and imperialism, the contradic-

tion between the great masses of the people and feudalism, the contradiction between the proletariat and the bourgeoisie, the contradiction between the peasantry together with the urban petty bourgeoisie on the one hand, and the bourgeoisie on the other, the contradiction between various reactionary ruling blocs, etc.; the situation is exceedingly complex. Not only do all these contradictions each have their own particularity and cannot be treated uniformly, but the two aspects of every contradiction also have each their own characteristics and cannot be treated uniformly. Not only should we who work for the Chinese revolution understand the particularity of each of the contradictions in the light of their totality, that is, from the interconnection of those contradictions, but we can understand the totality of the contradictions only by a study of each of their aspects. To understand each of the aspects of a contradiction is to understand the definite position each aspect occupies, the concrete form in which it comes into interdependence as well as conflict with its opposite, and the concrete means by which it struggles with its opposite when the two are interdependent and yet contradictory, as well as when the interdependence breaks up. The study of these problems is a matter of the utmost importance. . . . As regards the problem of the particularity of contradiction, there are still two sides which must be specially singled out for analysis, that is, the principal contradiction and the principal aspect of a contradiction. In the process of development of a complex thing, many contradictions exist; among these, one is necessarily the principal contradiction whose existence and development determine or influence the existence and development of other contradictions.

So in studying any process—if it is a complicated process in which more than two contradictions exist—we must do our utmost to discover its principal contradiction. Once the principal contradiction is grasped, any problem can be readily solved. This is the method Marx taught us when he studied capitalist society. When Lenin and Stalin studied imperialism and the general crisis of capitalism, and when they studied Soviet economy, they also taught us this method.[3]

But of all his writings perhaps the most successful in its impact on the Chinese people was a funeral speech composed for a common soldier, later published under the title "Serve the People":

Our Communist party and the Eighth Route and New Fourth Armies led by our party are battalions of the revolution. These battalions of ours are wholly dedicated to the liberation of the people and work

---

[3] De Bary, *Sources of Chinese Tradition*, 2:236, 239.

entirely in the people's interests. Comrade Zhang Side was in the ranks of these battalions.

All men must die, but death can vary in its significance. The ancient Chinese writer Sima Qian said, "Though death befalls all men alike, it may be weightier than Mount Tai or lighter than a feather." To die for the people is weightier than Mount Tai, but to work for the fascists and die for the exploiters and oppressors is lighter than a feather. Comrade Zhang Side died for the people, and his death is indeed weightier than Mount Tai.

If we have shortcomings, we are not afraid to have them pointed out and criticized, because we serve the people. Anyone, no matter who, may point out our shortcomings. If he is right, we will correct them. If what he proposes will benefit the people, we will act upon it. The idea of "better troops and simpler administration" was put forward by Mr. Li Dingming, who is not a Communist. He made a good suggestion which is of benefit to the people, and we have adopted it. If, in the interests of the people, we persist in doing what is right and correct what is wrong, our ranks will surely thrive.

We hail from all corners of the country and have joined together for a common revolutionary objective. And we need the vast majority of the people with us on the road to this objective. Today, we already lead base areas with a population of 91 million, but this is not enough; to liberate the whole nation more are needed. In times of difficulty we must not lose sight of our achievements, must see the bright future and must pluck up our courage. The Chinese people are suffering; it is our duty to save them and we must exert ourselves in struggle. Wherever there is struggle there is sacrifice, and death is a common occurrence. But we have the interests of the people and the sufferings of the great majority at heart, and when we die for the people it is a worthy death. Nevertheless, we should do our best to avoid unnecessary sacrifices. Our cadres must show concern for every soldier, and all people in the revolutionary ranks must care for each other, must love and help each other.

From now on, when anyone in our ranks who has done some useful work dies, be he soldier or cook, we should have a funeral ceremony and a memorial meeting in his honor. This should become the rule. And it should be introduced among the people as well. When someone dies in a village, let a memorial meeting be held. In this way we express our mourning for the dead and unite all the people.[4]

---

[4] Mao Tse-tung, *Serve the People* (Beijing, n.d.).

Another famous piece is a poem, possibly written during the Long March, possibly at the end of the war when he flew to Chongqing to negotiate with Chiang Kai-shek, that summarizes his responses to the terrible glories of the Chinese landscape and his enduring ambivalence about the heroes of China's past:

SNOW
The scene is the northern lands.
Thousands of *li* sealed in ice,
Ten thousand *li* of blowing snow.
Inside and outside the Great Wall,
There is nothing but wasteland.
Up and down the Yellow River,
The gurgling river is frozen.
The mountains dance like silver snakes,
The highlands roll like waxen elephants,
As if they want to contest their height with heaven.
And on a sunny day
It's like a red robe thrown over white.
Such beauty in our rivers and mountains
Has caused unnumbered heroes to bow in homage.
But alas these heroes!—the First Qin Emperor
and Wu of the Han
Were rather lacking in culture;
Rather lacking in literary talent
Were the Taizong of Tang and Taizu of Song,
And Chinggis Khan,
Man of his age, proud as heaven,
Only knew how to bend his bow at the golden eagle.
Now they are all past and gone:
To find men truly great and noble-hearted
We must look here in the present.[5]

In 1945 the national government emerged from its years in Chongqing sadly weakened. The Communists, an insignificant force in the nation in 1937, now claimed that one-fourth of all China's people lived under resistance authorities and special governments they controlled; this probably was a high estimate, but not wildly unrealistic. The Yan'an policies had been immensely successful. The united front had been dead since 1941, and it was clear that Kuomintang–Communist warfare was likely to re-

---

[5] Modified from Barnstone, *The Poems of Mao Tse-tung*, pp. 74–75.

sume. American efforts to mediate the impending conflict led nowhere, and the Communists became convinced that the United States had been intending to support the Kuomintang all along. The Soviet Union occupied "Manchuria" as Japan collapsed and facilitated the entry of Communist troops there, but at the same time the Soviet troops looted the area of huge amounts of industrial supplies and equipment as "war reparations" from the Japanese. From 1946 to 1948 the scale of military operations grew steadily, and the Communist armies swept south. On October 1, 1949, Mao Zedong stood on the reviewing platform of the Gate of Heavenly Peace (Tiananmen), the front entrance to the imperial palaces of Beijing, and proclaimed the founding of the People's Republic of China: "The Chinese people have stood up."

The early years of the People's Republic were supposed to be a moderate "New Democracy," and in fact they were less distinctively "Maoist" than those between 1955 and 1976. Much attention was given to establishing law and order, controlling inflation, and reviving transportation, irrigation, and industry. In all of this the new Communist elite showed amazing zeal and political competence, but in many ways they followed common-sense reconstruction policies that were pragmatic and downplayed class struggle. Redistribution of land had resumed after 1945, but it was not clear how rapidly it would be implemented all across the huge country. Then the outbreak of the Korean War in June 1950 changed all the equations of Chinese policy making. Once the United States had intervened in Korea it made Taiwan part of its defense perimeter in the Far East, placing American ships in the Taiwan Strait, so that the Communists could not invade Taiwan without embroiling themselves with the world's only nuclear power. Thus the Kuomintang would have a secure base for subversion and possible invasion of the mainland for the foreseeable future. The situation became still more grave at the end of 1950 as the Americans and South Koreans rolled up the Korean peninsula and approached the Chinese border, and then were pushed back by a massive counterthrust of Chinese "volunteers." Under the circumstances it is not surprising that there was a harsh crackdown on political and intellectual dissent, especially when it seemed tainted by American ideas or connections. More important, the threat of Nationalist subversion stimulated a speedup in efforts to crush the remains of the old local elite who might be tempted to cooperate with the Taiwan regime. Redistribution of land and the elimination of an idle landlord class make good sense in many versions of economic development, but in China it was clear that the main goals were political. Land was redistributed not by administrative action but by "mass action" campaigns in which villagers became actively and emotionally involved, decades of grievances were aired, and frequently landlords and their families were shot. In many areas the elite families had managed to change their hats and survive every political change since 1911, but now were replaced by a new leadership drawn from those who had become active in the land redistribution struggles.

In defeating the Kuomintang and in consolidating their power, the Chinese Communists had demonstrated the combination of coherent organization of revolutionary leadership and effective exploitation and mobilization of the grievances of ordinary people that still makes Communist and crypto-Communist movements so politically formidable in many areas of the Third World today. The achievements of these movements after they come to power in mass education and public health generally are as impressive as their records on human rights and vigor of intellectual life are dismal, and China was no exception. Their efforts at economic development, following more or less closely patterns developed in the Soviet Union, have some successes in heavy industry, transport, and other infrastructure, but little in producing consumer goods. Collectivized agriculture, thought necessary for planning and control and to overcome peasant individualism and conservatism, all too frequently also has destroyed initiative and incentives to produce more. The Chinese agricultural economy is by no means the worst case; with the exception of one terrible period, it has kept pace with the tremendous population growth set off by improvements in public health. The Chinese leaders do not seem to have questioned the necessity of collectivizing agriculture eventually, but many thought the process would take decades. But from the early 1950s on, Chinese farmers were pushed into more and more elaborate forms of cooperation as preparation for collectivization.

In 1954–55, many ex-soldiers, including veterans of the Korean War, became available for assignment as local cadres, giving the Communists the local leadership manpower that would be needed for a massive collectivization effort. At meetings in the summer and fall of 1955 Mao overcame considerable opposition in the high command, apparently sometimes by packing "enlarged" meetings with people who would do his bidding, and there was a radical speedup of collectivization, so that almost all Chinese agriculture had been fully collectivized by the end of 1956. There was a good deal of resistance, and some farmers slaughtered their animals instead of turning them over to the collectives, but the whole process went much more smoothly than it had in Stalin's forced collectivization in the early 1930s and produced nothing like the food shortages and loss of life that had been seen in Russia.

In the fall of 1956 Mao had every reason to be pleased with the accomplishments of the party and government. Collectivization of agriculture made economic sense in some ways. Its execution had been amazingly rapid, found many local allies and aroused only scattered resistance, cut off the possibility of the emergence of a new elite of independent farmers, and put the central authorities more thoroughly in control of rural China than any Chinese rulers had been since the early Tang. But many were uneasy about the Soviet model of economic organization and development, wondering if its rigid centralization was really appropriate for China. And events far from China also reminded Mao of the possible strains among an aroused and involved people, a highly organized party, and a supreme leader. In February 1956 Nikita Khrushchev denounced the tyrannies of Stalin; in the fall, Poland and Hungary erupted in futile revolts. Mao was appalled by Khrushchev's attack on the "cult of the leader," believing the Chinese people very much in need of images of heroic leadership; by his failure to acknowledge the historical circumstances that to him justified some of Stalin's deeds; and by his charging ahead into such sensitive changes without consulting the leaders of other Communist parties or considering the possible repercussions of his actions in their countries. Mao had no use for the Hungarian rejection of communism, but some sympathy for Polish desires for autonomy within the Communist camp. China, he thought, could avoid such upheavals if it could go its own way. Vital as party organization and discipline were to any Communist movement, in his view the new China had many other sources of strength. Its ordinary people and its non-Communist intellectuals and technicians were as devoted to the building of the new China, as capable of intelligent initiative and self-sacrificing commitment, as were its party cadres. Mao himself embodied the dramatic history of the revolution's many brushes with disaster and its ultimate triumph, the pride and idealism of a great people, the capacity of its collective will and enthusiasm to overcome limitations of organization and technology.

From May 1956 on, Mao repeatedly called for open discussion of the problems and policy alternatives China was facing, using the slogan "Let a hundred flowers bloom, let a hundred schools of thought contend." The latter phrase was an allusion to the immense intellectual creativity of the "Hundred Schools" of the Warring States period. Some of his colleagues in the party high command, especially Liu Shaoqi, opposed Mao's call, and—somewhat like the ancient Legalists—feared subversion and disorder more than they valued creativity. Mao argued for his policy in a major speech of February 1957 on "The Correct Handling of Contradictions among the People," in which he elaborated his theory of contradictions into an insistence that force should be used only against enemies of the people and counterrevolutionaries, while differences among the people, including bourgeois supporters of the new China, should be resolved by free and open discussion. Later he commented that "sometimes it is necessary to have even this poisoned fruit to know what we are fighting against. We must know exactly what the reactionaries want and what they represent."

Despite the obvious ambiguities of this policy, for about ten weeks in the spring of 1957 there was an unprecedented outpouring of debate and public criticism. Many useful suggestions were made about economic policy, many mistakes and rigidities of party leadership pointed out, all very much in spirit of contributing to the growth of the new China, as Mao had intended. But the flowers did produce some poisonous fruit, probably more than Mao had expected. One minor-party politician asked why Mao should not be limited to a fixed term of office, as the president of a capitalist country was. A young lecturer at Beijing University wrote, "China belongs to the six hundred million people. . . . It does not belong to the Communist party alone. . . . If you carry on satisfactorily, well and good. If not, the masses may knock you down, kill the Communists, overthrow you." No Communist leader could tolerate such challenges. Party leaders at all levels, comfortable in their privileges and their unquestioned authority, were not willing to accept even constructive criticism from outside the party apparatus. The leaders who from the beginning had opposed the blooming and contending felt completely vindicated. The result was a quick reversal of course in the summer of 1957 that led to a massive nationwide Anti-Rightist Campaign in which large numbers of people who had spoken out in the spring or who were otherwise suspect were rounded up, subjected to vicious public criticism, and in many cases sent off for long years of confinement in prisons and labor camps.

In the winter of 1957–58, Mao's China began its metamorphosis from a fairly predictable and coherently managed Marxist-Leninist state into one of the greatest sources of bafflement and surprise in the late twentieth-century world. Between 1958 and 1980 China produced the Great Leap Forward, a vast effort at forced-pace industrial and agricultural growth that was so badly mismanaged that millions died of the effects of widespread crop failures; the Great Proletarian Cultural Revolution, in which Mao turned the mass movement strategy against the structure of the Communist party itself; and, after Mao's death in 1976, a sharp reversal of economic and social policies and return to power of those attacked during the Cultural Revolution. Clearly all were closely linked to the life and death of Mao: the first two represent phases in his effort to lead his people in a continuing struggle of revolutionary will against all material limitations and regular procedures, while the third great change could not begin while he was alive. Drawing back a bit from the focus on Mao, it is possible to see a series of solutions to the questions of what elements in China's new Communist elite would rule in alliance with what elements outside it.

The Anti-Rightist Campaign placed the party hierarchy thoroughly in control again, but offered no solution to the search for a strategy of economic development that would be more appropriate to China than the rigidities of Soviet central planning and would better suit Chinese national pride and the search for Chinese forms of socialism. Some nonparty intellectuals had been arguing for decentralization with more autonomy for enterprise managers and more reliance on market mechanisms and profit incentives—very roughly the basic policies that have been adopted since 1979. But these policies would violate a prejudice against the profit motive that is deeply rooted in Marxism–Leninism and also has Confucian echoes. They would also accept the proposals and rely of the expertise of those nonparty experts who had produced so much poisonous fruit in the days of the Hundred Flowers and would challenge the total control of the party hierarchy over every enterprise, every activity in the country.

The first suggestion of an alternative decentralizing policy came in the energetic rediscovery of a practice as old as Yu, the mobilization of off-season farmers in big flood-control and irrigation projects. If only the diligence and moral fervor of China's huge rural population could be as directly harnessed to all kinds of improvements in productivity as they were to the digging of canals and the building of earth dams! What was needed was a new form of rural organization in which planning of capital improvements, small-scale industry, and health and educational facilities all were at the same level as day-to-day management of agricultural labor. The new form emerged in Henan, in the experimental amalgamation of twenty to thirty cooperatives into a centrally managed unit called a commune (*gong-she*). Chairman Mao visited one and declared it good, which was enough to set party committees all over the country to work forming communes. Expectations rose rapidly, not only of great leaps forward in production but of the emergence of a radically new kind of society. Since industry would be developed in every commune, each would be fairly self-sufficient, the distinction between city and country gradually would disappear, and the importance of large-scale planning, controls, and exchange relations would decline. Farmers would have their mental horizons widened by working within the larger units. The family unit would lose many of its functions to communal nurseries, old-age homes, and dining halls. Labor would be motivated not by wages or work points but by selfless concern for the good of all and response to moral exhortation. Each would work according to his or her ability and receive according to his or her needs, and the state would wither away. This final utopia of "communism," which orthodox Marxist-Leninists see as the result of a long and difficult evolution in a stage of "socialism," would be achieved in just a few years.

The Great Leap Forward thus was another outburst of that moral utopianism which Confucians frequently justified by references to the early

Zhou and the well-field system, and which had appeared again in Taiping collectivism and in Kang Youwei's dreams of a "great harmony." Although many party leaders had their doubts about it, it was a recipe for change in which local party representatives had absolutely critical roles to play, and thus the organizational primacy and integrity of the party was preserved. It was a Chinese innovation, a sharp break with Soviet patterns, and in its goal of rapid transition to "communism" a clear challenge to Soviet ideological supremacy in the Communist world. In all this and in its reliance on moral incentives and human will, its forced pace and reckless disregard of regular planning, it was very much Mao's, and it was no accident that in 1958 public adulation of Mao rose to unprecedented heights.

Among the many schemes for rapid increase in production were one for dense planting of seed so that two or more stalks of grain would grow where one had grown before, and one in which every commune would build small blast furnaces and begin to produce its own iron. Many experts and farmers knew these were crazy ideas, but as a result of the Anti-Rightist Campaign of 1957 few experts would speak up, and farmers either were too thoroughly intimidated by the two upheavals of land reform and collectivization to speak up or were silenced by party activists who in turn either shared the utopian fervor or feared being labeled rightists if they opposed it. Rural people were exhausted by double-duty work on fields, factories, and blast furnaces. Much of the iron produced was worthless. In some places where excess seed had been planted none of it produced grain, and a whole village lost its entire crop; since food was short everywhere, there was no place to go, and there were places where everyone starved. Early optimistic production figures, more political than statistical, soon were revised downward, and by the end of 1958 the scope of the disaster was apparent. That year had seen good weather for the crops; it was followed by three bad years. It is not easy to estimate the death toll that results from a great food shortage; many do not starve to death but are weakened by malnutrition and die of diseases they would have survived if they had been well fed. Estimates of excess mortality over the normal levels in 1958–62 now are around ten to fifteen million people.

Mao Zedong had pushed the Great Leap policies through over much opposition in the party high command, and he had to take full responsibility for them. In December 1958 he was forced to step down as chairman of the People's Republic and was replaced by the much more cautious and bureaucratic Liu Shaoqi. Mao remained immensely prestigious as chairman of the Chinese Communist party. Liu and his ministers preserved the forms of the communes but not the substance of centralized control within them, and they abandoned many other Great Leap policies. Soviet criticism of the Great Leap policies became increasingly open. In July 1959 Mao, sleepless, incoherent, comparing attacks on his policies to traditional criticisms of the vast building projects of the First Emperor of Qin, forced the dismissal from the post of defense minister of Marshal Peng Dehuai, who some suspected had Soviet backing for his outspoken criticism of Mao's policies. In August 1960 the Soviets ordered the withdrawal of most of their technical advisers from China; they took their blueprints with them.

Mao's leadership had been characterized by a skillful balancing, abstractly and turgidly expressed in his writings on "contradiction," between the exploitation of tensions and conflicts in Chinese society on the one hand and the building of national unity and strength on the other. The changes of 1958–60 destroyed this balance. Mao and those closest to him came to see the world as radically and symmetrically polarized, they leading the forces of world revolution against an array of counterrevolutionary forces that included not only the United States and other capitalist powers but also the "revisionist" Soviet leadership, mired in privilege, devoid of revolutionary zeal, eventually bound to betray the revolution and restore capitalism, and those in the Chinese leadership who also were "leading China down the capitalist road." The most important task of Mao and his followers was to bring the next generation up in true revolutionary values; their most important political support came from the People's Liberation Army, where Peng Dehuai had been replaced in command by Lin Biao.

The early 1960s were a time of extremely confusing cross-currents of Maoist rhetoric and pragmatic policies, of campaigns that looked radical but then were dampened down by Liu Shaoqi's people in the party and bureaucracy. In 1964 a campaign to "learn from the People's Liberation Army" held up the selfless dedication of the soldier as a model for the younger generation, enhanced the prestige of Mao's most important political allies, and became the first occasion for the printing and distribution of the "little red book," the *Selections from the Writings of Mao Zedong*, soon to become one of the greatest best-sellers in the history of the world.

Mao, a poet with intellectual pretensions and a keen sense of the power of ideas in China, particularly resented some of the veiled criticisms directed at him by China's intellectuals. For example, Wu Han, one of China's leading historians, had written a play about Hai Rui, a mid-Ming official who scolded his incompetent ruler and was dismissed; educated Chinese took this as an allegory for Mao and Peng Dehuai and others who had opposed his policies. Late in 1965 an article attacking Wu Han and this work appeared in a Shanghai newspaper. Mao had approved it, and the author and the Shanghai party official who had arranged for its publication became two of his closest allies in the terrible conflict he was about to unleash.

Mao had already begun to criticize China's educational system, especially its elite universities, suggesting in rambling speeches full of bits of information about Chinese history that students should get a better grade for having a few good ideas than for answering all questions exactly according to their textbooks. He began to call for a "Cultural Revolution," but had found his efforts frustrated by his colleagues in the high command, who seemed to agree with what he said but managed to turn his calls for basic changes into academic discussions supervised by party "work teams." Now in May 1966 he began to find ways to reach beyond the high command, when a group of Beijing University students put up a wall poster calling for a Cultural Revolution and attacking the party and university authorities. When Mao ordered the *People's Daily* to carry a report of the poster, the excitement spread to other campuses. Mao posted his own poster on August 5, calling on China's youth to "bombard the headquarters" of the party; later in August he appeared before a huge rally of young people and accepted the red armband of one of their new "Red Guard" organizations. He had decided that the party high command was irrevocably "revisionist" and that he would have to lead a mass movement of China's youth against it. In the fall of 1966 he appeared repeatedly before crowds of hundreds of thousands of young people who were weeping hysterically and chanting passages from his works. Party and government leaders, school and university authorities, scientists, scholars, artists, all were violently attacked as representing elite structures of power and culture that would destroy China's revolutionary zeal. Government was disrupted, schools and universities closed. Many monuments and historic buildings were defaced in chaotic attacks on everything connected with China's past and its elite culture. Jiang Qing, the former film actress who had become Mao's fourth wife, carried through a sweeping "revolutionary" reform of the Chinese cinema and theater that left the people with nothing to watch for almost ten years but a small number of bombastic "revolutionary dramas."

At the end of 1966 disorder began to interfere with factory production and the functioning of China's railroads and water transport, and both Mao and the army decided things had gone too far. In February 1967 a new system of government was announced that would consolidate the gains of the Cultural Revolution and prevent the revival of centralized systems of authority. At every level of government there would be individually worked-out "three-way alliances" among army people, Red Guard leaders, and Maoist party leaders. None of these Revolutionary Committees would be subordinate to those at higher levels. The actuality seems to have been an increase in the political power of the army at all levels, with its commander, Lin Biao, emerging as Mao's second in command and designated successor. The unleashed passions and commitments of China's youth

11. Mao Zedong, 1966

continued to produce many conflicts with other powers in the country and among Red Guard factions, some fought with screamed Mao slogans and some with bullets, until 1969, when millions of young Chinese were neutralized politically by being sent to the countryside to learn from the peasants and from labor. Many of them remained there for fifteen years or more.

Mao was seventy-six in 1969, and it is not clear how active a role he was playing in the later stages of the Cultural Revolution. His wife and his other close associates, vilified after his death as the Gang of Four, may have been increasingly in control of day-to-day decisions. As the party hierarchy pulled itself back together, it came into conflict with army power, and in September 1971 there was some kind of bizarre high-level intrigue that ended with Lin Biao dead. There then followed a campaign to "Criticize Lin Biao and Criticize Confucius," based on the claim that Lin had been the kind of elitist who had so long dominated China through the Confucian tradition; this probably represented an attack by Jiang Qing and her allies on the reviving influence of some of the high party leaders who had managed to survive the Cultural Revolution, especially Zhou Enlai and Deng Xiaoping.

Education was slowly reviving, and some cautious openings were being made to the outside world, but there could be no fundamental political change while Mao lived. Zhou Enlai died in January 1976. In April public mourning for him in Tian'anmen Square turned into protests against the disasters of the Cultural Revolution. The protests were brutally suppressed, but their point had been made. The leader who had used a funeral oration so effectively to summon his people to selfless devotion to their country now found the emotions aroused by mourning and idealization of the selfless dead turned against him. Mao died on September 9, 1976. The "Gang of Four" were arrested in October, and there were huge spontaneous celebrations in the cities. The Cultural Revolution had disrupted science, technology, and education, but had had no such radical effects on production as the Great Leap had. Every elite family had stories to tell of suicides, beatings, years of humiliating imprisonment or exile to remote rural areas, careers disrupted and young lives wasted. In comparison, the millions who died as a result of the Great Leap famine have no one to speak for them. There are fewer portraits of Mao to be seen as the years go by, and his mistakes are more and more candidly criticized by the current leadership, but he remains the founder of the People's Republic, and many statues of him still stand. His body still lies in the great mausoleum so boldly erected in the direct line south from the Gate of Heavenly Peace. For many years, they say, people would come to weep for the lost days when he led his people to dream of a new age and a new humanity.

NAMES IN THE NEWS

······

FROM CONFUCIUS preserving the Literary Heritage of the sages to Su Dongpo discovering the political power of poetry to Liang Qichao inventing modern Chinese journalism, this somewhat episodic survey of the Chinese past has discussed many forms of hope for influence and immortality through the written word. Sima Qian and many others have told and retold stories of good and evil, of short-lived base success and of noble failure that brings everlasting renown, that enshrine so many names in the Chinese historical memory.

We are too close to the years since the death of Mao, and can only guess what names will remain in the stories and memories of the Chinese people in centuries to come. But there is no shortage of possibilities. The Chinese people remain fascinated, as all people are, by stories of individual lives. They probably still are more inclined than most peoples to cast their moral and political principles and arguments in terms of individuals who are idolized or reviled. Their appetite for names is fed by the big national newspapers like the *People's Daily*, by the provincial newspapers that reprint key stories from the national editions and add some of their own, and by a half-hour nightly television news broadcast seen all over the vast country. In the heady days of liberalization in the mid-1980s a huge range of journals of opinion sprang up. Outside the People's Republic, some influential Hong Kong magazines are especially important as collectors and purveyors of stories of China's intellectual and political leaders.

The most prominent political figure of the post-Mao period, Deng Xiaoping, has not often been as prominent in the newspapers and in the television news as he is in fact and as most Chinese recognize him to be. This is largely because he has only occasionally permitted anything like the cult of personality that surrounded Mao, and because he has not held the posts of state and party leadership that would get him in the news day after day receiving foreign guests, touring the country, and making major public statements on behalf of a more or less collective leadership. Only occasionally has he allowed collections of his speeches and papers to be widely distributed and studied, and there has been nothing remotely approximating a little red book of his teachings. If Mao was a hero riding the chaos like Guan Yu or a willful emperor like the First Emperor of Qin or Taizong of the Tang, and if Zhou Enlai was the Zhuge Liang of the Communist Revolution, charming the enemy, bridging impossible differences with his powers of negotiation and persuasion, Deng has been the organization man, something like Li Si of Qin or the conscientious ministers of Qianlong, working to keep decision making clear and implementation consistent, wary of public emotion and moral extremism.

Deng's career has been strikingly parallel to Mao's and strikingly different. Born eleven years after Mao, in 1904, he was a very young participant in the ferment of the May Fourth period of 1919–20, in which Mao, already in his late twenties, finally found his voice and his sphere of action. When thousands of Chinese laborers were recruited to work in French factories, desperately short of men during and immediately after the First World War, Mao thought of going but stayed in China. Deng went, staying in France from 1920 to 1925, working in an arms factory in which ten thousand of the thirty thousand workers were Chinese. He was a great admirer of the power of modern industrial civilization; it is interesting that even in his factory work he was experiencing modern industry in its most direct connection with military power. He absorbed the militant Marxism of his French fellow-workers, joining a special Chinese unit of the French Communist party that soon became a unit of the newly formed Chinese Communist party. He enjoyed wearing French clothes and sitting in cafes. He got no formal education but participated actively in a small but lively circle of Chinese radical intellectuals in France of which Zhou Enlai was a central figure. Deng's colleagues called him "Dr. Mimeograph"; his particular contribution to their activities and their ephemeral little journals was not to write brilliant theoretical essays or rousing calls to action but to prepare neat, legible mimeograph stencils of the writings of others and take care of their reproduction.

On his way back to China in 1925–26, he spent some several months at the Sun Yat-sen University in Moscow, the Soviet training school for Chinese revolutionaries, including some members of the Kuomintang; Chiang Ching-kuo, it will be recalled, also studied there. Thus by the time he returned to China he had been thoroughly schooled in the disciplined proletarian unionism of the French Communist party and in Leninist organizational discipline. His first assignment in China was as a political officer at a military academy training officers for the army of the colorful Christian warlord Feng Yuxiang, who at this time was friendly to Moscow and was presenting himself as a radical nationalist. Deng's role, like the parallel role that Zhou Enlai played in Chiang Kai-shek's Whampoa Academy, was to work within an environment where military discipline and the forming of personal loyalties within the modern military were unchallengeable realities, and his task was to work within them for the goals of his own organization, the Chinese Communist party.

When the Communists and the Kuomintang split and Feng Yuxiang sided with the Kuomintang, Deng participated in an effort to organize a rural base in the mountains of Guangxi, then became closely allied with Mao Zedong during the Jiangxi Soviet period, viewing Mao as a "brother-teacher." This personal tie would inhibit Deng's opposition to Mao's policies at several times and would shield him from the worst excesses of the Cultural Revolution. During the Sino-Japanese War Deng served very effectively as Mao's man in the command structure of some important forces that had ties to a potential rival of Mao. He was not a field commander but was a brilliant strategist and a capable administrator of a major "liberated area." Thus he remained consistently an organization man, with a special talent for staying close to the wielders of military power and keeping them under political control.

In 1949 Deng was placed in charge of the party structure in the Southwestern Region, centered in Sichuan, his native province. A highly capable administrator, he gave priority to the beginnings of the modernization of transportation, agriculture, and industry. He gathered around him a group of loyal and talented junior officials. Savoring his sweeping power in his homeland, he sometimes identified himself with Song Jiang, the central hero of the great tale of noble outlaws *Water Margin*, and referred to his associates by the names of other *Water Margin* heroes.

In 1952 Deng was summoned to Beijing and made a vice-premier. From 1956 to 1965 he served as general secretary of the Communist party. This was in theory a post that involved not the making of policy but its execution and the maintenance of orderly administrative, personnel, and record-keeping procedures for the vast party apparatus. Deng was extremely well-suited to such a post. With control of files, decision-making procedures, and implementation, it also was a post of potentially immense power. Stalin had risen to absolute dominance of the Soviet Union from such a position. In Moscow in November 1957, Mao pointed to Deng and said to Khrushchev, "See that little man there? He's highly intelligent and has a great future ahead of him." In the aftermath of the Great Leap, Deng supported Mao against Peng Dehuai, but insisted on speaking bluntly about the terrible mistakes that had been made: "Not only will the people blame us, we also should blame ourselves." He was an important shaper of the retreat from the worst excesses of the Great Leap in rural policy. But still he stayed close to Mao when he could, and was especially proud of having stood firm in his debates with the Soviets in a 1963 meeting that made the Sino-Soviet split irreparable.

No measure of closeness to Mao could keep Deng, the quintessential organization man and disciplinarian, from a prominent place among the targets of the Cultural Revolution. He disliked all forms of spontaneous, uncontrolled activity; he had criticized Mao's "Hundred Flowers" initiative in 1956–57. Now he was one of those who tried to keep the Cultural Revolution under control by sending work teams to take charge of it at the universities. But by early 1967 he was among those being dragged out for public denunciations. In a final public "trial" in August 1967, he removed his hearing aid so that he could not hear what was being said about him, and admitted rather mockingly to being a counterrevolutionary. But he was treated much less harshly than Liu Shaoqi, who eventually died of the public and private beatings and tortures he suffered. From 1968 to 1973 Deng and his wife lived very quietly under guard in a small house on the outskirts of Nanchang, Jiangxi. Deng's younger brother killed himself. His eldest son Deng Pufang was pushed down a staircase in Beijing and has been confined to a wheelchair ever since.

Deng resurfaced rather dramatically in 1973, after the death of Lin Biao, and soon was filling important responsibilities as a close associate of Zhou Enlai. There was no secret to his return, he told an interviewer: "At a certain moment they thought that I could be useful again and they took me out of the grave. That's all." In 1975 he was very powerful, serving as first vice-premier, supervising the drafting of documents that called for "Four Modernizations," of industry, agriculture, science and technology, and national defense, and bluntly attacking the disasters of the Cultural Revolution. Mao and the Maoists counterattacked with a campaign against *Water Margin*, which they said glorified capitulation of popular leaders to the class enemy. In 1976, after the death of Zhou and the Tiananmen demonstrations, Deng was criticized by name and the stories of his fascination with *Water Margin* were given wide publicity. Neither Deng nor the candidate of the Cultural Revolution group was named to succeed Zhou as premier; Hua Guofeng, a somewhat pragmatic Maoist, was a shaky compromise choice. Finally, Deng was stripped of all his high offices.

Deng was restored to his offices in July 1977. Despite the arrest of the Gang of Four, politics still were in a condition of near stalemate, with most positions of power occupied by those who had risen during the Cultural Revolution. In the fall of 1978, big-character posters sharply criticizing Mao Zedong and the Cultural Revolution and calling for "democracy" appeared on walls in Beijing; Deng encouraged or protected some of this activity to gain leverage against Hua and other surviving Maoists, but he had little use for any expression of opinion that was hard to control. However, a few Maoists were eased out of high positions, and in December 1978 the party moved decisively to emphasize economic modernization and to abandon Maoist emphases on mass mobilization and class warfare.

These decisions of the third plenum of the party's Central Committee were recognized in later years as a turning point, but at the time they were criticized as abandoning too much of central importance to communism. Deng responded by continuing to crack down on the "Democracy Wall" movement, so that by March 1979 it was on its last legs and its leaders were in jail. He also proclaimed Four Cardinal Principles, toward which no dissent or challenge would be tolerated: socialism, government by proletarian dictatorship, the unique dominant position of the Communist party, and Marxism–Leninism–Mao Zedong Thought. In 1980–81 Hua Guofeng was dismissed from his high positions and replaced by Deng's men, Zhao Ziyang as premier and Hu Yaobang as party chairman.

It also was in 1980–81 that the new leadership moved with striking speed to reform the overcentralized command economy, introducing substantial measures of profit motivation and market-driven production and pricing. Some foreign observers have described these changes as an abandonment of socialism and a return to capitalism. So have some diehard Chinese opponents of the changes. Deng and his associates certainly retain their basic collectivist values and rhetoric, but one of Deng's few famous sayings is that it doesn't matter if a cat is black or white as long as it catches mice.

The reversal of collectivization is most nearly complete for agricultural land, where under the "responsibility system" families have been assigned plots of land, in return for agreed-on deliveries to the state, and may grow what they see fit on them, keeping whatever they earn beyond the agreed-on deliveries. The length of the assignments has been increased, and they have been made saleable and inheritable, so although the cooperative remains the formal owner, the difference from private ownership has been hard to detect. Specialized rural functions and productions—transportation, fish-farming, handicraft products, and so on—similarly have been assigned to individual families or to associations of members of the cooperative. Rising prices for agricultural products, first by increased state subsidies and more recently by allowing consumer prices to rise, have stimulated rapid increases in production. Some of the most conspicuously prosperous people in China in the 1980s have been farm families who have profited from selling their produce in a nearby city or specialized rural households who have found their services, such as transportation, in great demand.

In the 1980s there was a small amount of genuine private enterprise, especially in the service sector, but most of the industrial and urban economy remained state-owned. Managers, however, were given much more autonomy to decide how much their factories would produce what goods and what prices they would charge. The resulting income, when it exceeded that of the old planned output for fixed prices, was available for investment in expansion and modernization and for the payment of bonuses to workers.

Anyone reading the newspapers in China in the 1980s was aware that entrepreneurship, whether private or as director of a collective or government enterprise, was one way to fame and fortune, but a risky one. Industrial managers might find their names in the papers one week as models, having reorganized their factories and increased production and profits, but the next week as criminals, having given their employees larger bonuses than was allowed, underpaid their taxes, bribed officials, or what have you. Some appeared only as models, like Xiao Shuigan, who, made director of his commune's shoe factory, bought machines and recruited retired shoemakers in Shanghai, and sold the first product on the sidewalk in the big city. Xiao attracted the attention and orders of shop managers and sent people regularly to the big cities to check on the latest fashions, so that in 1984 the factory earned a profit twelve times its goal when he took over in 1981.

But then there was Li Rencai, a rural transportation entrepreneur who finally decided to give up his growing business because of the endless red tape of getting permits for his vehicles and because the rural people kept asking him for free rides on his new bus and tore up the seats when he refused. Nian Guangjiu, a private entrepreneur, started out selling roasted melon seeds on the street, discovered a tasty new seasoning, and eventually had a registered trademark, several factories with modern equipment, over one hundred employees, and wide distribution of his product. But his prosperity attracted government attention, and he was accused of failure to pay his full tax obligation. All the gray areas of private and semiprivate enterprise, all the confusion of old rules for collectives and half-formed new policies, made it hard to see just how seriously he had offended. Nian's case received nationwide publicity, and the government forced him to reduce the scale of his business, but did not convict him of tax evasion.

These changes have been accompanied by equally sweeping changes in China's relations with the outside world and its cultural life. Foreign trade has been promoted and investment in joint ventures encouraged. Thousands of Chinese have gone abroad to study, and foreign teachers and consultants are welcome in China. The educational system, so badly disrupted by the Cultural Revolution, at its best once again is very good, but as uneven in quality and inequitable in its provision of opportunity as that of the 1950s. In the mid-1980s the variety of books and periodicals published was immense, and state control of their contents was uneven. The accessibility of foreign ideas, the great popularity in the cities of foreign music and dress, added up to a lively ferment in China's cities that frequently made the rulers uneasy but seemed hard to stop as long as they sought market-driven economic growth and continued involvement in the worldwide circulation of goods and knowledge.

The strains of rapid change in Deng's China in the 1980s were obvious even to outside observers. Expectations and wants rose much more rapidly than opportunities and incomes. Opportunities for advanced education were limited, and many young people who did not get admitted to a university waited a long time for a job opening. Price inflation was very hard on professionals on fixed incomes. In rural areas, many resented their newly rich neighbors. In politics, all these strains were compounded by the resistance and resentment of a Communist party elite that saw its absolute control over every organization disappearing and its values and ideals challenged everywhere. The results included a campaign against "bourgeois liberalization" in 1981 and one against "spiritual pollution" in 1983, neither of which seems to have had much effect except to spread an ever-deepening cynicism about the official values of the regime, especially among students.

At the end of 1986 all these tensions boiled over into a round of student demonstrations and party reassertions of authority that at the time seemed of rather modest scale and quickly ended but in retrospect can be seen to have put Deng Xiaoping's leadership and China's young intellectuals on a collision course. Among the catalysts of dissent, the names in the news that articulated and symbolized an increasingly fundamental and principled opposition to the Communist party's monopoly of power, were a number of senior intellectuals who embody in various ways ideals of intellectual courage and honesty, of the special political responsibilities of scholars, and of the power of the written word that are universal but have special resonance among the heirs of Confucius, Su Dongpo, and Liang Qichao. One of them was Fang Lizhi, an astrophysicist of international reputation. Fang was a challenger of authority even when he was a brilliant physics student at Beijing University in the 1950s. He was expelled from the party in the Anti-Rightist Campaign of 1957, but his work was so highly valued that he continued to get good teaching and research assignments in the early 1960s. Imprisoned and then sent to work on a farm in Anhui during the Cultural Revolution, he had only one book with him, *Classical Theory of Fields* by the Soviet physicist Lev Landau. Reading and rereading this book, he began to shift from his previous specialty in particle physics to a focus on relativity, theoretical astrophysics, and theories of the early universe. His approach to social and political questions is what one might expect from a scientist capable of creative contributions to these fearfully difficult areas of physics. The fullest freedom of argument and mutual criticism of ideas is absolutely necessary. Obvious truths must be stated, stupidity and obstruction dismissed with a scornful laugh; sometimes he seems to be looking at them from thousands of light years away.

Politically exonerated in 1978, Fang was able to attend several international scientific conferences. His essays show him to be a quick and witty observer, learning a great deal from his new opportunities to see the world, even including the famous Christmas service at King's College, Cambridge. He published many scientific papers, and his work is internationally recognized. In 1986 he spent a few months at the Institute for Advanced Study in Princeton, where Einstein, von Neumann, and many others had worked. He also became a professor and eventually vice-president of the Chinese University of Science and Technology in Hefei, Anhui (Zhongguo Keji Daxue, or Keda), which had an unusually large number of scientists who had been attacked during the Cultural Revolution; the national leaders seem to have been hoping to isolate them and their students, so that they could get on with their important work and neither be distracted by nor contribute to dissent in the capital.

Fang made his name in the 1980s largely as a university reformer. At Keda he made administrative changes that broke up rigid centralization, reduced party control, and increased faculty decision-making power. He also insisted on freedom of speech at Keda and worked hard to arrange as many exchanges and connections with foreign universities and institutes as possible. But he did not hesitate to state the need for analogous changes in society at large or to claim a special role for scientists as those who are the first to become conscious of the emergence of a major social crisis. Students and scholars, he said, must speak out against the abuses they see around them. They must think independently, overcoming their tendency to think like officials or aspiring future officials. For the most part his ideas were presented in speeches to university audiences and thus lacked the instant nationwide impact they would have had if they had been published in widely circulating journals. In October and November 1986, however, a series of articles appeared in the *Guangming Daily*, which has a nationwide intellectual audience, praising Fang's reforms at Keda; an article in *People's Daily* seemed a bit more wary, but still declared the reforms in harmony with the party's present policies. In November 1986 the Shanghai *World Economic Herald* quoted some of his opinions on the need for intellectuals of independent spirit. And soon after that the pot boiled over.

Another great contributor to the ferment of the mid-1980s was the writer Liu Binyan, the developer of what the Chinese call "reporting literature" (*baogao wenxue*), which combines investigative reporting, with its pathos of the search for truth and its efforts to uncover well-hidden crimes and corruptions of society and spirit, with the storytelling skills and devices and the vivid presentation of individuals equal to the best fiction. Liu's contribution is complementary to Fang Lizhi's; Fang deals in clarity, basic principles, the very long view, while Liu shows, usually in the stories of modest people and petty tyrants, how deeply lying, exploitation, and obstruction are built into the system. Perhaps his message sometimes has been as daunting to would-be reformers as Fang's has been clarifying and inspiring, but it is vital as a warning to those who might hope for quick fixes or be tempted to compromise. And because he is such a storyteller, so acute about motives and relations, outsiders can learn a great deal from his works.

Liu Binyan was born in 1925 near Shenyang, where the Manchus had founded their state before they began their conquest of China in the 1600s. In the twentieth century the surrounding area and the wide plains farther north were being rapidly settled by Chinese farmers. It was a violent frontier world of bandits, warlords, and rapidly increasing Japanese power. Liu remembers watching proud, defiant bandits being paraded through the streets on their way to the executioner. He grew up farther north, in Harbin, where there were many Russians who had settled there during earlier Russian expansion into the area or had come as refugees from the Russian Revolution. Liu's father had been a laborer in Siberia during World War I, later worked as an interpreter on the Russian-owned Chinese Eastern Railway that cut across northeast China to Vladivostok, and knew and loved Russian literature. The Japanese occupied all of northeast China in 1931, setting up a puppet empire under the last of the Qing emperors. In Harbin, young Liu Binyan had a teacher who told stirring stories of Yue Fei and other patriotic heroes, and had no trouble obtaining anti-Japanese publications, many of which were from Communist sources. Liu thought he might grow up to be an actor or a writer. By 1943 he was in Japanese-occupied Tianjin, the port nearest Beijing, working with the Communist underground, scattering anti-Japanese leaflets in the city, eventually joining the party. He also got a teaching post at a very early age and was popular with his students because of his free and easy manner, his acting and storytelling skills, and his frankness about his political views.

In the early 1950s Liu's knowledge of the Russian language and his background in youth work for the Communist party earned him several trips to the Soviet Union and Eastern Europe and a position as a reporter for the *China Youth News*. Russian society and social life seemed to him more relaxed, less restricted than that of the tightly disciplined Chinese Communist elite; only afterward did he learn about the scale of the Stalinist terror of these years. He also noted the Soviet practice of exposing examples of bureaucratic abuse in the press; there was nothing like that in the Chinese Communist press in these early years.

Liu's recollections of his life in China at this time in his autobiography, *Di er zhong zhongcheng* (A Higher Kind of Loyalty), form the first stage of his wonderfully astute and honest depiction of the moral decline of a set of values and a vision of the future he himself fully shared. People threw themselves into every new campaign with real enthusiasm. When a colleague was secretly arrested, no one had any misgivings; the party knew best. When a campaign was launched to denounce a new film for "denigrating the peasant revolution," Liu thought the criticisms were excessive, but his faith in Mao's judgment was such that he put his own doubts aside and strove to strengthen his own commitment to class struggle. Looking back, he comments that no one could have imagined how much the "all to the party" spirit of those days would corrupt the party.

After several years of routine reporting work, in 1954 Liu for the first time wrote something similar to the exposés that he had noted in the Soviet press. "On the Bridge Construction Site" paints contrasting portraits of two construction supervisors, one of whom maintains rigid control and always awaits orders from above, while the other is more ready to act on his own and encourages his workers to take do the same; the former sees his men's work washed away in a flood while he is awaiting orders. No more a challenge to the political order than the similar Russian stories were, it was an innovation in China and the first step in Liu's development of "reporting literature." Before the story appeared in 1955, Liu had been again to Warsaw and Moscow, had read widely in the foreign press, and had learned much from the Russian writer Valentin Ovechkin, in whose house he stayed for some days. Ovechkin was writing many exposés of the Stalinist terror and the dreadful consequences of the forced collectivization of the 1930s. Many people now were writing to thank him and tell their own stories; while he worked, he let Liu read these letters. Thirty years later, it would be Liu's turn to tell people in his own country bitter stories of the recent past and to be besieged by visitors and letter-writers with their own stories.

Liu published another important piece in 1956, about an ignorant and tyrannical newspaper editor. But in 1957 he was among the targets of the Anti-Rightist Campaign. He had written to Mao Zedong pleading with him not to reverse the new openness of the "Hundred Flowers," but of course he accomplished nothing except to make his fate even more certain. He was expelled from the party and sent to do manual labor in the countryside. In the study and reform sessions with fellow "rightist" intellectuals, he noted wryly that they, "rightists" all, still judged each other by the standards of Communist party members.

Liu's conspicuous Russian connections probably delayed his full rehabilitation in the early 1960s; it finally came just in time for him to get back to work, publish a little, and then come under attack in the Cultural Revolution and be sent off to the countryside again. Appalled by the situation of the country as a whole and by the vicious attacks of his fellow victims on each other, he tried to find some clue to what had gone wrong and how

China might escape its present dreadful impasse. He read widely in the great European Marxists and also in Chinese history, using the great general history written by Wang Anshi's opponent Sima Guang. He was not fully rehabilitated until January 1979, over twenty years after he fell victim to the Anti-Rightist Campaign.

Liu's long years of absence from the political life of the Chinese elite seem to have enabled him to sense with unusual clarity just how deep the moral damage of the Cultural Revolution had been, how great the change was from the high hopes and real commitments of the 1950s. In 1979 he visited Harbin and became interested in the biggest embezzlement scandal in the history of the People's Republic, which had been uncovered in nearby Binxian and already widely publicized in 1978. Liu suspected that there was more to the case than had been told. As he made his own investigations he found that many people in Binxian still respected the embezzler, and that she had gotten many people on her side by diverting scarce coal and food to them. Such exchanges of supposedly state-owned goods for protection from investigation and exposure, Liu saw, had become an endemic and basic form of corruption in a society where most important economic assets "belonged to the people." Also, all the campaigns against various forms of "rightism" had created a climate in which ungrounded accusation of any kind could destroy anyone; one man who had twice stumbled on a powerful local official copulating with different women was himself almost destroyed by groundless accusations of sexual immorality; the official had started them to destroy the witness before his own acts could be reported. All this Liu reported in a long and vivid piece called "People or Monsters?" published in September 1979.

In the early 1980s Liu published one important piece after another, on the continued strength of Cultural Revolution leftovers in Shandong, on a vicious political clique in Shaanxi, and so on. Despite the apparent victory of Deng Xiaoping's moderate policies and personnel on the national level, he found "leftists" and surviving Cultural Revolution supporters all too often immune from dismissal or prosecution on the local level, and the systems of corruption and informing that had grown up still thoroughly entrenched. There were times when he could even publish his reports in the *People's Daily*. Many people wrote to him or came to see him; a visit to a provincial capital would turn into an exhausting ordeal of listening to terrible stories. Sometimes he met brave men of principle who would not rest until injustice was righted, even injustice done to others. In "A Higher Kind of Loyalty," published in January 1985, he described one such man, Chen Shizhong. Chen, an orphan who owed everything to the party, was completely devoted to it, could not bear to see it take a course he thought was mistaken, and as a result had written to urge Mao not to break with the

Soviet Union. Later he had sought justice on behalf of a fellow prison-camp inmate who had been tricked and shot in cold blood by the guards. Liu wrote that in China today most people's loyalty emphasizes meekness, deference, perhaps an occasional bit of personal sacrifice. Chen's was of another kind, which does not seek approval and for which the loyal individual often must pay a bitter price; it was a miracle that this kind of loyalty had survived at all in China.

Liu's essays were widely excerpted and reprinted, but of course they also aroused a great deal of resentment in official circles. Every year there were rumors that he had been dismissed from the party or arrested. Hu Yaobang generally tried to maintain the greatest possible freedom of expression, but that led to attacks on him, and early in 1985 he became more cautious, and no more exposés were published in the *People's Daily*. Liu continued his work, following the case of a worker who had been thrown into an insane asylum after he came to tell Liu about the crimes of a local party secretary. But before he could publish that report he was swept up in the upheaval of the end of 1986.

In December 1986 students at the University of Science and Technology in Hefei began demonstrating over local issues of curriculum and living conditions, but soon turned to demands for "democracy" and harsh criticisms of the national leaders. The demonstrations quickly spread to universities elsewhere in China. Deng and others responded by condemning "bourgeois liberalization" and blaming Fang Lizhi and other outspoken intellectuals. Fang, Liu Binyan, and several others were expelled from the party. Hu Yaobang, the most sympathetic to political liberalization of the Communist high command, was dismissed as general secretary of the party. A new campaign against "bourgeois liberalization" was begun but was met with nearly universal loathing and apathy and was not continued very long.

A party Congress in October–November 1987 reaffirmed Deng Xiaoping's economic reform policies and accepted the retirement of many of the aged Long March generation of leaders; Deng Xiaoping set the stage by resigning from all his positions except his chairmanship of the Central Military Commission. It also seems likely that these elders were willing to relinquish some of their formal roles because they knew they still would have much influence and because Li Peng, no friend of political reform, was likely to be the new premier. A National People's Congress in March 1988 confirmed an ambiguous and fragile political balance, as Li Peng became premier, the hard-line general Yang Shangkun president, and Wan Li, a Deng ally admired by Liu Binyan and many other liberals, chairman of the National People's Congress.

Many thoughtful people seem to have been willing, or at least resigned, to seeing Deng Xiaoping continue these intricate political maneuvers as long as his economic reforms stayed in place and produced positive results. But there too there were major difficulties, as growth slowed and the decontrolling of prices, a necessary step to increase incentives for production, caused much hardship and resentment among people living on fixed incomes in the cities, including students, intellectuals, bureaucrats, and workers. Price decontrol finally was slowed down, but the strains remained. Workers slowed down and stole on the job; bureaucrats made the most of their special privileges and accepted bribes from anyone with access to money or goods, including foreigners doing business in China. Intellectuals and students got poorer and more frustrated and sent off sheaves of letters of inquiry and application to foreign universities. Important parts of international trade, including sales of arms to foreign countries, were said to be under the corrupt control of the children of high officials, including the crippled Deng Pufang. The situation was ripe for an explosion of demands for genuine political liberalization, combined with expressions of a highly personalized moral indignation at the corruption of the leaders that had about it more than a faint echo of the Confucian political heritage.

Hu Yaobang died on April 15, 1989. Previously many Chinese intellectuals had viewed him as the only man in the high command with any real understanding of the need for freedom of expression and genuine political change. Mourning for him now turned, as it had for Zhou Enlai in 1976, into an occasion for renewal of commitment and emotional protest against current abuses. And as in 1976 the center of activity was Tiananmen Square, and especially the Monument to the People's Heroes. The monument has on its sides several very effective low-relief sculptures of scenes from modern Chinese history, such as the burning of the opium seized from the English during the Opium War. The most moving of them, almost unbearable to recall after 1989, shows the young orators and followers who gathered in this same area to protest against another corrupt government in May 1919. The men and women seem very young, very fresh, very determined. They are creating modern Chinese intellectual radicalism in the service of nationalism, and many of them will follow their commitments into the Communist party. Echoes of 1919 were very much on people's minds in 1989; the May Fourth values of science and democracy seemed still vital and hard to attain. Fang Lizhi wrote an important commemorative essay that ended with a ringing proclamation: "The dharma wheel of science has already come rolling into China, and that of democracy is starting to turn as well. The problems we face today are merely the creaking sounds it makes as it begins to roll. This is the basis of my confidence and strength."

Almost seventy years after the 1919 demonstrations depicted on the monument, and two days after Hu Yaobang's death, students from the Beijing universities had placed mourning wreaths and declarations around the base of the monument, and Central Art Academy students had hoisted a big memorial portrait of Hu to a higher level. From this time on, the monument became the central point for speeches, posting of statements, and later for the organization of the vast demonstrations in the square.

This great movement was almost entirely led by university undergraduates and a few graduate students. Several of them had organized open discussion forums on their campuses the previous winter and spring, but until the movement began they had no experience at all in any kind of autonomous organizing or political activity. A few individuals showed real qualities of intellect and leadership and became names in the news worldwide, if not in the *People's Daily*. Among them were Wang Dan, a history major at Beijing University; Wuer Kaixi, a Uighur from Xinjiang and a student at Beijing Normal University; and Chai Ling, a former graduate student at Beijing Normal. But the movement was chaotic, many of its most important and interesting pronouncements were collective or anonymous, and it is altogether likely that some heroic names are lost to us forever and others will become known only many years later.

On April 18 a huge crowd gathered on the square, and a student leader read a series of requests, including the reevaluation of Hu Yaobang's achievements (implying that they had been unfairly criticized); freedom of speech and the press; increased spending on education and improvement of students' living conditions; and disclosure of the incomes of government leaders and their families. Some individual leaders began to emerge, especially as autonomous student unions were formed in the next few days. (The previously existing student unions were under party control.) The leaders of the new unions, including Wang Dan and Wuer Kaixi, now demanded an opportunity to discuss their grievances with Li Peng and other government leaders. Ignored, on April 22 they defied government prohibitions and gathered in front of the Great Hall of the People on the west side of the square, while Hu Yaobang's funeral was being conducted inside. Several representatives knelt on the steps, one holding a petition above his head as he would have done to present it to an emperor or high official of the old imperial state. This was apparently meant to show that the leadership was just as undemocratic as the imperial rulers had been, but some did not get the point, thinking that the kneelers were themselves reverting to "feudal" ways. Wuer Kaixi refused to kneel.

Deng Xiaoping and many other senior officials had been victims of the Cultural Revolution. They had suffered, and so had the country, from the excesses of uncontrollable masses of enthusiastic young people condemning the corruption and authoritarianism of government leaders. It was easy to lose sight of the fact that in the Cultural Revolution the students frequently had been cynically manipulated by central and provincial leaders, while this was a genuinely spontaneous movement. In any case, Deng feared spontaneity, prized order and discipline. On April 24 the leaders moved to get the situation under control. Deng proclaimed that "this is no ordinary student movement, but an episode of turmoil. . . . We cannot allow their objectives to be achieved." "Turmoil" was the term often used in official documents to refer to the Cultural Revolution. Deng's remarks became the basis for an editorial in the *People's Daily* on April 26.

The students reacted with anger and defiance. Demonstrations continued in Beijing and spread to other cities. Among the leaders who emerged at this stage was a young woman named Chai Ling, not as fiery a speaker as some others but a fine organizer and always deeply concerned about the dangers and difficulties through which the movement was trying to make its way. On May 1, she recalled later, her father came to visit her and found her already deep in the movement. He reminded her that he owed the party everything, having begun life as a peasant and become a doctor. "I don't believe in the party," Chai Ling replied. "You should be getting so much more." The father understood: "You haven't gone through what we have gone through. But you can have your own way of thinking."

The demonstrations reached another peak on May 4, with a great celebration of the seventieth anniversary of the May Fourth Movement, so well commemorated on the Monument to the People's Heroes. But then confusion and dissension spread, as various student leaders and organizations competed for leadership or opted for different strategies. No doubt government agents were doing all they could to promote these troubles. More and more students were getting tired, worrying about their studies, and going back to class. The leaders, including Chai Ling, Wuer Kaixi, and Wang Dan, now sought to revive the movement by calling for volunteers for a truly brave gesture of selfless commitment, a hunger strike until their demands were met. Once again, they sought recognition of their autonomous unions, freedom of speech and the press, "systematic democratic reform," and an end to elite privileges and corruption. Soon three thousand hunger strikers were lying in tents in Tiananmen Square, watched over by medical personnel. The revival of organization and morale was striking. Some hunger strikers wrote their wills before they set out for the Square. Many carried signs or wrote slogans on their shirts: "We have the hearts to serve the country, but we have no power to restore the heavenly order." In English, "I ♥ life, I need food, but I'd rather die without democracy," and then in Chinese: "The sons and daughters of the people will die for the people."

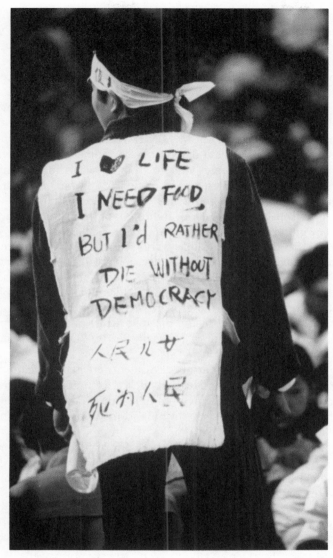

12. Beijing, Spring, 1989

Just as the hunger strike was getting under way, Mikhail Gorbachev arrived in Beijing on May 15, marking a turning point away from thirty years of Sino-Soviet hostility. The leaders had to have the welcoming ceremonies at the airport, not in the square, and Gorbachev was unable to tour the imperial palaces north of the square. The Gorbachev visit also led to the presence in Beijing of television crews from around the world, ready to report on the dramas that would follow in the square. Zhao Ziyang still may have argued for a "soft" approach to the students, but on May 19 Deng Xiaoping met with the Military Commission in Wuhan and secured its support, while on the same day Li Peng finally met with Wuer Kaixi and other student leaders in a televised meeting that produced no real dialogue. On May 20 martial law was proclaimed for Beijing.

No immediate action followed, but by May 28 morale was sagging and disputes were emerging among the demonstrators. Some university administrators and professors, deeply concerned about what might come next, were urging their students to return to their campuses, and some student leaders agreed. But now thousands of new demonstrators were arriving in Beijing from provincial cities, full of fervor, not about to back down before they got involved in the great drama, and subject to no single organization. The Beijing student leaders were trying to keep control and at the same time trying to make sure that decisions were made in some "democratic" fashion, that everyone had a voice. At the end of May Chai Ling emerged as the number one coordinating leader, but she was deeply worried about the confusion and the growing menace of military action. Attacks on the national leaders became more strident; one photograph shows a huge sign across the Gate of Heavenly Peace: "Deng Xiaoping resign! Li Peng resign!"

On May 29 students from the Central Art Academy erected in the north end of the square, facing the Gate of Heavenly Peace, a large statue of foam plastic called the Goddess of Democracy. On June 2 the student leadership issued a new call for a hunger strike. But by now armed troops were closing in on the city in large numbers.

Ever since the May 20 martial law declaration, efforts had been made to bring troops into the city. The first truckloads of unarmed and bewildered young soldiers had been surrounded and stopped by crowds of ordinary people who were very friendly, gave them food and cigarettes, and would not let them go forward. Soon there were reports that this or that military unit was advancing, mixed with hopes that some of them might be sympathetic to the students, that there might even be a full-scale split in the military establishment. But Deng Xiaoping seems to have pretty well taken care of that possibility. The demonstrations of the sympathy of the common people of Beijing for the students, and the arrival of groups of workers to join the demonstrations in the square, must have hardened the determination of Deng and his allies; such a broadening of support would make the movement much more dangerous than when it was confined to the students.

From the predawn hours of June 3, army units, including many with tanks and armored personnel carriers, began to move from several directions toward central Beijing. Everywhere people brought food and water to the students and tried to blockade intersections and main avenues by parking, overturning, and burning trucks and buses. By the end of the day the police were getting very rough as they tried to clear parts of the main avenue just west of the square, and the crowds were starting to throw rocks at police and soldiers. Troops opened fire on civilians on the west side of the city about ten o'clock that night, and soon there was indiscriminate firing by infantry and from tanks and personnel carriers on many major avenues as the troops attacked ordinary people trying to block their advance and fought their way toward the square. Then the fighting got heavy in the north end of the square itself, and the Goddess of Democracy was destroyed. Finally, in the predawn hours of June 4, there was an ominous pause, when the authorities offered the last remaining groups of hunger strikers around the monument free passage out of the square. After a confused debate most of them agreed, and it seems that some of them did at least get out of the square unharmed. Then the army simply ran its vehicles back and forth across the remaining tents, crushing everything, including perhaps a few hunger strikers who had decided against leaving. Estimates of civilian dead on June 3–4 range from one thousand to ten thousand, including many who had not been directly participating. Soon the square was cleaned up, and for a time it was empty, off limits to the people of the city. In the weeks that followed, the dissident leaders finally got their names on Chinese television, in the form of bulletins on wanted criminals.

Deng Xiaoping still is formally in control but is in poor health, and others are doing most of the actual governing. Zhao Ziyang was dismissed as party general secretary. Fang Lizhi and his wife took refuge in the American Embassy, where they stayed for just over a year until an agreement was reached allowing them to leave; they now live in the United States. Liu Binyan was in the United States when the crisis began and has remained abroad. Both Fang and Liu seem to find a kind of hope in the widespread disillusionment in China; it represents to them a final loss of faith in the potentialities of the present political system that must precede serious efforts to build something new. Wang Dan was arrested, eventually expressed regret for his actions, was given a relatively light sentence of four years, and has been released. Wuer Kaixi and Chai Ling managed to get out of China. Liu Binyan, Wuer Kaixi, and several others have formed a Chinese Democratic Front to coordinate prodemocracy activities in exile and when possible to keep in touch with like-minded people in China. Liang Qichao would be delighted with the international phone links and the fax machines, but in many other ways he would feel right at home.

When we tell stories we want to know how they came out. But for our own lives, or the stories of great peoples, the end always is a question mark. The modern Chinese word for "future," *weilai*, literally means "not yet come." Confucius and his followers for two millennia had faith in the possibility of a future regenerated by human goodness, but that was in large measure because they believed that the record of the past proved that a good society was possible. Liang Qichao, confronting a world in which he no longer could be sure how much guidance the past offered, was fascinated by Japanese fiction about the future and tried his hand at writing some himself. As the 1990s pass, it remains hard to imagine a short-term bearable future for the people of China. Recent visitors report that only in Beijing does repression weigh really heavily, and in many places people of all classes are openly contemptuous of their government and its pronouncements. But that does not imply that they know what to do except to wait for a few old men to die, which is of course a kind of personalization of politics and abdication of thought about the institutions that must some day be built that is all too common everywhere in the world, and is a particular plague among the heirs of the political culture traced in this book.

The heirs of Yu never have feared hard work. The heirs of Confucius and of two millennia of aspiring scholars have known how to link ambition with moral earnestness and care for the public welfare. Su Dongpo's mother in the cloth business, the future Hui Neng selling firewood, Zheng Chenggong's father mastering the hazards of his maritime world, have not feared poverty and uncertainty. Liang Qichao's search for a viable set of values and political forms that will bring so many energies and excellences together to provide the dynamism and social solidarity needed for effective participation in the modern world has not yet come to any resolution effective for the vast area and population of twentieth-century mainland China. Nor is it clear just how the lessons of economic growth and democratization on Taiwan may be applicable to the search for a viable future for the People's Republic. Taiwan and Hong Kong investment in factories in south China, especially in Guangdong, is powering impressive regional economic growth. Deng Xiaoping has given wary approval to these economically promising but perhaps politically destabilizing developments. The collapse of communism in Eastern Europe and the Soviet Union will be no surprise to the many in China who quietly or noisily abandoned faith in Marxism–Leninism years ago, but it will not necessarily stimulate a new round of efforts to organize an open opposition. Despite all the difficulties and cross-currents of China's efforts to shift to a market- and profit-oriented economy, they are years ahead of those in the former Soviet Union. Looking at the economic and political chaos of their huge neighbor, quite a few Chinese are willing to keep their heads down for a few years to maintain order and hold on to their economic gains. And of course everyone knows how elusive order and political unity for all of China's vast area were from 1911 to 1949.

But there also are many who cannot forget June 4. On August 21, 1991, a foreign visitor approached the barricade of burned-out streetcars on the Ring Road near Smolenskaya square in Moscow, where three young patriots had died in resisting the forces of the junta the night before. Many people were leaving flowers and notes of tribute. The visitor spotted a sheet torn out of a ringed note pad, the ink smeared by rain. He could not read the Chinese characters scrawled on it, but below them was written in Russian, "CHINA. From a participant in Tiananmen, June 1989."[1]

Most of those who will help to find a way past the terrible contradictions of post-Mao China are still nameless, perhaps unborn. Somewhere in a provincial city, we might imagine a hard-working mother, like Su Dongpo's, grieving for the brave child who boarded the train to Beijing in May 1989 and never was heard from again. She looks at the younger child, head down, studying for the college entrance exam, and thinks, "What next? What next?"

[1] Jamey Gambrell, "Seven Days that Shook the World," *New York Review of Books*, September 26, 1991, p. 58.

SOURCES AND SUGGESTIONS FOR FURTHER READING

• • • • • •

THE FOLLOWING is intended as a guide to basic sources of information and insight, and as a list of the most important sources from which I worked in each chapter. Most of the books listed provide further bibliographic guidance.

1. YU

On the legends and their interpretation see Derk Bodde, "Myths of Ancient China," in Samuel Noah Kramer, ed., *Mythologies of the Ancient World* (New York, 1961); Sarah Allan, *The Heir and the Sage: Dynastic Legend in Early China* (San Francisco, 1981); and K. C. Chang, *Early Chinese Civilization: Anthropological Perspectives* (Cambridge, Mass., 1976), chaps. 8, 9. For the classical texts see James Legge, *The Chinese Classics* (Oxford, 1893; reprint, Hong Kong, 1960). The constantly developing story of modern Chinese archaeology can be followed in the many publications of Kwang-chih Chang; see especially *The Archeology of Ancient China*, 4th ed. (New Haven and London, 1987), and *Art, Myth, and Ritual: The Path to Political Authority in Ancient China* (Cambridge, Mass.: 1983).

2. CONFUCIUS

On early Zhou see, in addition to the works of Kwang-chih Chang, Herrlee G. Creel, *The Origins of Statecraft in China*, Vol. I: *The Western Chou* (Chicago, 1970), and Edward L. Shaughnessy, *Sources of Western Zhou History: Inscribed Bronze Vessels* (Berkeley, Los Angeles, and London, 1991). An excellent survey of the economic, political, and cultural changes around the time of Confucius is Cho-yun Hsu, *Ancient China in Transition: An Analysis of Social Mobility, 722–222 B.C.* (Stanford, 1965). Useful studies of the life of Confucius are Herrlee G. Creel, *Confucius: the Man and the Myth* (paperback ed., New York, 1960), and D. C. Lau's translation of the *Analects* (Harmondsworth, 1979), appendix 1. Richard Wilhelm, *Confucius and Confucianism* (New York, 1931), translates and draws on the biography of Confucius in Sima Qian's *Records of the Grand Historian*, the most influential early compilation of the legends that grew up around the life of the Master. Two excellent surveys of Zhou thought are Benjamin I. Schwartz, *The World of Thought in Ancient China* (Cambridge, Mass., 1985), and A. C. Graham, *Disputers of the Tao* (La Salle,

Ill.: 1989). For a searching and in many ways very persuasive reinterpretation of Confucius, see David L. Hall and Roger T. Ames, *Thinking Through Confucius* (Albany, N.Y., 1987). My own rethinking takes Confucius's conservative utterances more seriously than Hall and Ames seem to but is in many ways sympathetic to their approach.

3. The First Emperor of Qin

For chapters 3 through 7, authoritative summary and extensive bibliography can be found in John K. Fairbank and Denis Twitchett, gen. eds., *The Cambridge History of China*, Vol. I: *The Ch'in and Han Empires, 221 B.C.–A.D. 220*, edited by Denis Twitchett and Michael Loewe (Cambridge, 1986). The chapter on Qin by Derk Bodde draws on his detailed studies of the biographies of Li Si and other Qin leaders. A useful translation of the Qin Basic Annals in Sima Qian's *Records of the Grand Historian* is in Li Yu-ning, ed., *The Politics of Historiography: The First Emperor of China* (White Plains, N.Y., 1975). A good popular account with much about the terra-cotta army near the First Emperor's tomb is Arthur Cotterell, *The First Emperor of China* (London, 1981). On Warring States thought see, in addition to the works listed for chapter 2, Joseph Needham, *Science and Civilization in China* (Cambridge, 1954 et seq.), vol. 2, which is especially helpful on the five powers and other "naturalist" trends of thought. Needham's multivolume work, still in progress, immensely intelligent, erudite, and bold in its interpretations, is one of the great monuments of scholarship in our century. The reader with some knowledge of science, taste for intellectual adventure, a bit of time, and about two thousand dollars to spare should consider simply buying the whole set and devoting the next decade of evenings and vacations to it.

4. Sima Qian

The interpretive issues on the reign of Emperor Wu have not been as well argued out in the Western-language literature as the importance of the period demands. See *The Cambridge History of China* for surveys and bibliography. On Sima Qian see Burton Watson, *Ssu-ma Ch'ien: Grand Historian of China* (New York, 1958), and Burton Watson, tr., *Records of the Grand Historian of China: Translated from the Shih-chi of Ssu-ma Ch'ien*, 2 vols (New York, 1961) 2d ed., 1993. For intelligent summaries of many aspects of Han history and culture, and especially for fine illustrations, see Michele Pirazzoli-t'Serstevens, Janet Seligman, tr., *The Han Dynasty* (New York, 1982).

5. Wang Mang

For politics and ideology in the first century B.C.E. see, in addition to *The Cambridge History of China*, Michael Loewe, *Crisis and Conflict in Han China* (London, 1974). On Huo Guang see Pan Ku (Ban Gu), Burton Watson, tr., *Courtier and Commoner in Ancient China* (New York, 1974), pp. 121–51. The Basic Annals of the *Han shu* and its long memoir on Wang Mang are translated in Pan Ku, Homer H. Dubs, tr.,

The History of the Former Han Dynasty, 3 vols. (Baltimore, 1938–55), vols 2 and 3. Dubs included in his third volume a number of substantial interpretive essays on Wang Mang's reforms, the reasons for his failure, and so on. Hans Bielenstein's *Cambridge History* chapter summarizes decades of research and thought on this period. On Bright Hall lore see Howard J. Wechsler, *Offerings of Jade and Silk* (New Haven, 1985), chap. 10.

6. BAN ZHAO

The main authority here is Nancy L. Swann, *Pan Chao: Foremost Woman Scholar of China* (New York and London, 1932). I also have drawn on the basic annals of these years in the *History of Later Han* (*Hou Han shu*) and on the biographies of Ban Zhao, Ban Gu, Ban Chao, and Dowager Empress Deng in *Han shu*, juan 100, and *Hou Han shu, ji*, juan 10, and *liezhuan*, juan 30, 37, and 74.

7. ZHUGE LIANG

A fine translation of the *San Guo yanyi* and extensive interpretive comments can be found in Moss Roberts, tr. *Three Kingdoms* (Berkeley and Los Angeles, 1992). The best modern literary study of the novel in English is Andrew H. Plaks, *The Four Masterworks of the Ming Novel* (Princeton, 1987), Chap. 5.

8. HUI NENG

For a fine translation, the Chinese text, and excellent analyses see Philip B. Yampolsky, tr., *The Platform Sutra of the Sixth Patriarch* (New York, 1967). For background and context see the various excellent studies by Heinrich Dumoulin, most recently *Zen Buddhism: A History* (New York, 1988). A sophisticated recent study is John McRae, *The Northern School and the Formation of Early Chan Buddhism* (Honolulu, 1987).

9. EMPRESS WU

The Cambridge History of China, vol. 3, has excellent chapters on Gaozong and on Empress Wu. The most important studies in English are C. P. Fitzgerald, *The Empress Wu* (Melbourne, 1955, reprinted Vancouver, 1968), and R. W. L Guisso, *Wu Tse-t'ien and the Politics of Legitimation in T'ang China* (Bellingham, Wash., 1978). I also have drawn on the great eleventh-century comprehensive history, Sima Guang, *Zizhi tongjian*.

10. SU DONGPO

Excellent biographies of Su Xun and Su Shi (Dongpo) by George Hatch are in Herbert Franke, ed., *Sung Biographies* (Wiesbaden, 1976), under Su Hsun and Su Shih. Michael A. Fuller, *The Road to East Slope: The Development of Su Shi's Poetic Voice* (Stanford, 1990), is excellent on the poetry and very helpful on every aspect of the life. For translations of Su's poetry, see also Burton Watson, *Su Tung-p'o* (New York and London, 1965). Superb accounts of the Song cultural transformation and Su's place in it can be found in chapters 2 and 3, both by Peter K. Bol, of Kidder Smith et al., *Sung Dynasty Uses of the I Ching* (Princeton, 1990). Bol does an excellent job of placing Su's thought in the succession of great thinkers of his times in Bol, *"This Culture of Ours": Intellectual Transitions in T'ang and Sung China* (Stanford, 1992), chap. 8. Lin Yutang, *The Gay Genius* (New York, 1947), makes Su too charming and accessible but is full of good information. These excellent works soon are to be joined by another, perhaps the most comprehensive of all in its account of this many-faceted man: Ronald C. Egan, *Word, Image, and Deed in the Life of Su Shi* (Cambridge, Mass., 1994).

11. YUE FEI

The most extensive study in a Western language is Edward H. Kaplan, "Yueh Fei and the Founding of the Southern Sung," Ph.D. dissertation, University of Iowa, 1970. Also very helpful are James T. C. Liu, "Yueh Fei (1103–1141) and China's Heritage of Loyalty," *Journal of Asian Studies* 31, 2 (1972): 291–97, and Hellmut Wilhelm, "From Myth to Myth: The Case of Yueh Fei's Biography," in Arthur F. Wright and Denis Twitchett, eds., *Confucian Personalities* (Stanford, 1962).

12. QIU CHUJI

The primary sources of this account are Li Chih-ch'ang, Arthur Waley, tr. and intro., *The Travels of an Alchemist* (London, 1931), and Tao-chung Yao, "Ch'üan-chen: A New Taoist Sect in North China During the Twelfth and Thirteenth Centuries," Ph.D. dissertation, University of Arizona, 1980. For interpretations of classical Daoism, see the books by Schwartz and Graham listed under chapter 2 above. Quotations from the *Dao De Jing* follow Victor H. Mair, trans., *Tao Te Ching* (New York, 1990). Aspects of the later history of Daoism are opened up in Holmes Welch and Anna Seidel, eds., *Facets of Taoism* (New Haven and London, 1979). I know of no fully satisfactory account of Inner Elixir Daoism in any language. In English by far the best approach is through the very rich translated materials and sophisticated commentary in Joseph Needham, *Science and Civilization in China* (see under chapter 3), vol. 5, parts 3, 4, 5.

13. WANG YANGMING

Excellent biographies of Wang (Wang Shou-jen) and his contemporaries are to be found in L. C. Goodrich, ed., *Dictionary of Ming Biography* (New York and London, 1976). The best linking of life and thought is Tu Wei-ming, *Neo-Confucian Thought in Action: Wang Yang-ming's Youth (1472–1509)* (Berkeley, Los Angeles, and London, 1976). There is nothing of comparable sophistication for the later phases of the life. The most important translation, accompanied by good biographical comments and some documents on his local reform measures, is Wing-tsit Chan, ed. and tr., *Instructions for Practical Living and Other Neo-Confucian Writings by Wang*

Yang-ming (New York, 1963). Another important study is Julia Ching, *To Acquire Wisdom: The Way of Wang Yang-ming* (New York and London, 1976). Landmarks in changing Western approaches to Neo-Confucianism are W. T. de Bary et al., *Self and Society in Ming Thought* (New York and London, 1970), and Thomas A. Metzger, *Escape from Predicament: Neo-Confucianism and China's Evolving Political Culture* (New York, 1977). De Bary's many writings and edited volumes have made a massive contribution to Neo-Confucian studies.

14. ZHENG CHENGGONG

For the political history of the Ming–Qing transition see Lynn A. Struve, *The Southern Ming* (New Haven and London, 1984), and Frederic Wakeman, *The Great Enterprise* (Berkeley, Los Angeles, and London, 1985). Various approaches to the period are opened up in Jonathan D. Spence and John E. Wills, Jr., eds., *From Ming to Ch'ing: Conquest, Region, and Continuity in Seventeenth-Century China* (New Haven and London, 1979). On the Cheng family and their milieu, see the Spence and Wills volume, "Maritime China from Wang Chih to Shih Lang." On Zheng's historical reputation, see Ralph D. Croizier, *Koxinga and Chinese Nationalism: History, Myth, and the Hero* (Cambridge, Mass., and London, 1977). For a sense of the richness and variety of information available on the Ming–Qing transition, see Lynn A. Struve, ed. and tr., *Voices from the Ming-Qing Cataclysm: China in Tigers' Jaws* (New Haven, 1993); chaps. 11 and 12 are on facets of Zheng Chenggong.

15. THE QIANLONG EMPEROR

For China since the mid-seventeenth century a particularly rich and absorbing survey is Jonathan D. Spence, *The Search for Modern China* (New York, 1990). Most basic on the Qianlong reign are Alexander Woodside, "The Ch'ien-lung Reign," *The Cambridge History of China*, vol. 9 (in press), and Harold L. Kahn, *Monarchy in the Emperor's Eyes: Image and Reality in the Ch'ien-lung Reign* (Cambridge, Mass., 1971). For brief biographies of the emperor (under his given name, Hung-li, i.e., Hongli) and the other individuals mentioned, see Arthur W. Hummel, ed., *Eminent Chinese of the Ch'ing Period (1644–1912)*, 2 vols. (Washington, 1943–44). For specific aspects see Susan Naquin and Evelyn S. Rawski, *Chinese Society in the Eighteenth Century* (New Haven, 1987); R. Kent Guy, *The Emperor's Four Treasuries: Scholars and the State in the Late Ch'ien-lung Reign* (Cambridge, Mass., 1987); Susan Naquin, *Shantung Rebellion: The Wang Lun Uprising of 1774* (New Haven, 1981); Madeline Zelin, *The Magistrate's Tael: Rationalizing Fiscal Reforms in Eighteenth-Century Ch'ing China* (Berkeley, Los Angeles, and London, 1984); Philip A. Kuhn, *Soulstealers: The Chinese Sorcery Scare of 1768* (Cambridge, Mass., and London, 1990); Beatrice S. Bartlett, *Monarchs and Ministers: The Grand Council in Mid-Ch'ing China* (Berkeley, Los Angeles, and Oxford, 1991); Pamela Kyle Crossley, "The Qianlong Retrospect on the Chinese-martial (*hanjun*) Banners," *Late Imperial China* 10, 1 (June 1989): 63–107; Morris Rossabi, *China and Inner Asia: From 1368 to the Present Day* (New York, 1975), chap. 6; Sven Hedin, *Jehol: City of Emperors* (New York, 1933); David S. Nivison, "Ho-shen and His Accusers: Ideology and

Political Behavior in the Eighteenth Century," in David S. Nivison and Arthur F. Wright, eds., *Confucianism in Action* (Stanford, 1959); David M. Farquhar, "Emperor as Boddhisattva in the Governance of the Ch'ing Empire," *Harvard Journal of Asiatic Studies*, vol. 38 (1978).

16. HONG XIUQUAN

For an accurate and thoughtful summary, see Philip A. Kuhn's chapter in *The Cambridge History of China*, vol. 10. This volume also provides excellent summaries of other aspects of the nineteenth century. The fullest narrative in English is Jen Yu-wen, *The Taiping Revolutionary Movement* (New Haven and London, 1973). Franz Michael et al., *The Taiping Rebellion*, 3 vols. (Seattle and London, 1966, 1971), provides a brief narrative and a large number of translated documents. See also Vincent Y. C. Shih, *The Taiping Ideology* (Seattle and London, 1967), and Rudolf G. Wagner, *Reenacting the Heavenly Vision: The Role of Religion in the Taiping Rebellion* (Berkeley, 1982).

17. LIANG QICHAO

There are three important biographies in English: Joseph R. Levenson, *Liang Ch'i-ch'ao and the Mind of Modern China* (Cambridge, Mass., 1959); Hao Chang, *Liang Ch'i-ch'ao and Intellectual Transition in China, 1890–1907* (Cambridge, Mass., 1971); and Philip C. Huang, *Liang Ch'i-ch'ao and Modern Chinese Liberalism* (Seattle, 1972). Levenson's is the work of an intellectually adventurous pioneer; Chang's is the richest of the three on Liang's thought; Huang's is very helpful on links between ideas and action. Also very perceptive is Andrew J. Nathan, *Chinese Democracy* (Berkeley and Los Angeles, 1985). The account of 1898 follows Luke S. K. Kwong, *A Mosaic of the Hundred Days* (Cambridge, Mass., 1984). For contexts and bibliography see *The Cambridge History of China*, vol. 11. The detail on Tokyo at the turn of the century is from Edward Seidensticker, *High City, Low City* (New York, 1983). In Chinese see Ding Wenjiang and Zhao Fengtian, *Liang Qichao nianpu changbian* (Shanghai, 1983), and Li Huaxing and Wu Jiaxun, eds., *Liang qichao xuanji* (Shanghai, 1984).

18. THE KUOMINTANG LEGACY

On Zou Rong see Tsou Jung, John Lust, tr., *The Revolutionary Army* (The Hague and Paris, 1968); on Qiu Jin, Mary Backus Rankin, *Early Chinese Revolutionaries: Radical Intellectuals in Shanghai and Chekiang, 1902–1911* (Cambridge, Mass., 1971); on Sun Yat-sen, Harold Z. Schiffrin, *Sun Yat-sen and the Origins of the Chinese Revolution* (Berkeley, Los Angeles, and London, 1970), and C. Martin Wilbur, *Sun Yat-sen: Frustrated Patriot* (New York, 1976). For English translations of the writings of Sun, see Leonard S. Hsu, *Sun Yat-sen: His Social and Political Ideals* (Los Angeles, 1933). Most of the many biographies of Chiang Kai-shek are unscholarly and strongly biased for or against him. Hollington K. Tong, *Chiang Kai-shek*

(Taipei, 1953), and Keiji Furuya, *Chiang Kai-shek* (New York, 1981), are thorough and useful pro-Chiang works. Pichon P. Y. Loh, *The Early Chiang Kai-shek* (New York and London, 1971), cites some fascinating material and makes uneven psychologizing use of it. The most important writings available in English are Chiang Kai-shek, *Soviet Russia in China* (New York, 1957) and *China's Destiny* (New York, 1947). The best survey of the changes on Taiwan after 1949 is Thomas B. Gold, *State and Society in the Taiwan Miracle* (Armonk, N.Y., and London, 1986). On the relevance of Sun's ideas to Taiwan government policies, see A. James Gregor, Maria Hsia Chang, and Andrew B. Zimmerman, *Ideology and Development: Sun Yat-sen and the Economic History of Taiwan* (Berkeley, 1981). Useful biographies of Sun, Chiang, Chiang, and other important figures who died after 1911 can be found in Howard L. Boorman, ed., *Biographical Dictionary of Republican China*, 4 vols. (New York and London, 1967). Some of the fullest narrative and analysis, and bibliography in English is to be found in *The Cambridge History of China*, vols. 12 and 13; key chapters from the latter also are in Lloyd E. Eastman, Jerome Ch'en, Suzanne Pepper, and Lyman Van Slyke, *The Nationalist Era in China, 1927–1937* (Cambridge and New York, 1991).

19. MAO ZEDONG

"Mao's China" has been the subject of an amazing number of good, bad, and uneven books, many of which focus too much on the man and too little on the contexts in economics, politics, and political culture that he sought to alter and that shaped and constrained him. Good starting points are Boorman, ed., *Biographical Dictionary*; *The Cambridge History of China*, vols. 12, 13, 14, 15; and the many works of Stuart Schram, especially *Mao Tse-tung* (New York, 1967), *The Political Thought of Mao Tse-tung* (New York, 1969), *Chairman Mao Talks to the People* (New York, 1974), and *The Thought of Mao Tse-tung* (Cambridge and New York, 1989). See also Roderick MacFarquhar et al., eds., *The Secret Speeches of Mao Tse-tung* (Cambridge, Mass., and London, 1989). A classic of detailed narrative and analysis is Roderick MacFarquhar, *The Origins of the Cultural Revolution*, 2 vols. (New York and London, 1974, 1983). For a balanced and sophisticated account of the Cultural Revolution years, see Hong Yung Lee, *The Politics of the Chinese Cultural Revolution: A Case Study* (Berkeley, 1978).

20. NAMES IN THE NEWS

Useful summaries of the post-Mao era include Immanuel C. Y. Hsu, *China Without Mao* (New York, 1990), and Harry Harding, *China's Second Revolution* (Washington, D.C., 1987). Ching Hua Lee, *Deng Xiaoping* (Princeton, 1985) is full of useful information. A fine collection of translations of Fang Lizhi's writings and speeches, with good biographical commentary, is *Bringing Down the Great Wall* (New York, 1990). Several important pieces of Liu Binyan's writings have been translated in Perry Link., ed., *People or Monsters? And Other Stories and Reportage from China after Mao* (Bloomington, Ind., 1983). The account of his life and views in this chapter is heavily dependent on his splendid autobiography, *A Higher Kind of Loyalty* (New York, 1990). His Harvard lectures of 1988–89 and related materials have been published as *China's Crisis, China's Hope* (Cambridge, Mass., 1990). Of the many books on the Tian'anmen Square events, see especially *Children of the Dragon* (New York, 1990), the fuller collection of texts in Han Minzhu, ed., *Cries for Democracy* (Princeton, 1990), and a lively eyewitness account, Shen Tong, *Almost a Revolution* (Boston, 1990).